FLY ME TO THE MOON

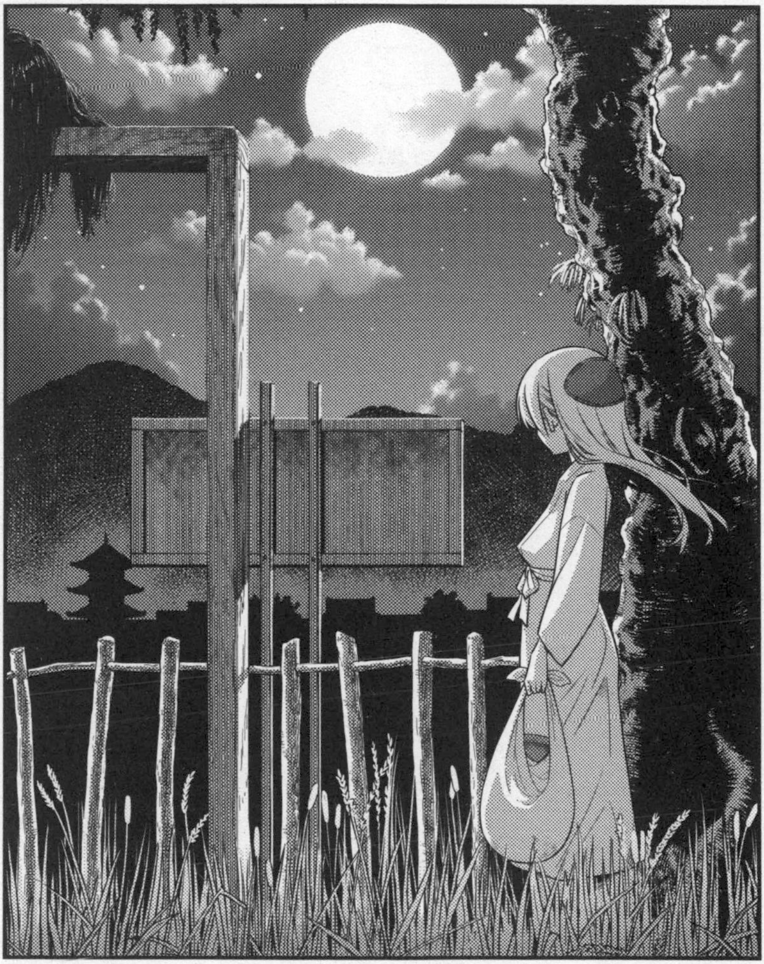

VOLUME 13

KENJIRO HATA

FLY ME TO THE MOON

Contents

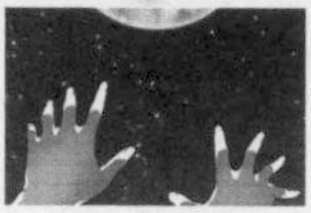

CHAPTER 121

"Entangled with Idiots"

43

CHAPTER 120

"Flower of Life"

23

CHAPTER 119

"Beyond 1,000 Nights"

5

CHAPTER 123

"Plenty of Nudity"

81

CHAPTER 122

"Sometimes
He Looks Cool"

61

CHAPTER 126

"Masakado and Kiyomori
Are Different People"

135

CHAPTER 125

"I Clicked on a Scary
Image and Crashed
My Browser"

117

CHAPTER 124

"At Paranormal Hot
Spots, You Have a Higher
Chance of Running into
Delinquents than Ghosts"

99

CHAPTER 123 ½

"Growing Girls
Need Sleep"

173

CHAPTER 127

"The Manga's Good,
but Watch the Anime
Too, Okay?"

154

Chapter 119: "Beyond 1,000 Nights"

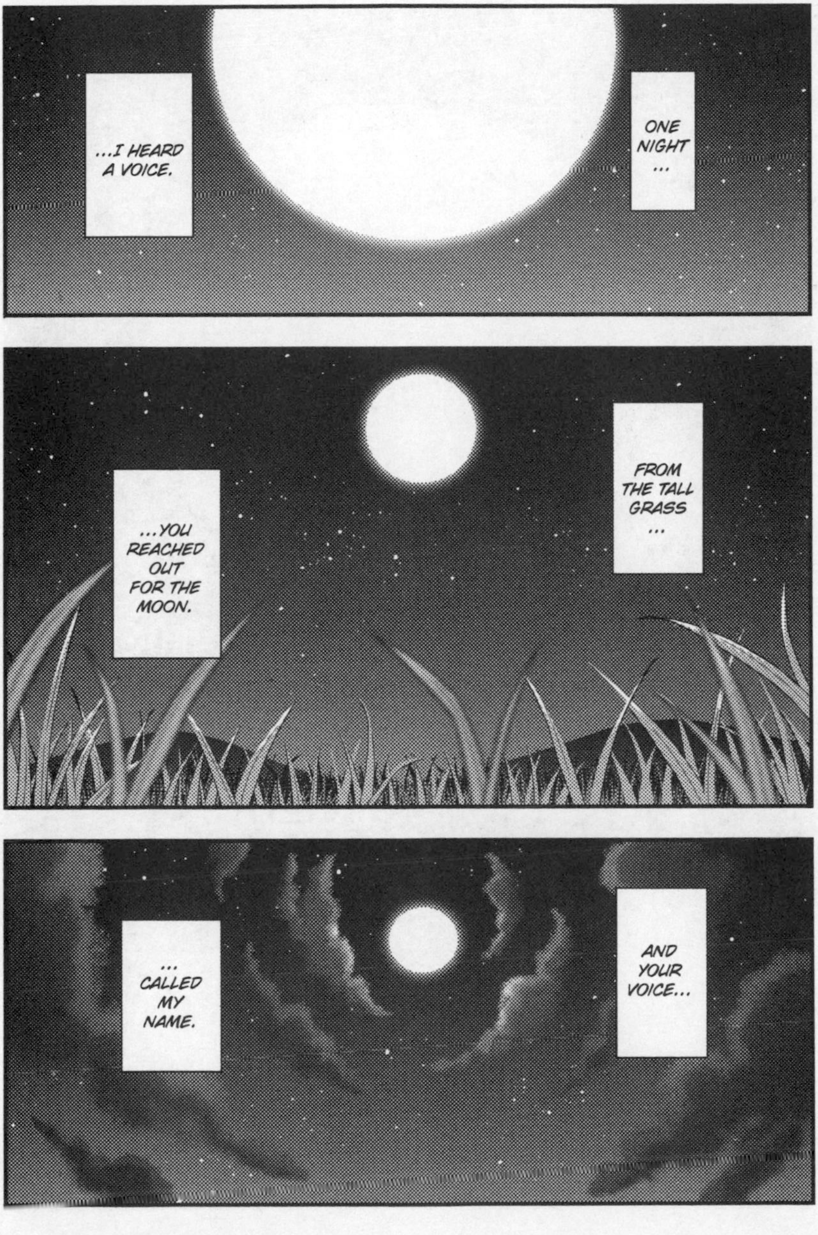
ONE NIGHT ...
...I HEARD A VOICE.
FROM THE TALL GRASS ...
...YOU REACHED OUT FOR THE MOON.
AND YOUR VOICE...
... CALLED MY NAME.

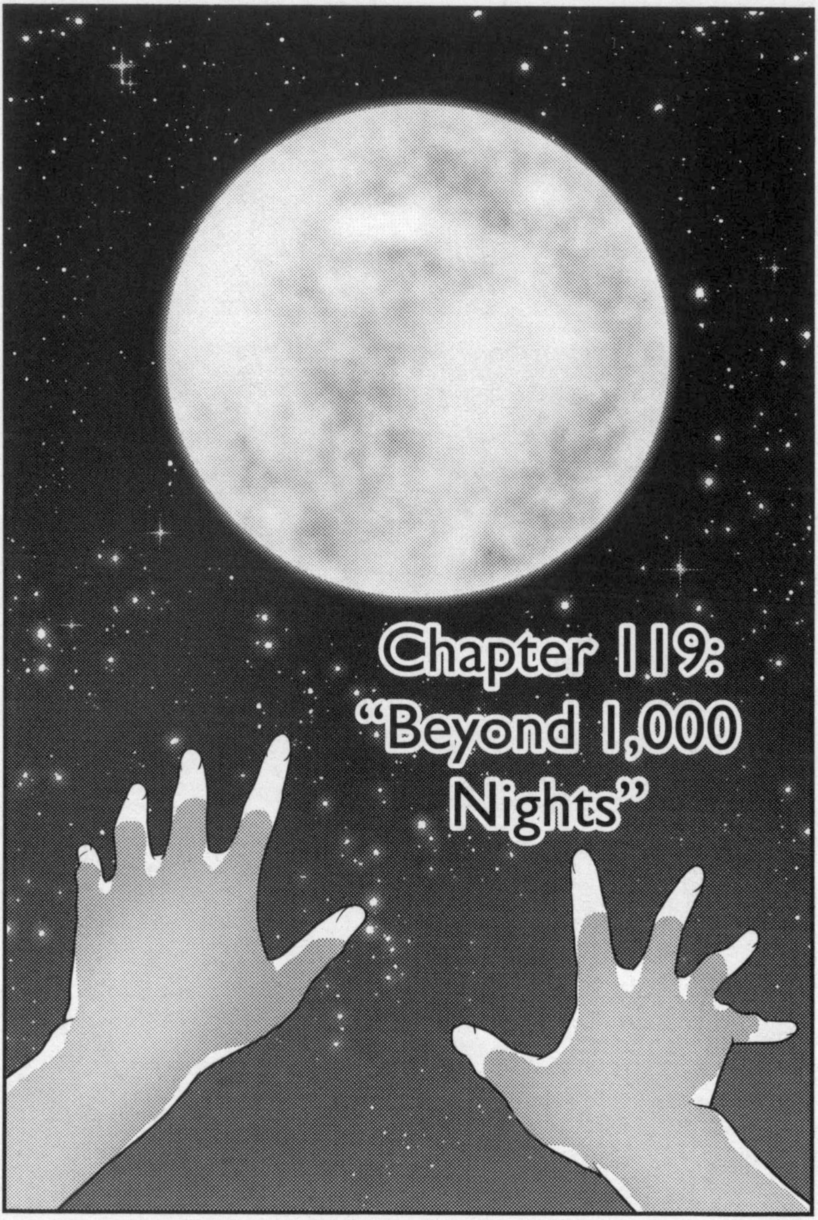
Chapter 119:
"Beyond 1,000
Nights"

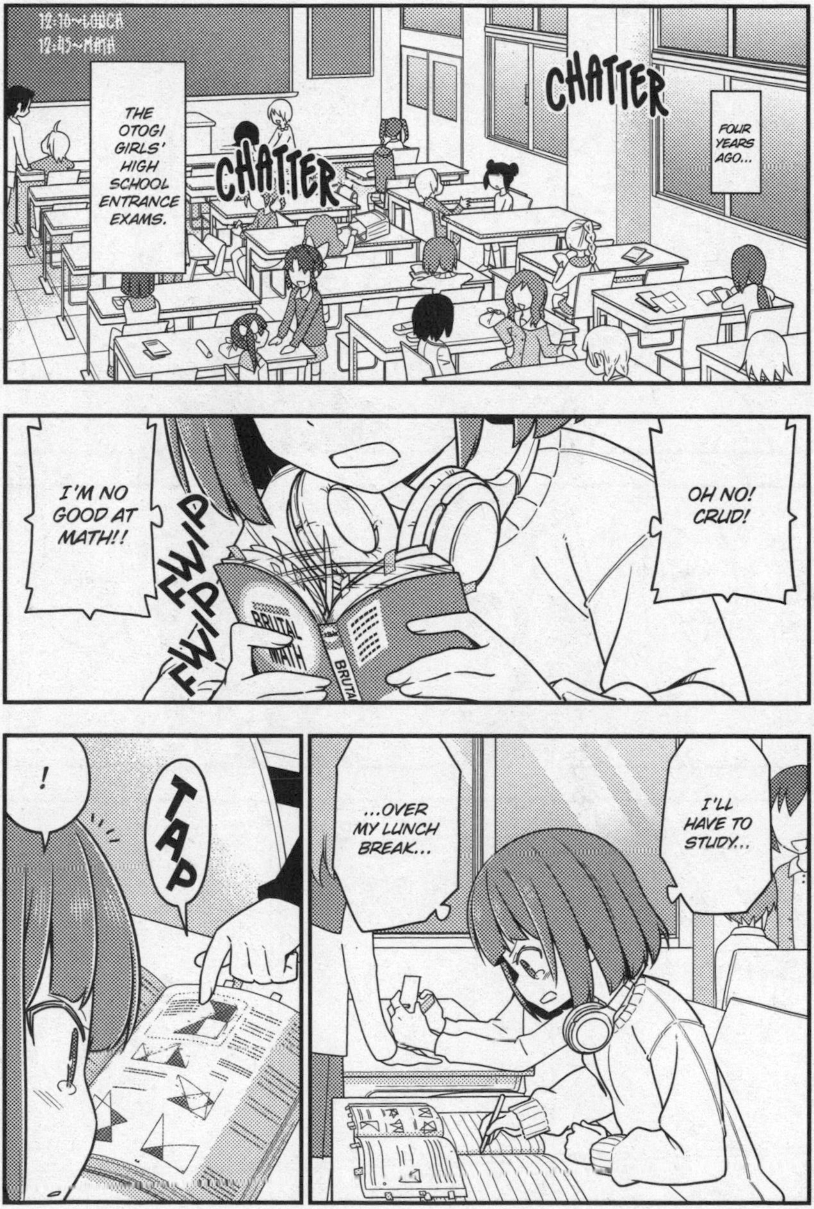
FOUR YEARS AGO...
CHATTER
CHATTER
THE OTOGI GIRLS' HIGH SCHOOL ENTRANCE EXAMS.
OH NO! CRUD!
FWIP FWIP
I'M NO GOOD AT MATH!!
BRUTAL MATH
I'LL HAVE TO STUDY...
...OVER MY LUNCH BREAK...
TAP
!

WHO ARE YOU?

UH...

AND HERE.

HERE...

HERE ...

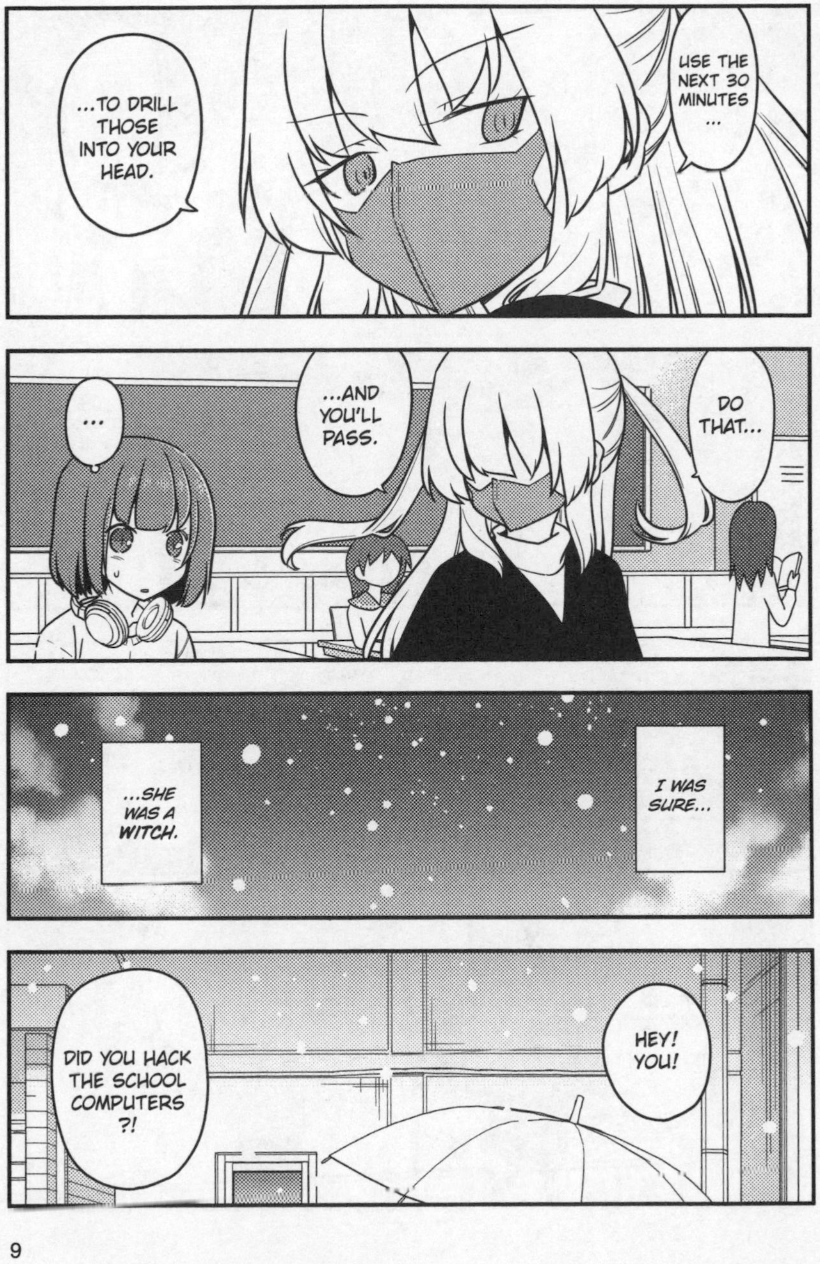
USE THE NEXT 30 MINUTES...
...TO DRILL THOSE INTO YOUR HEAD.
DO THAT...
...AND YOU'LL PASS.
...
I WAS SURE...
...SHE WAS A WITCH.
HEY! YOU!
DID YOU HACK THE SCHOOL COMPUTERS?!

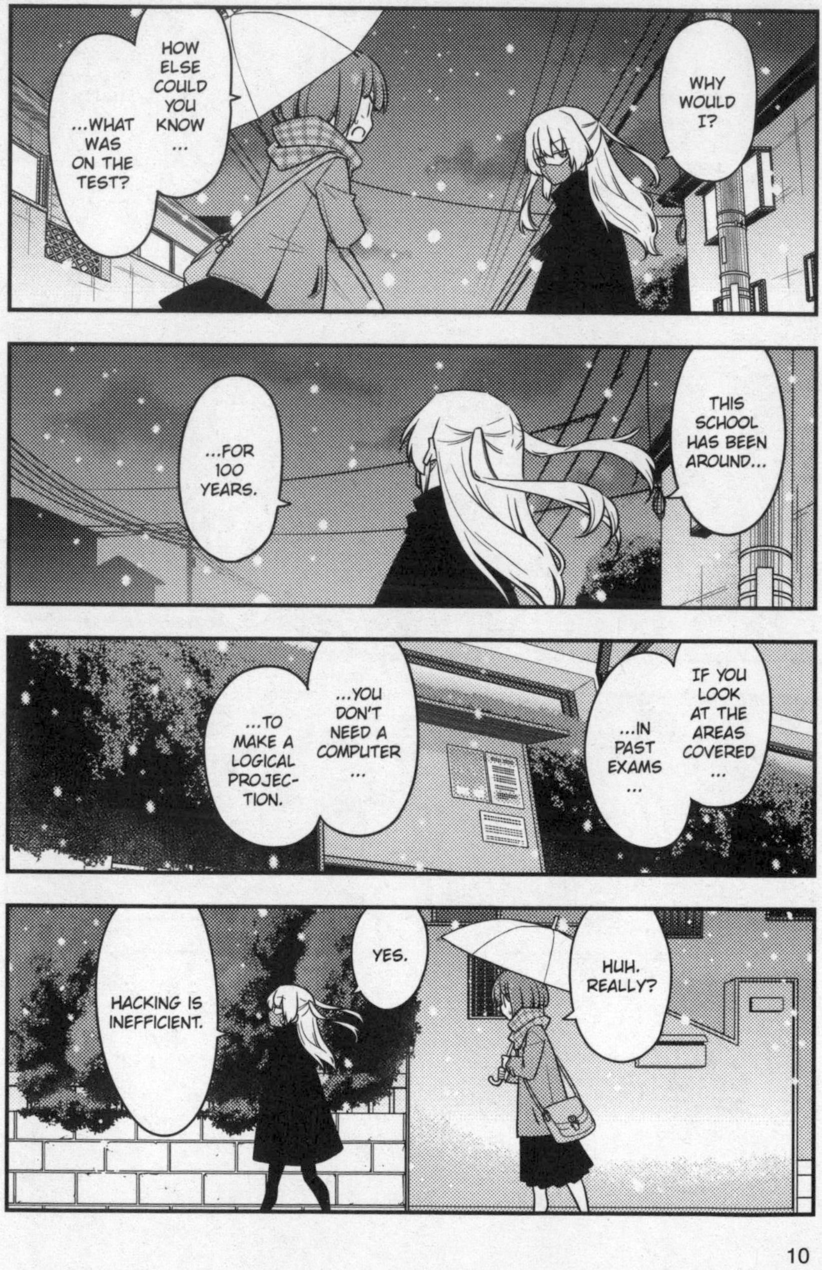
WHY WOULD I?
HOW ELSE COULD YOU KNOW ... ...WHAT WAS ON THE TEST?
THIS SCHOOL HAS BEEN AROUND...
...FOR 100 YEARS.
IF YOU LOOK AT THE AREAS COVERED ... ...IN PAST EXAMS ...
...YOU DON'T NEED A COMPUTER ... ...TO MAKE A LOGICAL PROJECTION.
HUH. REALLY?
YES.
HACKING IS INEFFICIENT.

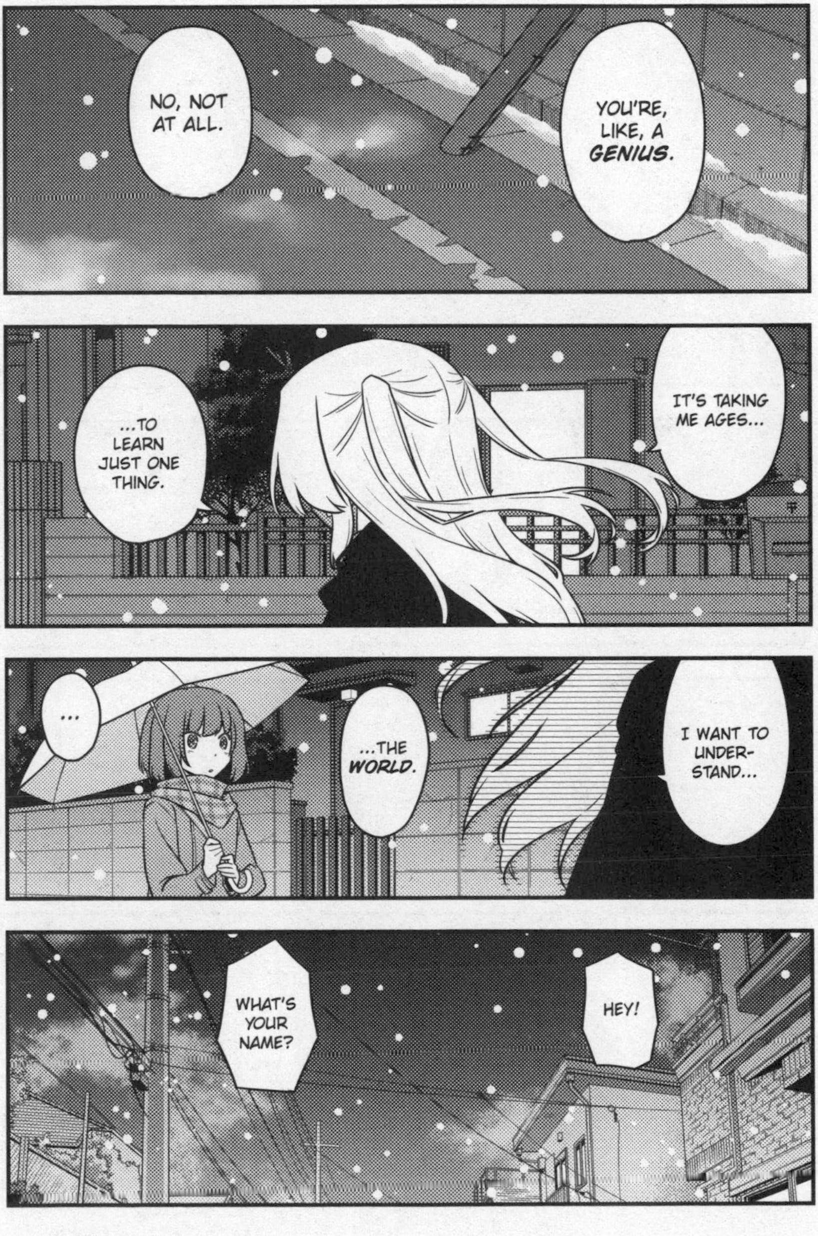
YOU'RE, LIKE, A *GENIUS*.
NO, NOT AT ALL.
IT'S TAKING ME AGES...
...TO LEARN JUST ONE THING.
I WANT TO UNDER-STAND...
...THE *WORLD*.
...
HEY!
WHAT'S YOUR NAME?

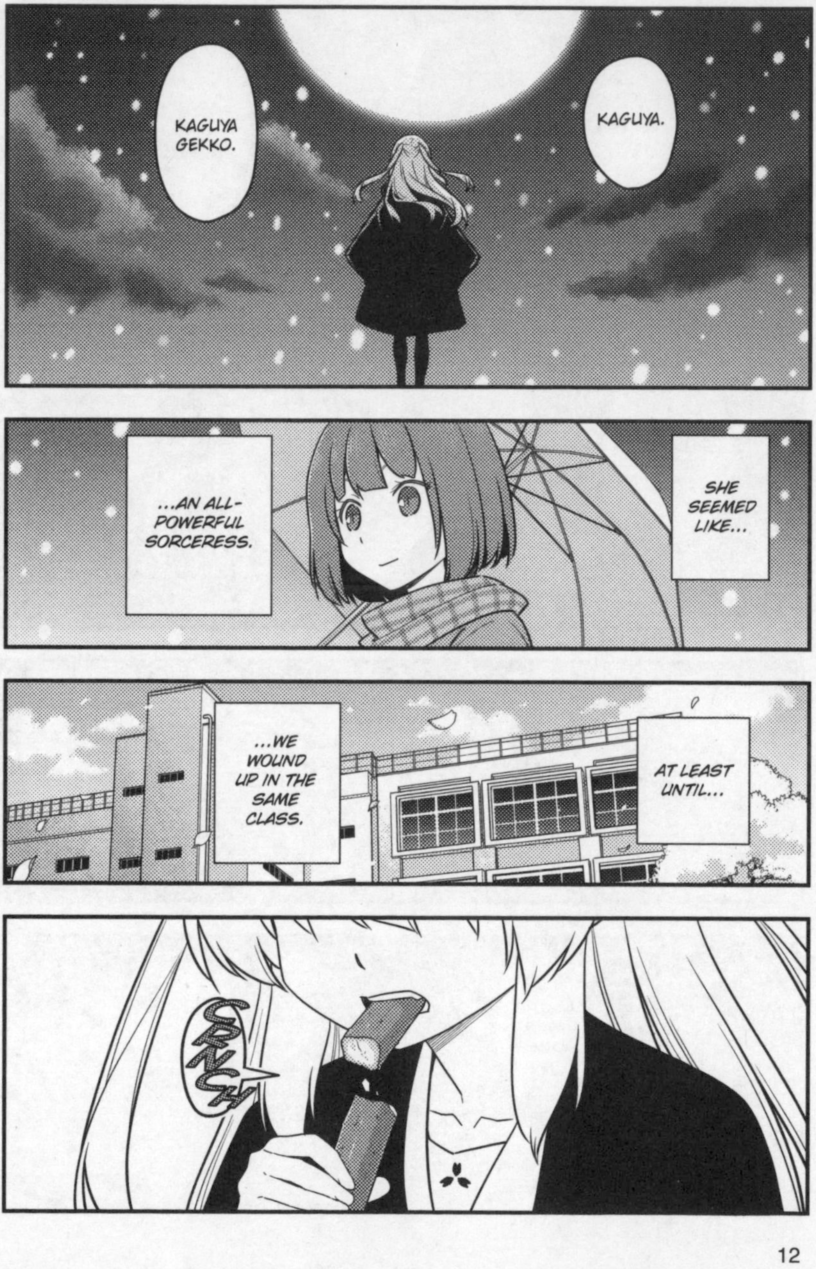
KAGUYA.
KAGUYA GEKKO.
SHE SEEMED LIKE...
...AN ALL-POWERFUL SORCERESS.
AT LEAST UNTIL...
...WE WOUND UP IN THE SAME CLASS.
CRNCH

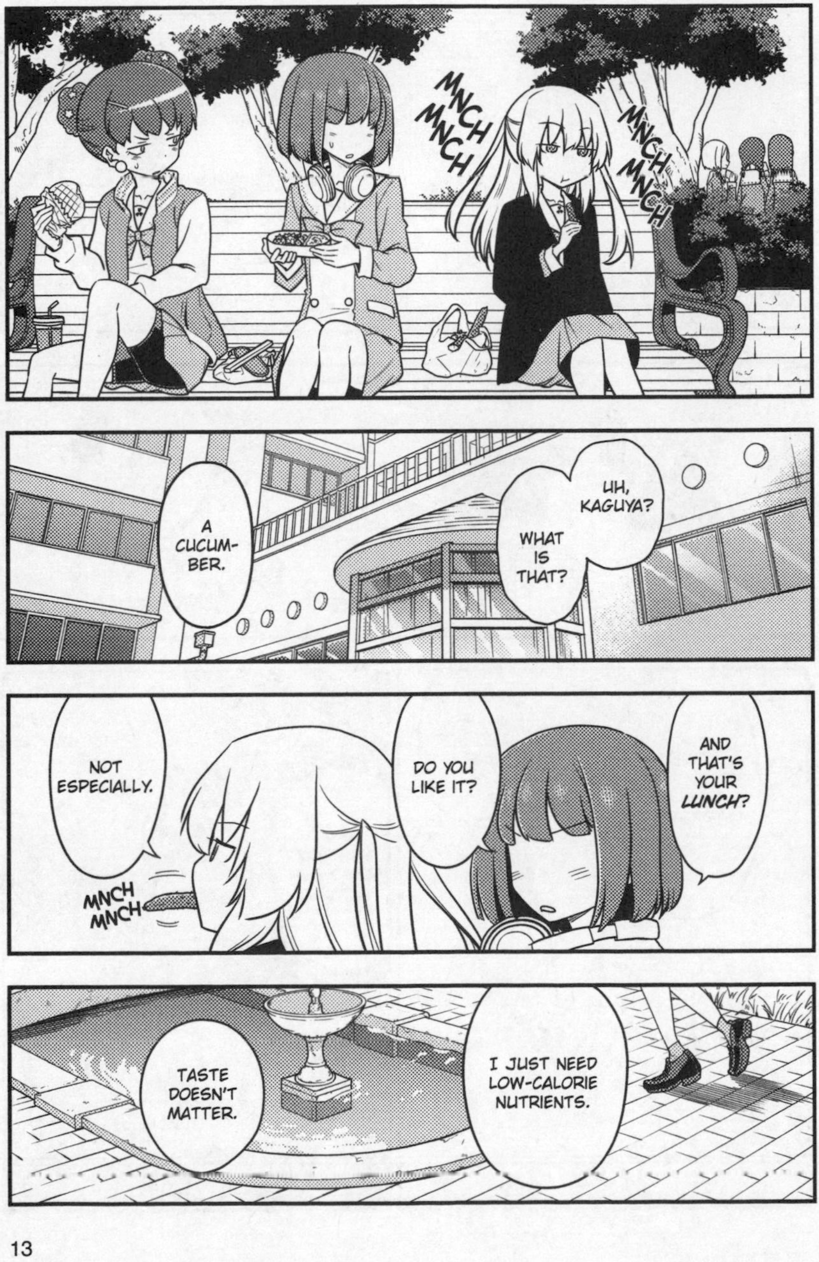
MNCH MNCH
MNCH MNCH
UH, KAGUYA?
WHAT IS THAT?
A CUCUMBER.
AND THAT'S YOUR *LUNCH*?
DO YOU LIKE IT?
NOT ESPECIALLY.
MNCH MNCH
I JUST NEED LOW-CALORIE NUTRIENTS.
TASTE DOESN'T MATTER.

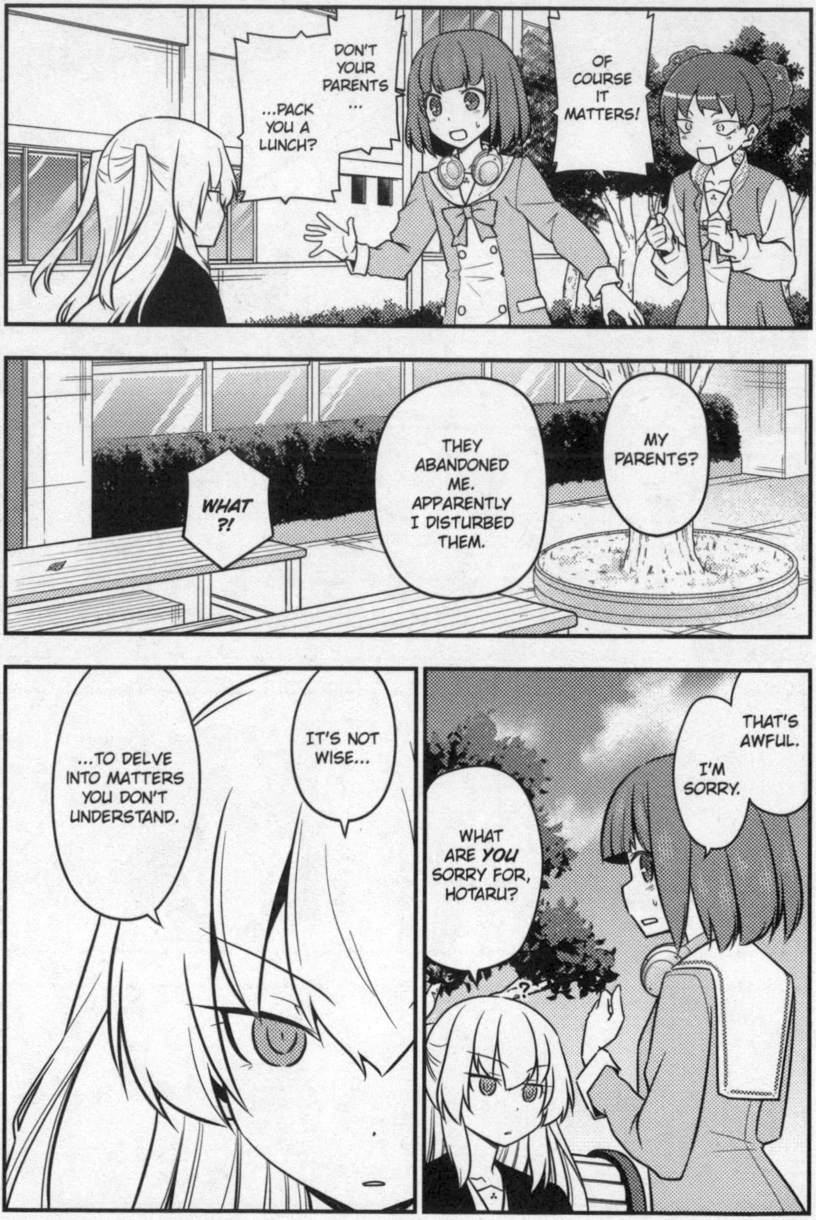
OF COURSE IT MATTERS!
DON'T YOUR PARENTS ...
...PACK YOU A LUNCH?
MY PARENTS?
THEY ABANDONED ME. APPARENTLY I DISTURBED THEM.
WHAT ?!
THAT'S AWFUL.
I'M SORRY.
WHAT ARE *YOU* SORRY FOR, HOTARU?
IT'S NOT WISE...
...TO DELVE INTO MATTERS YOU DON'T UNDERSTAND.

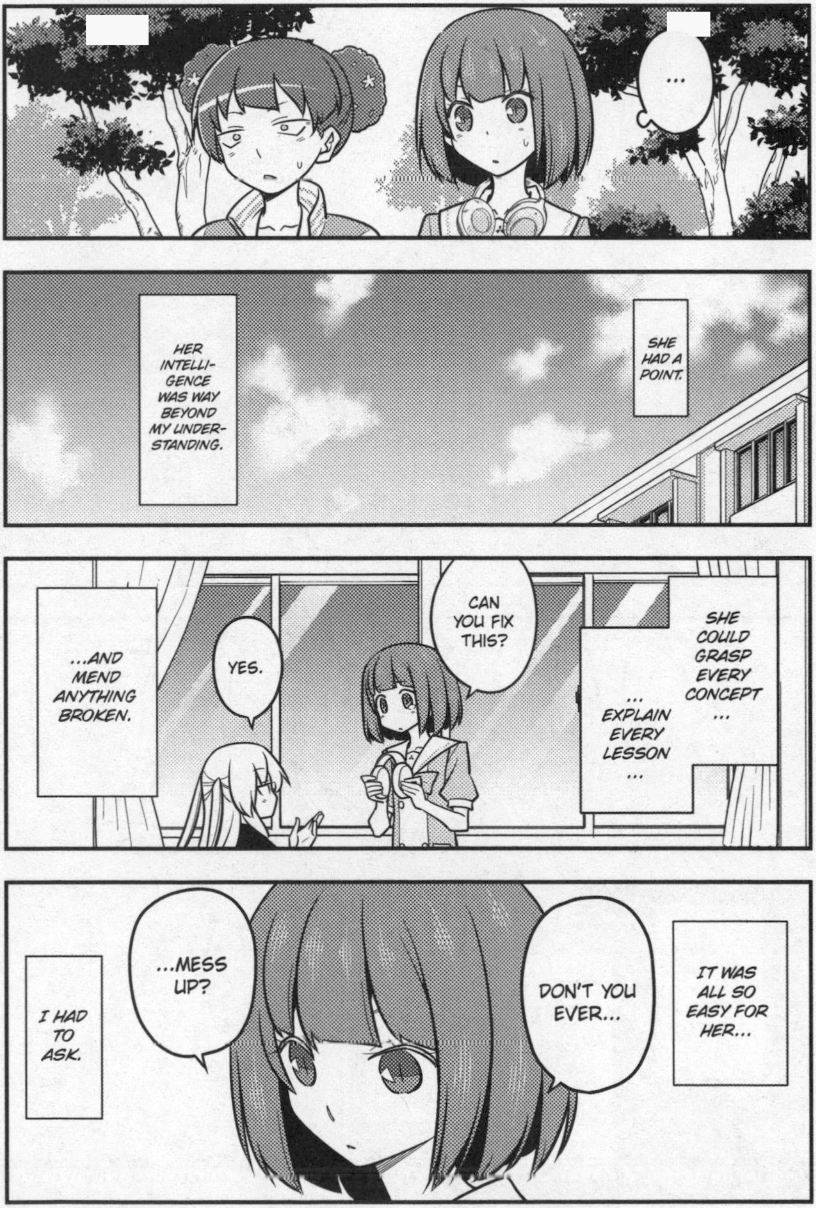
...
SHE HAD A POINT.
HER INTELLIGENCE WAS WAY BEYOND MY UNDERSTANDING.
SHE COULD GRASP EVERY CONCEPT...
...EXPLAIN EVERY LESSON...
CAN YOU FIX THIS?
YES.
...AND MEND ANYTHING BROKEN.
IT WAS ALL SO EASY FOR HER...
DON'T YOU EVER...
...MESS UP?
I HAD TO ASK.

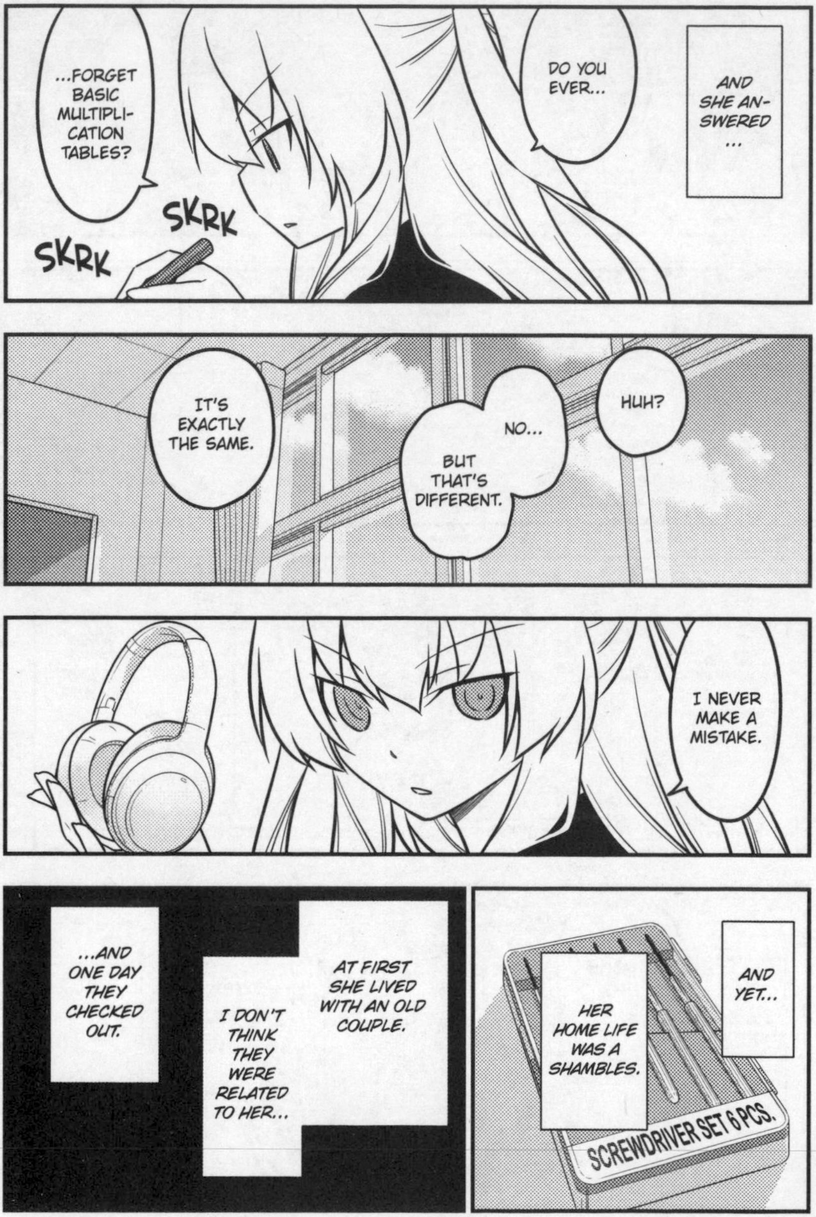
AND SHE ANSWERED...
DO YOU EVER...
...FORGET BASIC MULTIPLICATION TABLES?
SKRK
SKRK
HUH?
NO...
BUT THAT'S DIFFERENT.
IT'S EXACTLY THE SAME.
I NEVER MAKE A MISTAKE.
AND YET...
HER HOME LIFE WAS A SHAMBLES.
SCREWDRIVER SET 6 PCS.
AT FIRST SHE LIVED WITH AN OLD COUPLE.
I DON'T THINK THEY WERE RELATED TO HER...
...AND ONE DAY THEY CHECKED OUT.

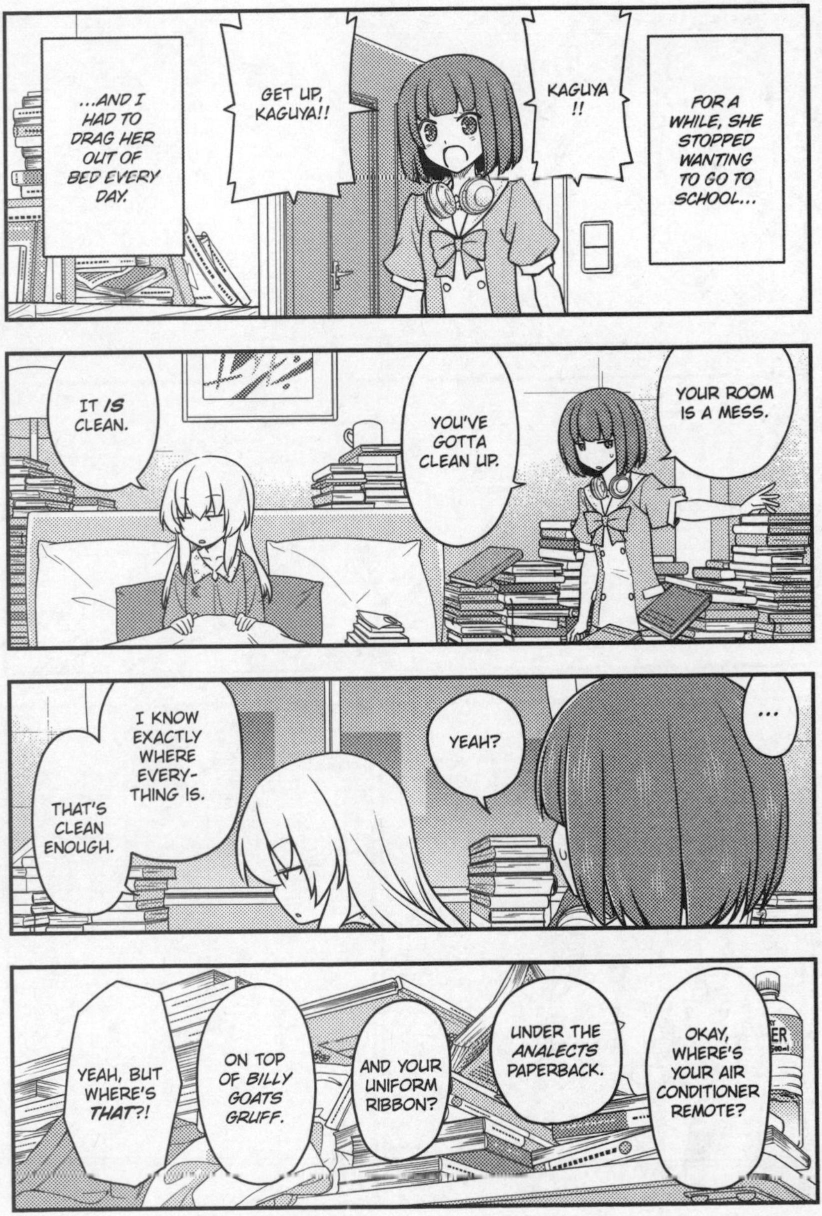
FOR A WHILE, SHE STOPPED WANTING TO GO TO SCHOOL...
KAGUYA !!
GET UP, KAGUYA!!
...AND I HAD TO DRAG HER OUT OF BED EVERY DAY.
YOUR ROOM IS A MESS.
YOU'VE GOTTA CLEAN UP.
IT *IS* CLEAN.
...
YEAH?
I KNOW EXACTLY WHERE EVERY-THING IS.
THAT'S CLEAN ENOUGH.
OKAY, WHERE'S YOUR AIR CONDITIONER REMOTE?
UNDER THE *ANALECTS* PAPERBACK.
AND YOUR UNIFORM RIBBON?
ON TOP OF *BILLY GOATS GRUFF*.
YEAH, BUT WHERE'S *THAT*?!

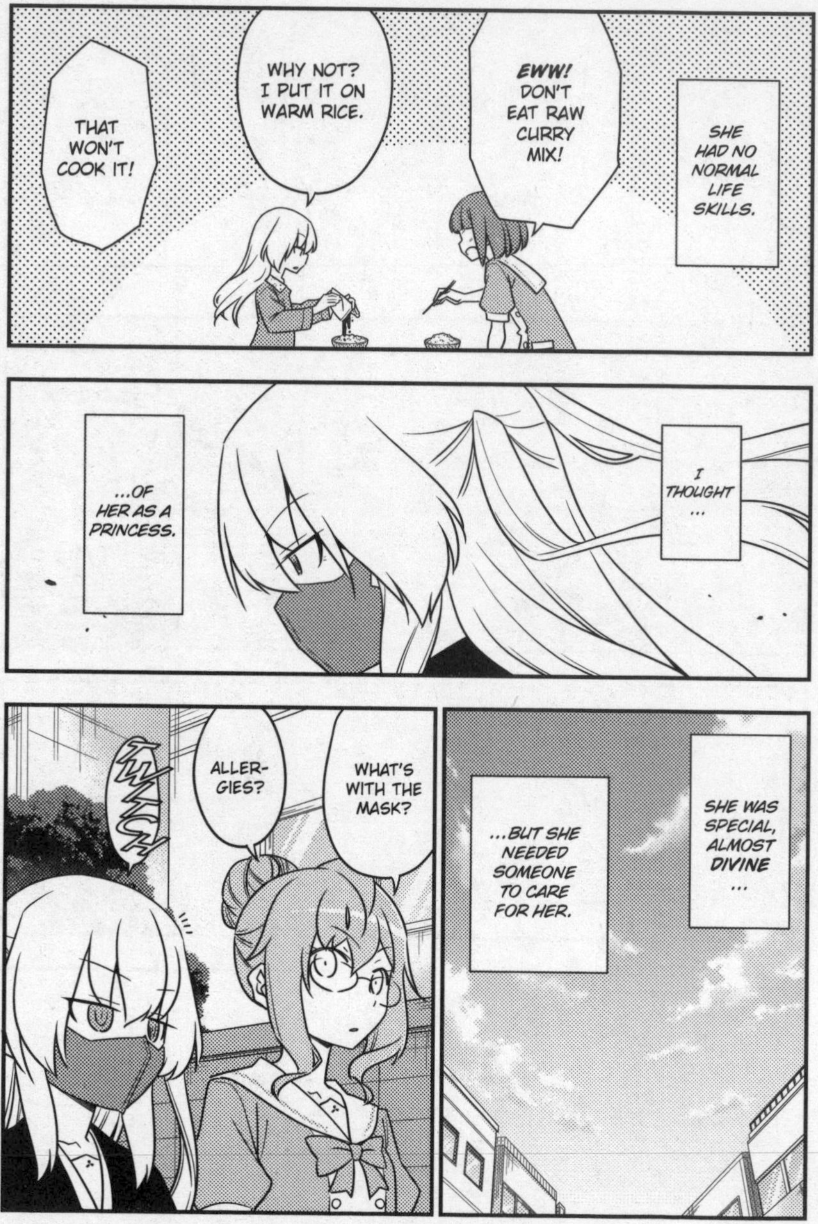
SHE HAD NO NORMAL LIFE SKILLS.
EWW! DON'T EAT RAW CURRY MIX!
WHY NOT? I PUT IT ON WARM RICE.
THAT WON'T COOK IT!
I THOUGHT ...
...OF HER AS A PRINCESS.
SHE WAS SPECIAL, ALMOST DIVINE ...
...BUT SHE NEEDED SOMEONE TO CARE FOR HER.
WHAT'S WITH THE MASK?
ALLER-GIES?
TWITCH

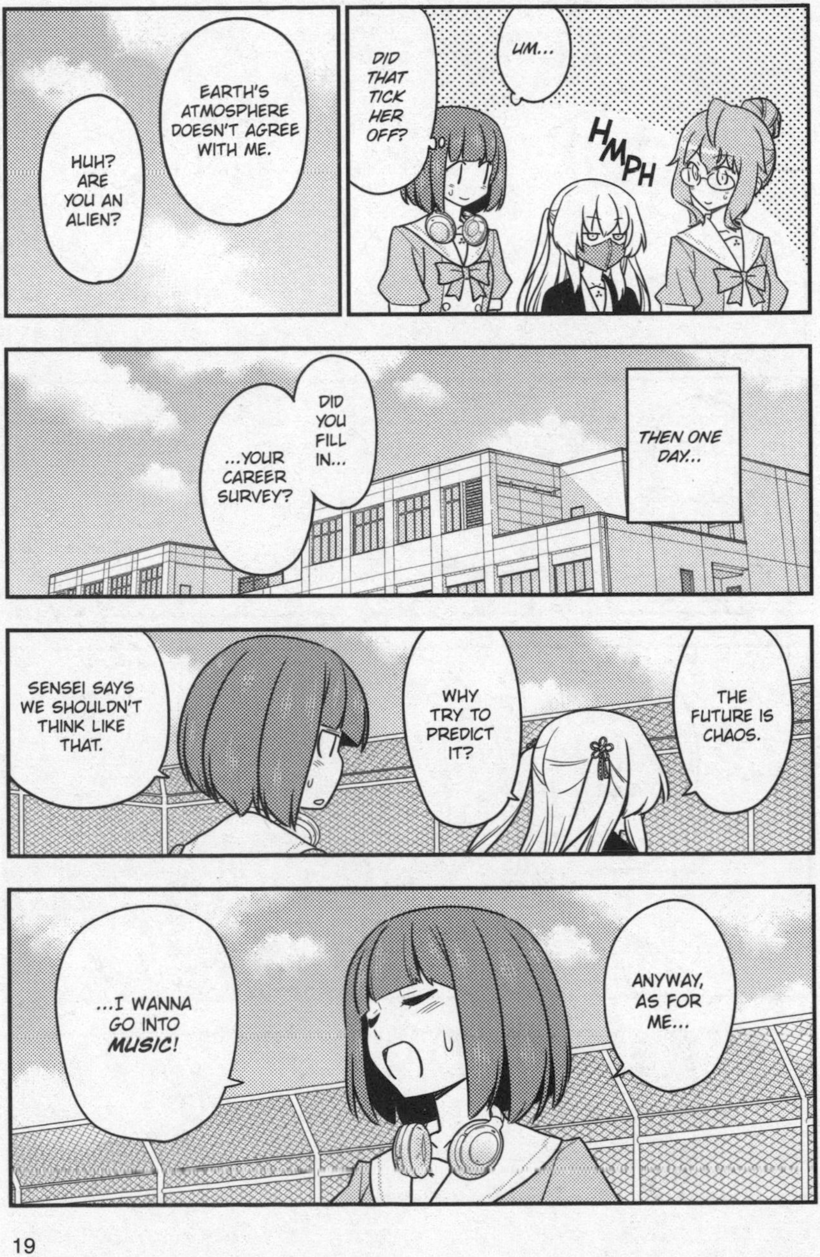
UM...
DID THAT TICK HER OFF?
HMPH
EARTH'S ATMOSPHERE DOESN'T AGREE WITH ME.
HUH? ARE YOU AN ALIEN?
THEN ONE DAY...
DID YOU FILL IN...
...YOUR CAREER SURVEY?
THE FUTURE IS CHAOS.
WHY TRY TO PREDICT IT?
SENSEI SAYS WE SHOULDN'T THINK LIKE THAT.
ANYWAY, AS FOR ME...
...I WANNA GO INTO ***MUSIC***!

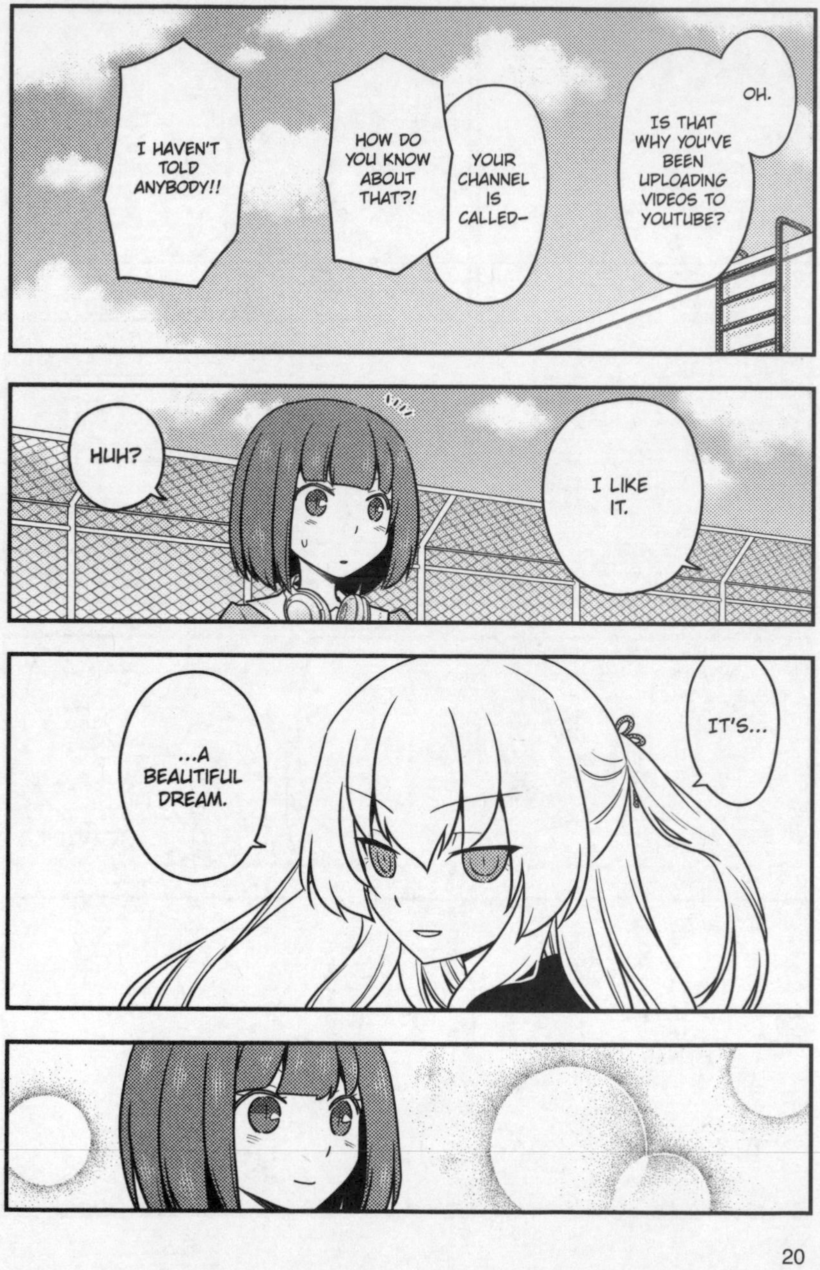
OH. IS THAT WHY YOU'VE BEEN UPLOADING VIDEOS TO YOUTUBE?
YOUR CHANNEL IS CALLED—
HOW DO YOU KNOW ABOUT THAT?!
I HAVEN'T TOLD ANYBODY!!
I LIKE IT.
HUH?
IT'S...
...A BEAUTIFUL DREAM.

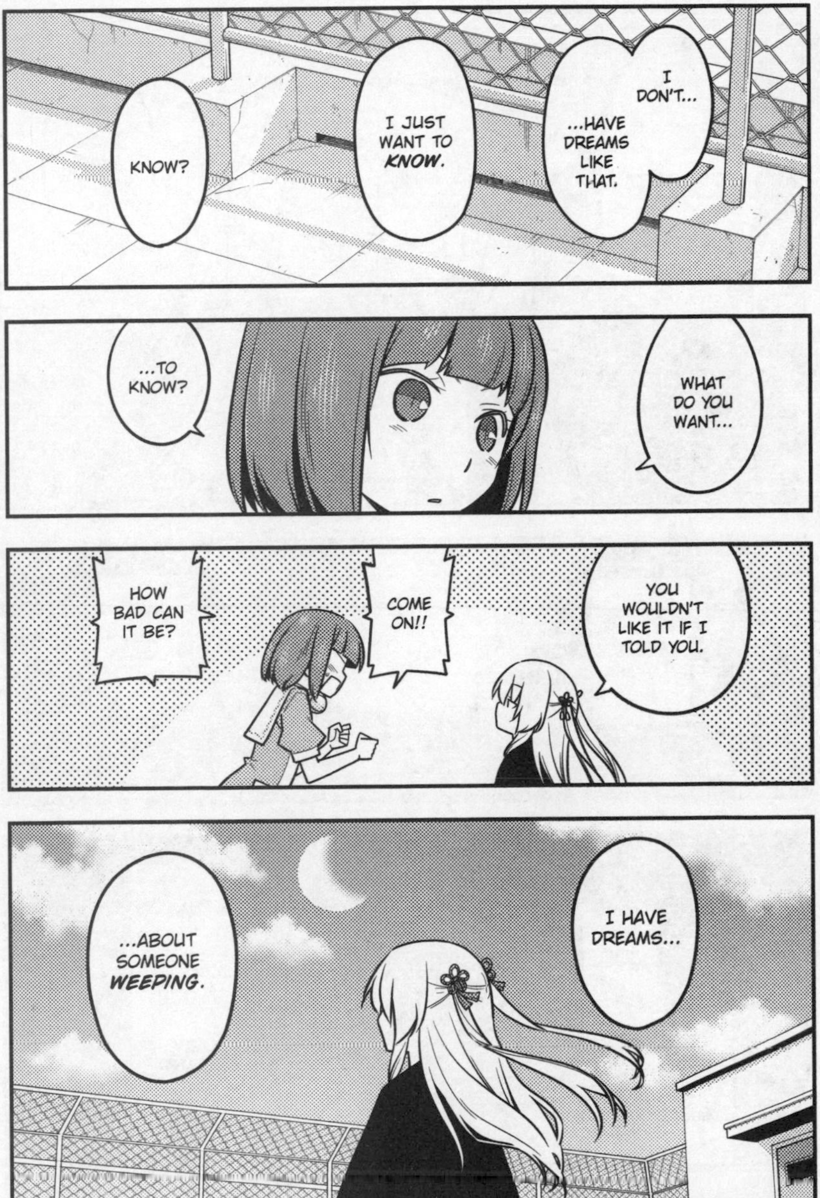
I DON'T...
...HAVE DREAMS LIKE THAT.
I JUST WANT TO **KNOW**.
KNOW?
WHAT DO YOU WANT...
...TO KNOW?
YOU WOULDN'T LIKE IT IF I TOLD YOU.
COME ON!!
HOW BAD CAN IT BE?
I HAVE DREAMS...
...ABOUT SOMEONE **WEEPING**.

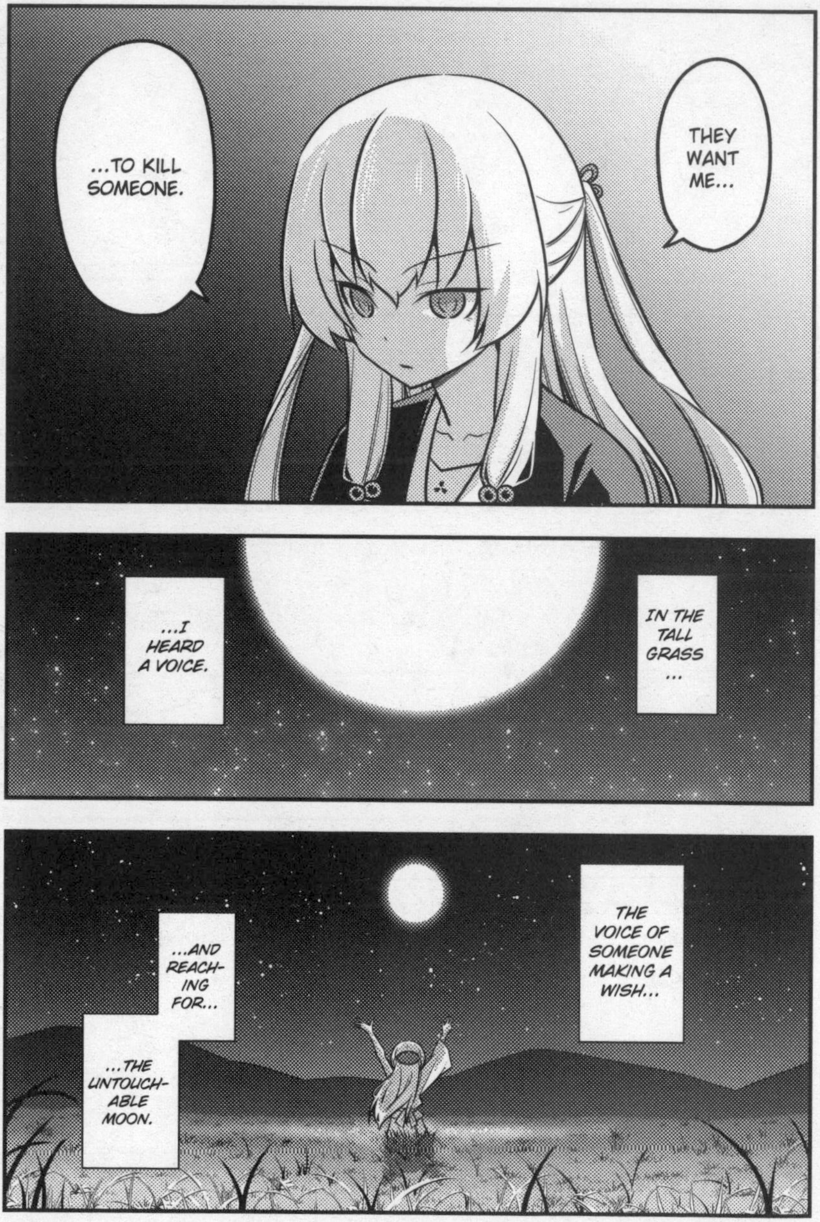
THEY WANT ME...
...TO KILL SOMEONE.
IN THE TALL GRASS ...
...I HEARD A VOICE.
THE VOICE OF SOMEONE MAKING A WISH...
...AND REACHING FOR...
...THE UNTOUCHABLE MOON.

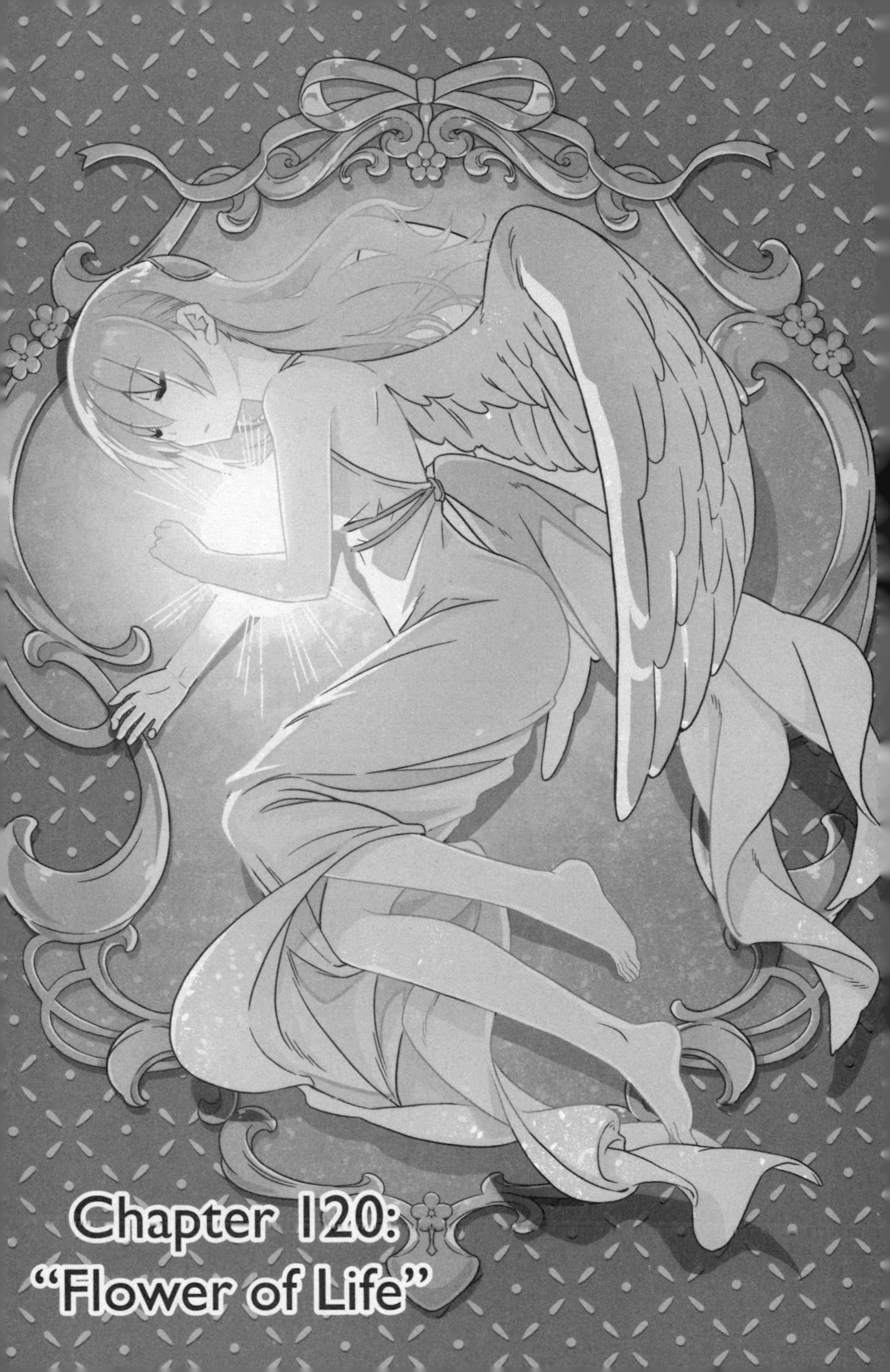

Chapter 120: "Flower of Life"

FLY ME ᵀᴼ ᵀᴴᴱ MOON

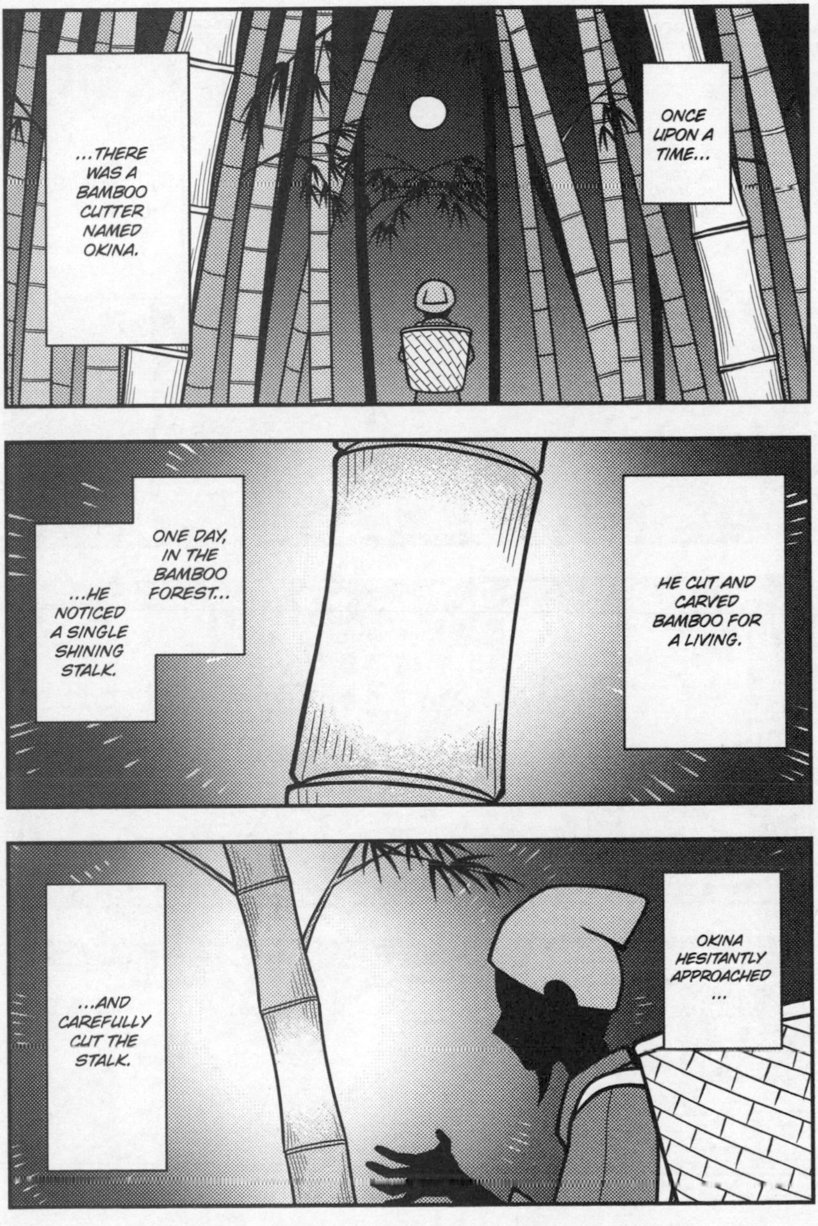
ONCE UPON A TIME...
...THERE WAS A BAMBOO CUTTER NAMED OKINA.
HE CUT AND CARVED BAMBOO FOR A LIVING.
ONE DAY, IN THE BAMBOO FOREST...
...HE NOTICED A SINGLE SHINING STALK.
OKINA HESITANTLY APPROACHED ...
...AND CAREFULLY CUT THE STALK.

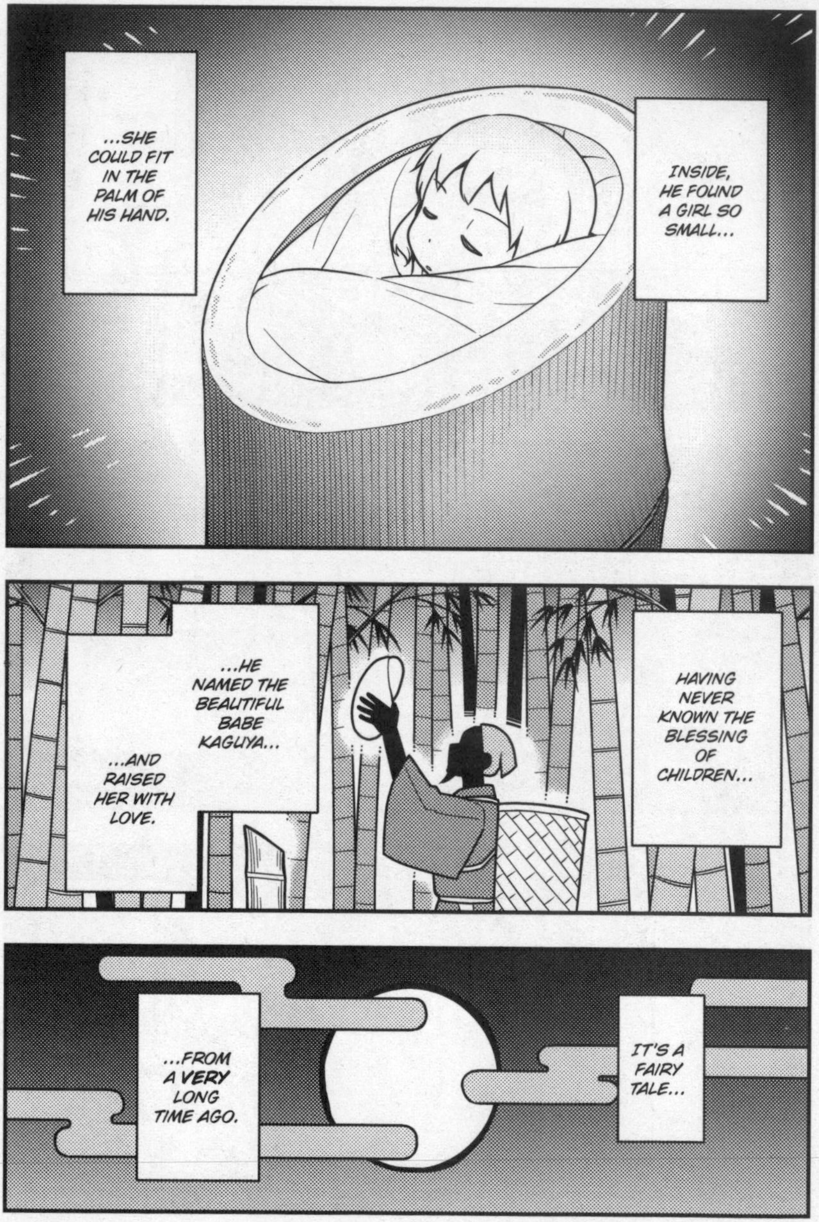
INSIDE, HE FOUND A GIRL SO SMALL...
...SHE COULD FIT IN THE PALM OF HIS HAND.
HAVING NEVER KNOWN THE BLESSING OF CHILDREN...
...HE NAMED THE BEAUTIFUL BABE KAGUYA...
...AND RAISED HER WITH LOVE.
IT'S A FAIRY TALE...
...FROM A VERY LONG TIME AGO.

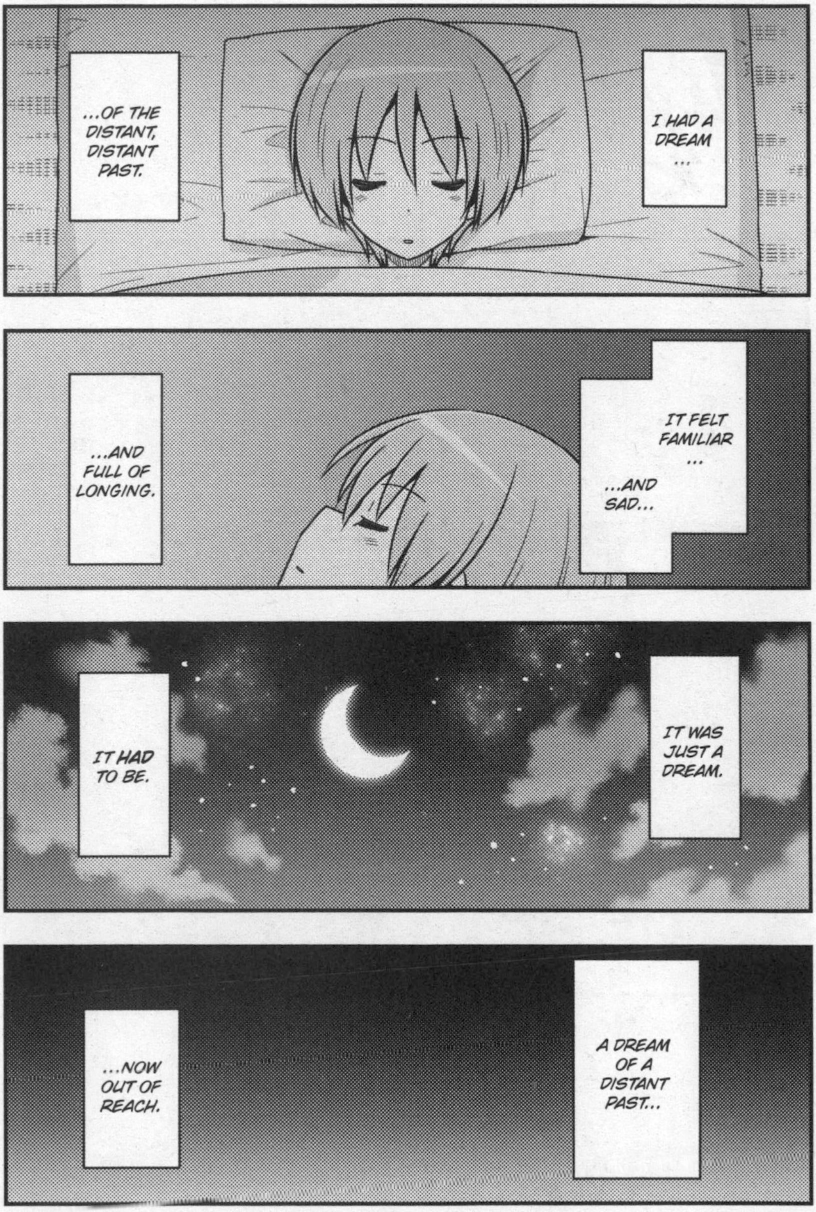
I HAD A DREAM ...
...OF THE DISTANT, DISTANT PAST.
IT FELT FAMILIAR ...
...AND SAD...
...AND FULL OF LONGING.
IT WAS JUST A DREAM.
IT HAD TO BE.
A DREAM OF A DISTANT PAST...
...NOW OUT OF REACH.

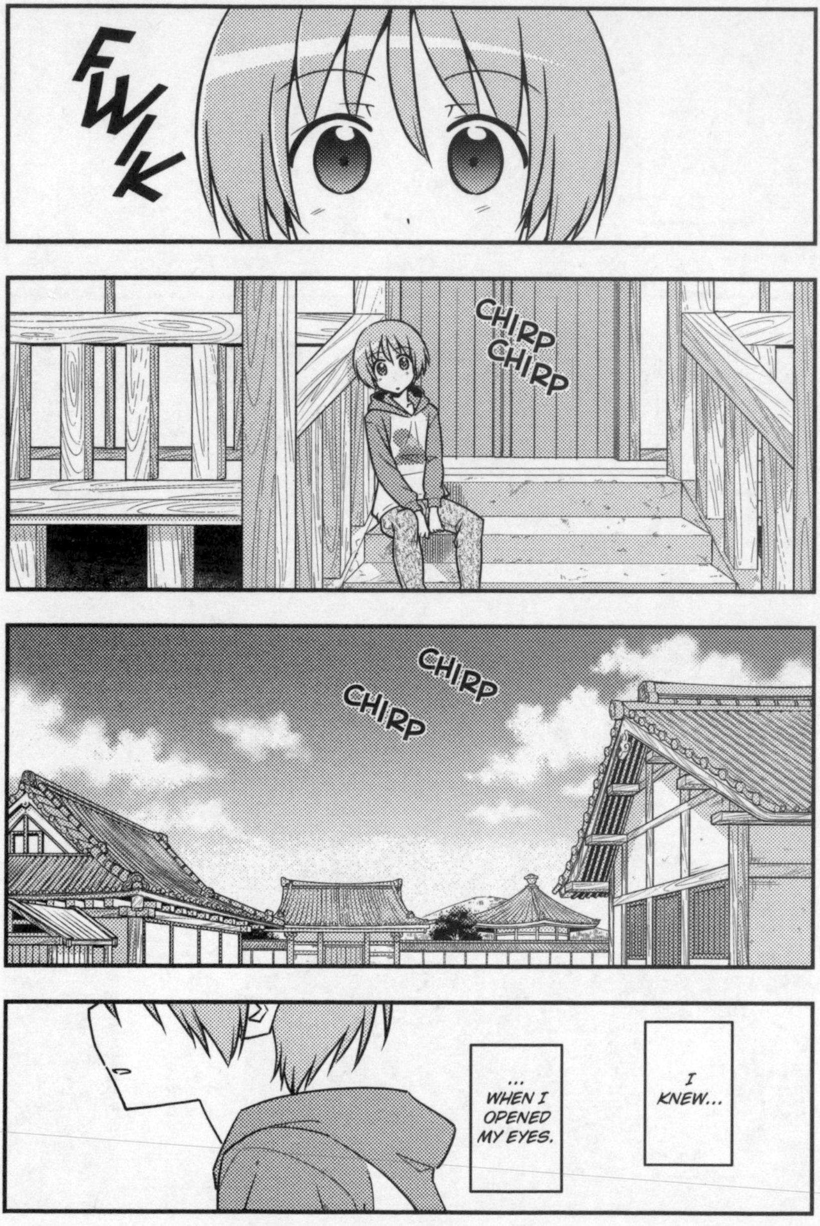
FWIK
CHIRP CHIRP
CHIRP
CHIRP
I KNEW...
... WHEN I OPENED MY EYES.

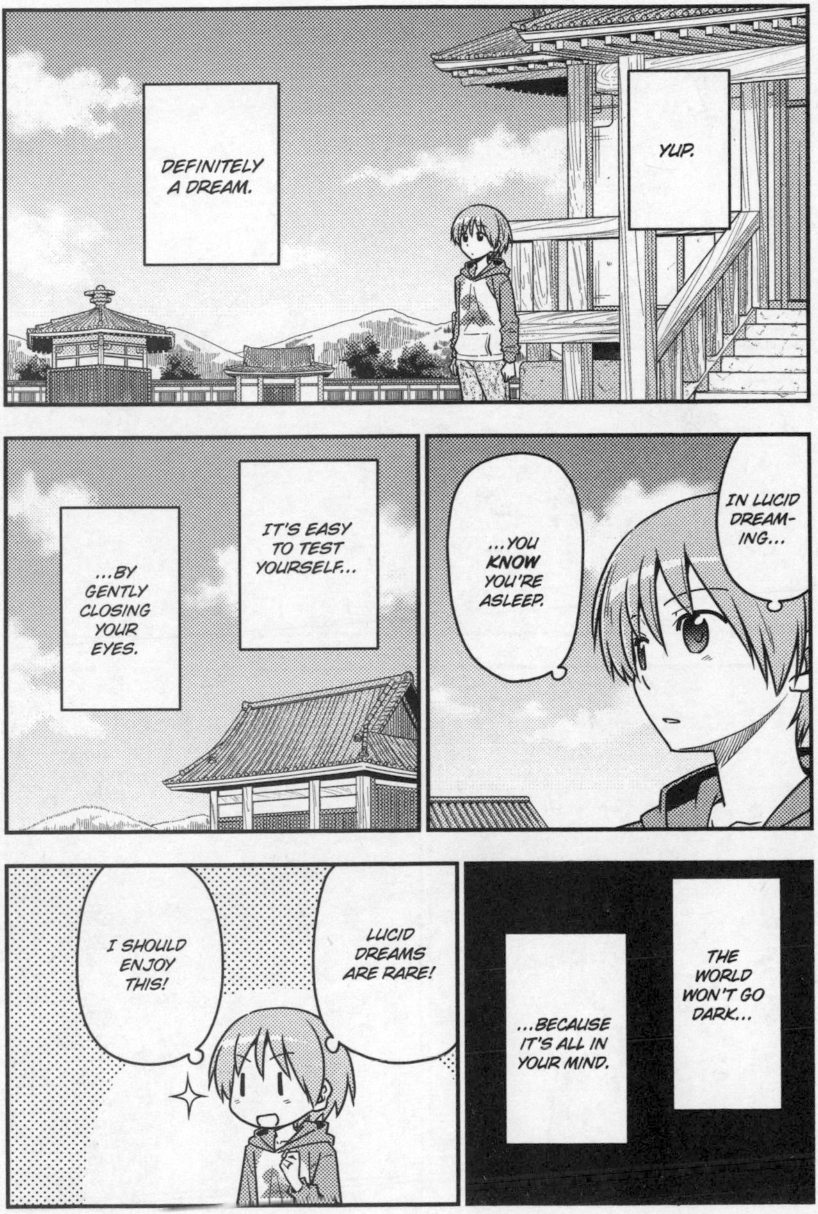
YUP.
DEFINITELY A DREAM.
IN LUCID DREAMING...
...YOU **KNOW** YOU'RE ASLEEP.
IT'S EASY TO TEST YOURSELF...
...BY GENTLY CLOSING YOUR EYES.
THE WORLD WON'T GO DARK...
...BECAUSE IT'S ALL IN YOUR MIND.
LUCID DREAMS ARE RARE!
I SHOULD ENJOY THIS!

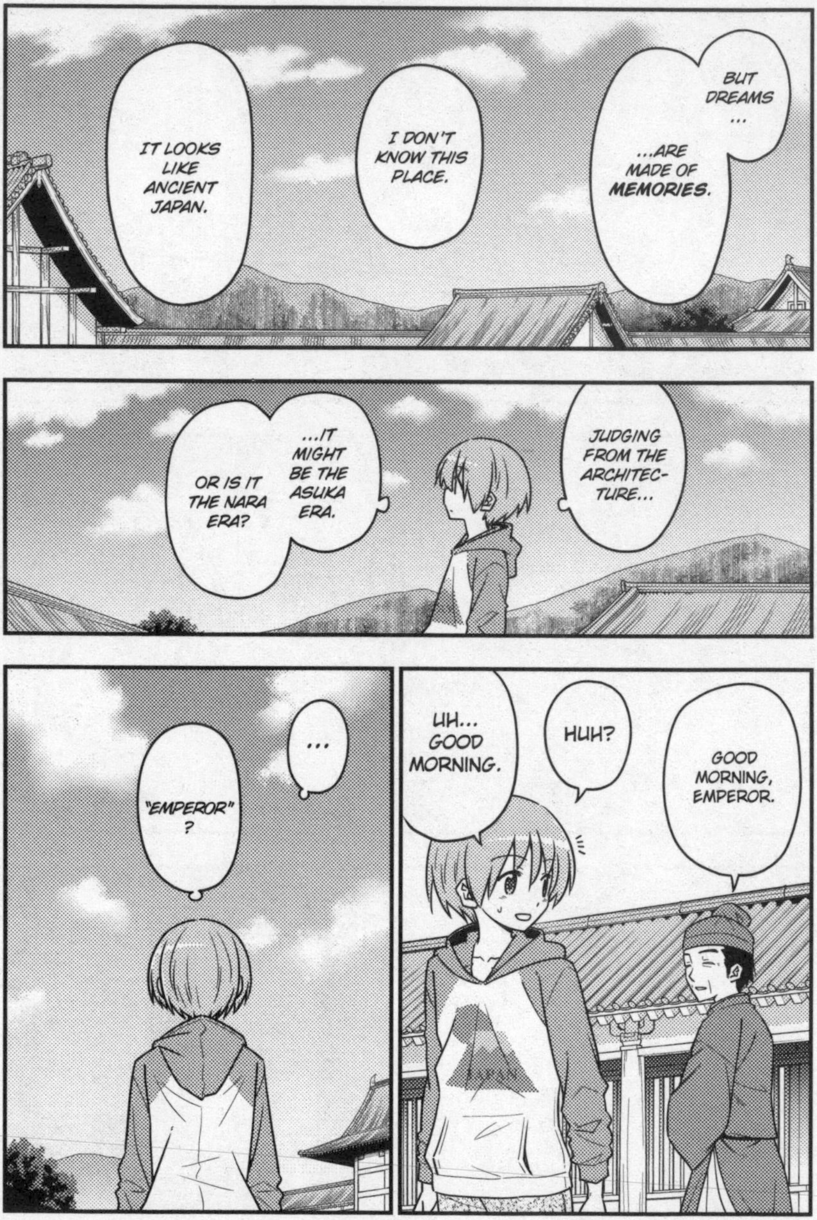
BUT DREAMS ...
...ARE MADE OF MEMORIES.
I DON'T KNOW THIS PLACE.
IT LOOKS LIKE ANCIENT JAPAN.
JUDGING FROM THE ARCHITEC-TURE...
...IT MIGHT BE THE ASUKA ERA.
OR IS IT THE NARA ERA?
GOOD MORNING, EMPEROR.
HUH?
UH... GOOD MORNING.
...
"EMPEROR"?

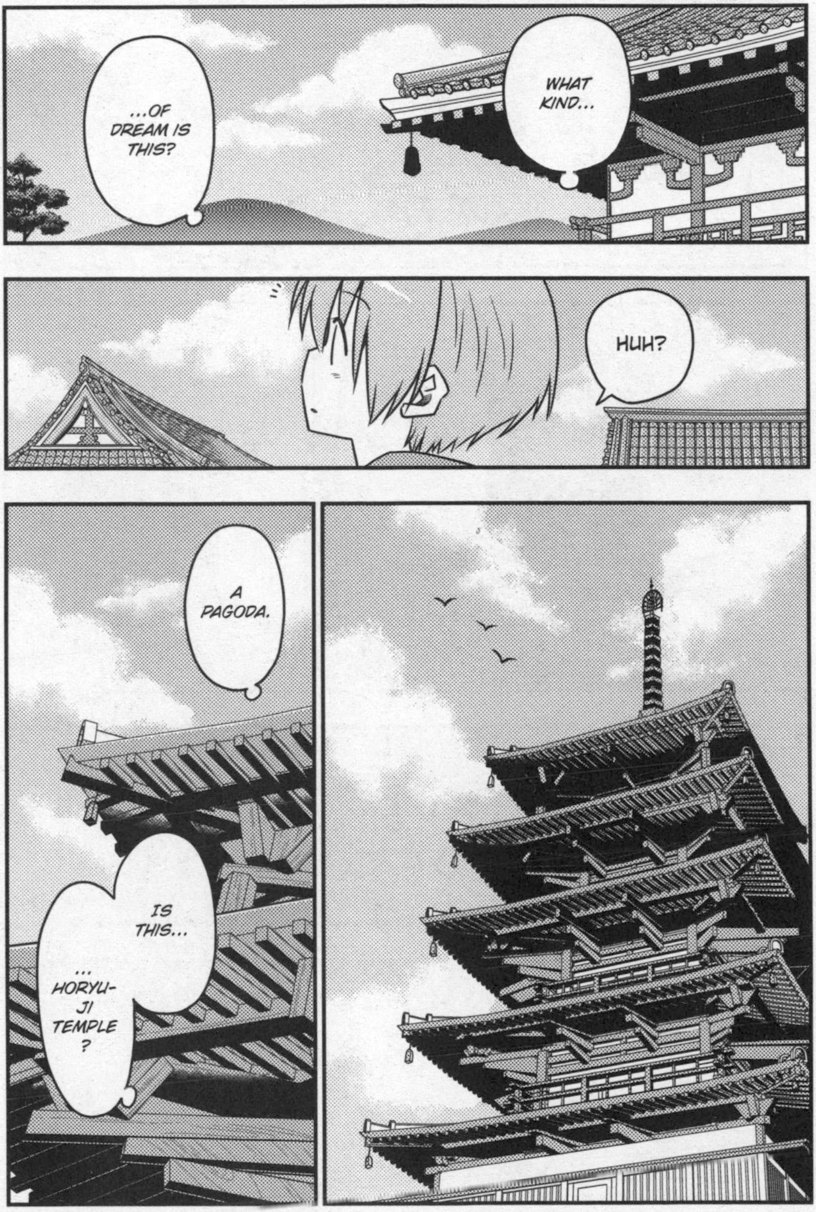
WHAT KIND...
...OF DREAM IS THIS?
HUH?
A PAGODA.
IS THIS...
...HORYU-JI TEMPLE?

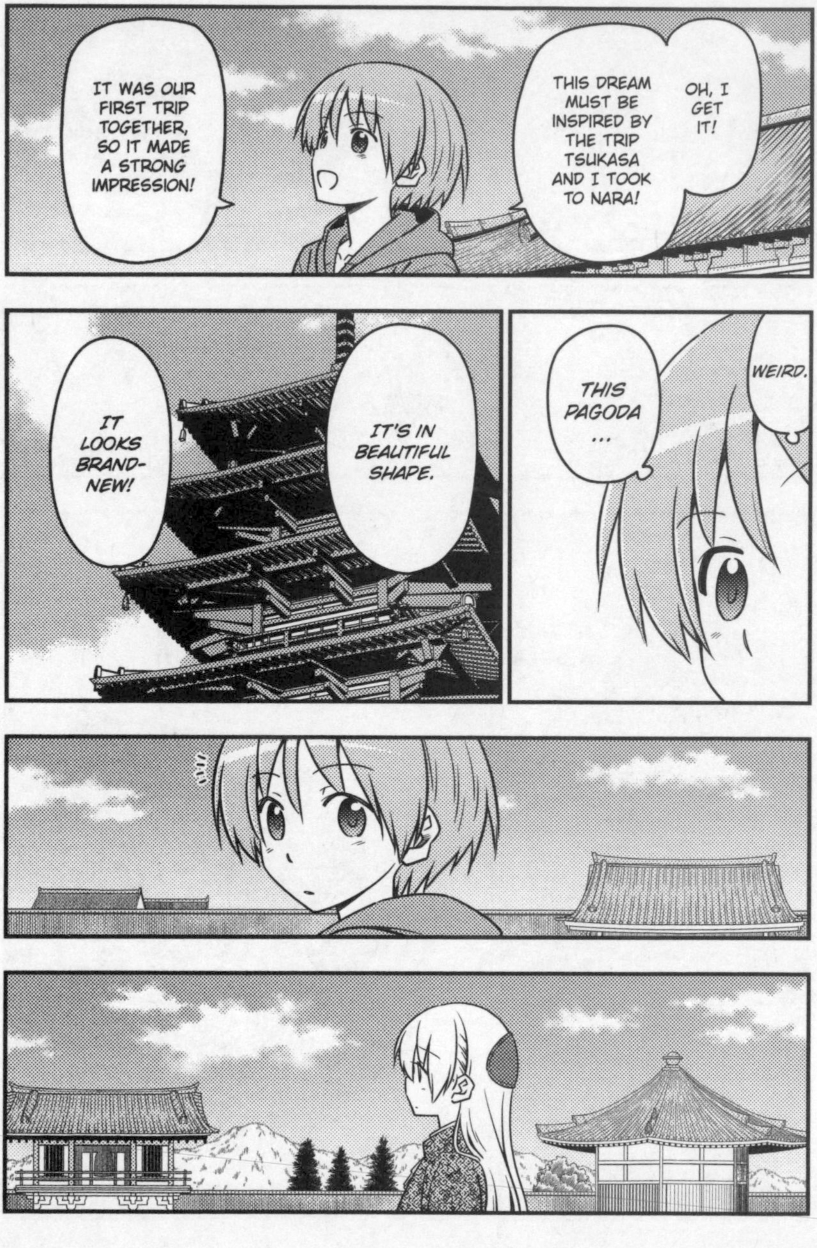
OH, I GET IT!
THIS DREAM MUST BE INSPIRED BY THE TRIP TSUKASA AND I TOOK TO NARA!
IT WAS OUR FIRST TRIP TOGETHER, SO IT MADE A STRONG IMPRESSION!
WEIRD.
THIS PAGODA ...
IT'S IN BEAUTIFUL SHAPE.
IT LOOKS BRAND-NEW!

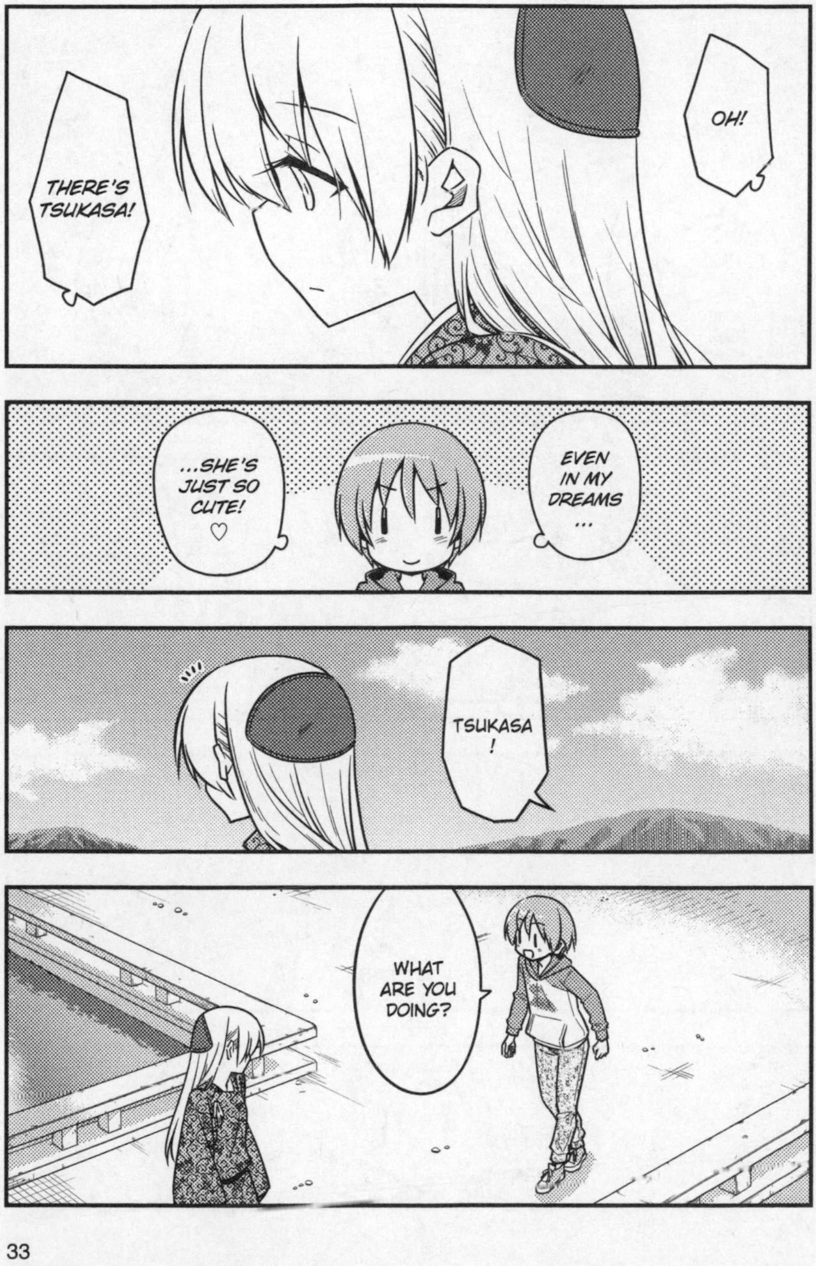
OH!
THERE'S TSUKASA!
EVEN IN MY DREAMS ...
...SHE'S JUST SO CUTE! ♡
TSUKASA !
WHAT ARE YOU DOING?

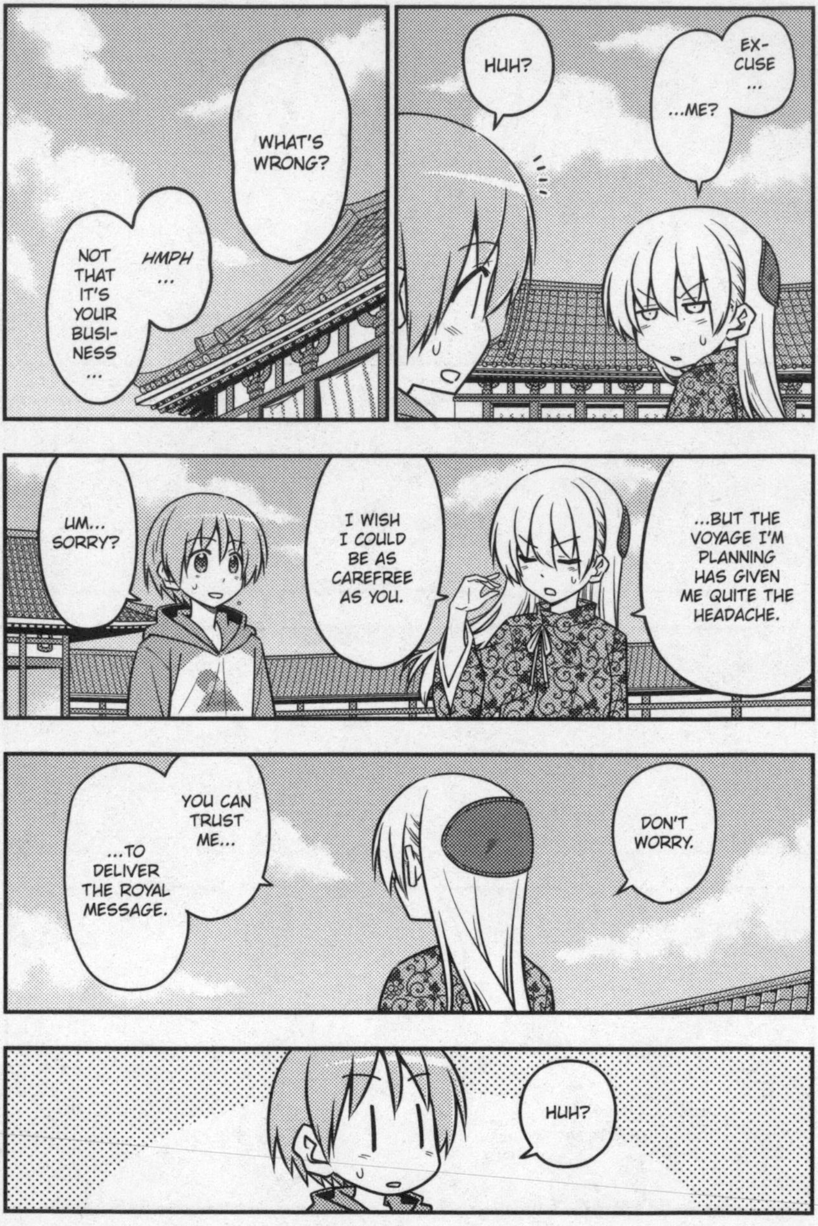
EXCUSE... ...ME?
HUH?
WHAT'S WRONG?
HMPH... NOT THAT IT'S YOUR BUSINESS...
...BUT THE VOYAGE I'M PLANNING HAS GIVEN ME QUITE THE HEADACHE.
I WISH I COULD BE AS CAREFREE AS YOU.
UM... SORRY?
DON'T WORRY.
YOU CAN TRUST ME...
...TO DELIVER THE ROYAL MESSAGE.
HUH?

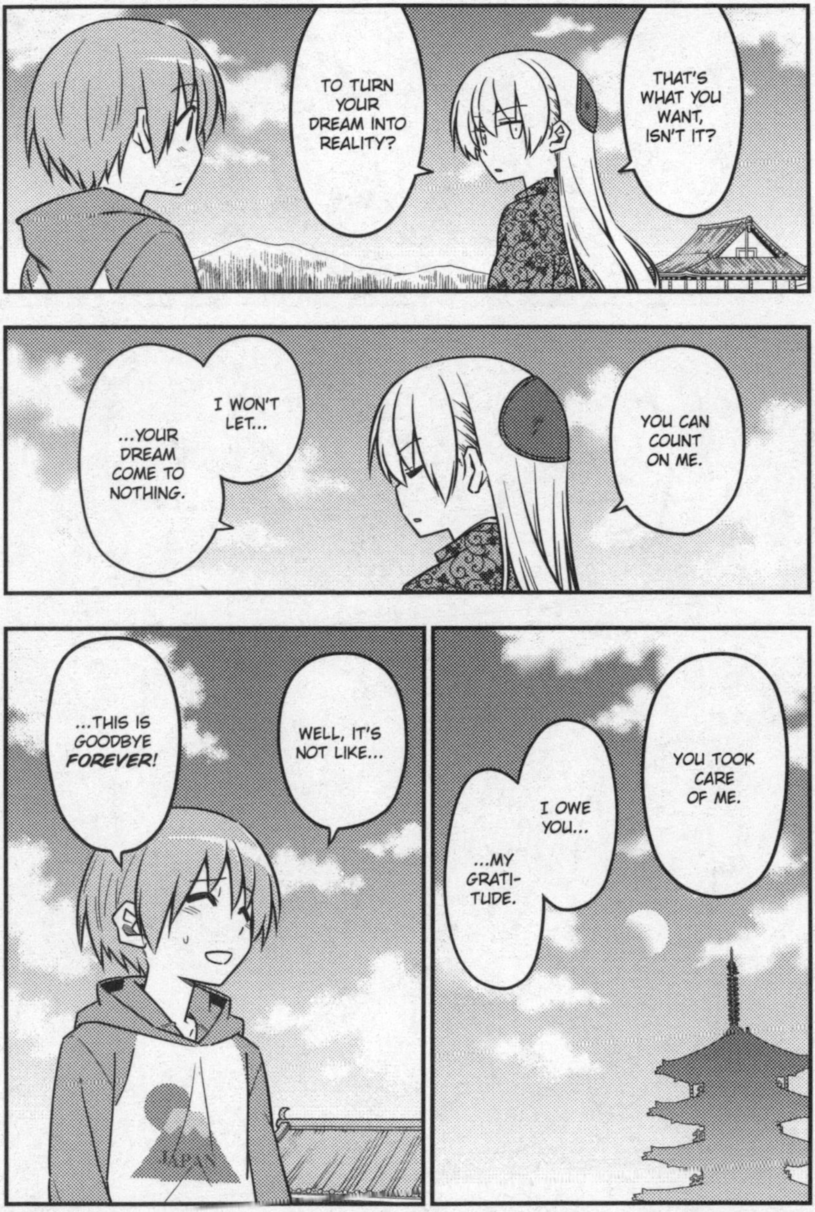
THAT'S WHAT YOU WANT, ISN'T IT?
TO TURN YOUR DREAM INTO REALITY?
YOU CAN COUNT ON ME.
I WON'T LET...
...YOUR DREAM COME TO NOTHING.
YOU TOOK CARE OF ME.
I OWE YOU...
...MY GRATI-TUDE.
WELL, IT'S NOT LIKE...
...THIS IS GOODBYE *FOREVER*!

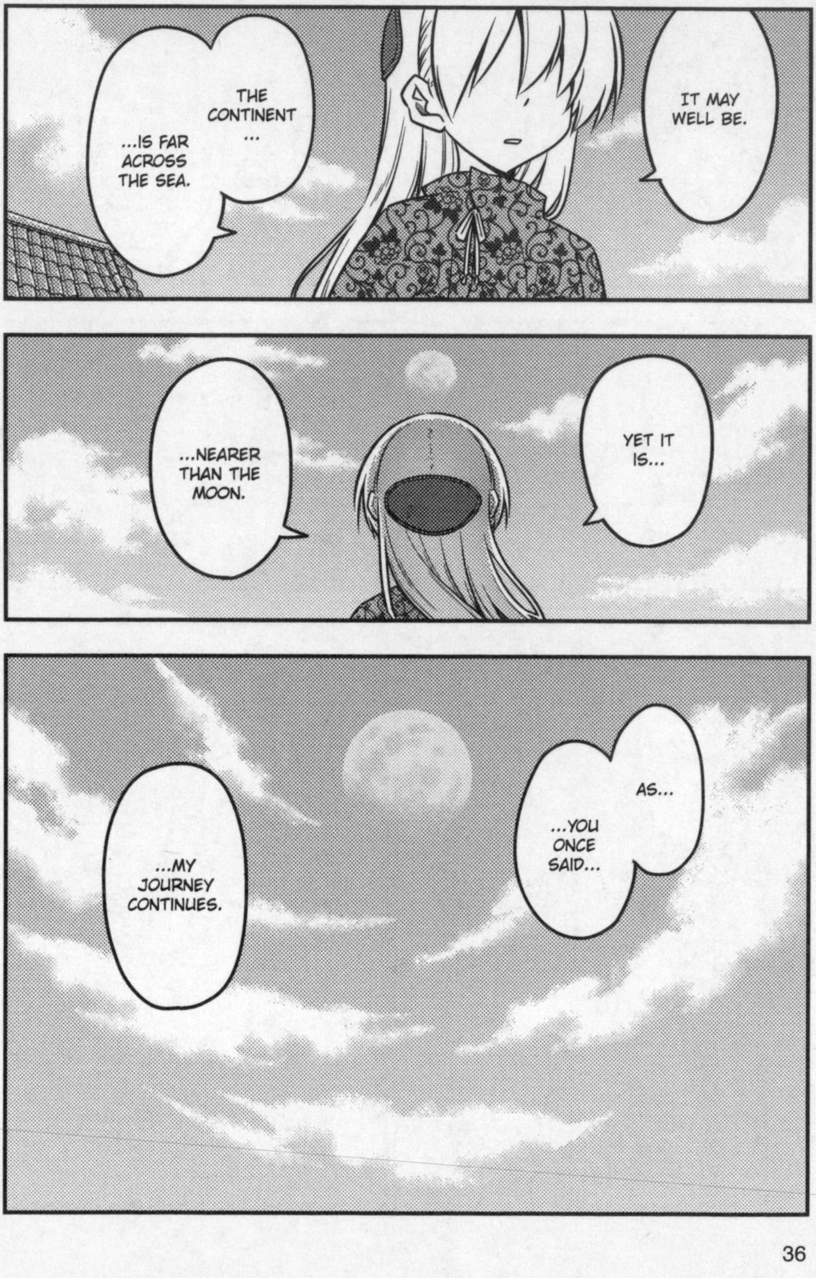
IT MAY WELL BE.
THE CONTINENT ...
...IS FAR ACROSS THE SEA.
YET IT IS...
...NEARER THAN THE MOON.
AS...
...YOU ONCE SAID...
...MY JOURNEY CONTINUES.

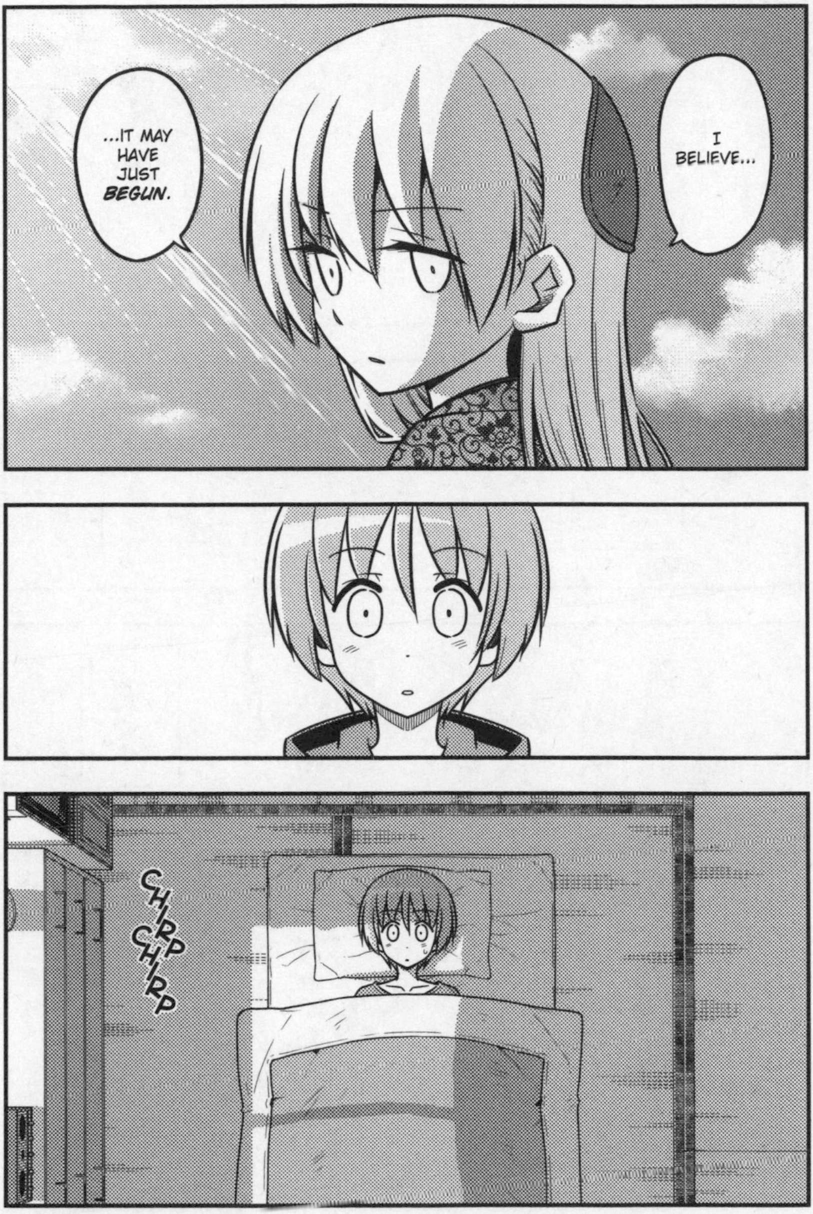
I BELIEVE...
...IT MAY HAVE JUST *BEGUN*.
CHIRP CHIRP

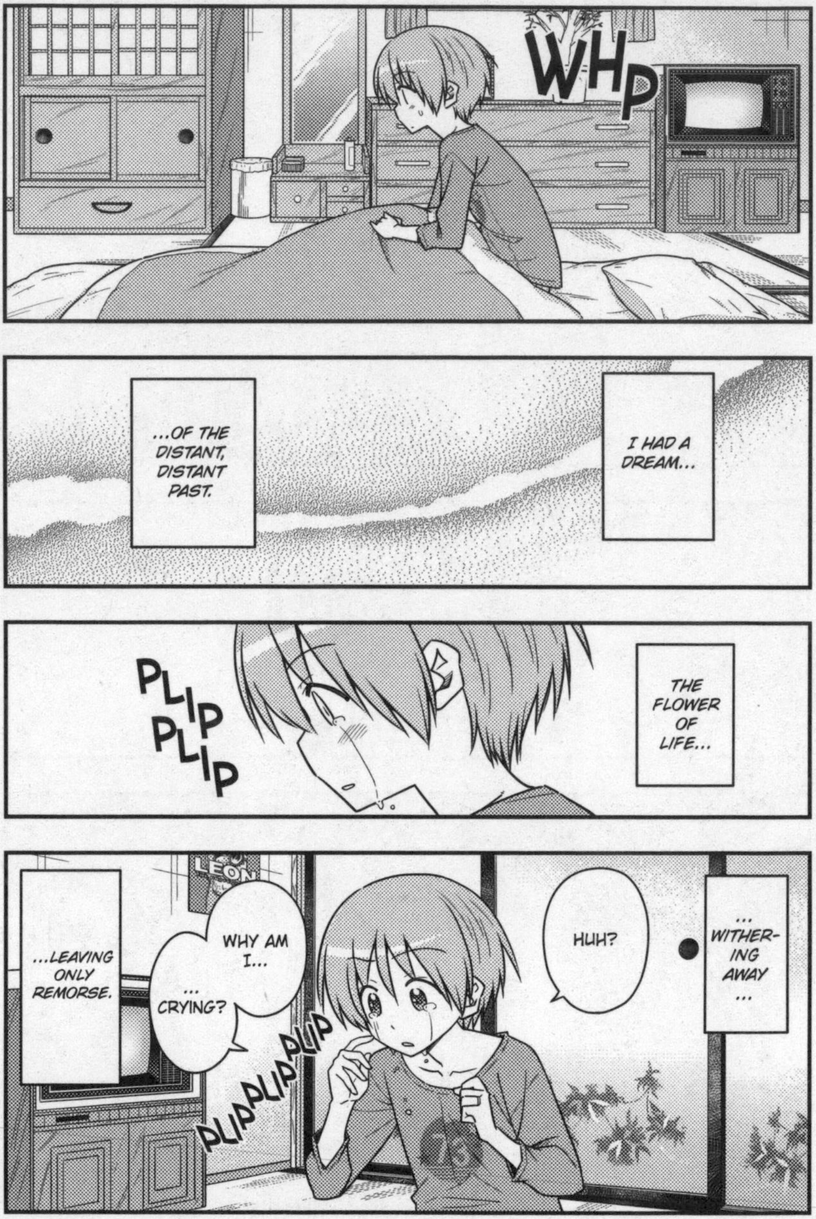
WHP
I HAD A DREAM...
...OF THE DISTANT, DISTANT PAST.
THE FLOWER OF LIFE...
PLIP PLIP PLIP
... WITHER-ING AWAY ...
HUH?
WHY AM I... ... CRYING?
PLIP PLIP PLIP PLIP
...LEAVING ONLY REMORSE.

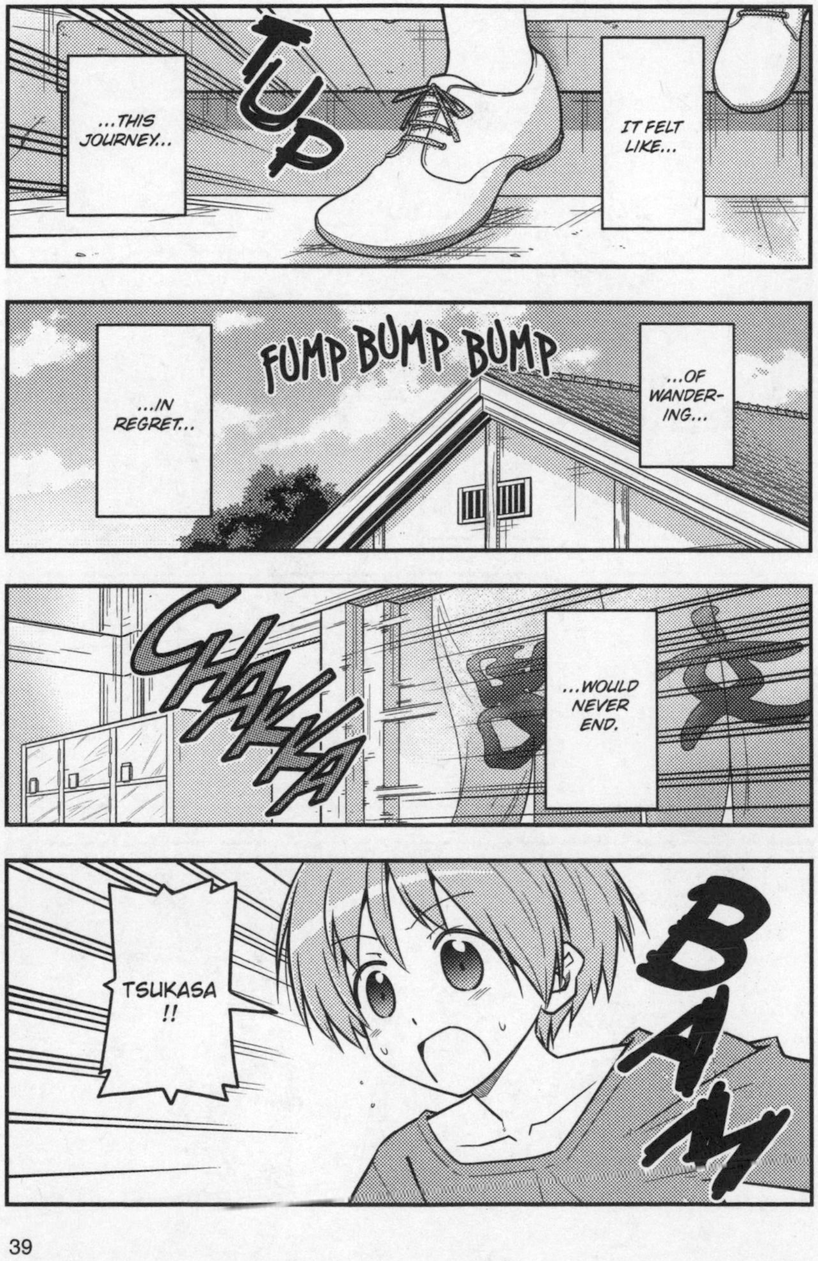
IT FELT LIKE...
TUP
...THIS JOURNEY...
...OF WANDER-ING...
FUMP BUMP BUMP
...IN REGRET...
...WOULD NEVER END.
CHAKA
BAM
TSUKASA !!

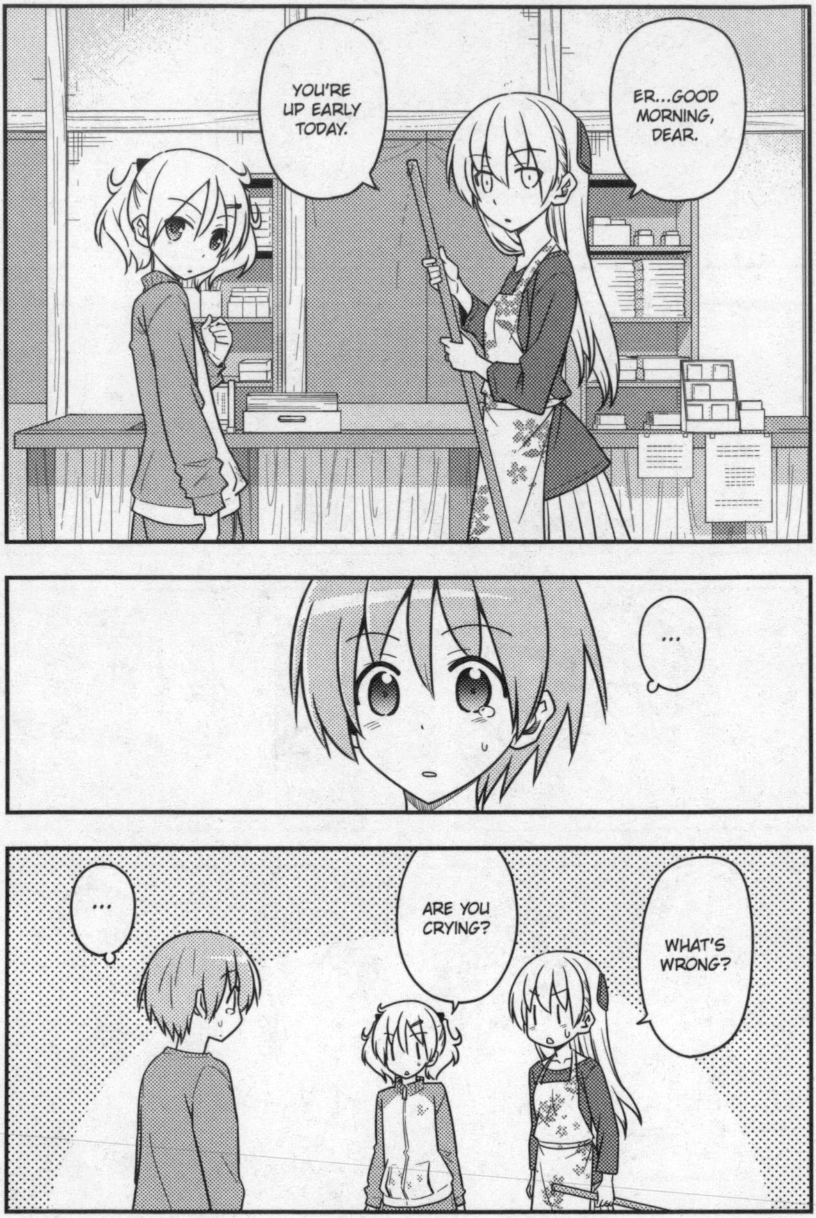
ER...GOOD MORNING, DEAR.
YOU'RE UP EARLY TODAY.
...
WHAT'S WRONG?
ARE YOU CRYING?
...

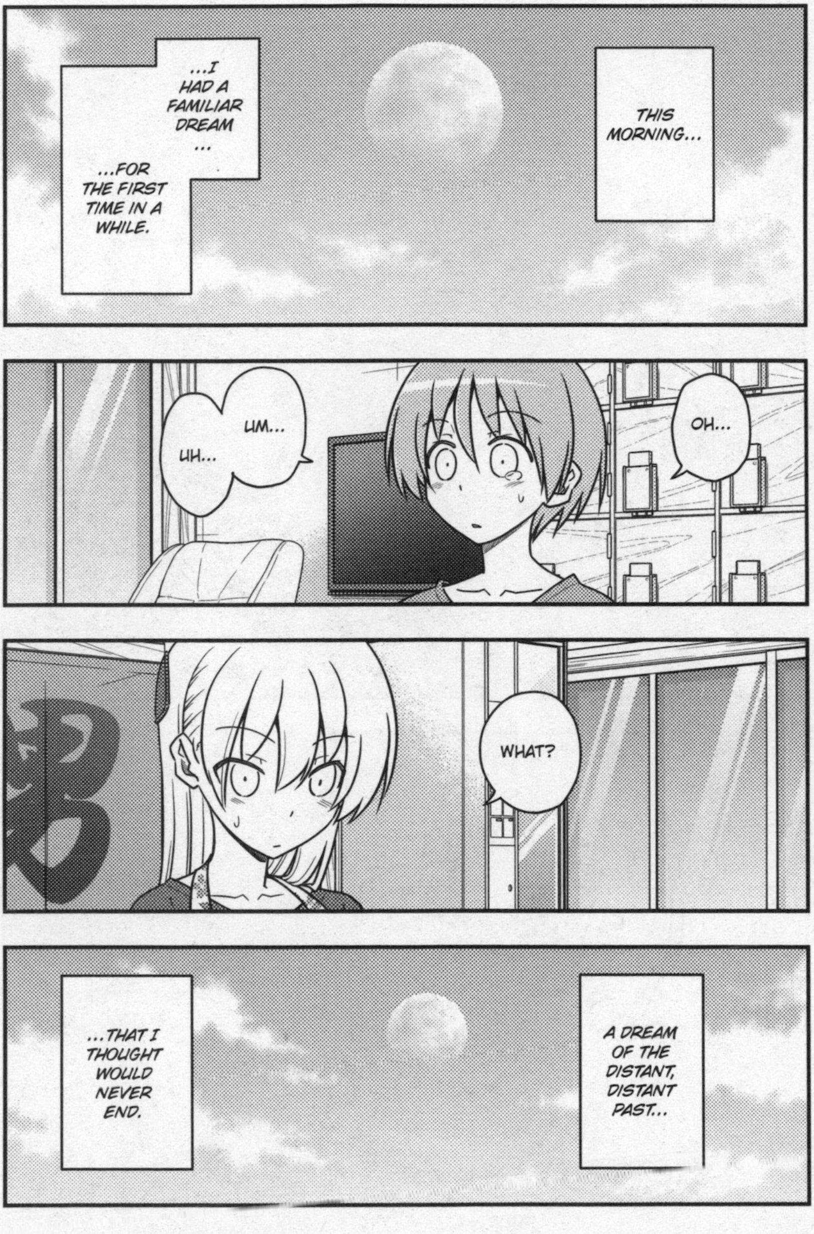
THIS MORNING...
...I HAD A FAMILIAR DREAM...
...FOR THE FIRST TIME IN A WHILE.
OH...
UM...
UH...
WHAT?
A DREAM OF THE DISTANT, DISTANT PAST...
...THAT I THOUGHT WOULD NEVER END.

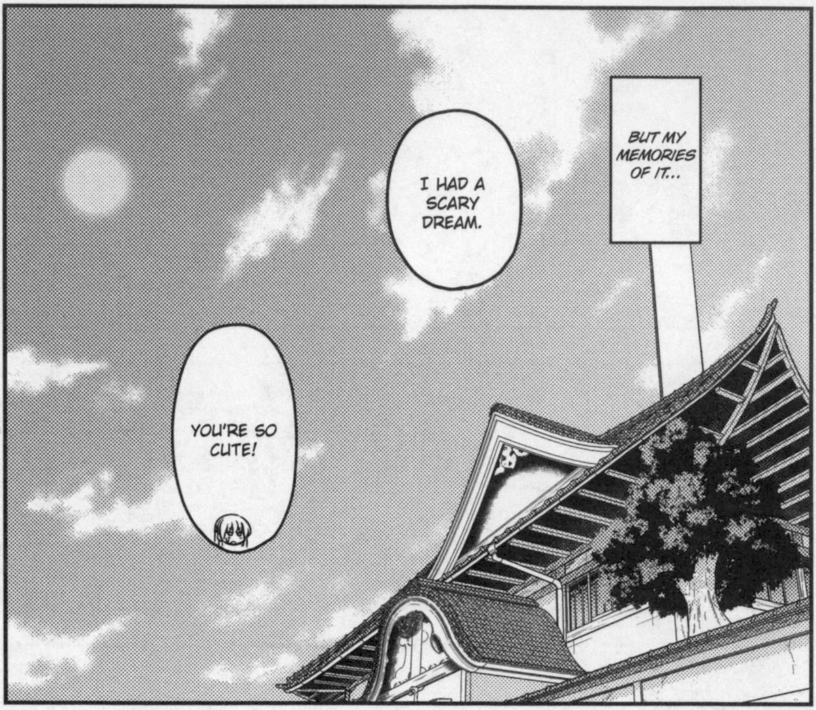
BUT MY MEMORIES OF IT...
I HAD A SCARY DREAM.
YOU'RE SO CUTE!
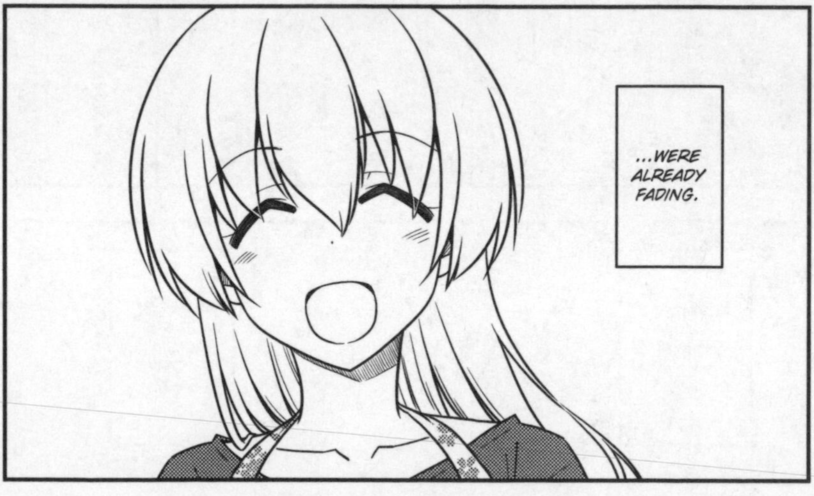
...WERE ALREADY FADING.

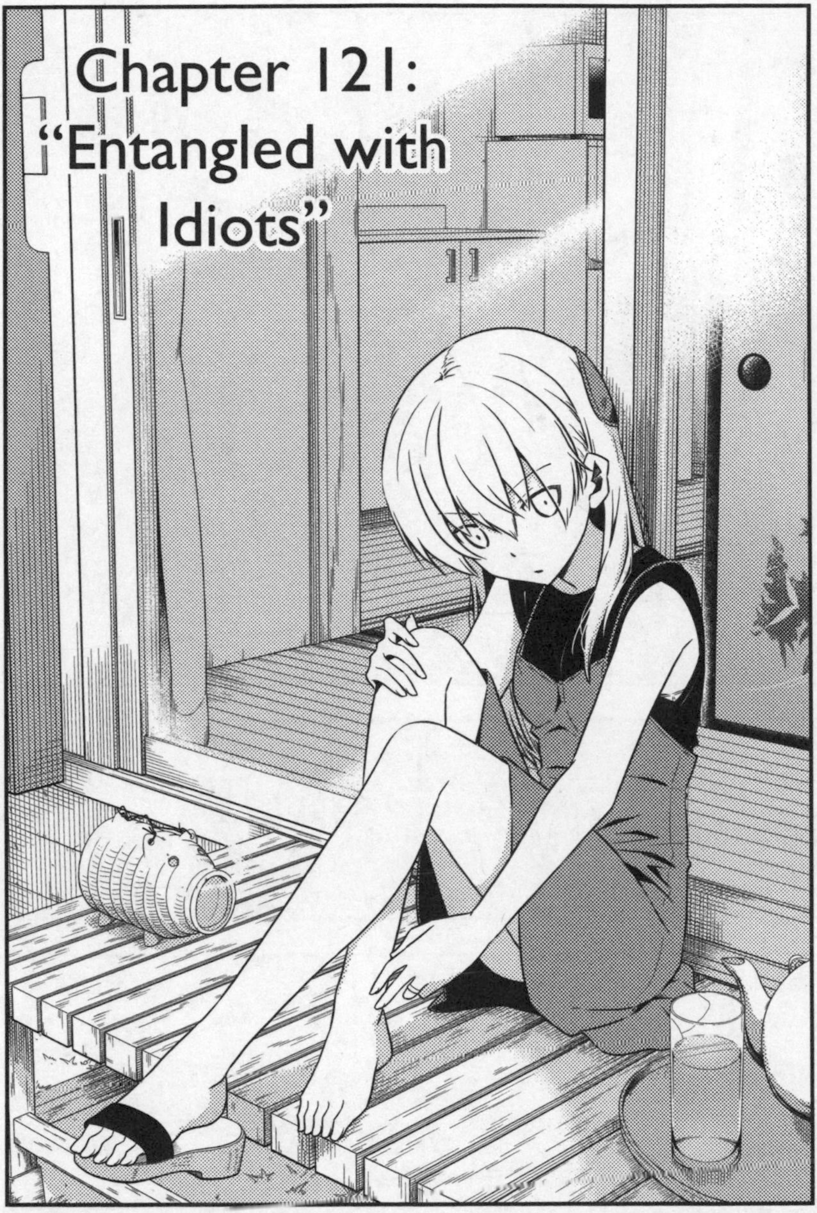
Chapter 121:
"Entangled with Idiots"

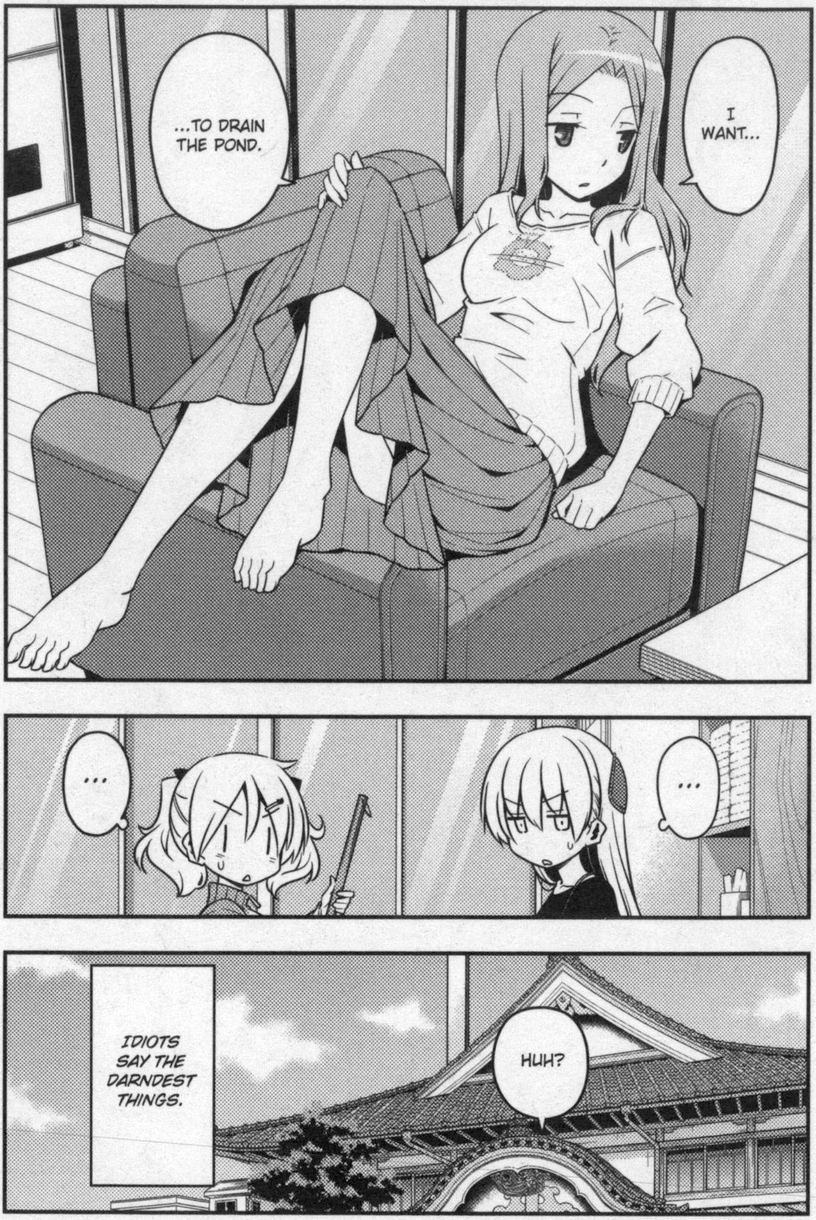
I WANT...
...TO DRAIN THE POND.
...
...
HUH?
IDIOTS SAY THE DARNDEST THINGS.

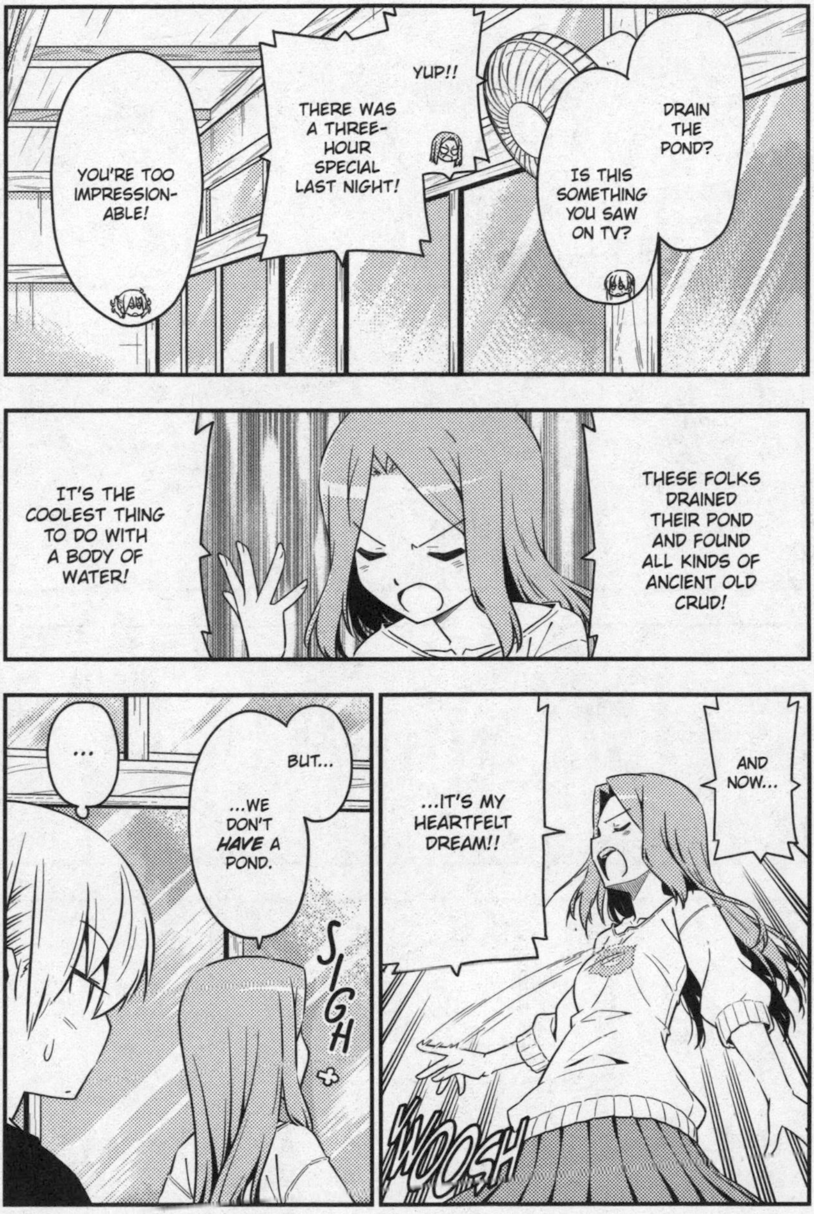
DRAIN THE POND?
IS THIS SOMETHING YOU SAW ON TV?
YUP!!
THERE WAS A THREE-HOUR SPECIAL LAST NIGHT!
YOU'RE TOO IMPRESSION-ABLE!
THESE FOLKS DRAINED THEIR POND AND FOUND ALL KINDS OF ANCIENT OLD CRUD!
IT'S THE COOLEST THING TO DO WITH A BODY OF WATER!
AND NOW...
...IT'S MY HEARTFELT DREAM!!
WOOSH
BUT...
...WE DON'T *HAVE* A POND.
SIGH
...

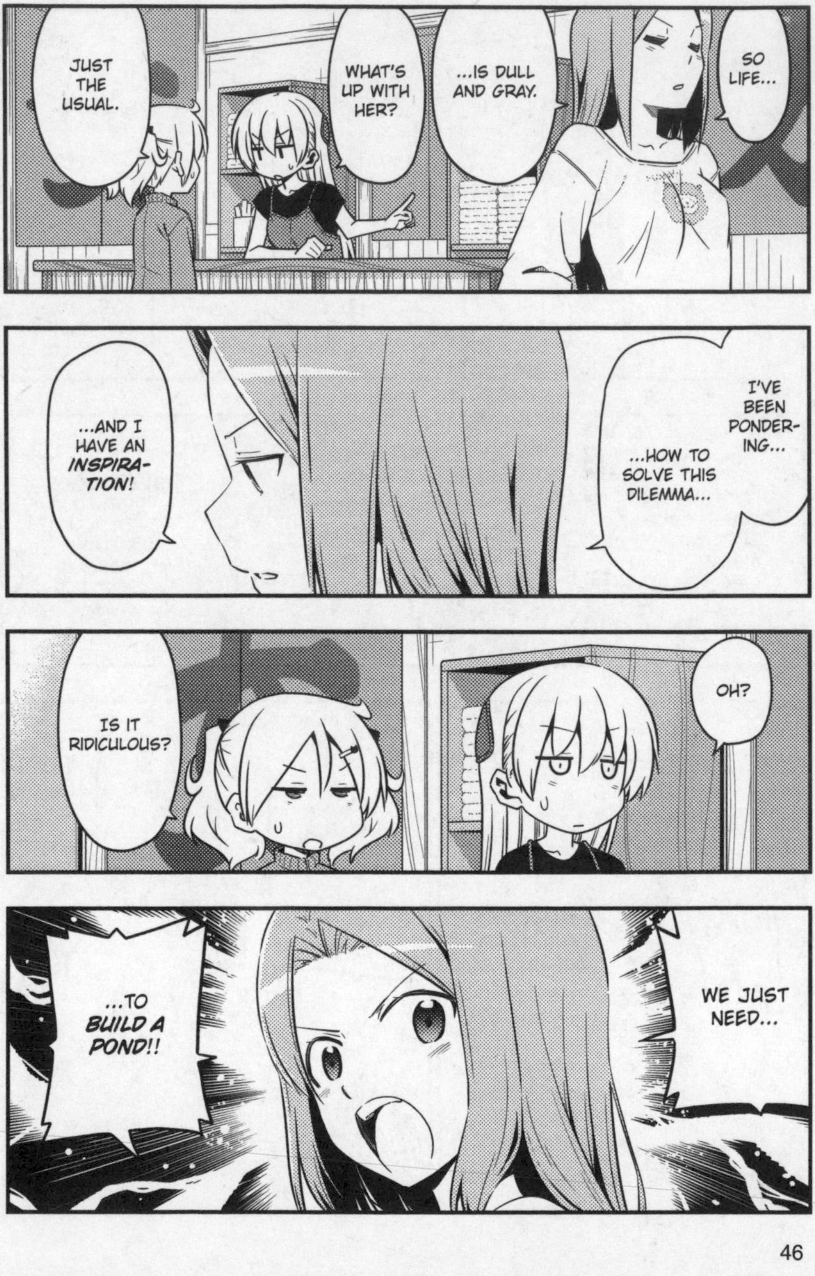
SO LIFE...
...IS DULL AND GRAY.
WHAT'S UP WITH HER?
JUST THE USUAL.
I'VE BEEN PONDER-ING...
...HOW TO SOLVE THIS DILEMMA...
...AND I HAVE AN INSPIRATION!
OH?
IS IT RIDICULOUS?
WE JUST NEED...
...TO BUILD A POND!!

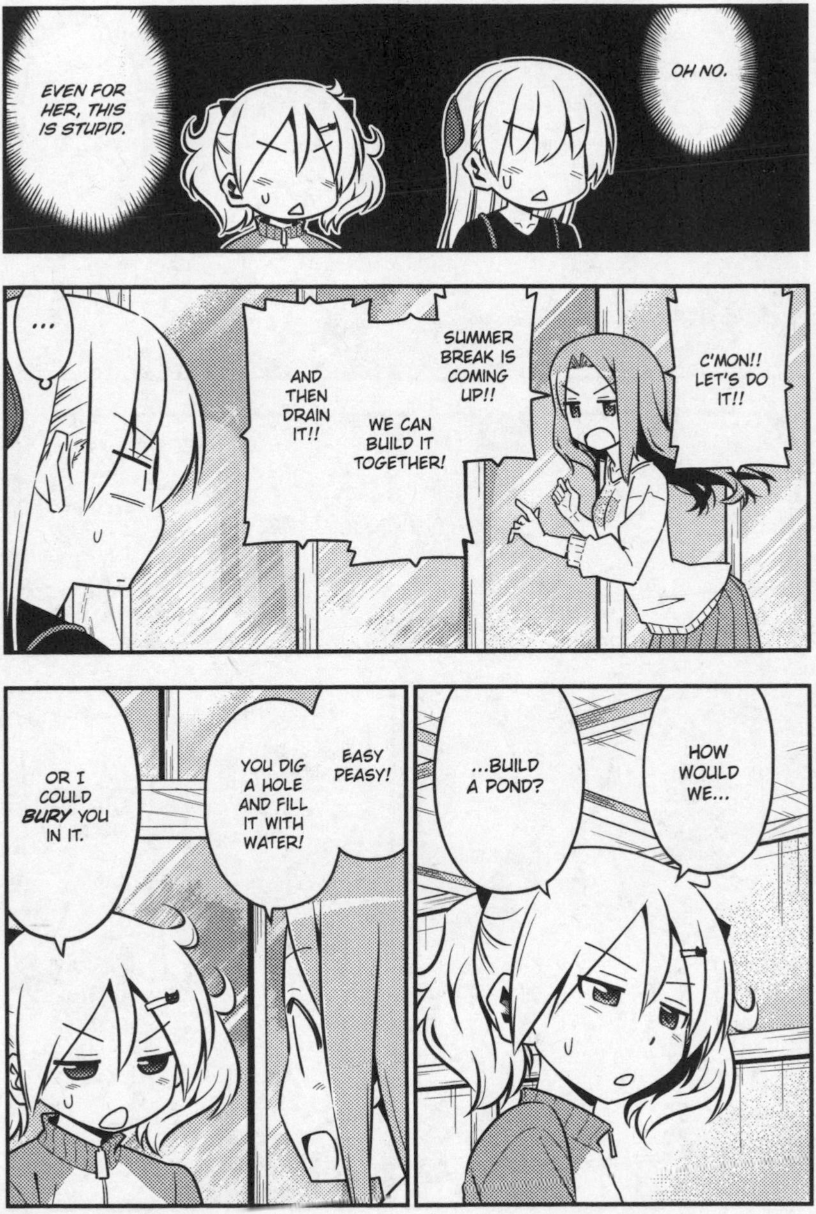
OH NO.
EVEN FOR HER, THIS IS STUPID.
C'MON!! LET'S DO IT!!
SUMMER BREAK IS COMING UP!!
WE CAN BUILD IT TOGETHER!
AND THEN DRAIN IT!!
...
HOW WOULD WE...
...BUILD A POND?
EASY PEASY!
YOU DIG A HOLE AND FILL IT WITH WATER!
OR I COULD *BURY* YOU IN IT.

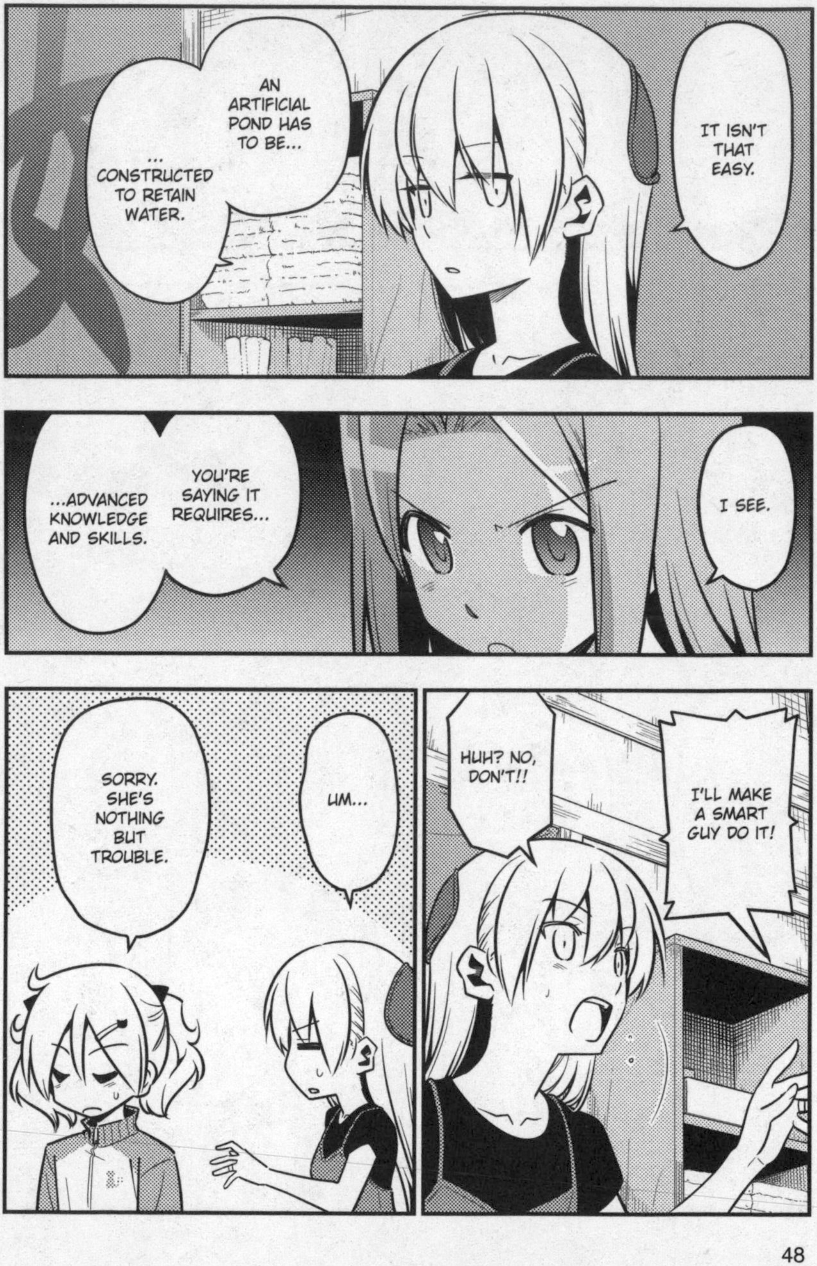
IT ISN'T THAT EASY.
AN ARTIFICIAL POND HAS TO BE...
...CONSTRUCTED TO RETAIN WATER.
I SEE.
YOU'RE SAYING IT REQUIRES...
...ADVANCED KNOWLEDGE AND SKILLS.
I'LL MAKE A SMART GUY DO IT!
HUH? NO, DON'T!!
UM...
SORRY. SHE'S NOTHING BUT TROUBLE.

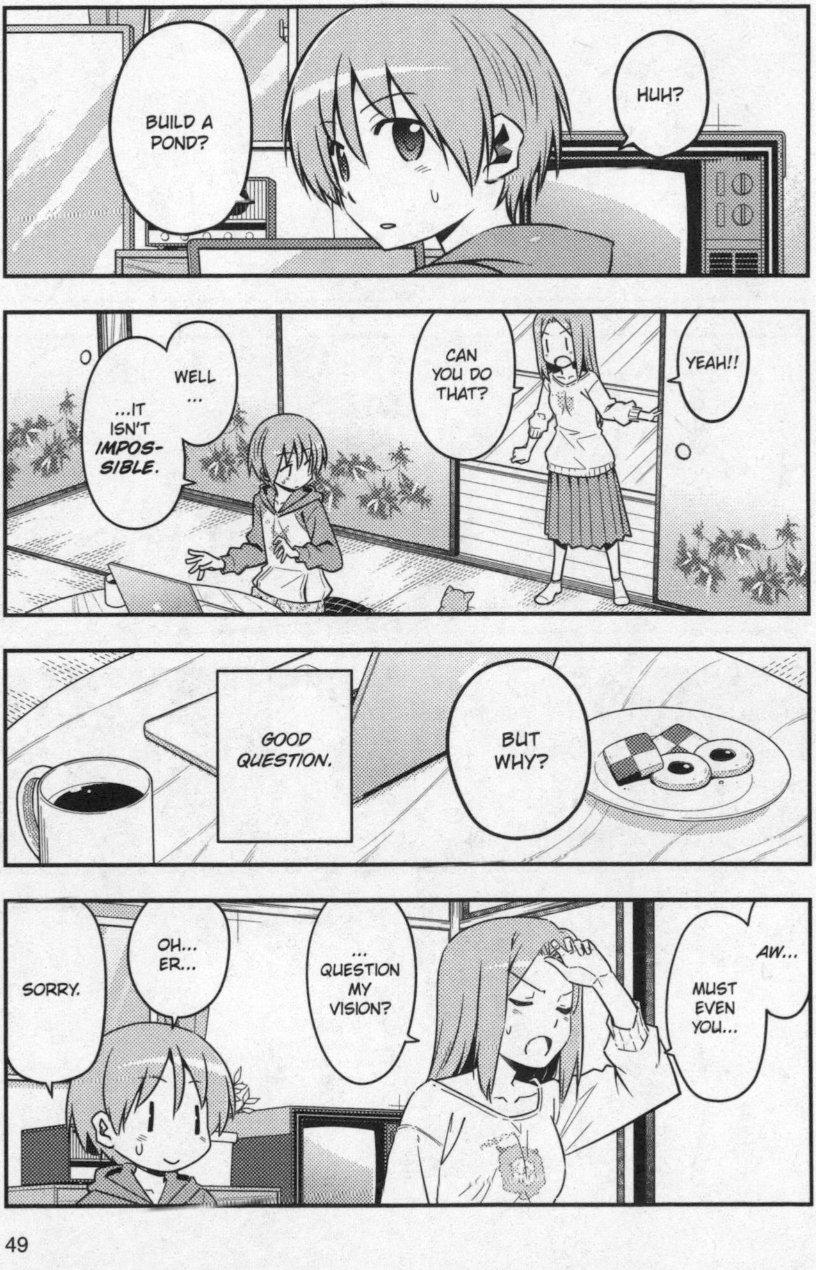
HUH?
BUILD A POND?
YEAH!!
CAN YOU DO THAT?
WELL...
...IT ISN'T *IMPOSSIBLE*.
BUT WHY?
GOOD QUESTION.
AW... MUST EVEN YOU...
...QUESTION MY VISION?
OH... ER...
SORRY.

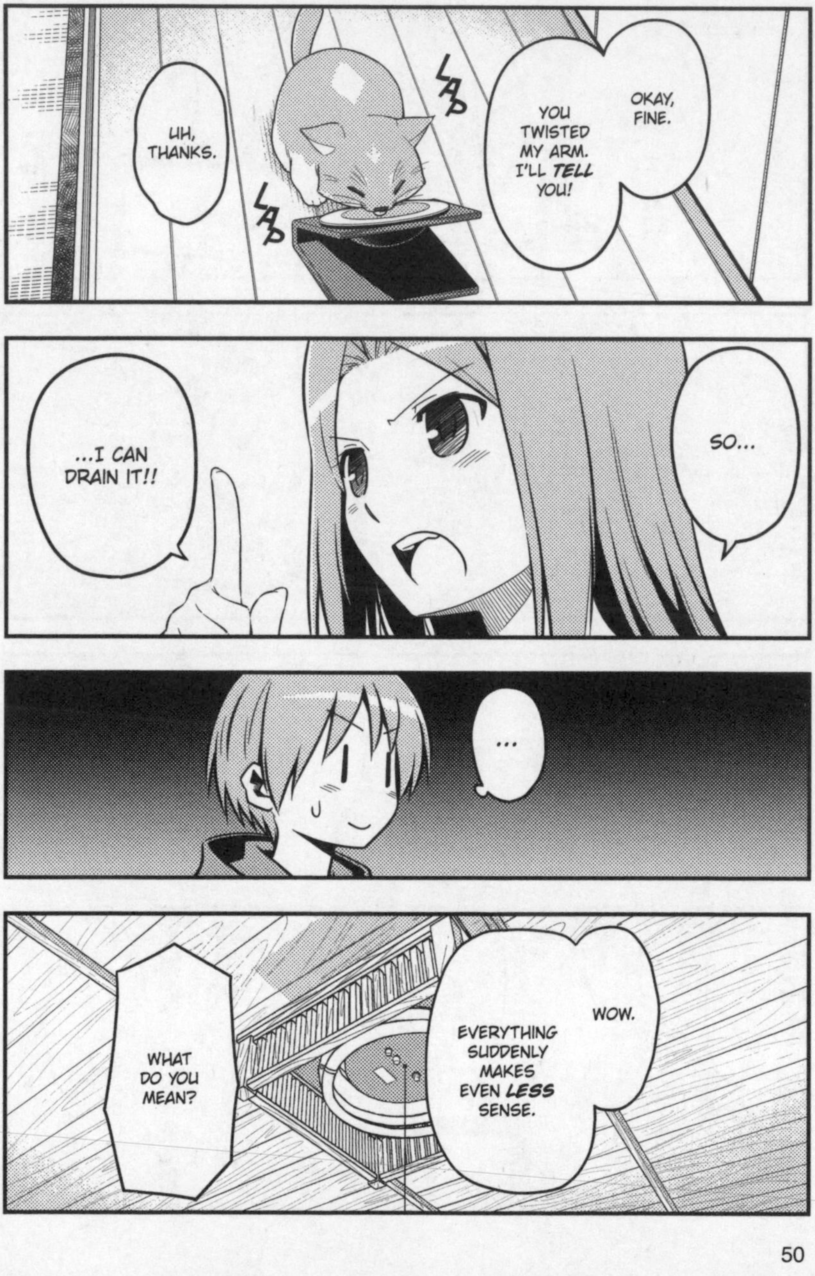
OKAY, FINE. YOU TWISTED MY ARM. I'LL TELL YOU!
LAP
LAP
UH, THANKS.
SO...
...I CAN DRAIN IT!!
...
WOW. EVERYTHING SUDDENLY MAKES EVEN LESS SENSE.
WHAT DO YOU MEAN?

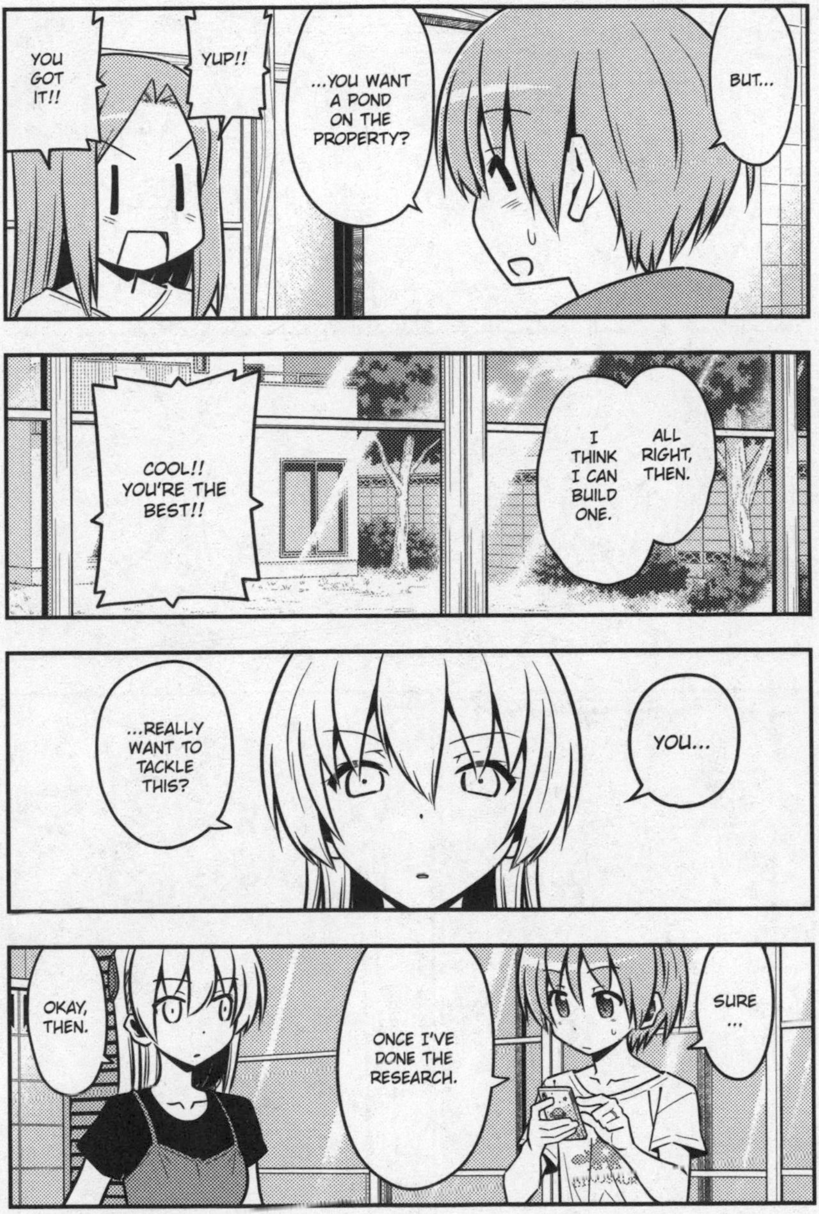
BUT...
...YOU WANT A POND ON THE PROPERTY?
YUP!!
YOU GOT IT!!
ALL RIGHT, THEN.
I THINK I CAN BUILD ONE.
COOL!! YOU'RE THE BEST!!
YOU...
...REALLY WANT TO TACKLE THIS?
SURE...
ONCE I'VE DONE THE RESEARCH.
OKAY, THEN.

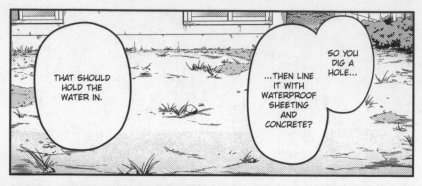

SO YOU DIG A HOLE...
...THEN LINE IT WITH WATERPROOF SHEETING AND CONCRETE?
THAT SHOULD HOLD THE WATER IN.
IN THE KAMAKURA ERA, PEOPLE USED TUFF LOAM AND CLAY...
...AND IN THE EDO PERIOD THEY USED MORTAR.
OH?
WELL, TIME TO START DIGGING!
READY?
YEAH! GET YOUR BUTT IN GEAR!!
DON'T BOSS HIM AROUND.

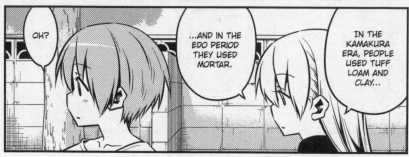

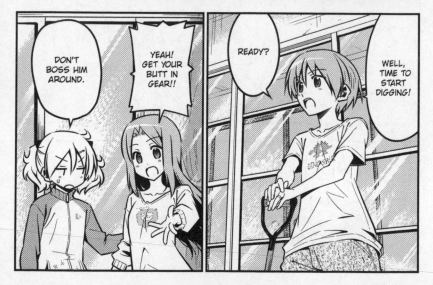

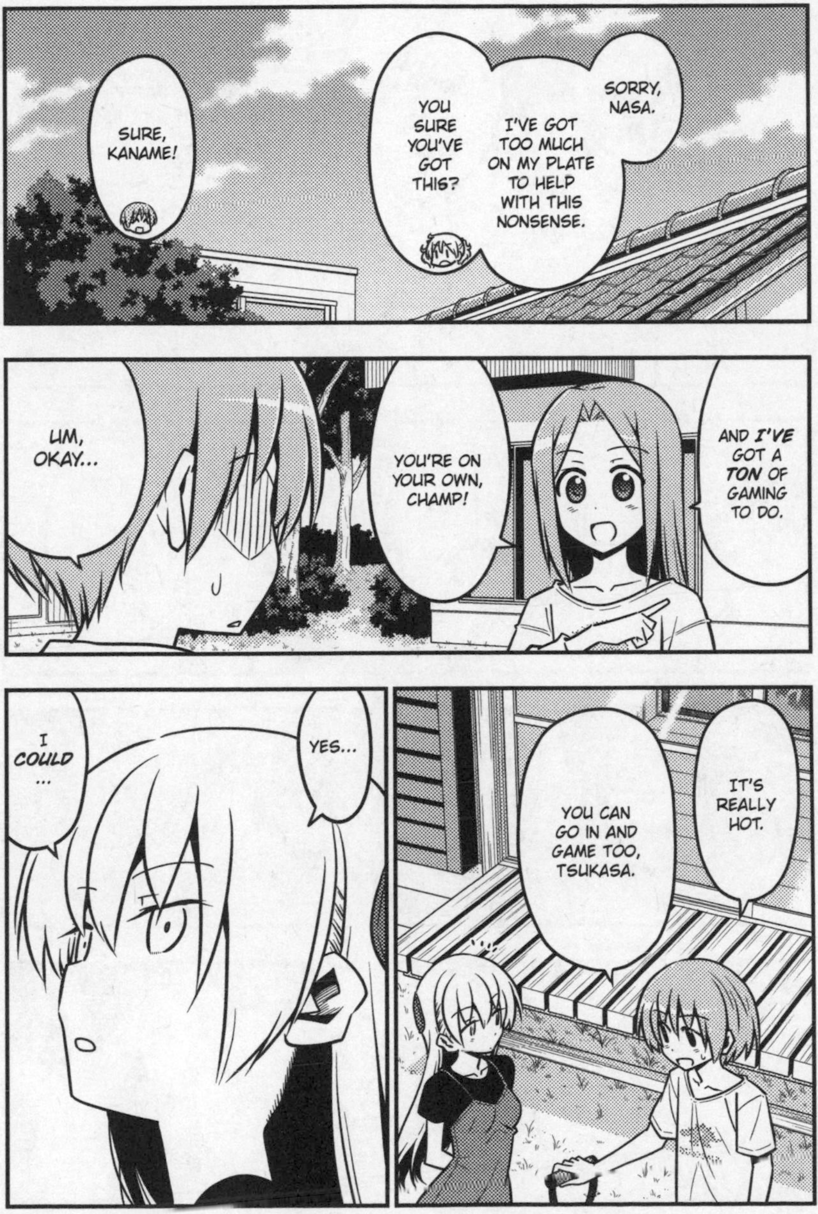
SORRY, NASA.
I'VE GOT TOO MUCH ON MY PLATE TO HELP WITH THIS NONSENSE.
YOU SURE YOU'VE GOT THIS?
SURE, KANAME!
AND *I'VE* GOT A *TON* OF GAMING TO DO.
YOU'RE ON YOUR OWN, CHAMP!
UM, OKAY...
IT'S REALLY HOT.
YOU CAN GO IN AND GAME TOO, TSUKASA.
YES...
I *COULD* ...

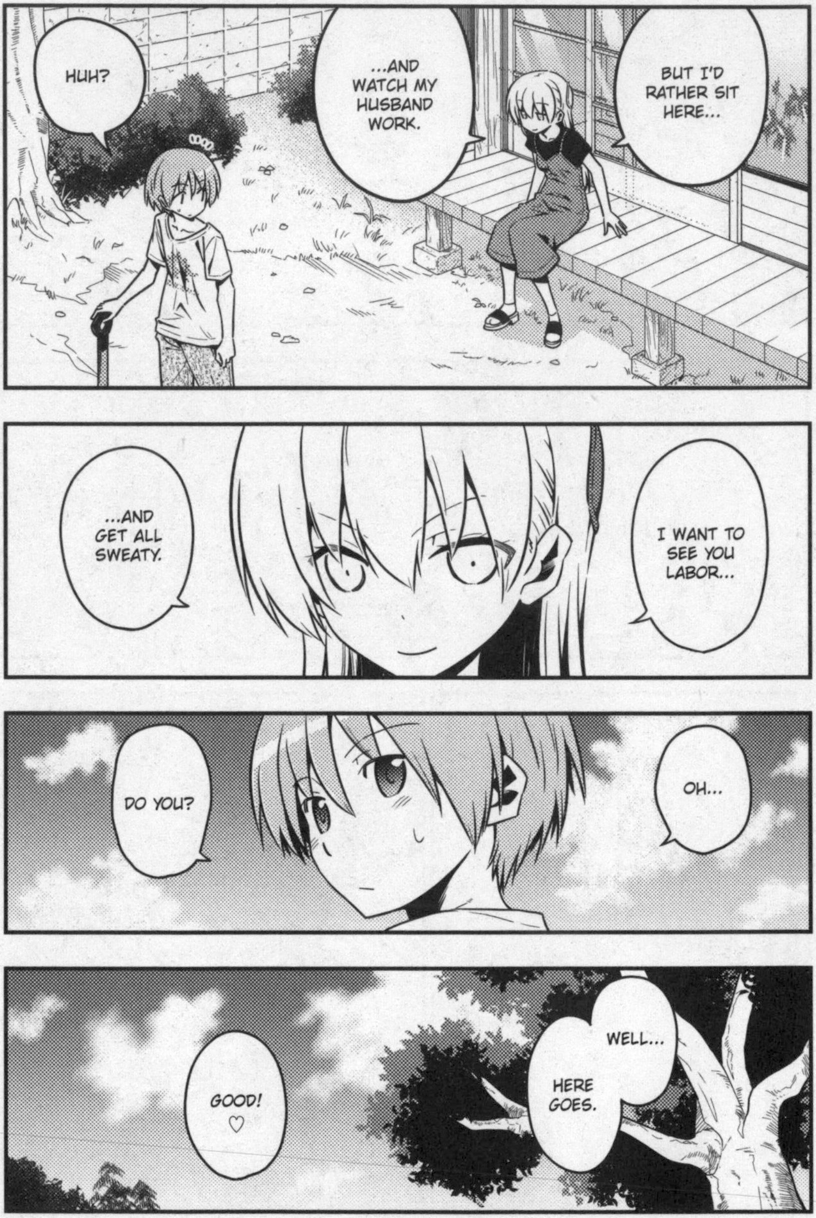
BUT I'D RATHER SIT HERE...
...AND WATCH MY HUSBAND WORK.
HUH?
I WANT TO SEE YOU LABOR...
...AND GET ALL SWEATY.
OH...
DO YOU?
WELL... HERE GOES.
GOOD! ♡

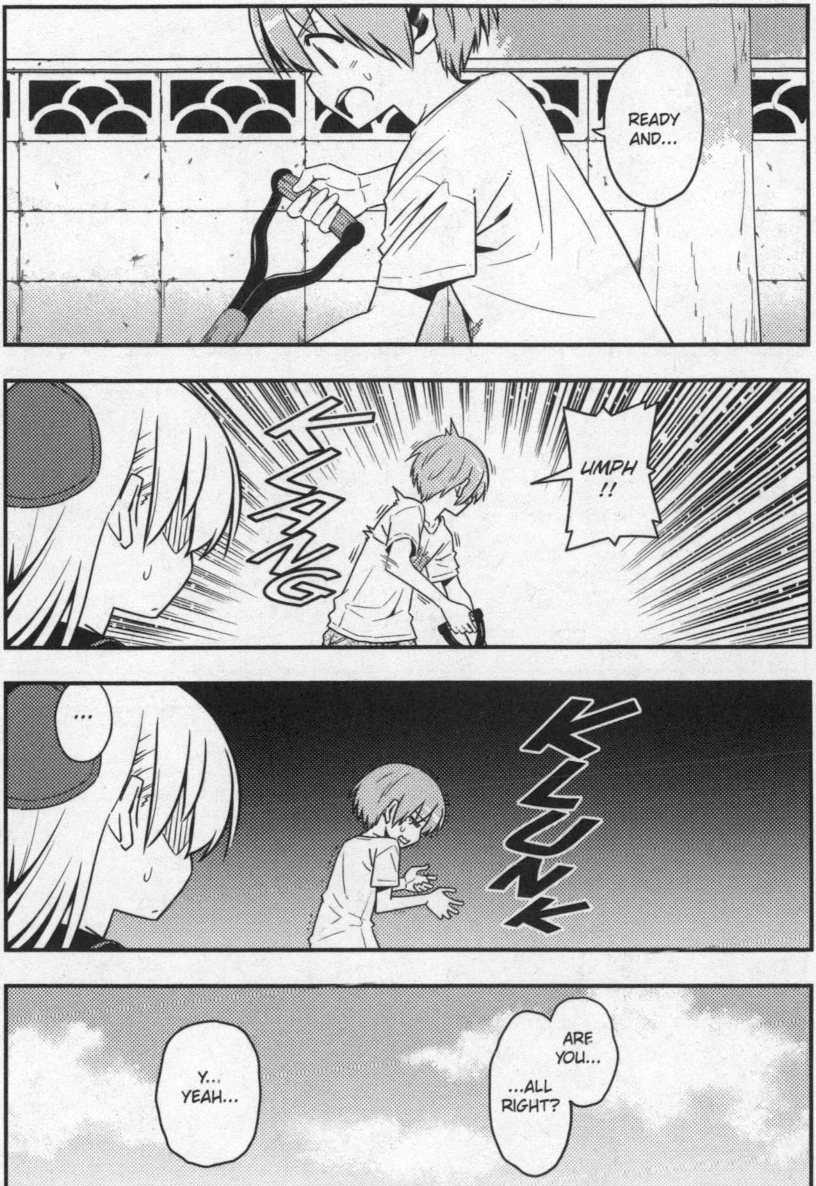
READY AND...
UMPH !!
KLANG
KLUNK
...
ARE YOU... ...ALL RIGHT?
Y... YEAH...

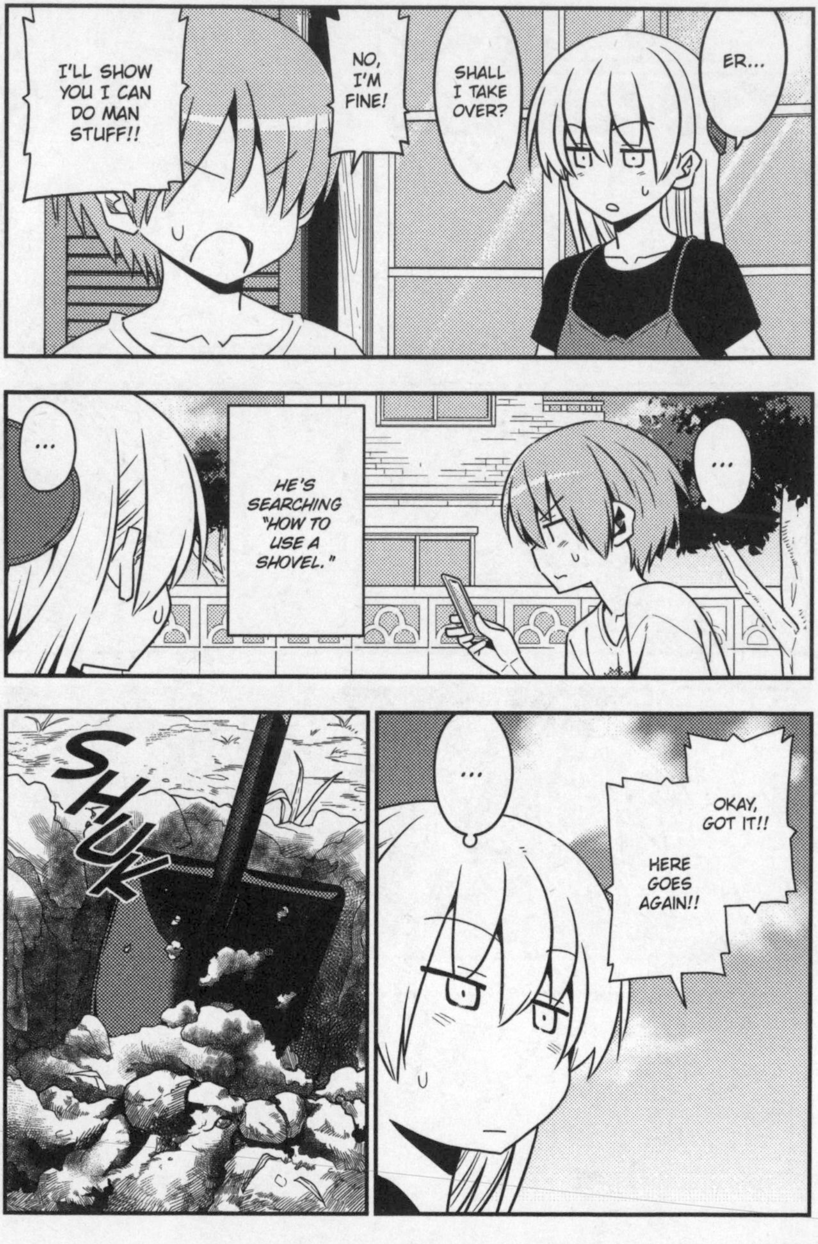
ER...
SHALL I TAKE OVER?
NO, I'M FINE!
I'LL SHOW YOU I CAN DO MAN STUFF!!
...
HE'S SEARCHING "HOW TO USE A SHOVEL."
...
OKAY, GOT IT!!
HERE GOES AGAIN!!
...
SHUK

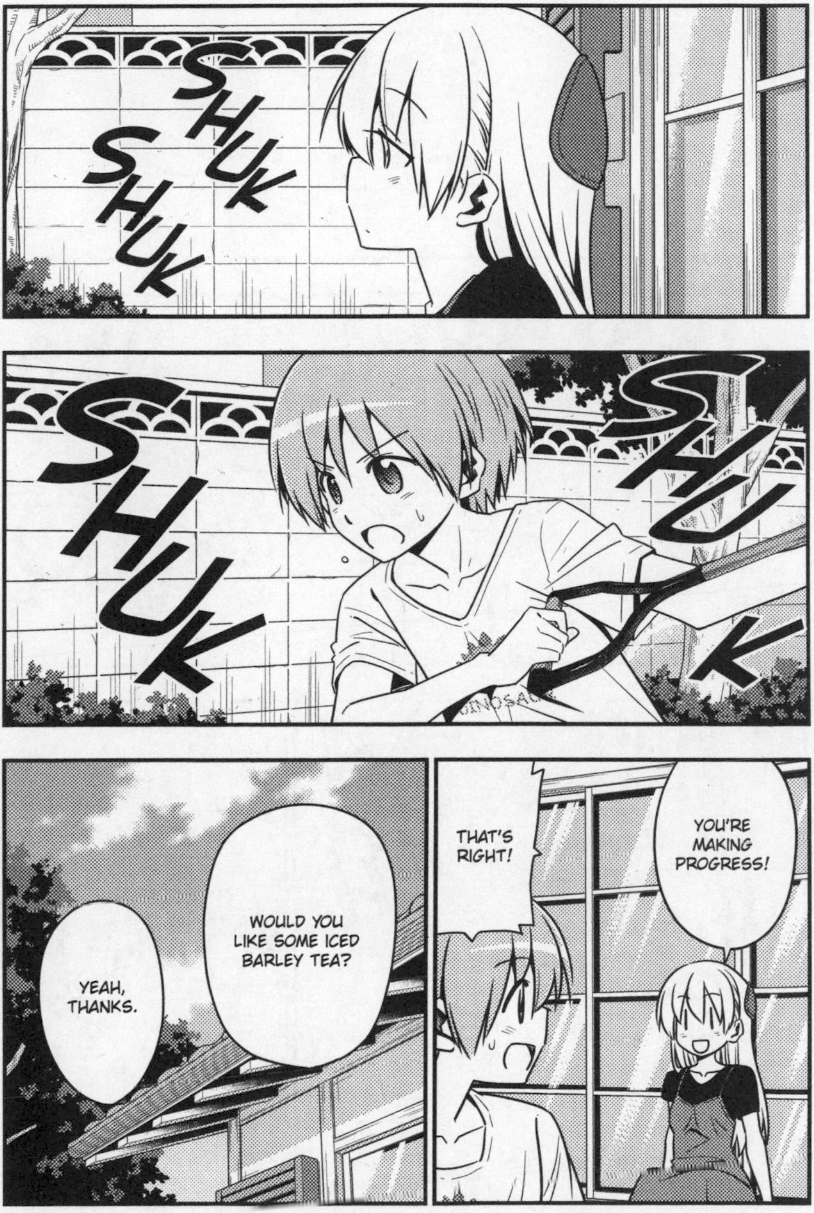
SHUK
SHUK
SHUK
SHUK
YOU'RE MAKING PROGRESS!
THAT'S RIGHT!
WOULD YOU LIKE SOME ICED BARLEY TEA?
YEAH, THANKS.

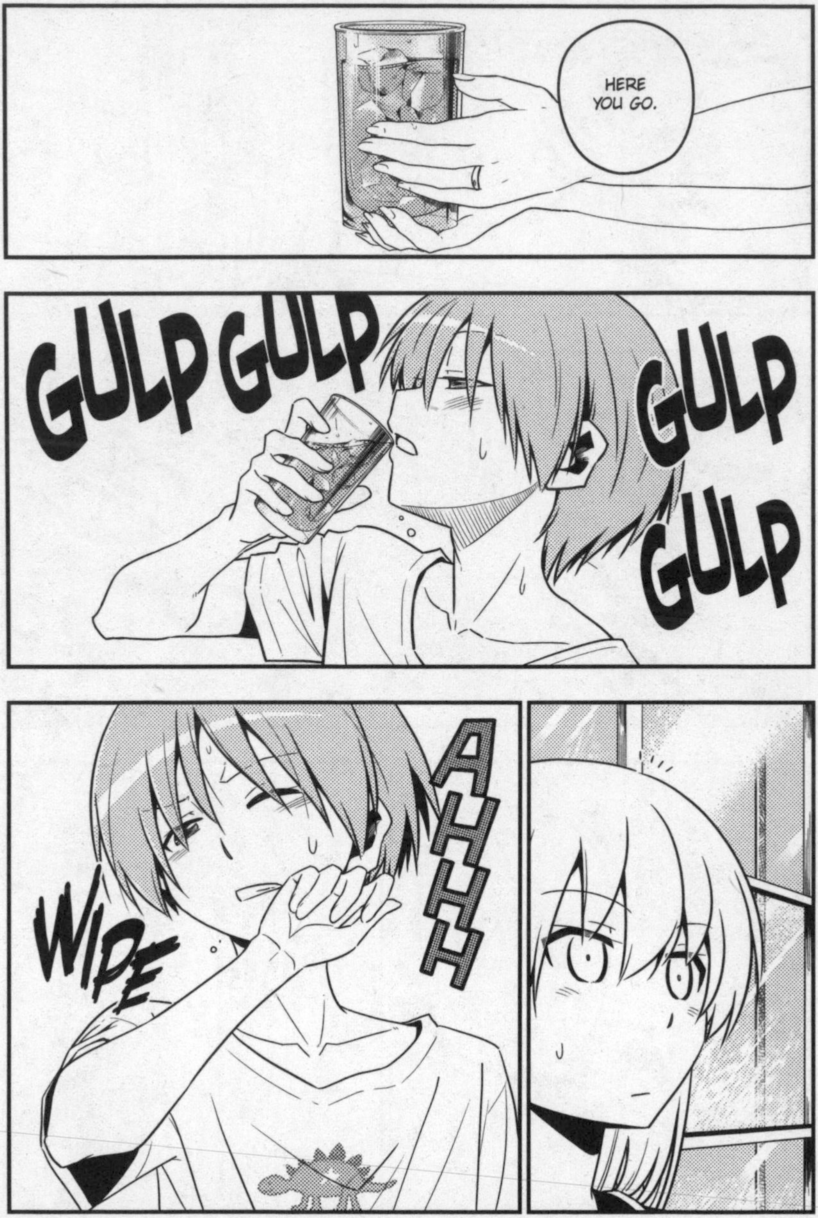
HERE YOU GO.
GULP GULP
GULP GULP
AHHHH
WIPE

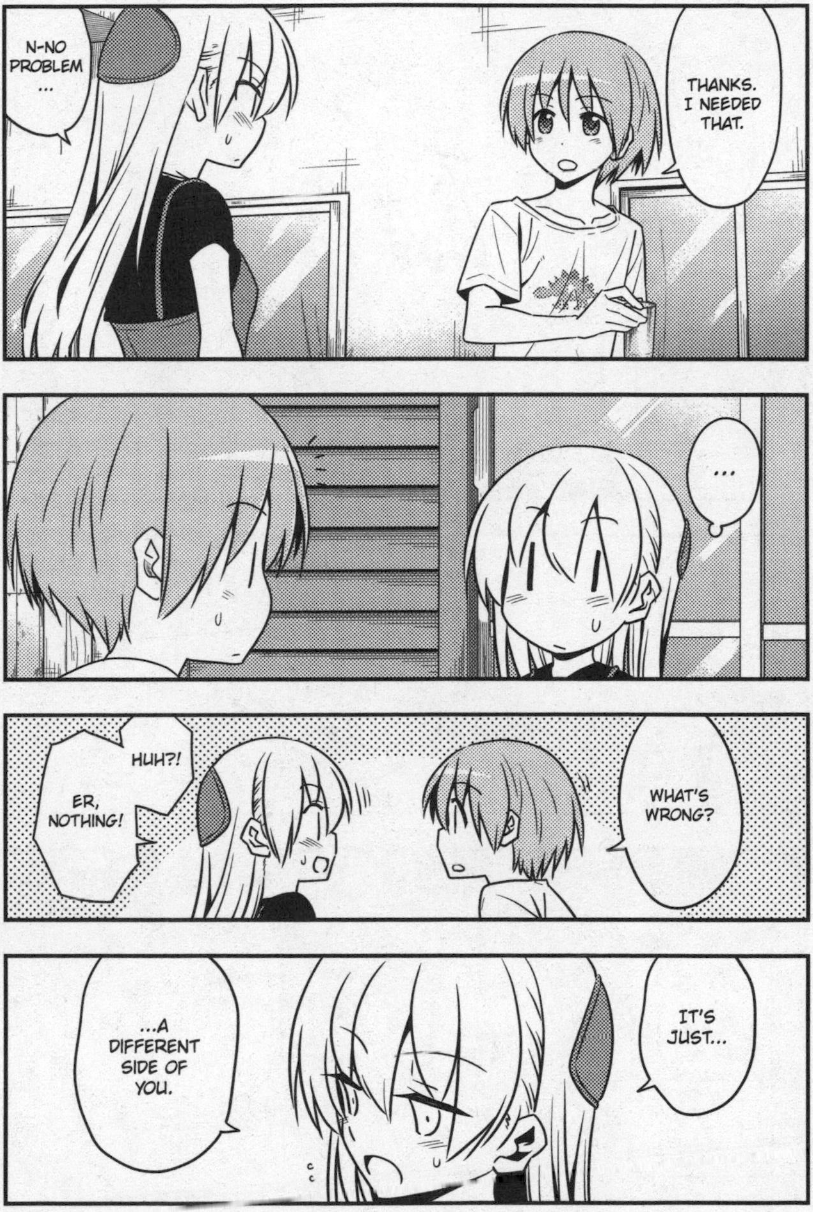
THANKS. I NEEDED THAT.
N-NO PROBLEM ...
...
WHAT'S WRONG?
HUH?! ER, NOTHING!
IT'S JUST...
...A DIFFERENT SIDE OF YOU.

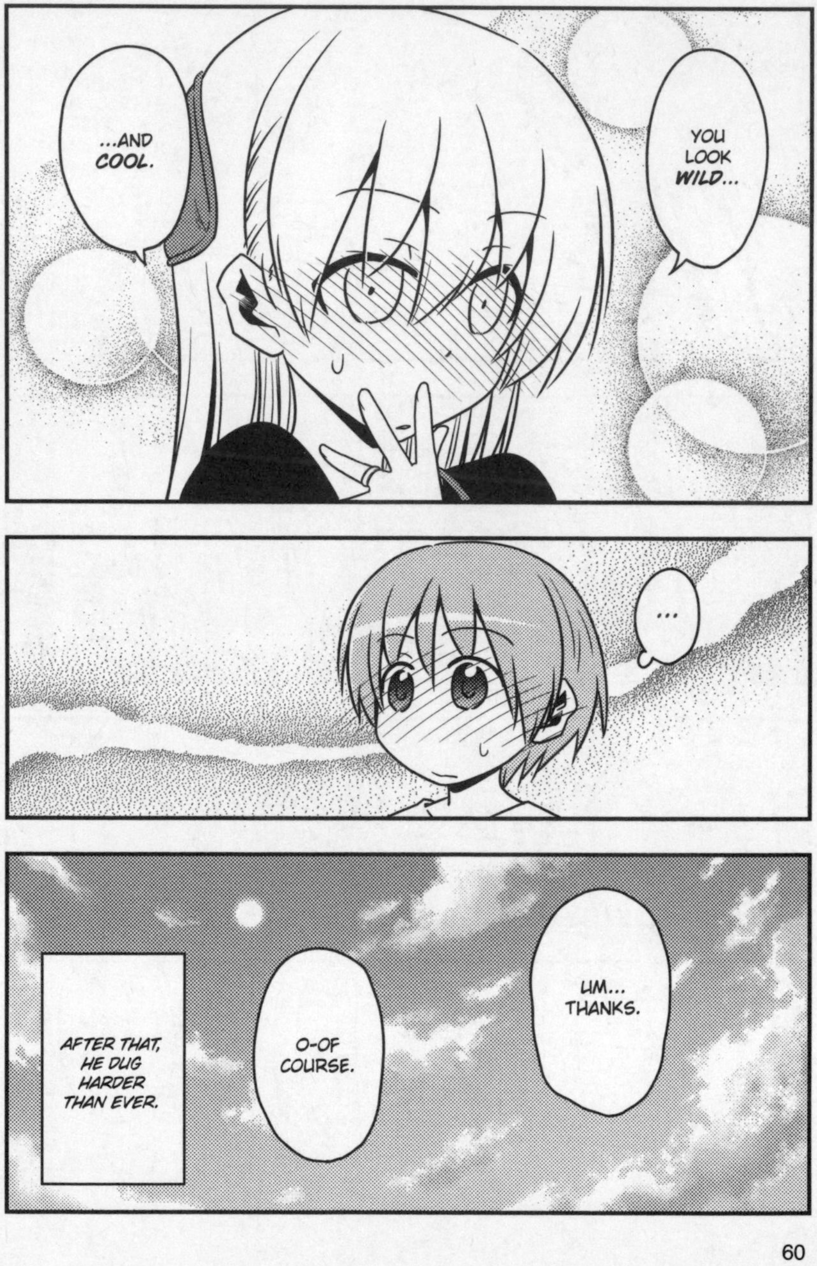
YOU LOOK WILD...
...AND COOL.
...
UM... THANKS.
O-OF COURSE.
AFTER THAT, HE DUG HARDER THAN EVER.

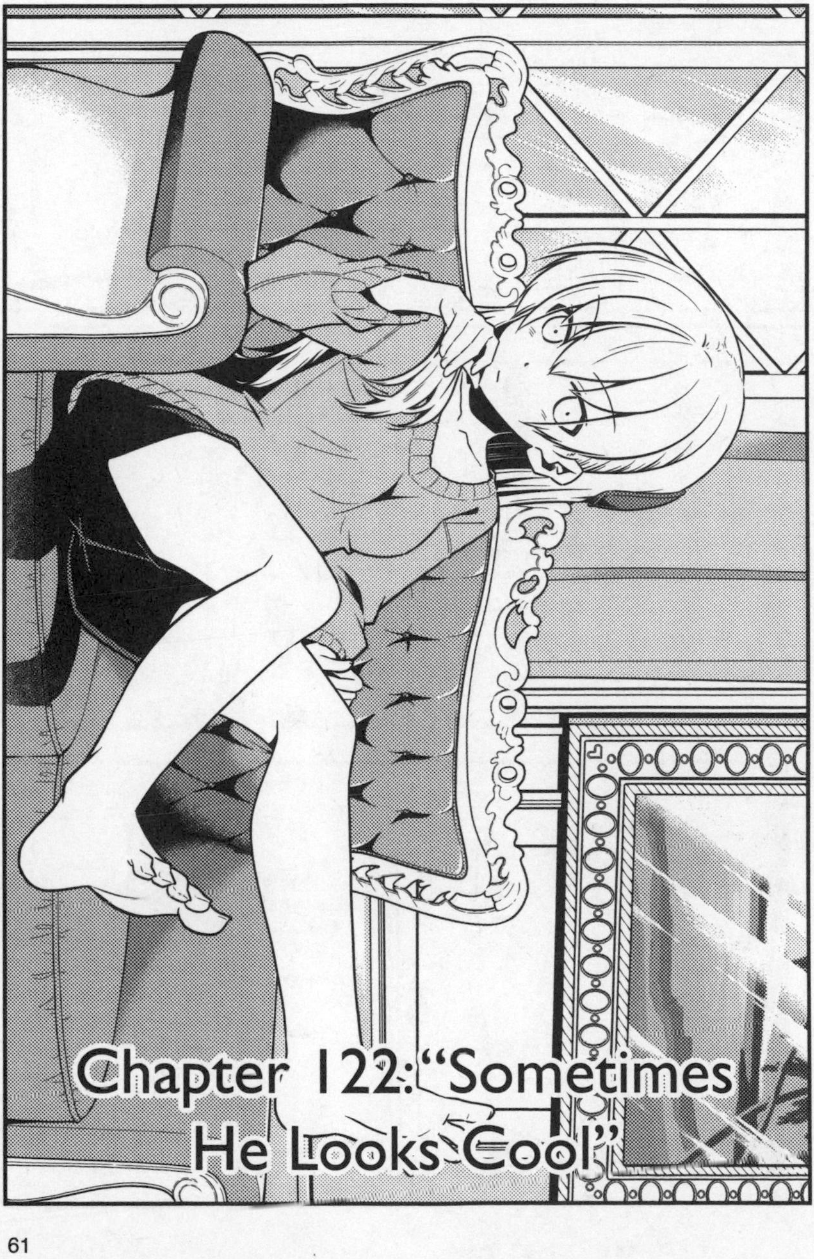
Chapter 122: "Sometimes He Looks Cool"

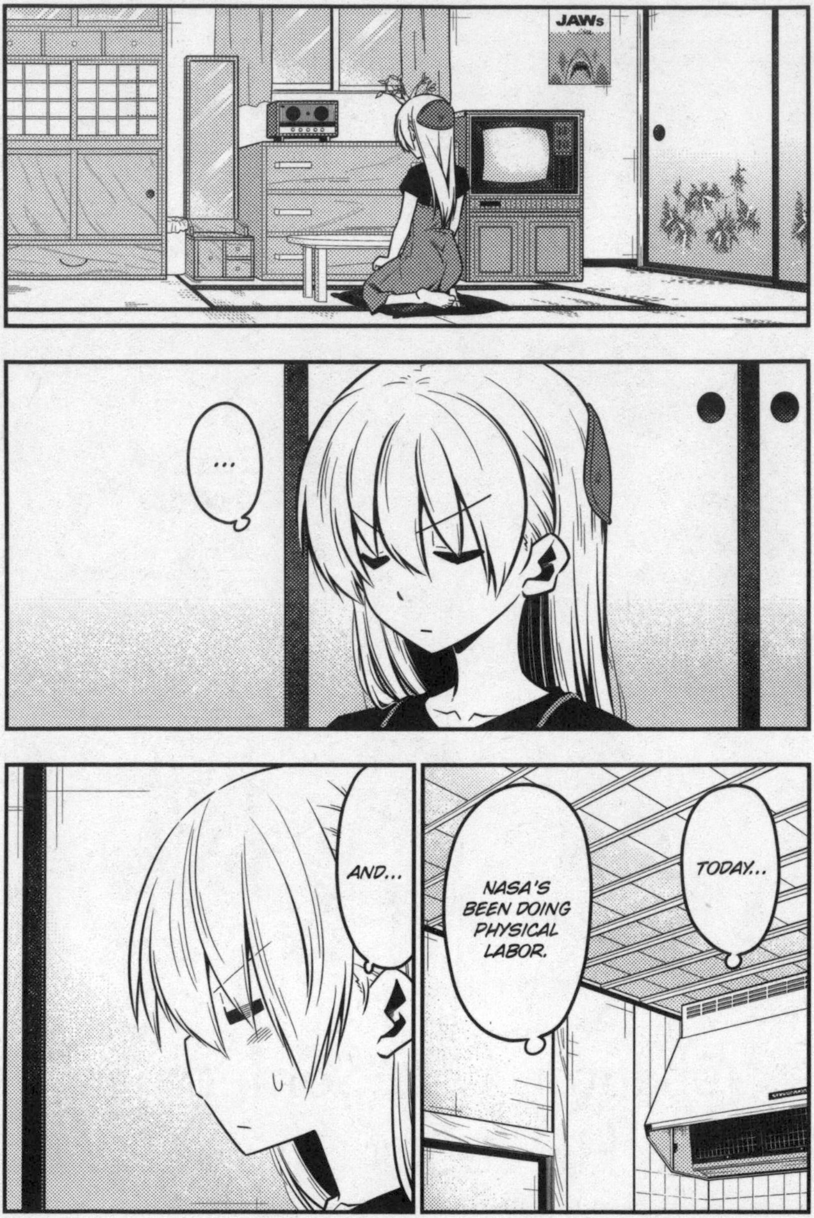
JAWs
...
TODAY...
NASA'S BEEN DOING PHYSICAL LABOR.
AND...

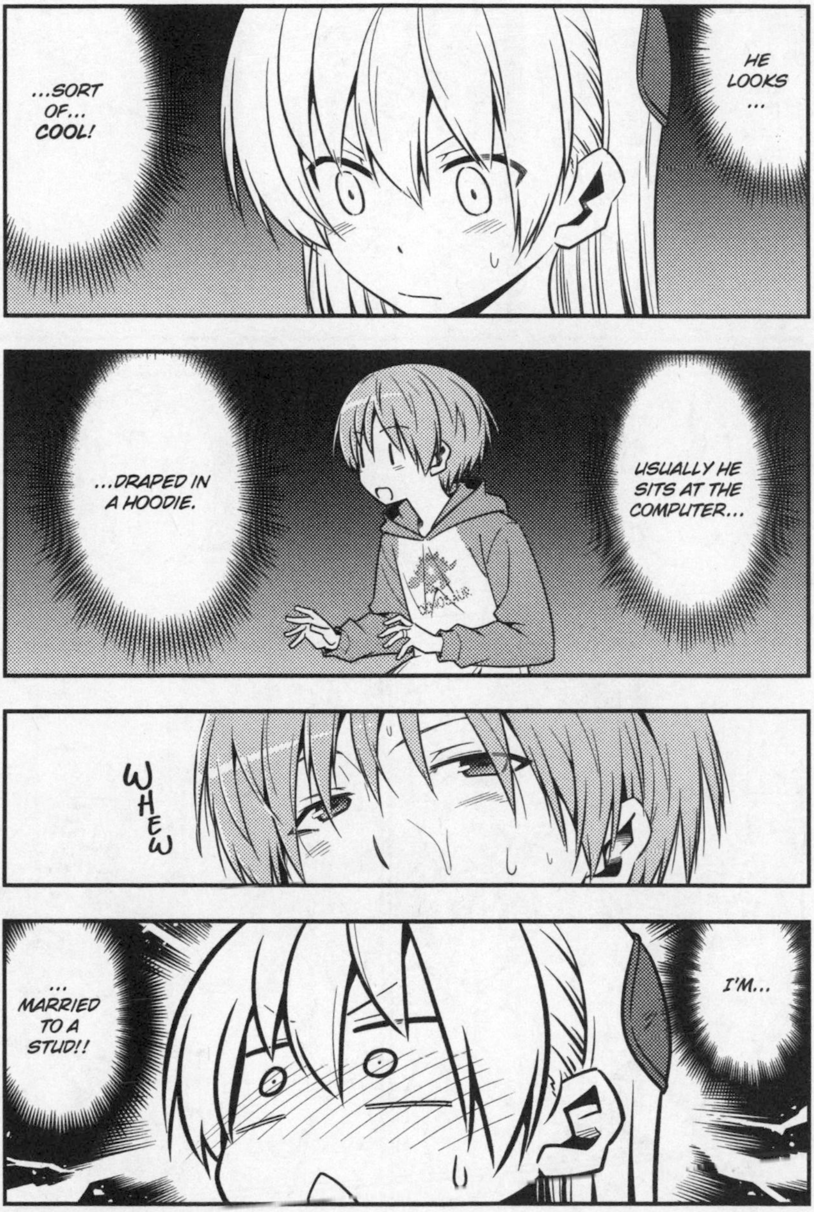
HE LOOKS ...
...SORT OF... COOL!
USUALLY HE SITS AT THE COMPUTER...
...DRAPED IN A HOODIE.
WHEW
I'M...
... MARRIED TO A STUD!!

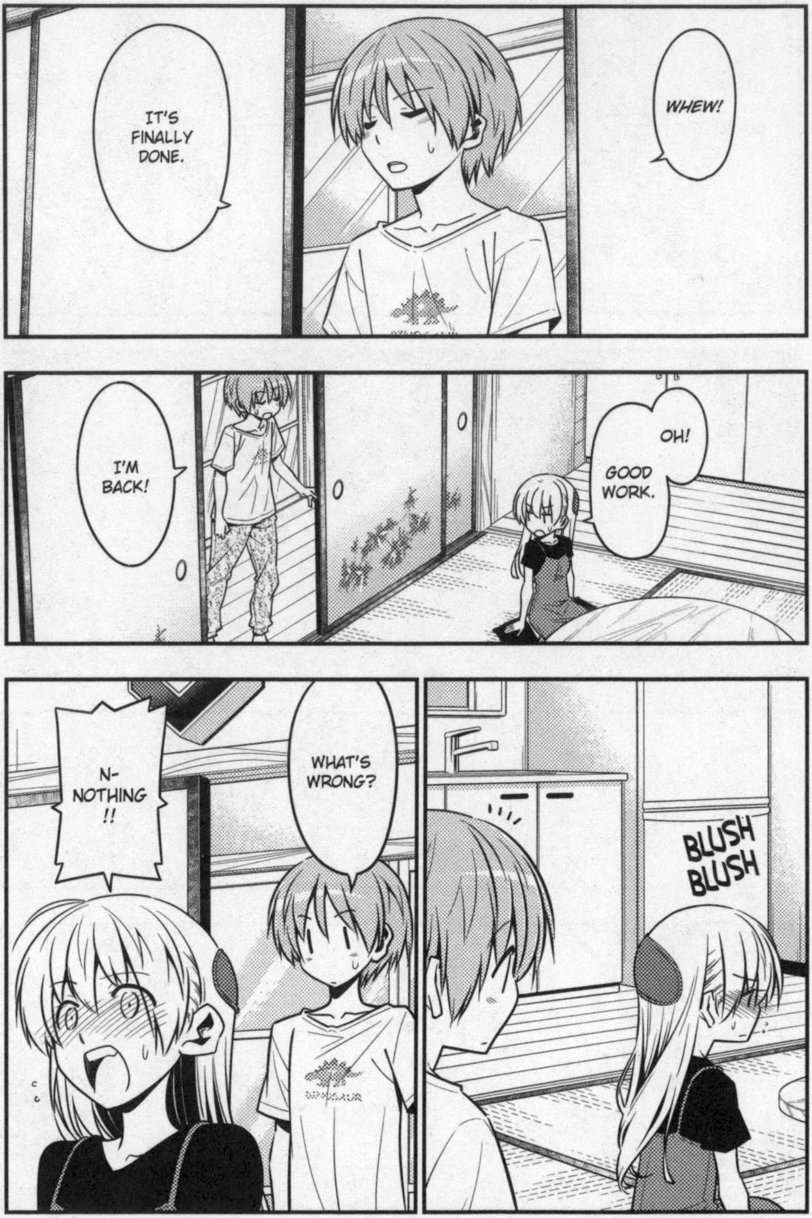
WHEW!
IT'S FINALLY DONE.
I'M BACK!
OH! GOOD WORK.
BLUSH BLUSH
WHAT'S WRONG?
N-NOTHING!!

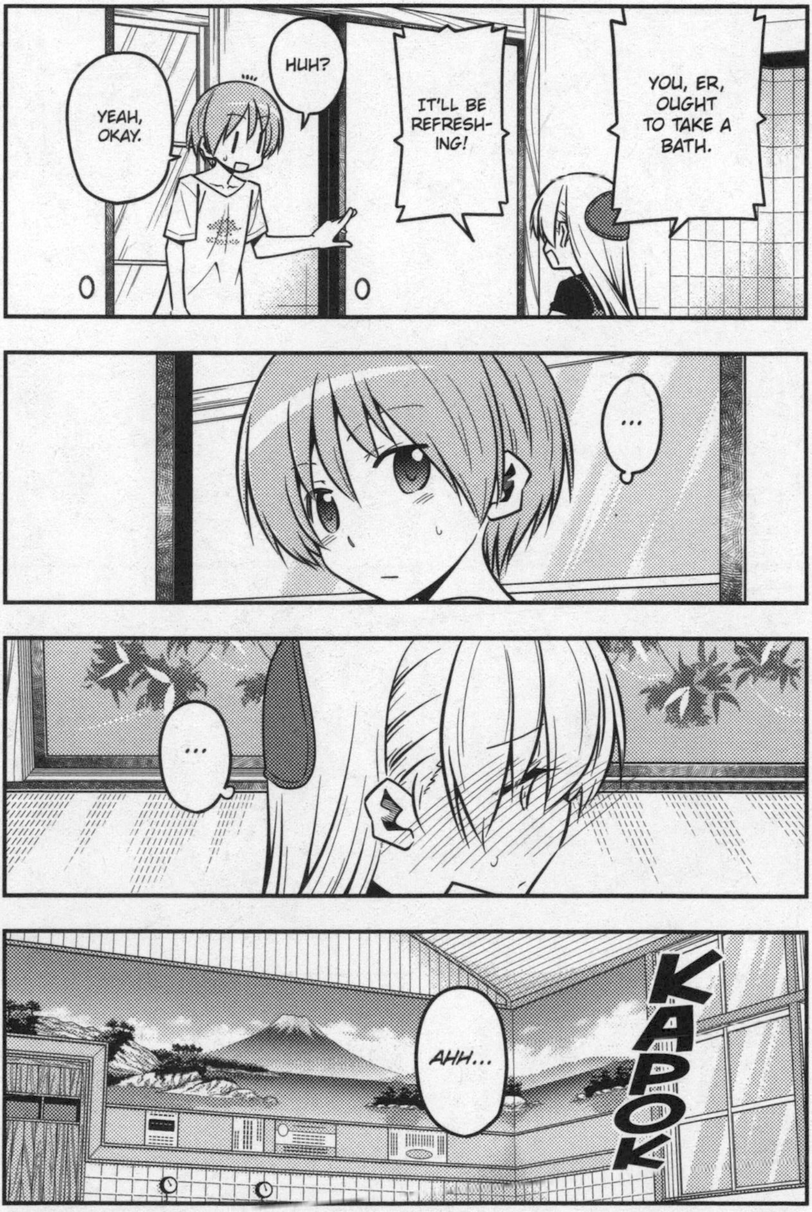
YOU, ER, OUGHT TO TAKE A BATH.
IT'LL BE REFRESH-ING!
HUH?
YEAH, OKAY.
...
...
KAPOK
AHH...

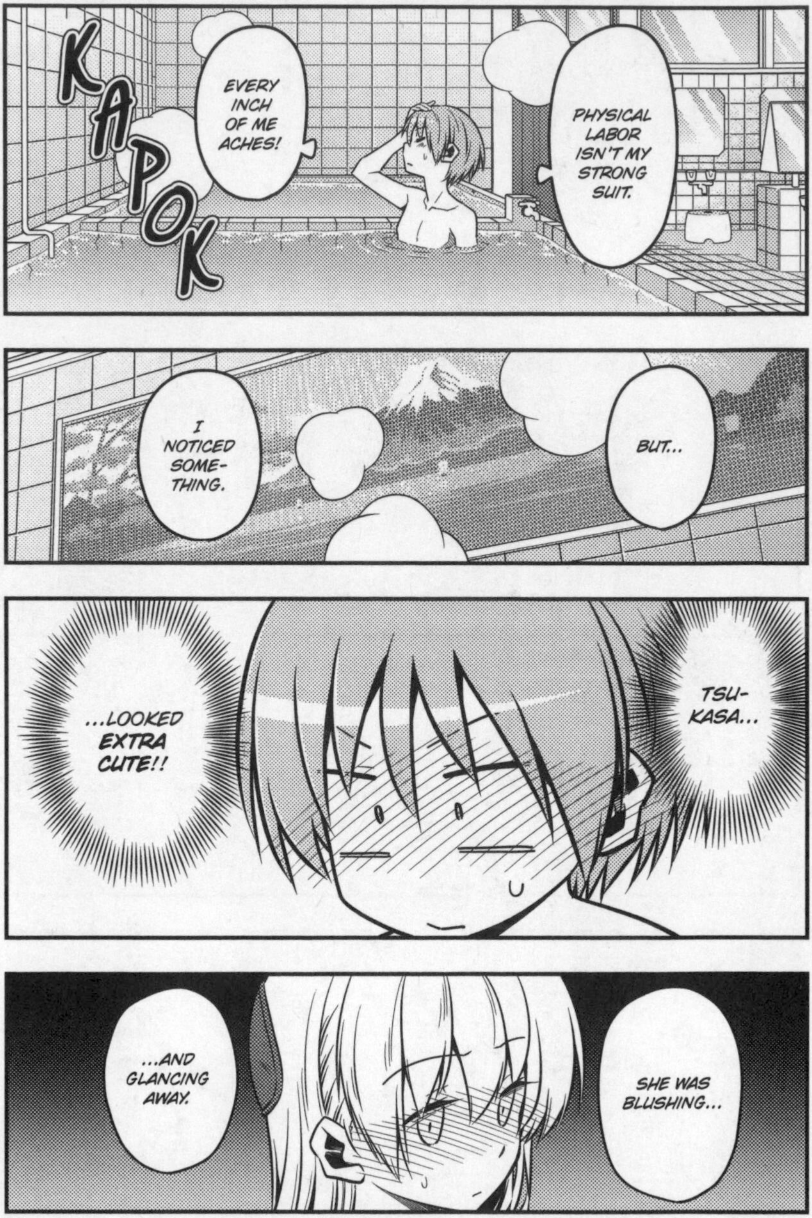
PHYSICAL LABOR ISN'T MY STRONG SUIT.
EVERY INCH OF ME ACHES!
KAPOK
BUT...
I NOTICED SOME-THING.
TSU-KASA...
...LOOKED EXTRA CUTE!!
SHE WAS BLUSHING...
...AND GLANCING AWAY.

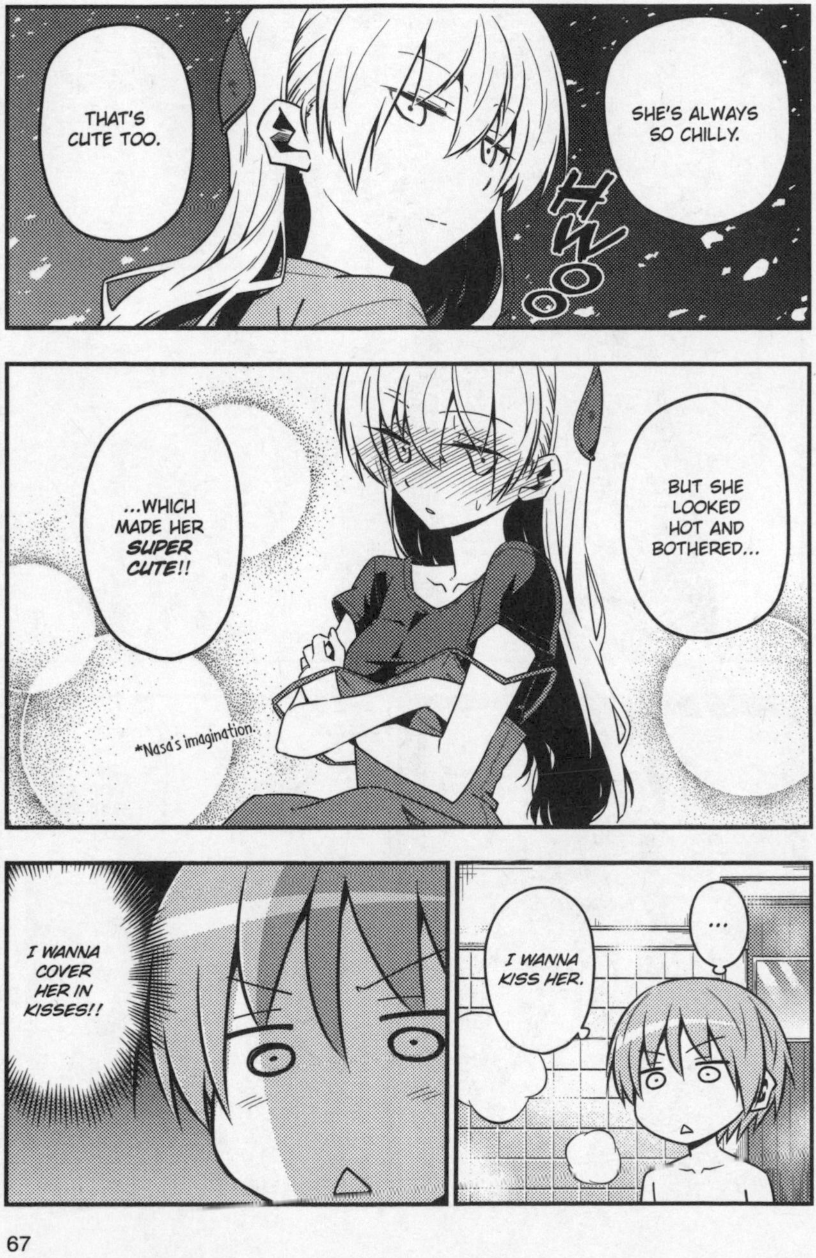

SHE'S ALWAYS SO CHILLY.
HWOO
THAT'S CUTE TOO.
BUT SHE LOOKED HOT AND BOTHERED...
...WHICH MADE HER SUPER CUTE!!
*Nasa's imagination.
...
I WANNA KISS HER.
I WANNA COVER HER IN KISSES!!

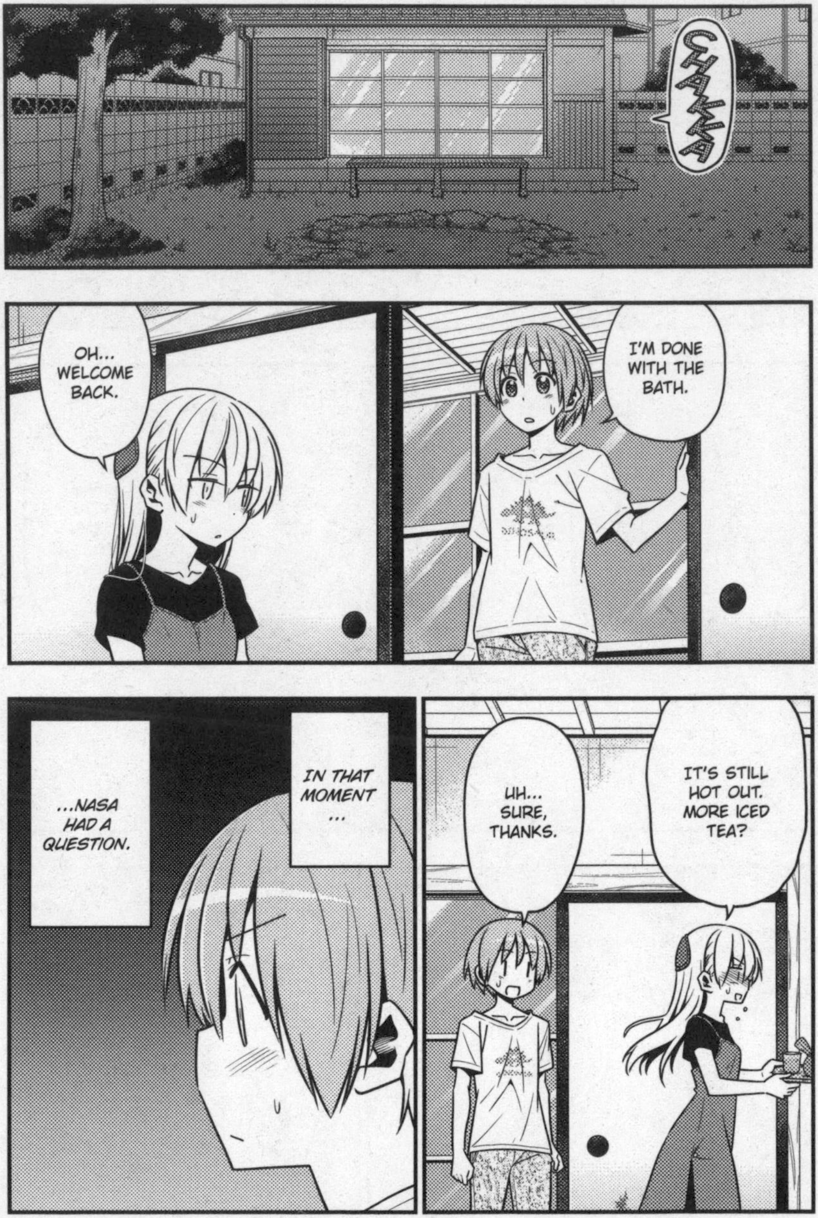
CHAKKA
I'M DONE WITH THE BATH.
OH... WELCOME BACK.
IT'S STILL HOT OUT. MORE ICED TEA?
UH... SURE, THANKS.
IN THAT MOMENT ...
...NASA HAD A QUESTION.

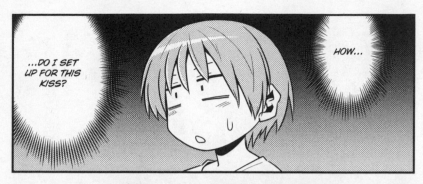

HOW...
...DO I SET UP FOR THIS KISS?
SHOULD I CREATE A ROMANTIC ATMOSPHERE?
GRRF
NAH, BAD IDEA.
OUR KISSES ARE USUALLY SPONTANEOUS. A SURPRISE!
THAT MEANS...
...I SHOULD JUST GO FOR IT!

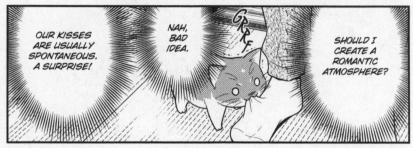

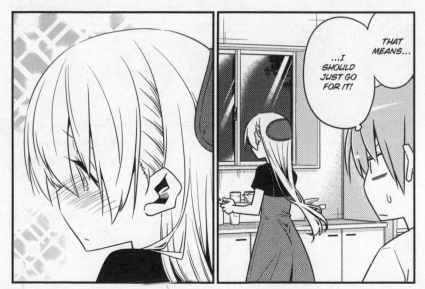

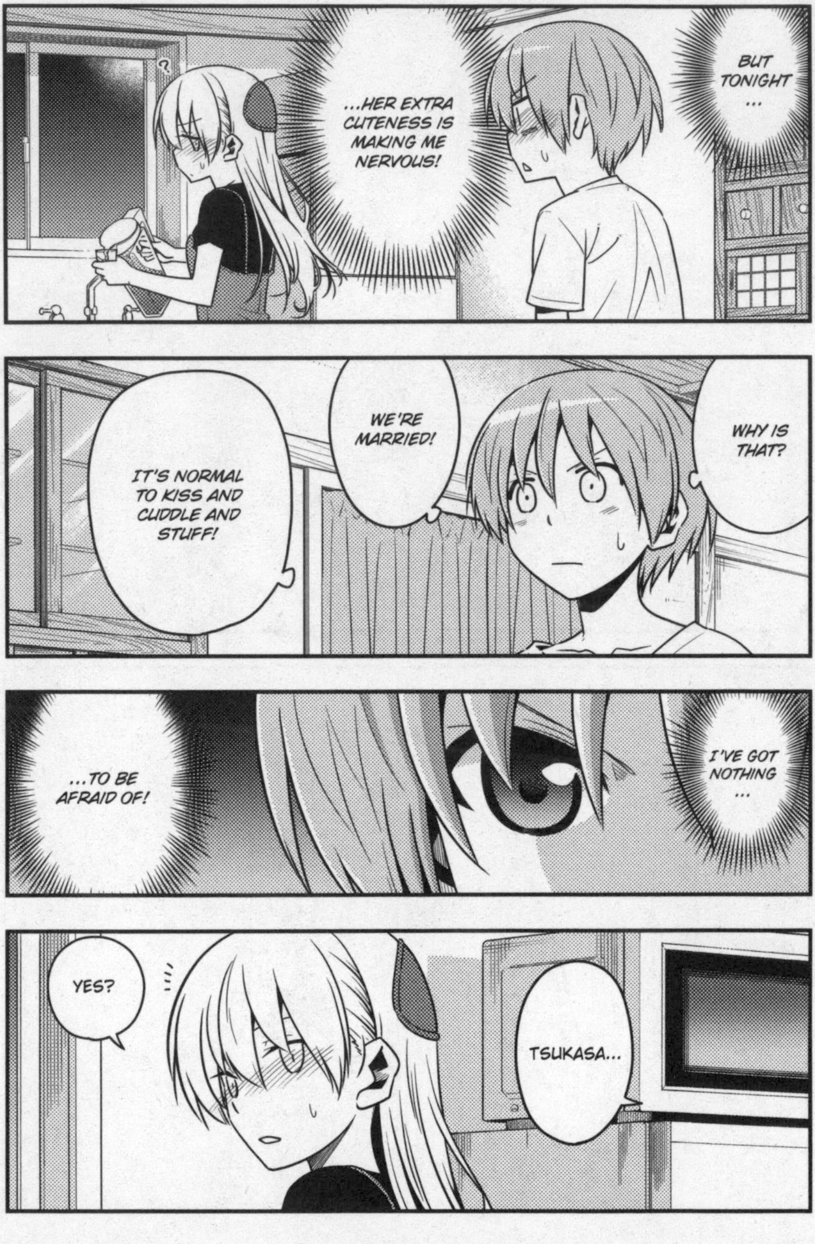
BUT TONIGHT...
...HER EXTRA CUTENESS IS MAKING ME NERVOUS!
WHY IS THAT?
WE'RE MARRIED!
IT'S NORMAL TO KISS AND CUDDLE AND STUFF!
I'VE GOT NOTHING...
...TO BE AFRAID OF!
TSUKASA...
YES?

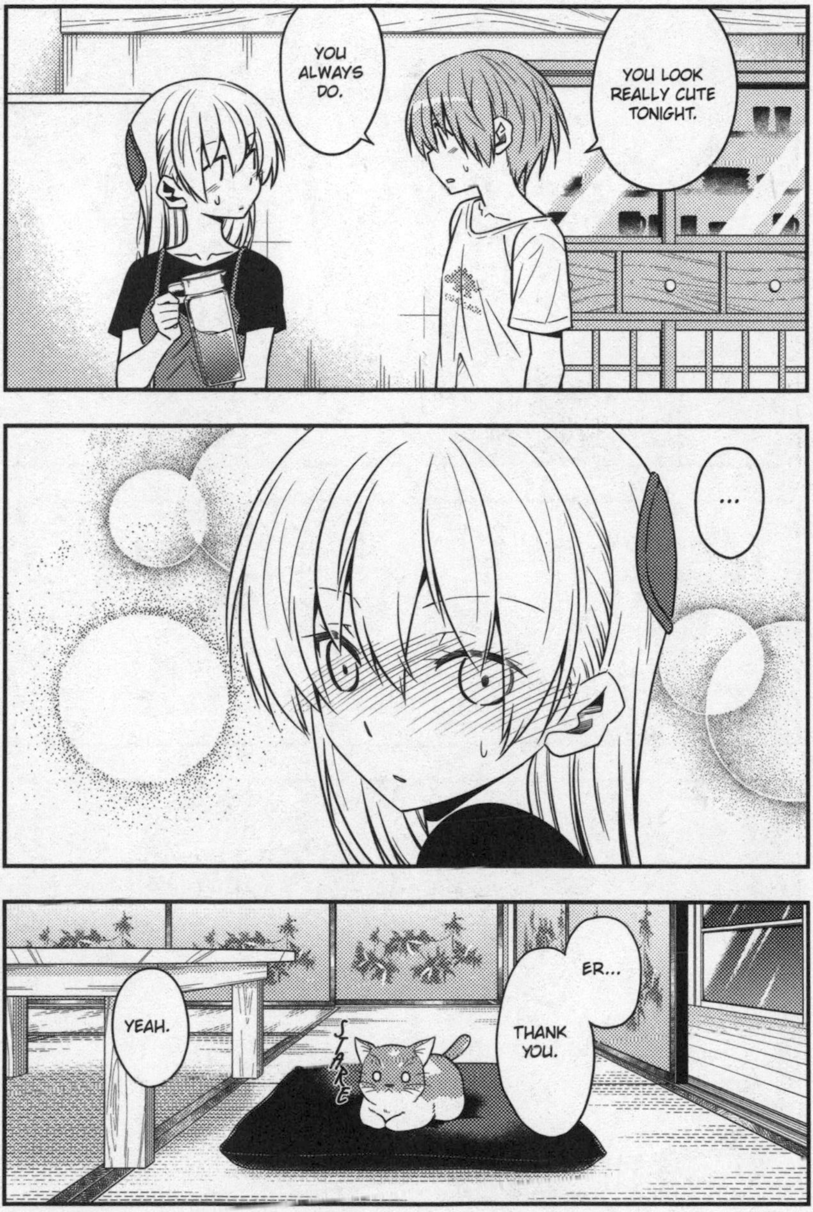
YOU LOOK REALLY CUTE TONIGHT.
YOU ALWAYS DO.
...
ER...
THANK YOU.
STARE
YEAH.

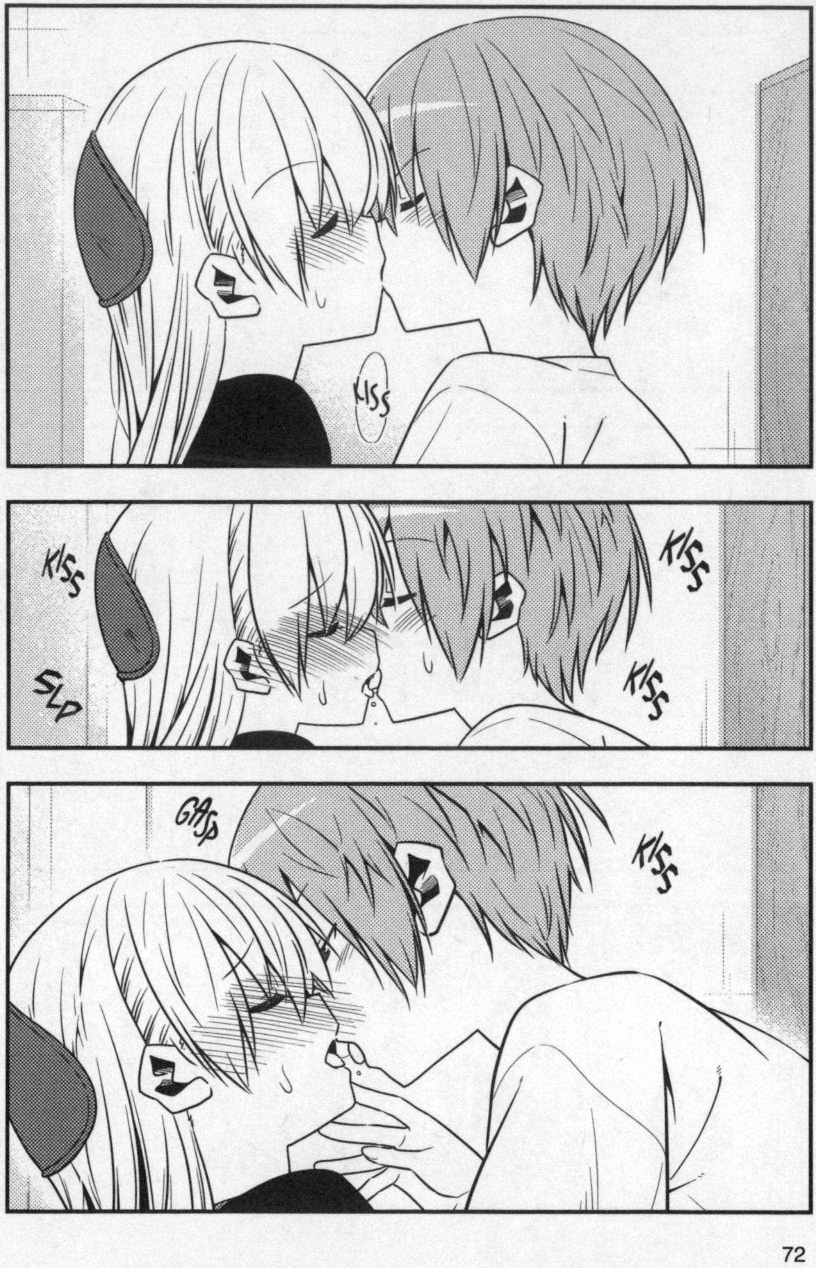
KISS
KISS
KISS
KISS
SLP
KISS
GASP

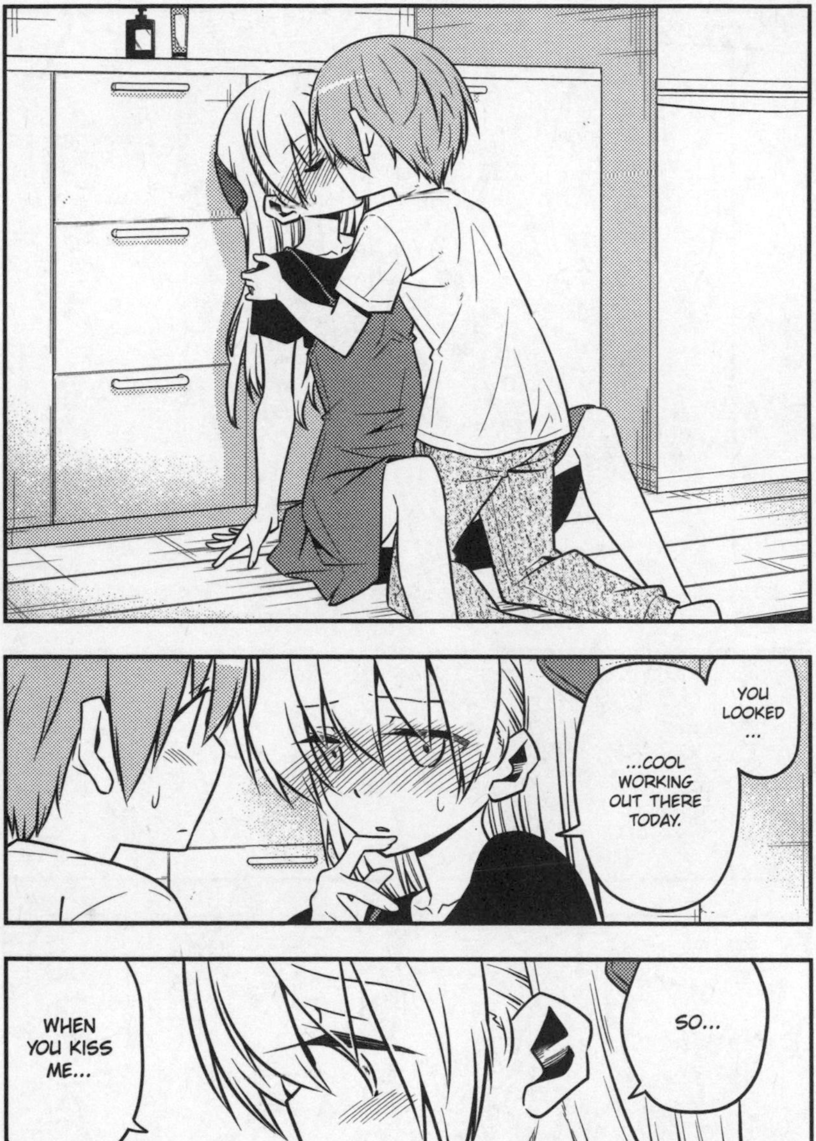
YOU LOOKED ...
...COOL WORKING OUT THERE TODAY.
SO...
WHEN YOU KISS ME...

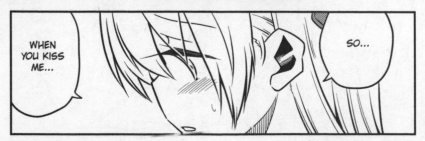

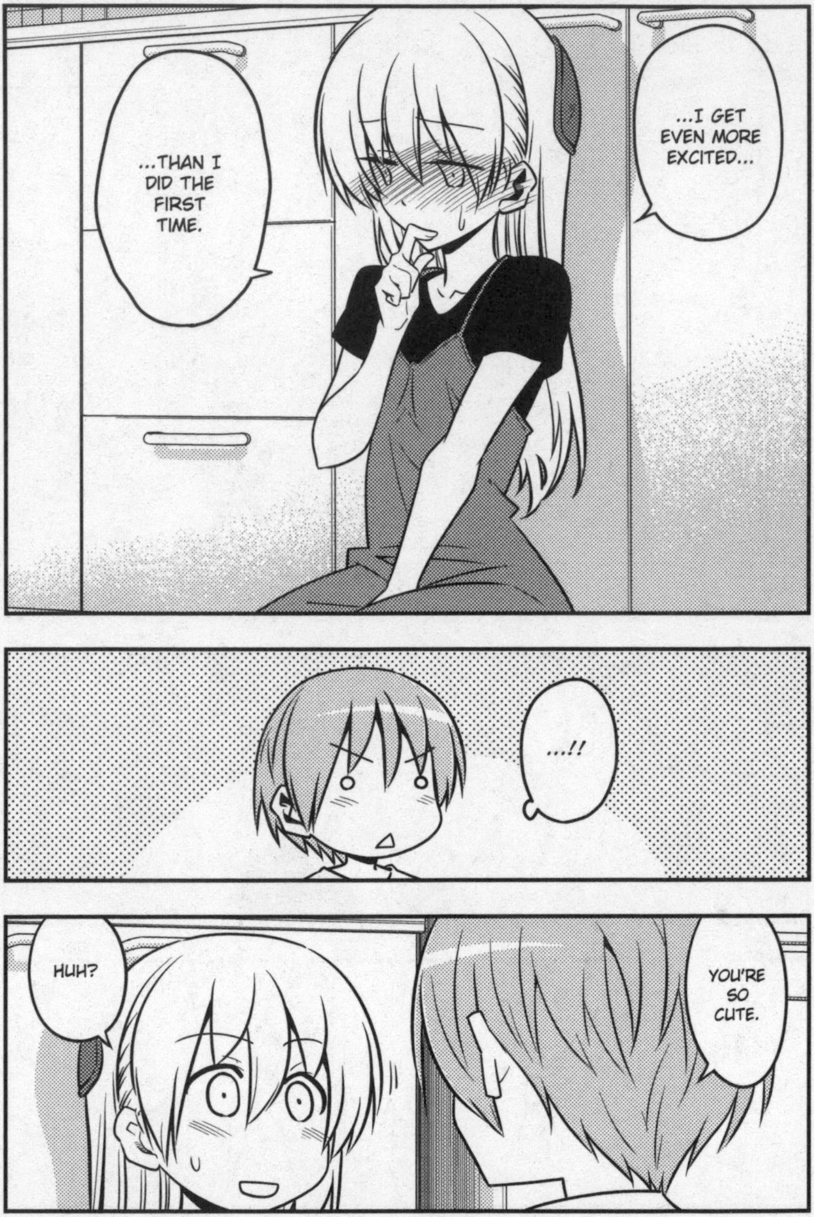
...I GET EVEN MORE EXCITED...
...THAN I DID THE FIRST TIME.
...!!
YOU'RE SO CUTE.
HUH?

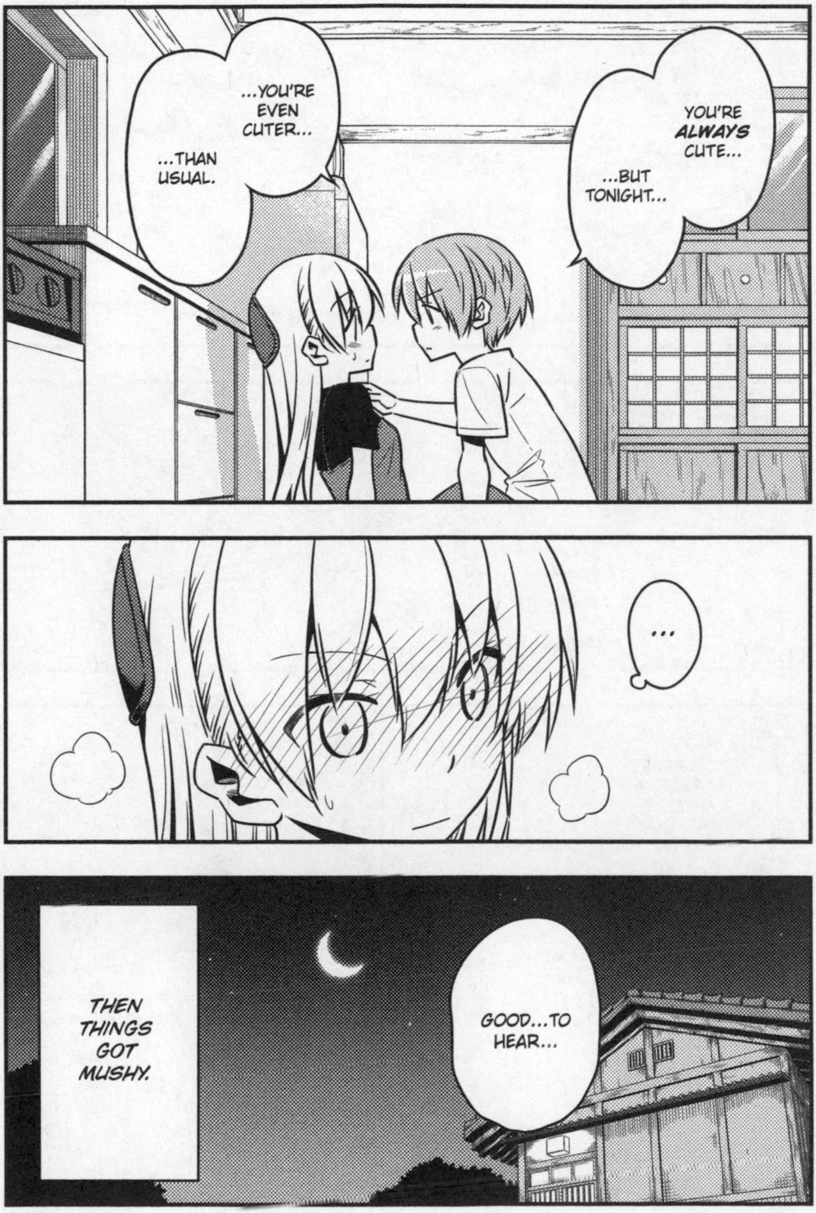
YOU'RE ALWAYS CUTE... ...BUT TONIGHT...
...YOU'RE EVEN CUTER... ...THAN USUAL.
...
GOOD...TO HEAR...
THEN THINGS GOT MUSHY.

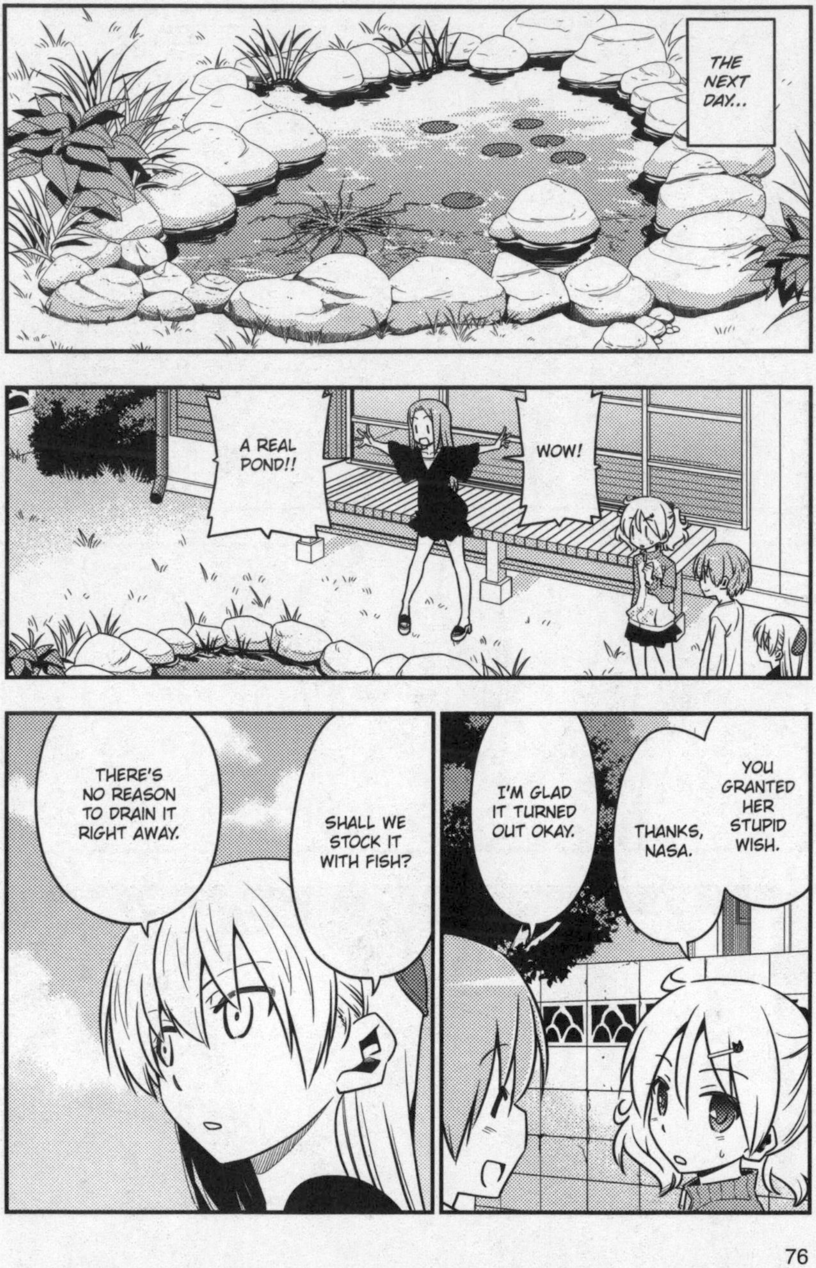
THE NEXT DAY...
WOW!
A REAL POND!!
YOU GRANTED HER STUPID WISH.
THANKS, NASA.
I'M GLAD IT TURNED OUT OKAY.
SHALL WE STOCK IT WITH FISH?
THERE'S NO REASON TO DRAIN IT RIGHT AWAY.

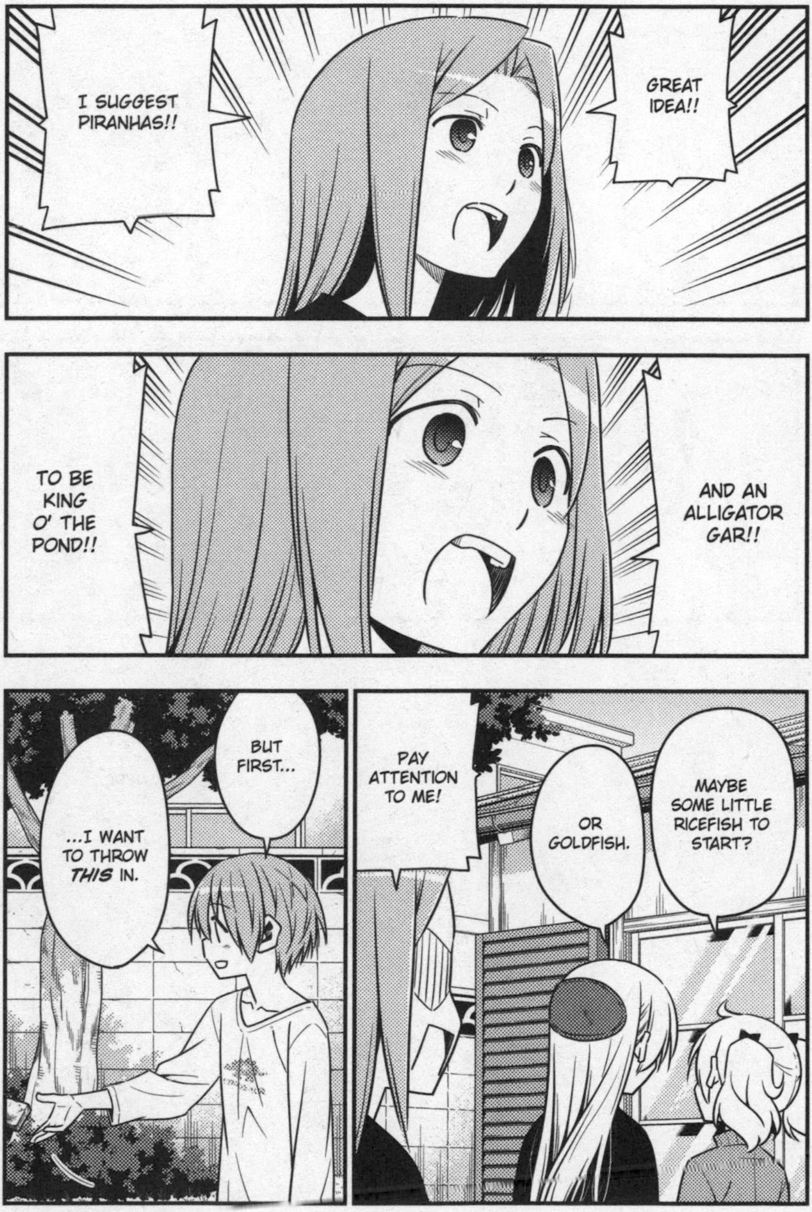
GREAT IDEA!!
I SUGGEST PIRANHAS!!
AND AN ALLIGATOR GAR!!
TO BE KING O' THE POND!!
MAYBE SOME LITTLE RICEFISH TO START?
OR GOLDFISH.
PAY ATTENTION TO ME!
BUT FIRST...
...I WANT TO THROW *THIS* IN.

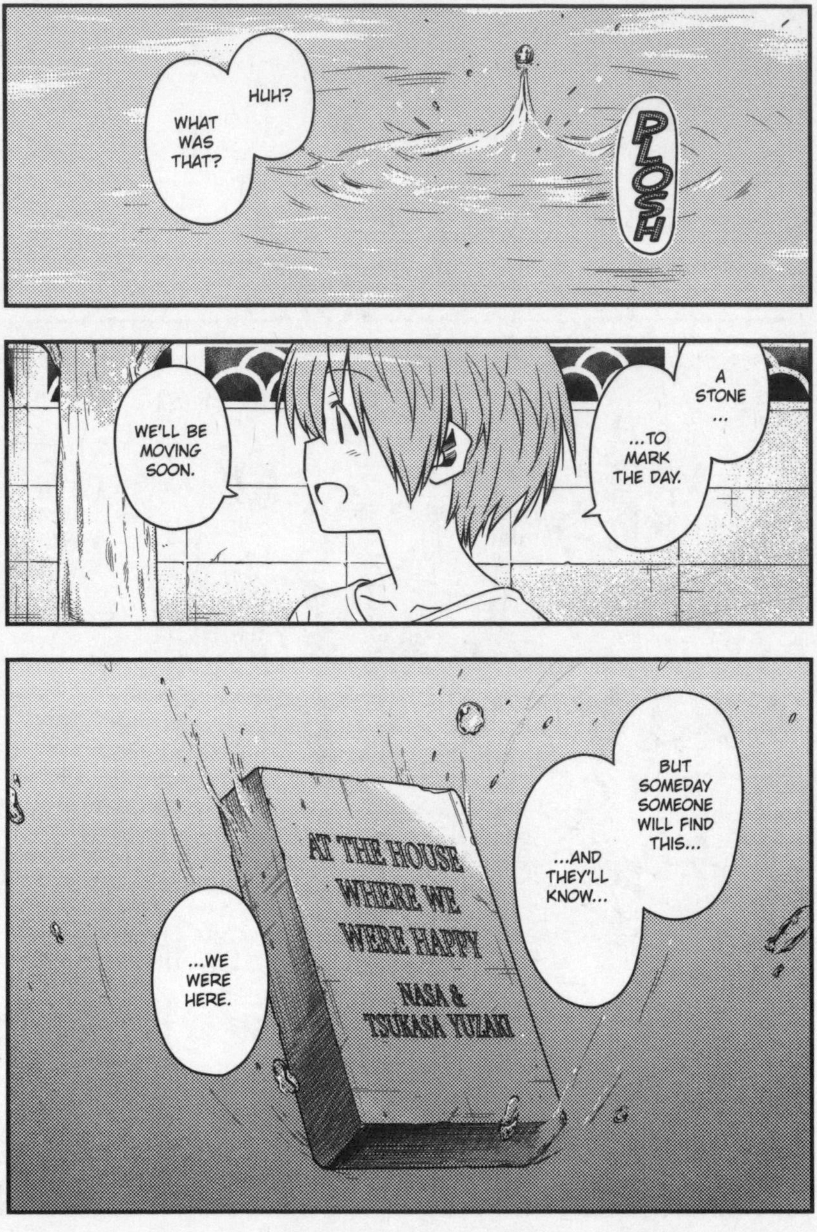
PLOSH
HUH? WHAT WAS THAT?
A STONE ... ...TO MARK THE DAY.
WE'LL BE MOVING SOON.
BUT SOMEDAY SOMEONE WILL FIND THIS... ...AND THEY'LL KNOW...
AT THE HOUSE WHERE WE WERE HAPPY
NASA & TSUKASA YUZAKI
...WE WERE HERE.

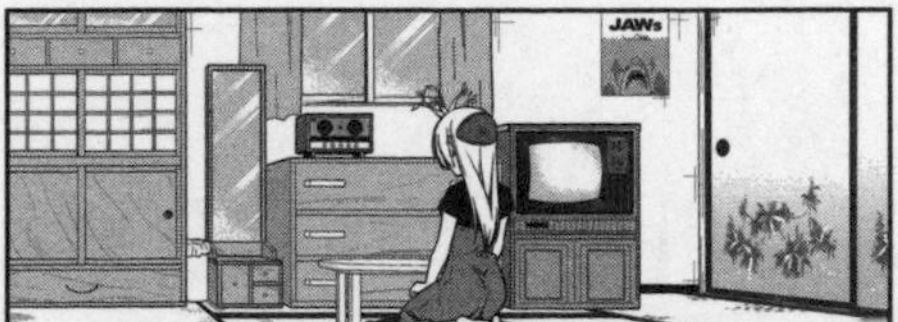
JAWS

FLY ME TO THE MOON

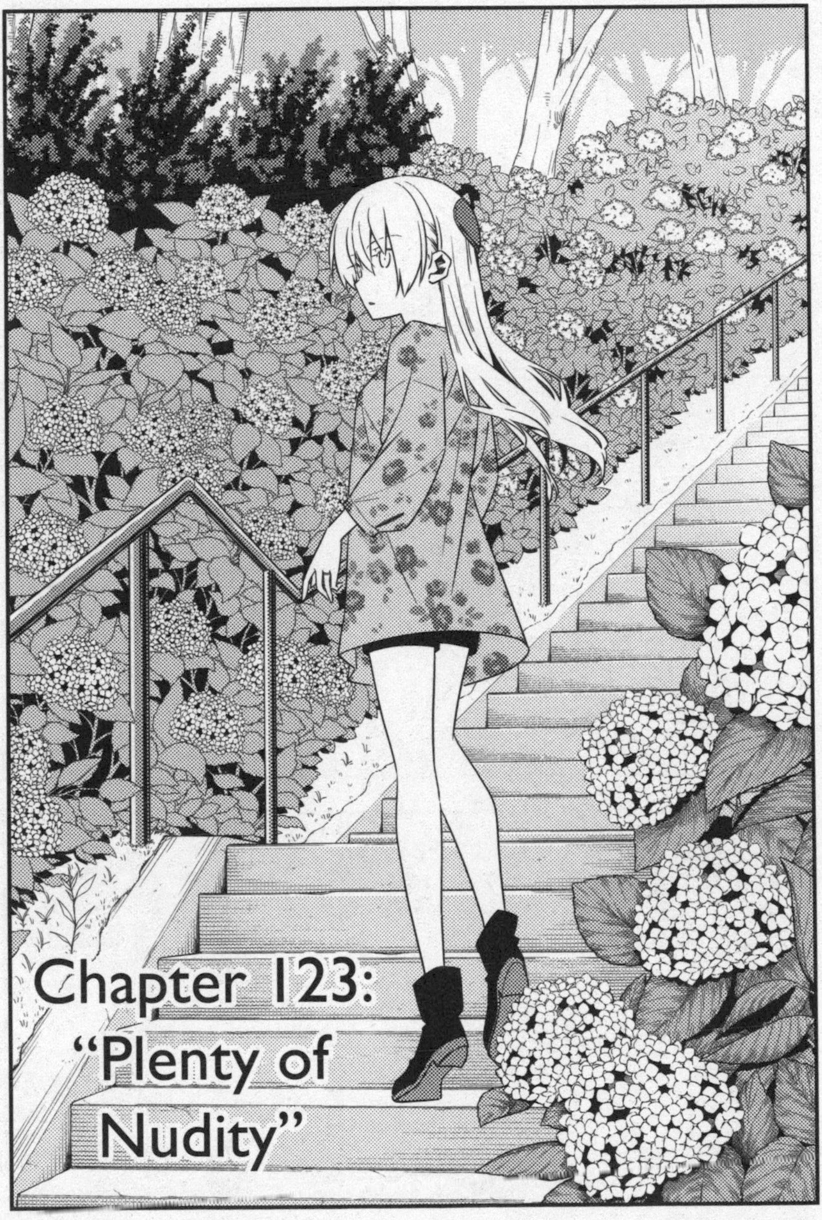
Chapter 123:
"Plenty of
Nudity"

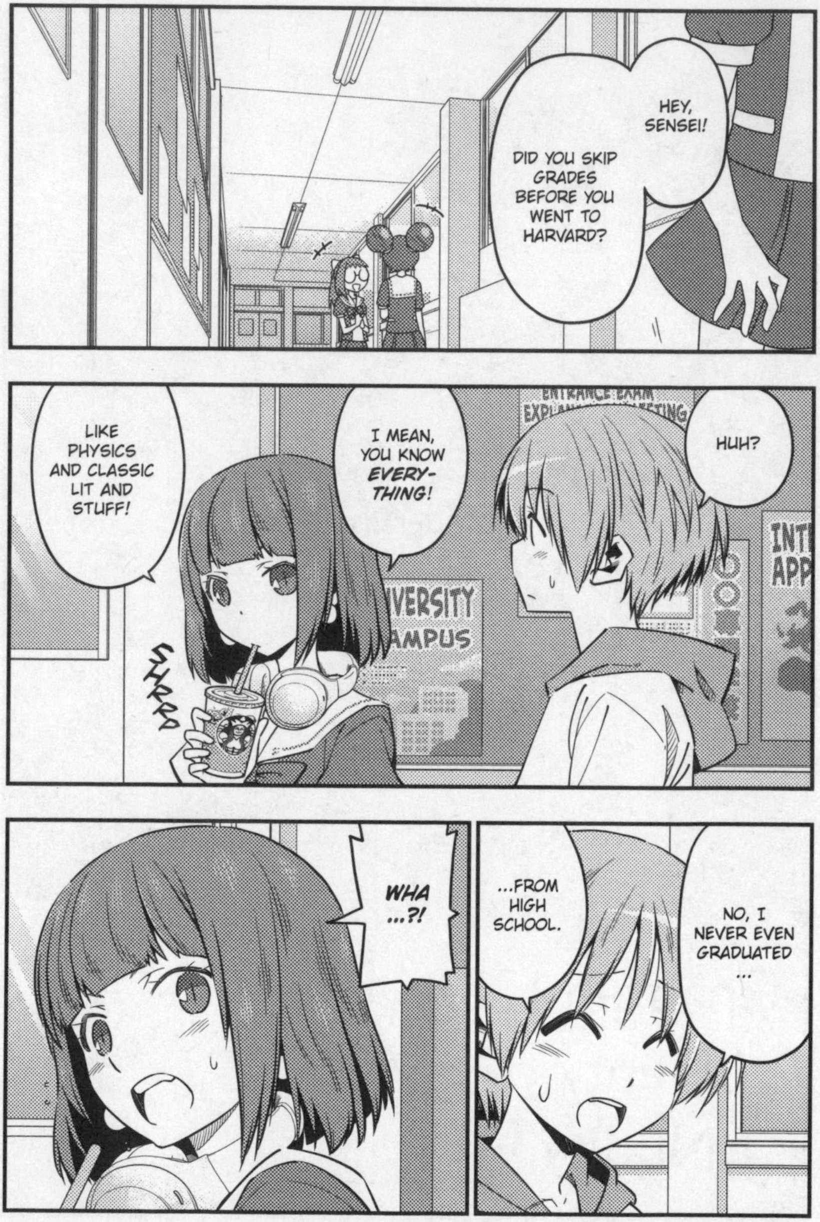
HEY, SENSEI!
DID YOU SKIP GRADES BEFORE YOU WENT TO HARVARD?
ENTRANCE EXAM
HUH?
I MEAN, YOU KNOW *EVERYTHING!*
LIKE PHYSICS AND CLASSIC LIT AND STUFF!
SHRRP
NO, I NEVER EVEN GRADUATED ...
...FROM HIGH SCHOOL.
WHA ...?!

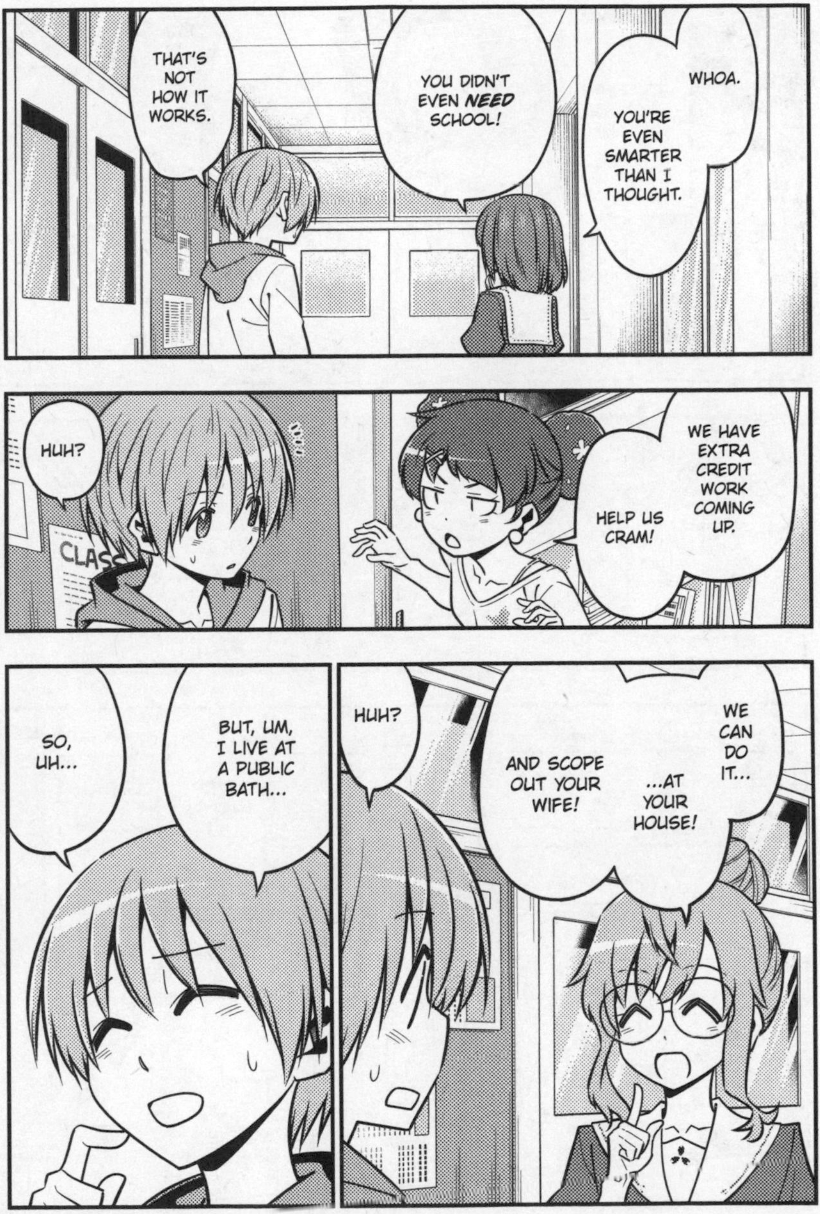
WHOA.
YOU'RE EVEN SMARTER THAN I THOUGHT.
YOU DIDN'T EVEN *NEED* SCHOOL!
THAT'S NOT HOW IT WORKS.
WE HAVE EXTRA CREDIT WORK COMING UP.
HELP US CRAM!
HUH?
WE CAN DO IT...
...AT YOUR HOUSE!
AND SCOPE OUT YOUR WIFE!
HUH?
BUT, UM, I LIVE AT A PUBLIC BATH...
SO, UH...

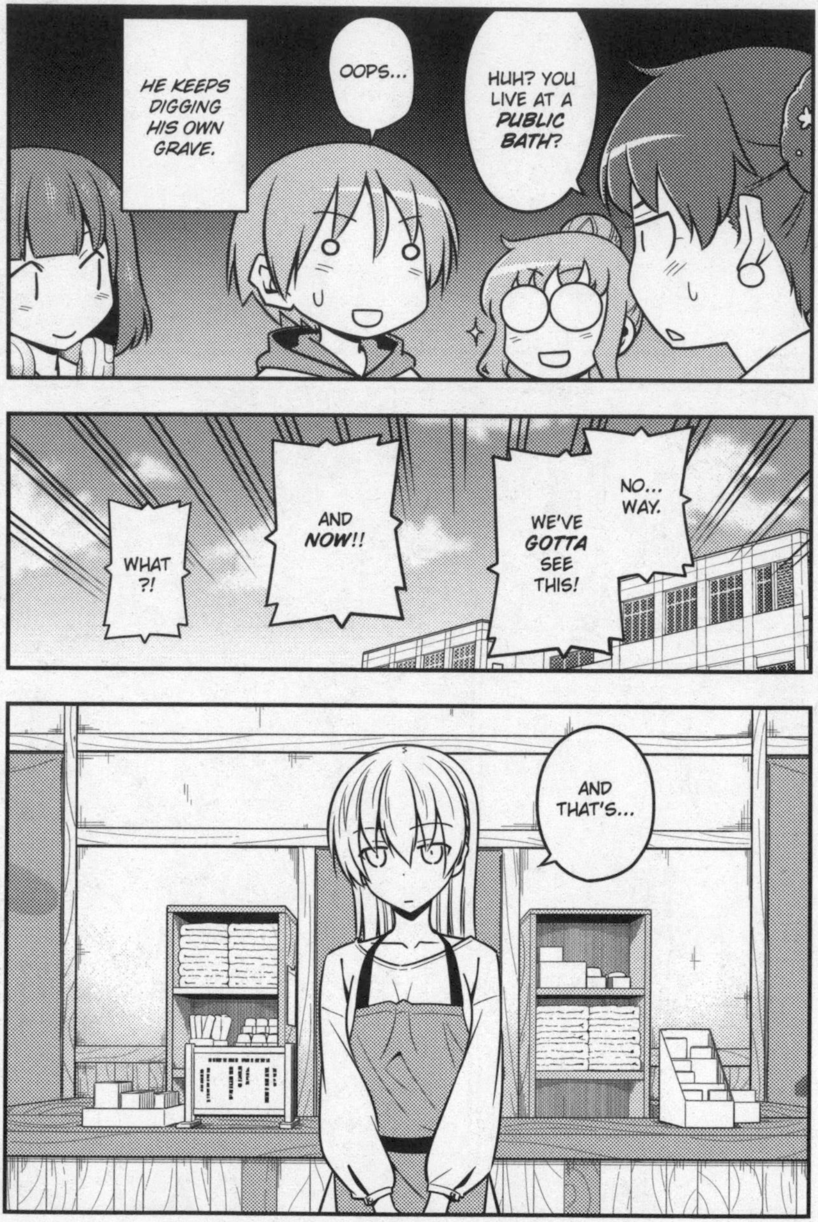
HUH? YOU LIVE AT A *PUBLIC BATH?*
OOPS...
HE KEEPS DIGGING HIS OWN GRAVE.
NO... WAY.
WE'VE *GOTTA* SEE THIS!
AND *NOW!!*
WHAT?!
AND THAT'S...

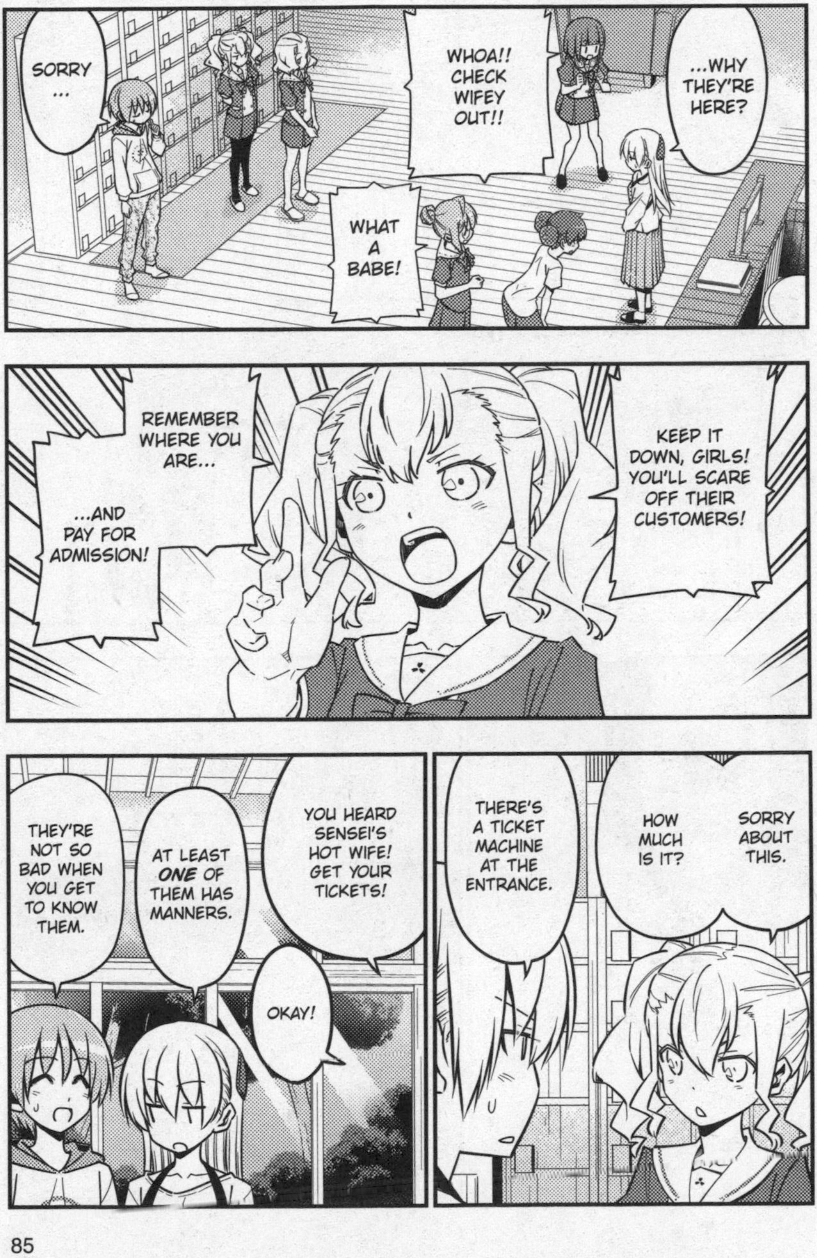
...WHY THEY'RE HERE?
WHOA!! CHECK WIFEY OUT!!
WHAT A BABE!
SORRY ...
KEEP IT DOWN, GIRLS! YOU'LL SCARE OFF THEIR CUSTOMERS!
REMEMBER WHERE YOU ARE...
...AND PAY FOR ADMISSION!
SORRY ABOUT THIS.
HOW MUCH IS IT?
THERE'S A TICKET MACHINE AT THE ENTRANCE.
YOU HEARD SENSEI'S HOT WIFE! GET YOUR TICKETS!
OKAY!
AT LEAST *ONE* OF THEM HAS MANNERS.
THEY'RE NOT SO BAD WHEN YOU GET TO KNOW THEM.

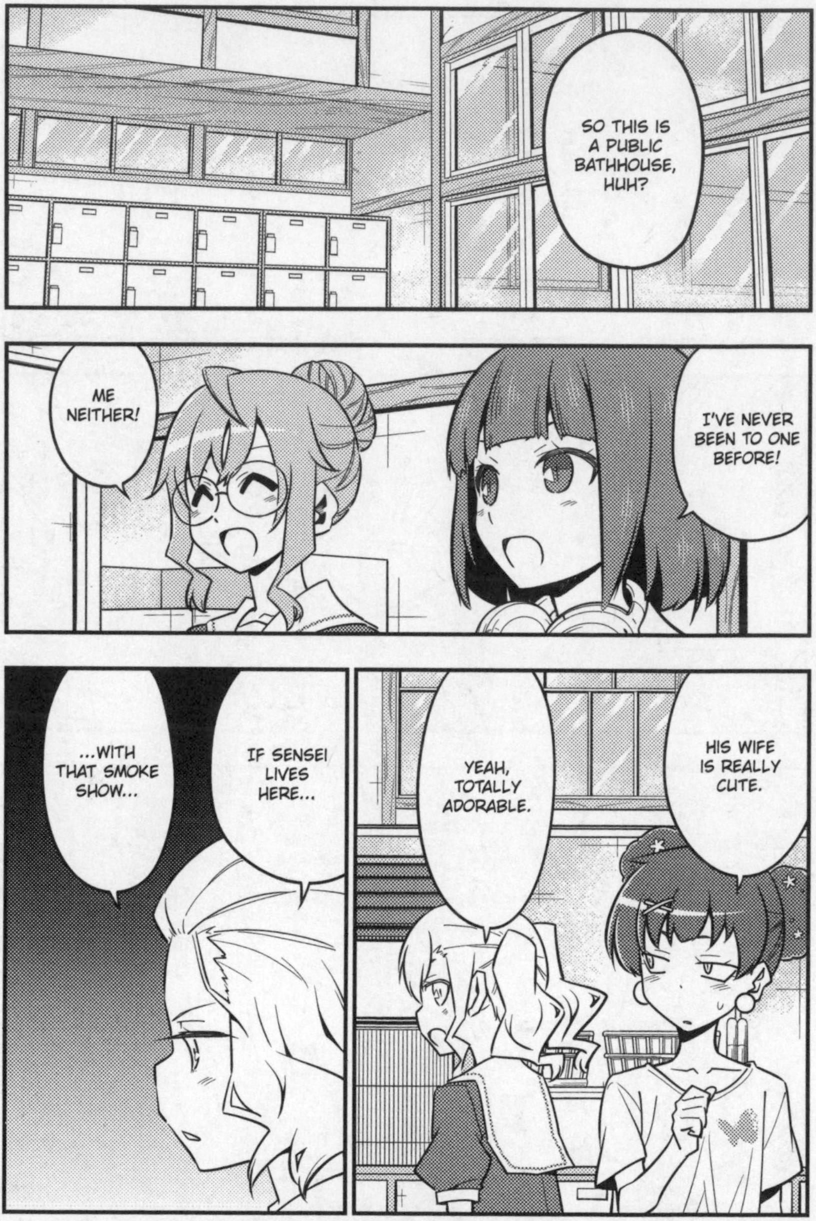
SO THIS IS A PUBLIC BATHHOUSE, HUH?
I'VE NEVER BEEN TO ONE BEFORE!
ME NEITHER!
HIS WIFE IS REALLY CUTE.
YEAH, TOTALLY ADORABLE.
IF SENSEI LIVES HERE...
...WITH THAT SMOKE SHOW...

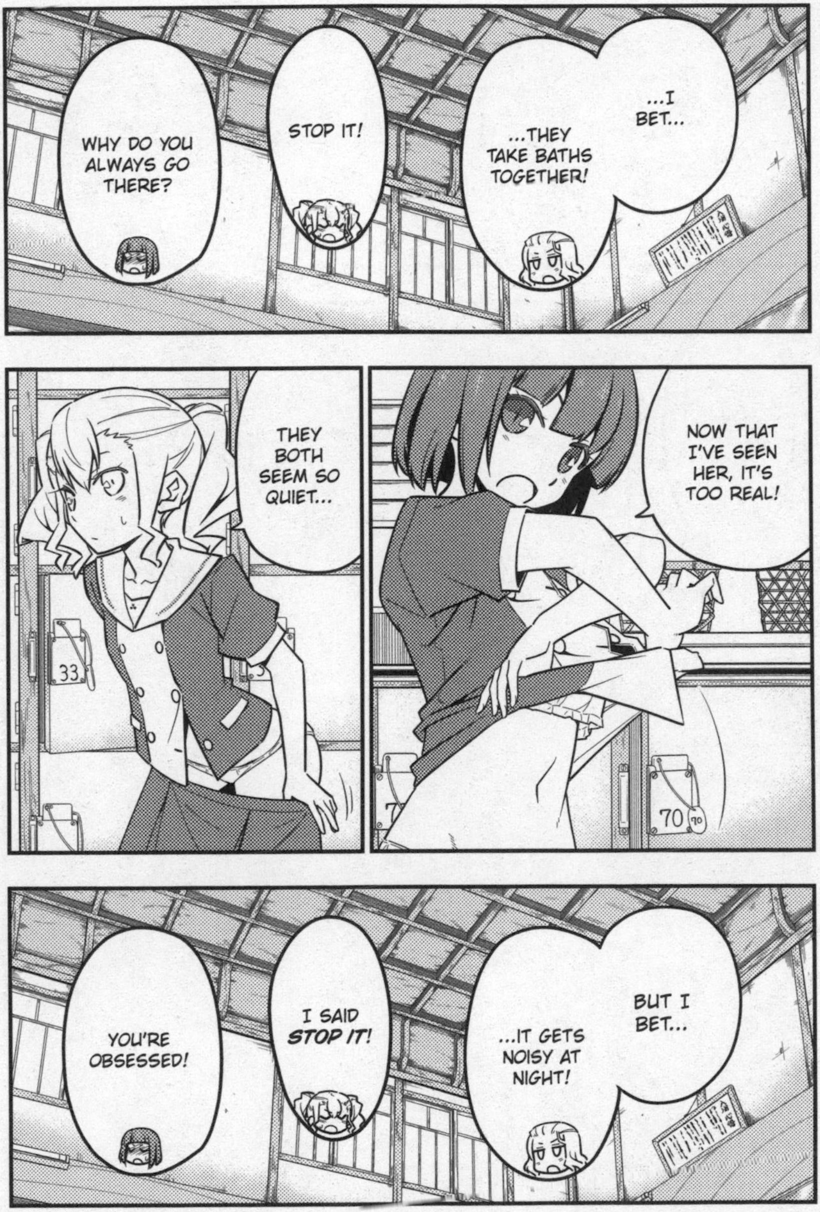
...I BET...
...THEY TAKE BATHS TOGETHER!
STOP IT!
WHY DO YOU ALWAYS GO THERE?
NOW THAT I'VE SEEN HER, IT'S TOO REAL!
THEY BOTH SEEM SO QUIET...
BUT I BET...
...IT GETS NOISY AT NIGHT!
I SAID *STOP IT!*
YOU'RE OBSESSED!

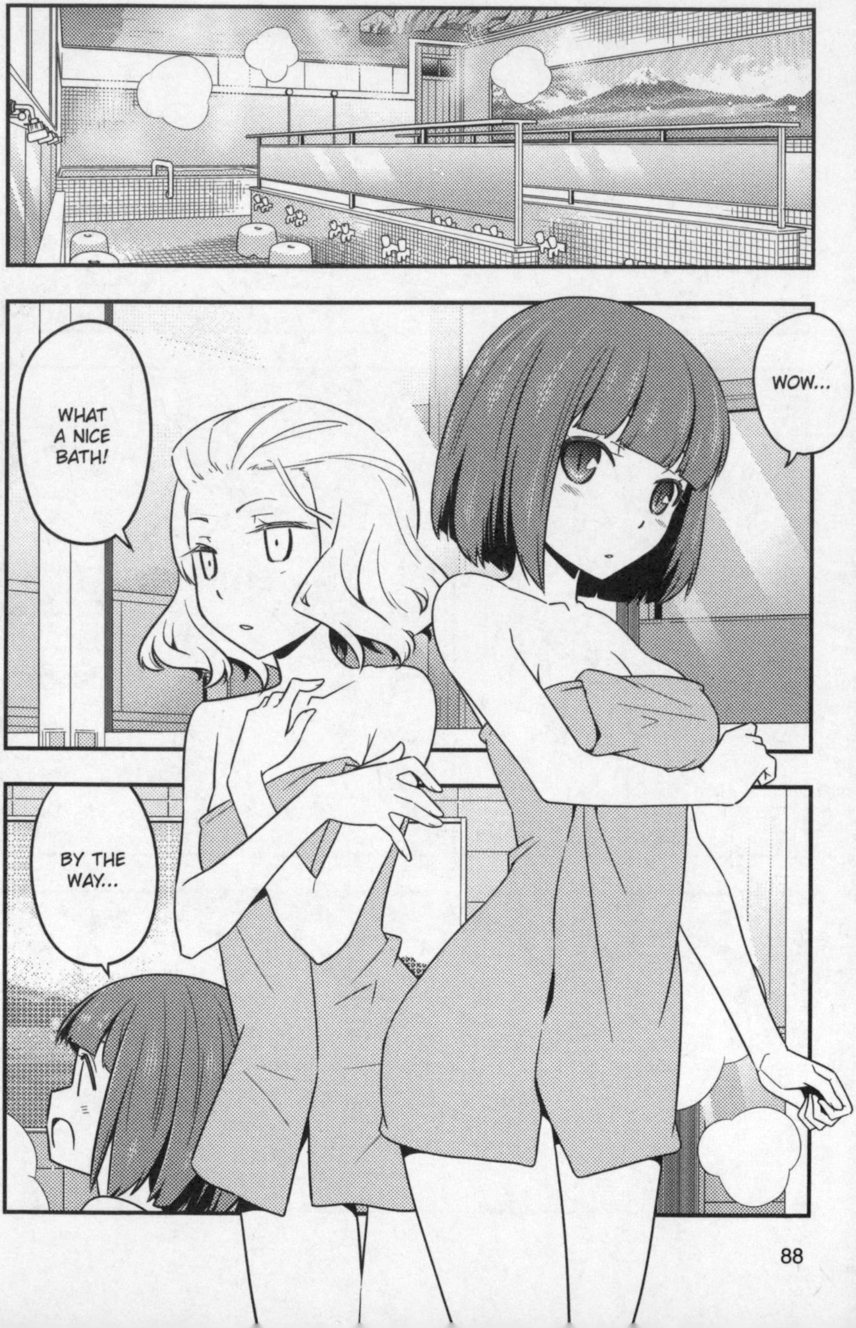
WOW...
WHAT A NICE BATH!
BY THE WAY...

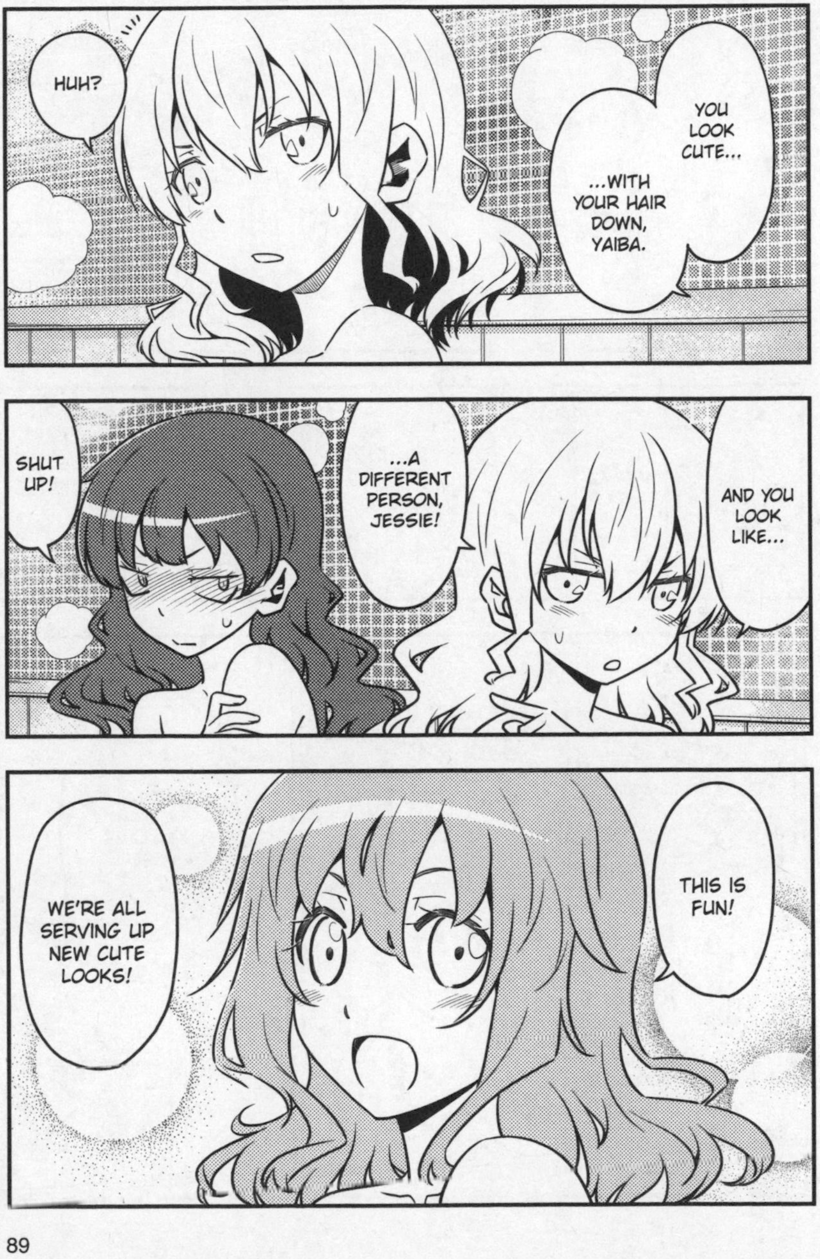
YOU LOOK CUTE...
...WITH YOUR HAIR DOWN, YAIBA.
HUH?
AND YOU LOOK LIKE...
...A DIFFERENT PERSON, JESSIE!
SHUT UP!
THIS IS FUN!
WE'RE ALL SERVING UP NEW CUTE LOOKS!

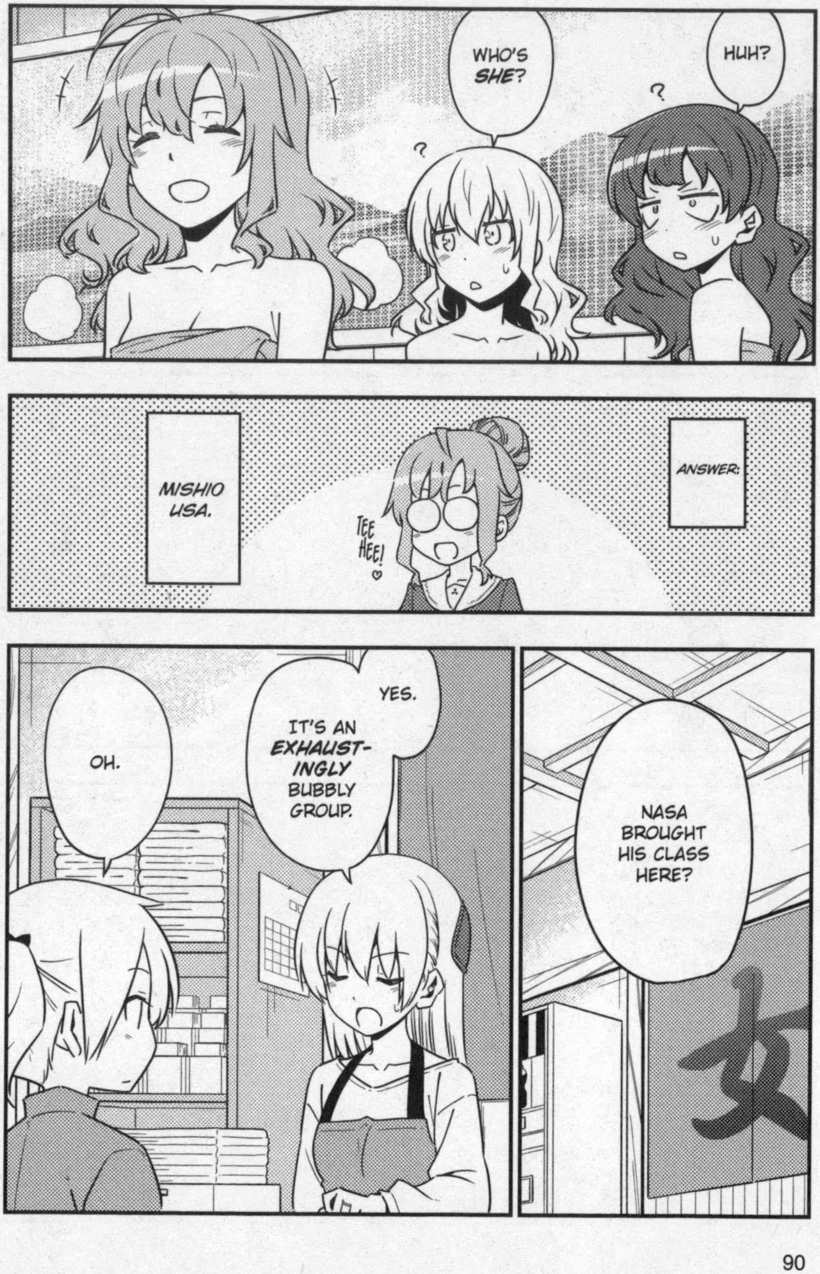
HUH?
WHO'S SHE?
ANSWER:
TEE HEE! ♡
MISHIO USA.
NASA BROUGHT HIS CLASS HERE?
YES. IT'S AN EXHAUSTINGLY BUBBLY GROUP.
OH.

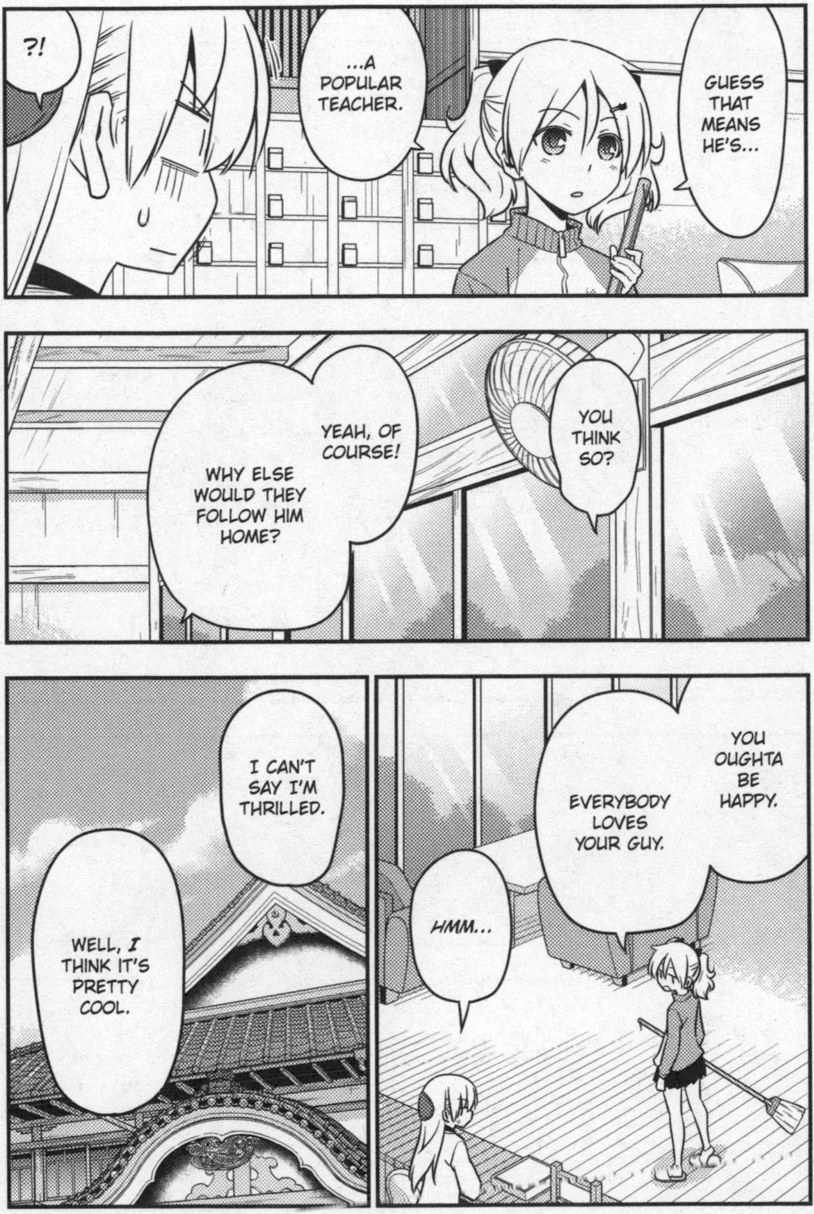
GUESS THAT MEANS HE'S...
...A POPULAR TEACHER.
?!
YOU THINK SO?
YEAH, OF COURSE!
WHY ELSE WOULD THEY FOLLOW HIM HOME?
YOU OUGHTA BE HAPPY.
EVERYBODY LOVES YOUR GUY.
HMM...
I CAN'T SAY I'M THRILLED.
WELL, I THINK IT'S PRETTY COOL.

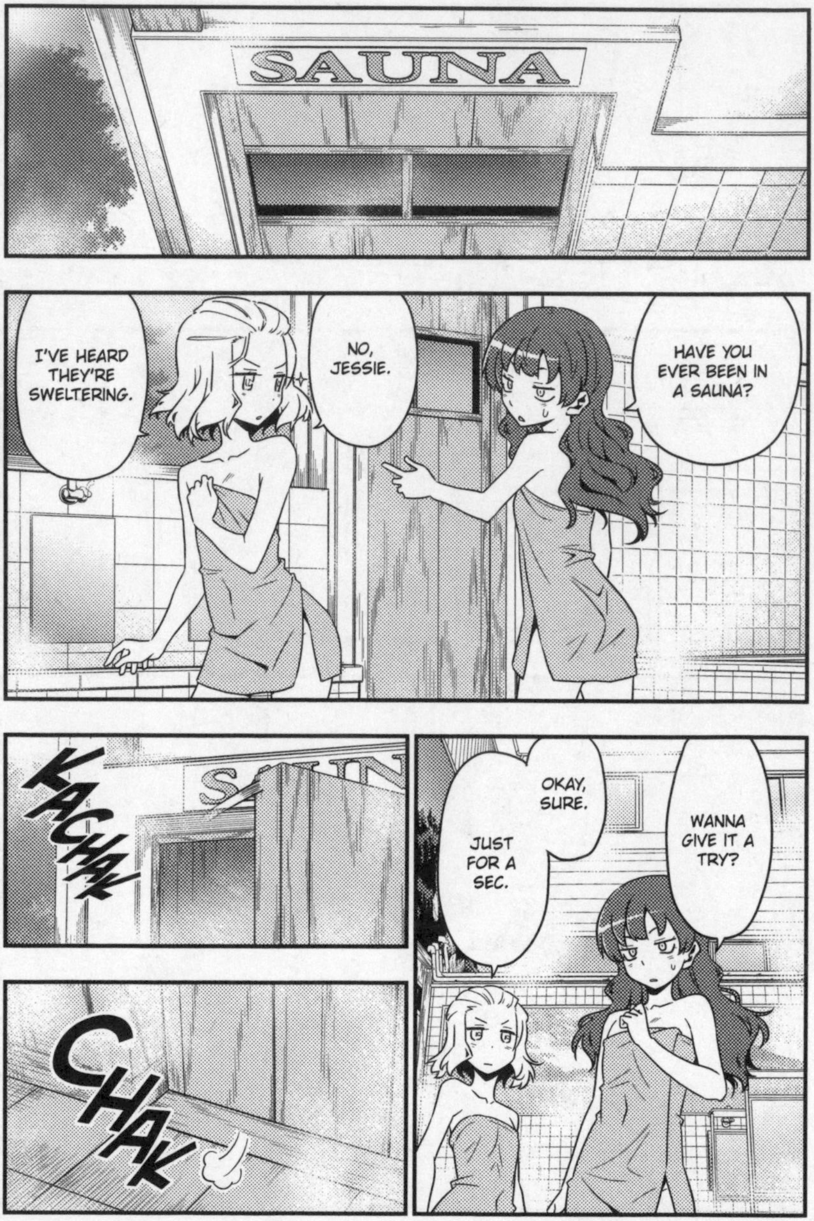
SAUNA
HAVE YOU EVER BEEN IN A SAUNA?
NO, JESSIE.
I'VE HEARD THEY'RE SWELTERING.
WANNA GIVE IT A TRY?
OKAY, SURE.
JUST FOR A SEC.
KACHAK
CHAK

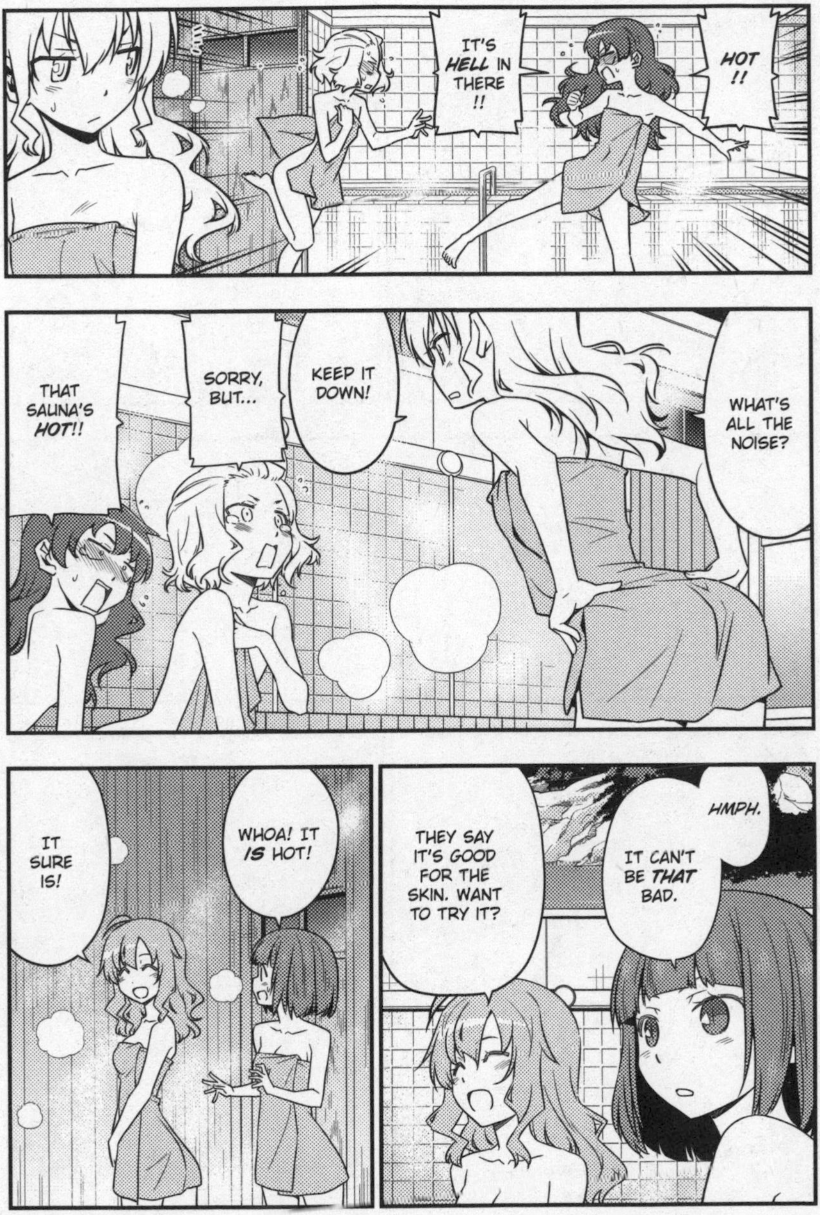
HOT!!
IT'S HELL IN THERE!!
WHAT'S ALL THE NOISE?
KEEP IT DOWN!
SORRY, BUT...
THAT SAUNA'S HOT!!
HMPH.
IT CAN'T BE THAT BAD.
THEY SAY IT'S GOOD FOR THE SKIN. WANT TO TRY IT?
WHOA! IT IS HOT!
IT SURE IS!

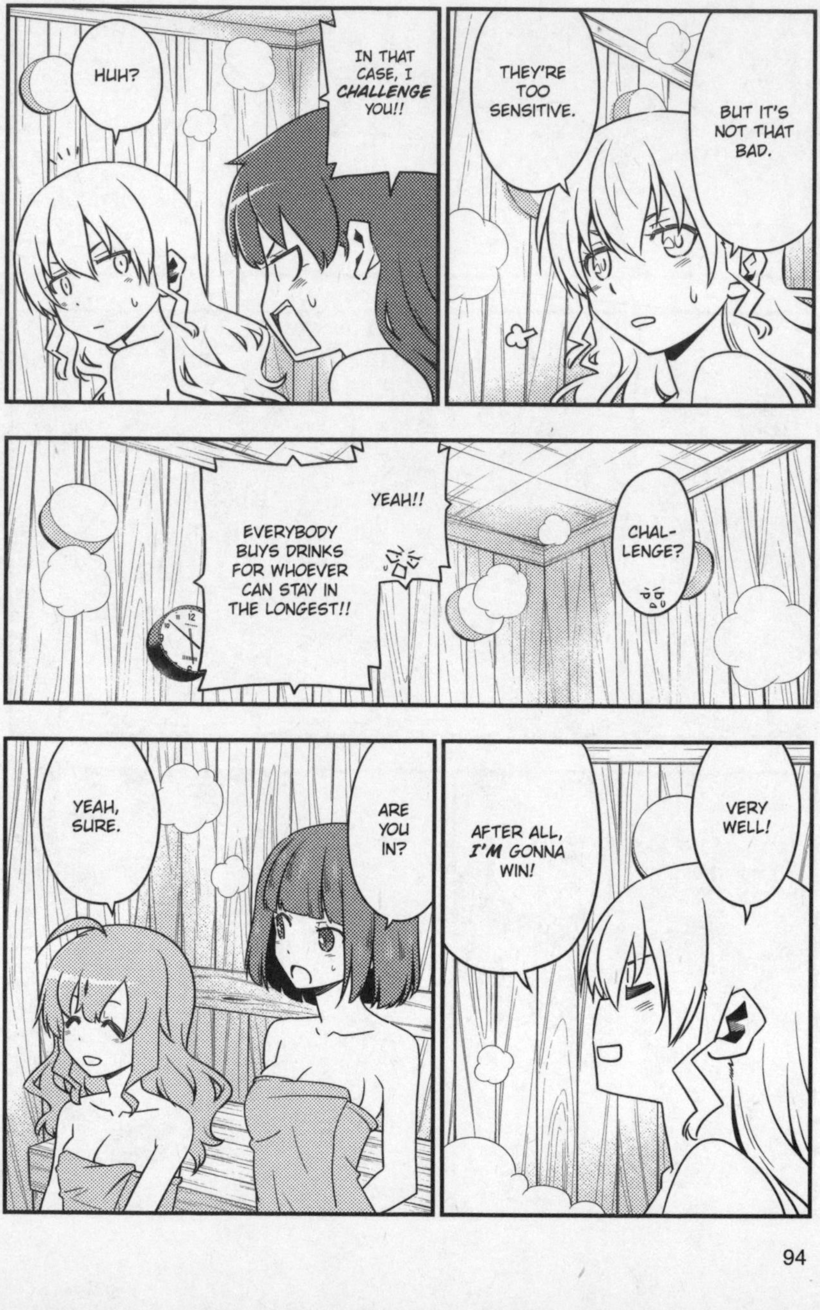
BUT IT'S NOT THAT BAD.
THEY'RE TOO SENSITIVE.
IN THAT CASE, I CHALLENGE YOU!!
HUH?
CHAL-LENGE?
YEAH!!
EVERYBODY BUYS DRINKS FOR WHOEVER CAN STAY IN THE LONGEST!!
VERY WELL!
AFTER ALL, I'M GONNA WIN!
ARE YOU IN?
YEAH, SURE.

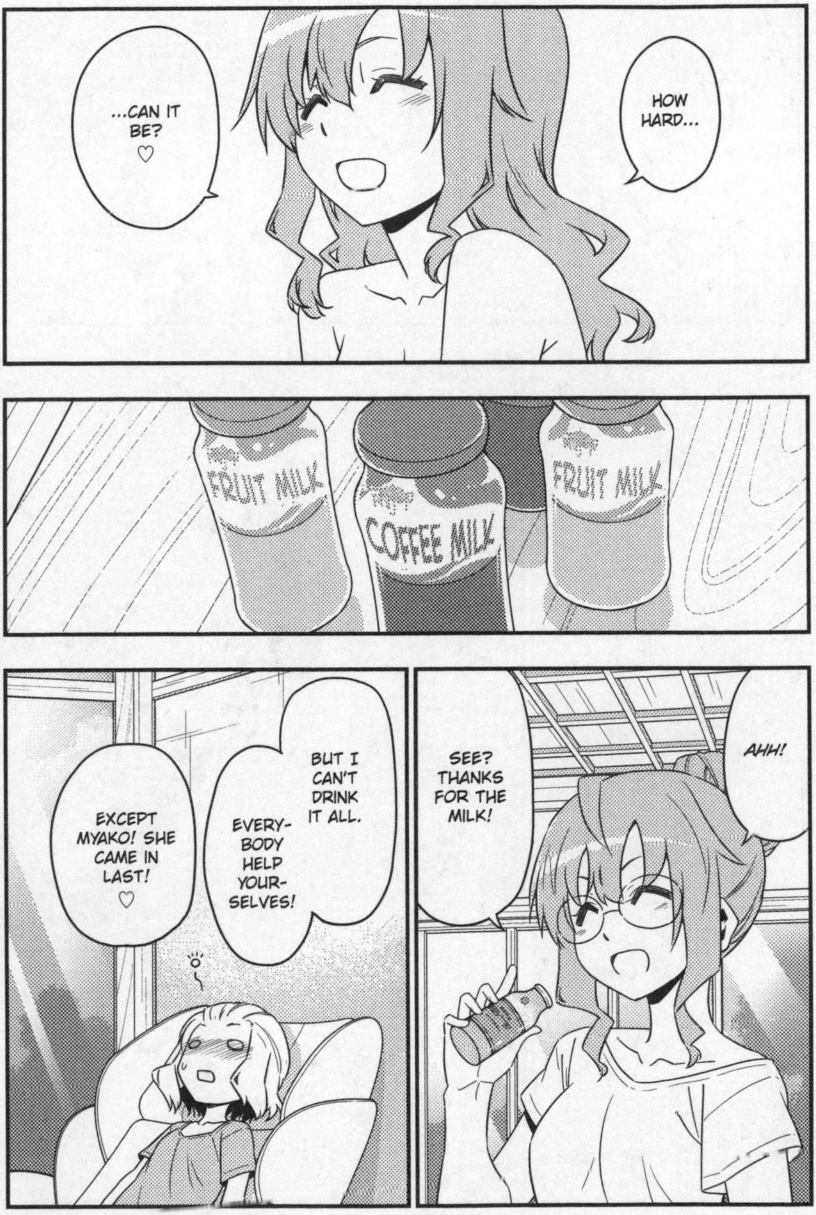
HOW HARD...
...CAN IT BE? ♡
FRUIT MILK
COFFEE MILK
FRUIT MILK
AHH!
SEE? THANKS FOR THE MILK!
BUT I CAN'T DRINK IT ALL.
EVERY-BODY HELP YOUR-SELVES!
EXCEPT MYAKO! SHE CAME IN LAST! ♡

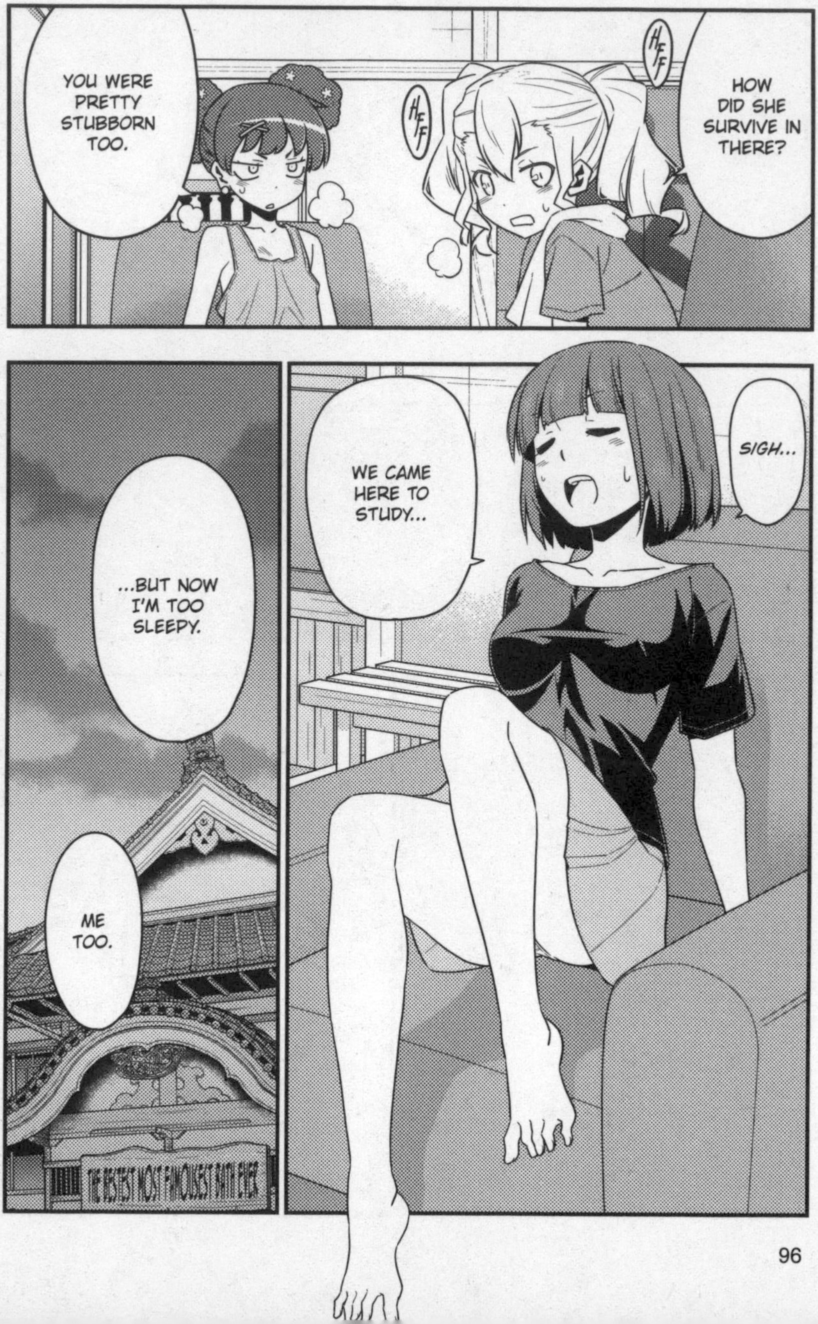
HEFF
HEFF
HOW DID SHE SURVIVE IN THERE?
YOU WERE PRETTY STUBBORN TOO.
SIGH...
WE CAME HERE TO STUDY...
...BUT NOW I'M TOO SLEEPY.
ME TOO.
THE BESTEST MOST FAMOUSEST BATH EVER

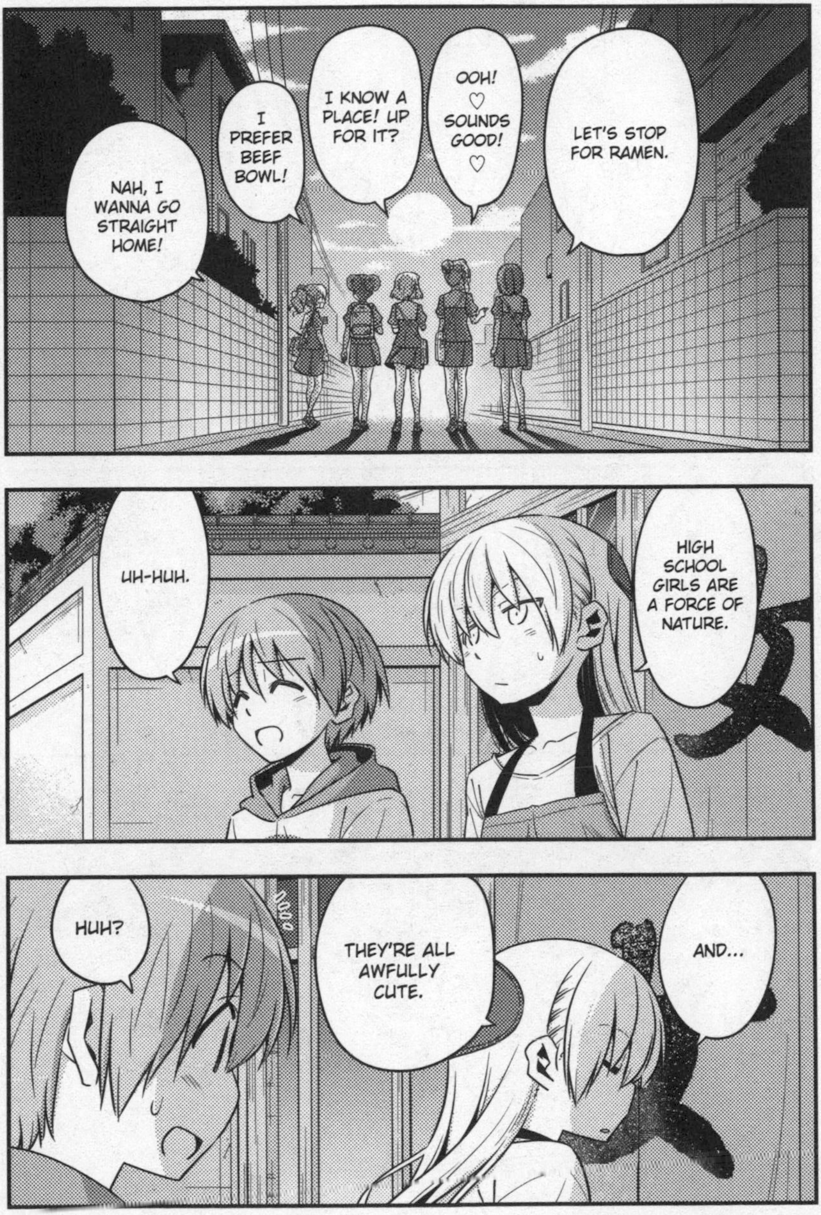
LET'S STOP FOR RAMEN.
OOH! ♡ SOUNDS GOOD! ♡
I KNOW A PLACE! UP FOR IT?
I PREFER BEEF BOWL!
NAH, I WANNA GO STRAIGHT HOME!
HIGH SCHOOL GIRLS ARE A FORCE OF NATURE.
UH-HUH.
AND...
THEY'RE ALL AWFULLY CUTE.
HUH?

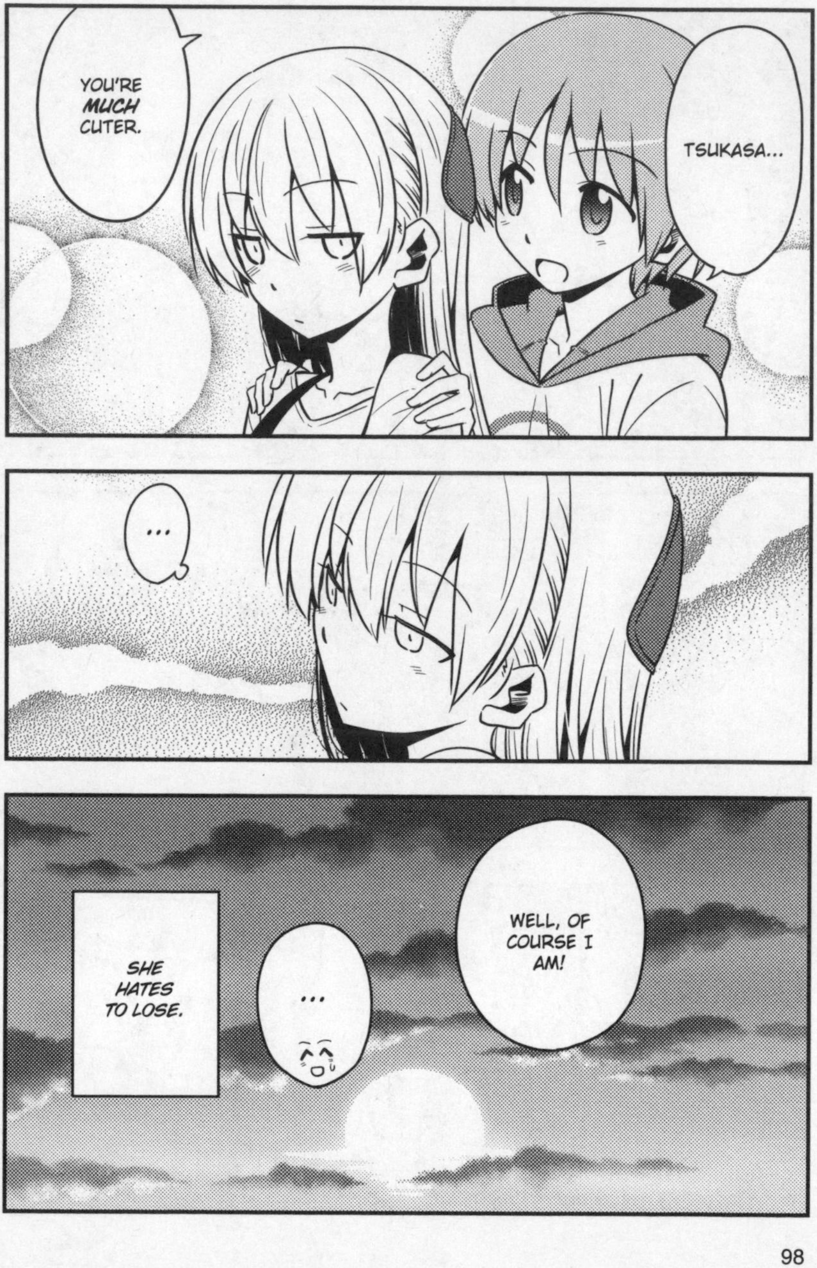
TSUKASA...
YOU'RE *MUCH* CUTER.
...
WELL, OF COURSE I AM!
...
SHE HATES TO LOSE.

Chapter 124: "At Paranormal Hot Spots, You Have a Higher Chance of Running into Delinquents than Ghosts"

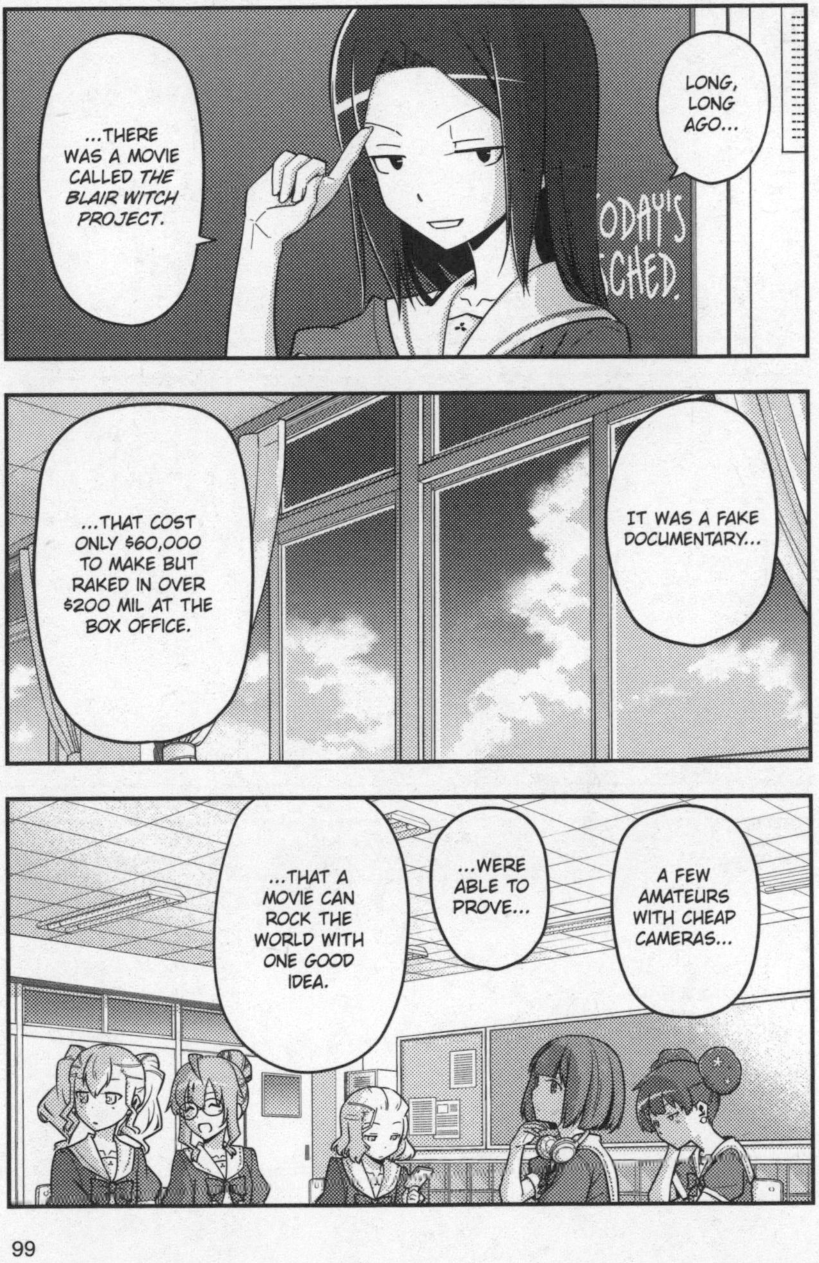
LONG, LONG AGO...
...THERE WAS A MOVIE CALLED *THE BLAIR WITCH PROJECT*.
IT WAS A FAKE DOCUMENTARY...
...THAT COST ONLY $60,000 TO MAKE BUT RAKED IN OVER $200 MIL AT THE BOX OFFICE.
A FEW AMATEURS WITH CHEAP CAMERAS...
...WERE ABLE TO PROVE...
...THAT A MOVIE CAN ROCK THE WORLD WITH ONE GOOD IDEA.

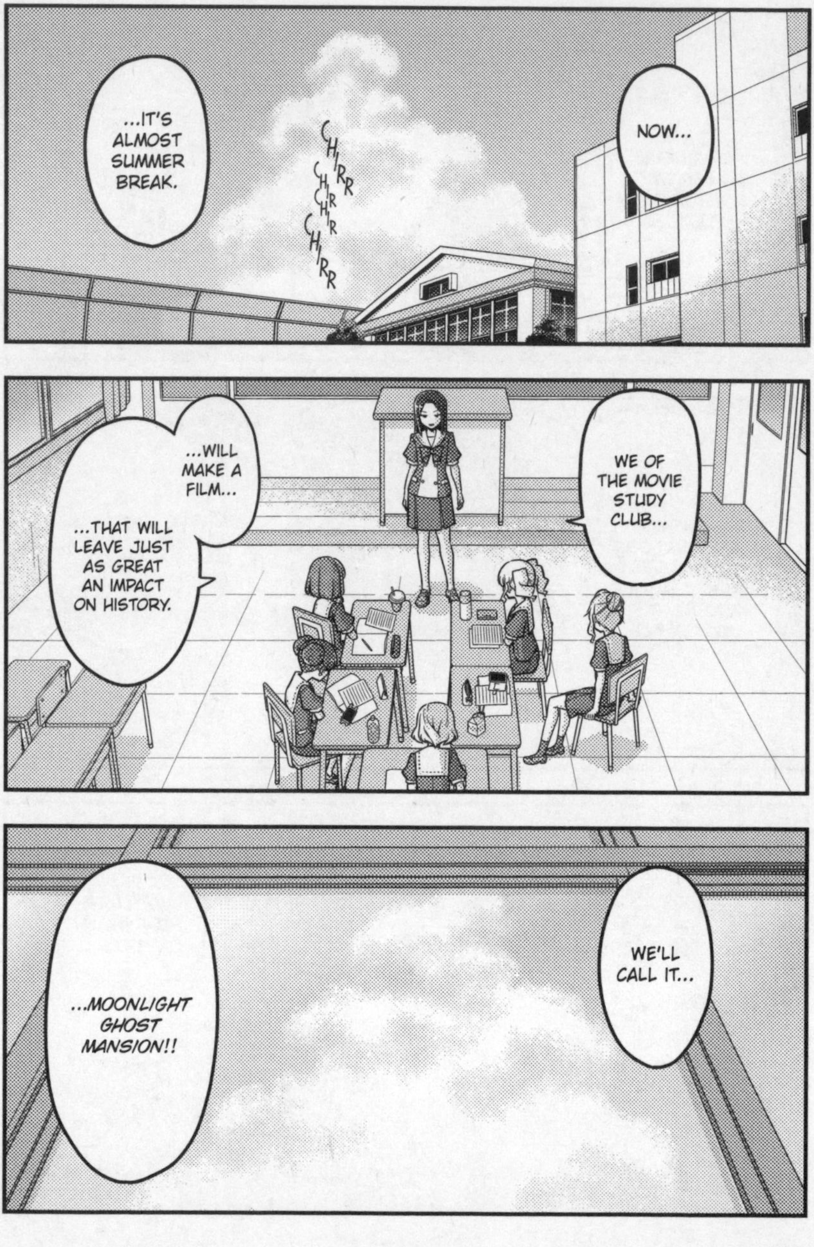
NOW...
CHIRR CHIR CHIR CHIRR
...IT'S ALMOST SUMMER BREAK.
WE OF THE MOVIE STUDY CLUB...
...WILL MAKE A FILM...
...THAT WILL LEAVE JUST AS GREAT AN IMPACT ON HISTORY.
WE'LL CALL IT...
...MOONLIGHT GHOST MANSION!!

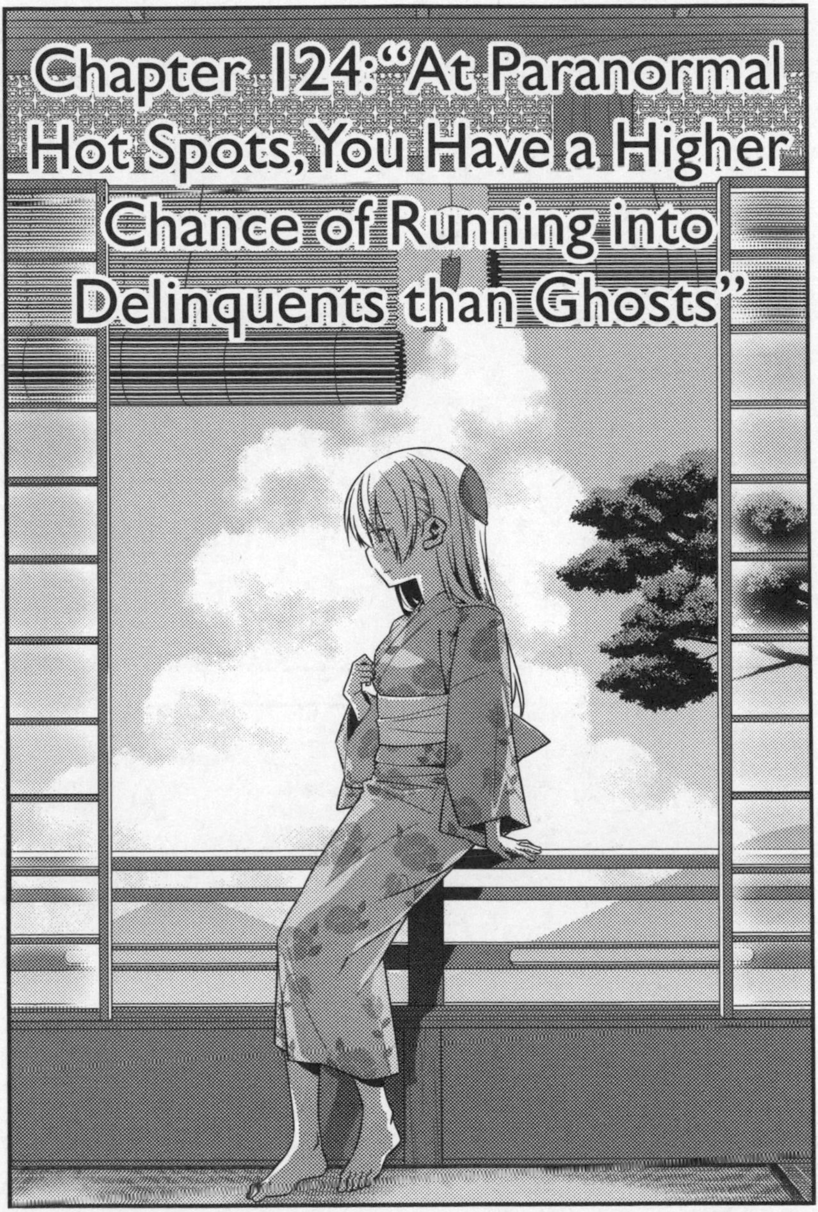
Chapter 124: "At Paranormal Hot Spots, You Have a Higher Chance of Running into Delinquents than Ghosts"

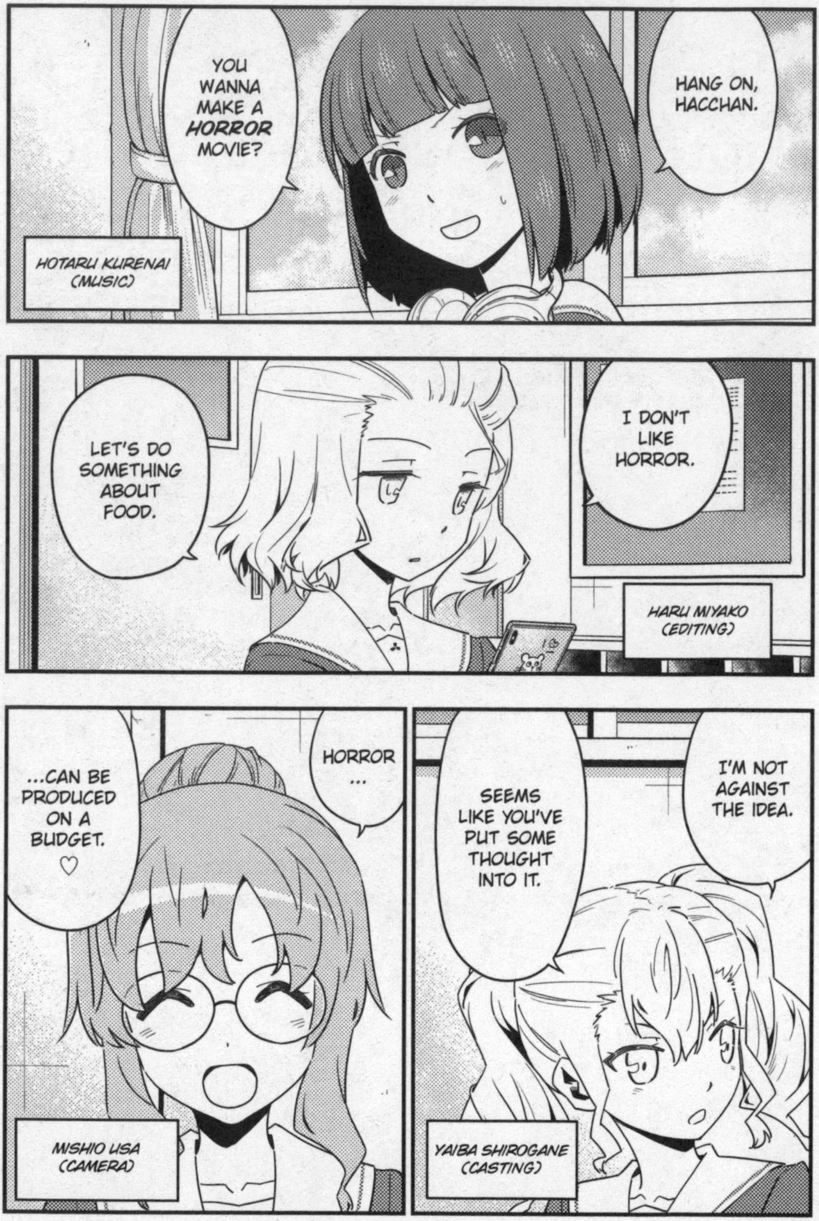
HANG ON, HACCHAN.
YOU WANNA MAKE A ***HORROR*** MOVIE?
HOTARU KURENAI (MUSIC)
I DON'T LIKE HORROR.
LET'S DO SOMETHING ABOUT FOOD.
HARU MIYAKO (EDITING)
I'M NOT AGAINST THE IDEA.
SEEMS LIKE YOU'VE PUT SOME THOUGHT INTO IT.
YAIBA SHIROGANE (CASTING)
HORROR ...
...CAN BE PRODUCED ON A BUDGET. ♡
MISHIO USA (CAMERA)

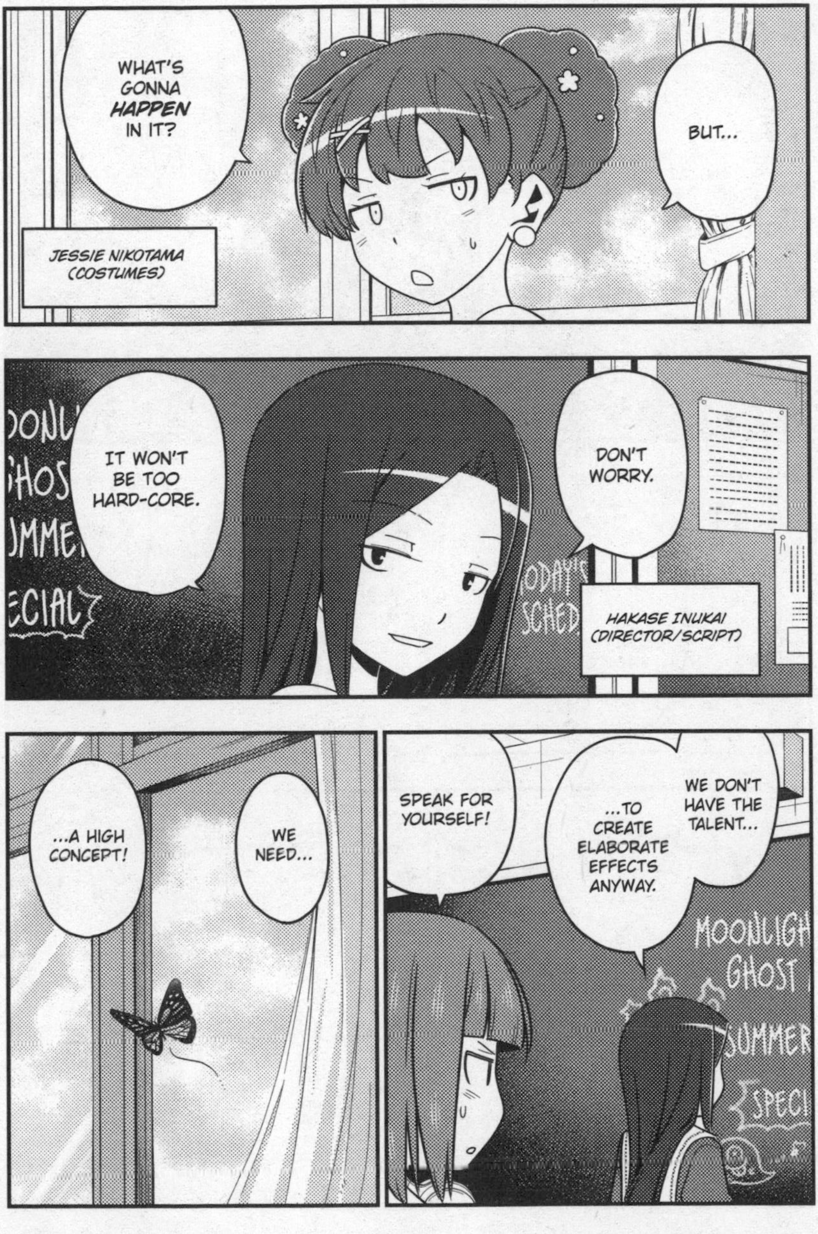
BUT...
WHAT'S GONNA HAPPEN IN IT?
JESSIE NIKOTAMA (COSTUMES)
DON'T WORRY.
IT WON'T BE TOO HARD-CORE.
HAKASE INUKAI (DIRECTOR/SCRIPT)
WE DON'T HAVE THE TALENT...
...TO CREATE ELABORATE EFFECTS ANYWAY.
SPEAK FOR YOURSELF!
WE NEED...
...A HIGH CONCEPT!

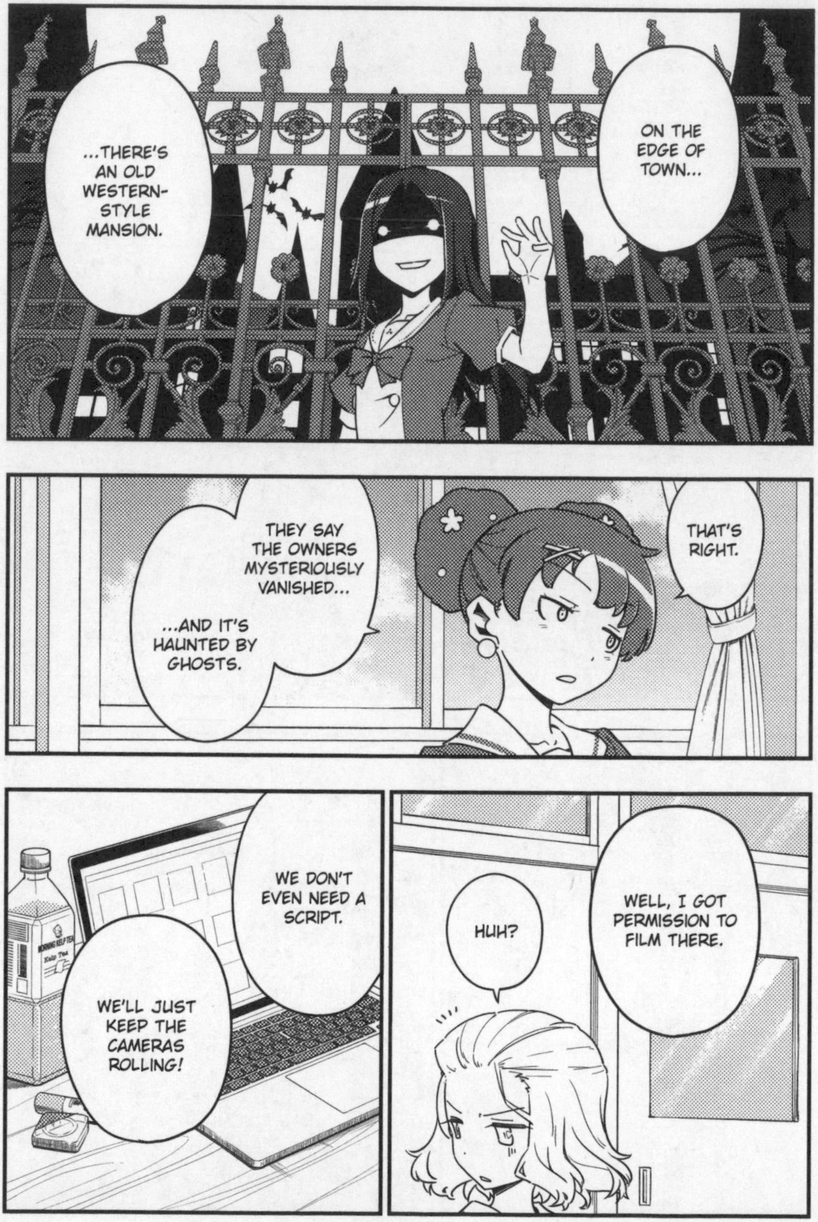
ON THE EDGE OF TOWN...
...THERE'S AN OLD WESTERN-STYLE MANSION.
THAT'S RIGHT.
THEY SAY THE OWNERS MYSTERIOUSLY VANISHED...
...AND IT'S HAUNTED BY GHOSTS.
WELL, I GOT PERMISSION TO FILM THERE.
HUH?
WE DON'T EVEN NEED A SCRIPT.
WE'LL JUST KEEP THE CAMERAS ROLLING!

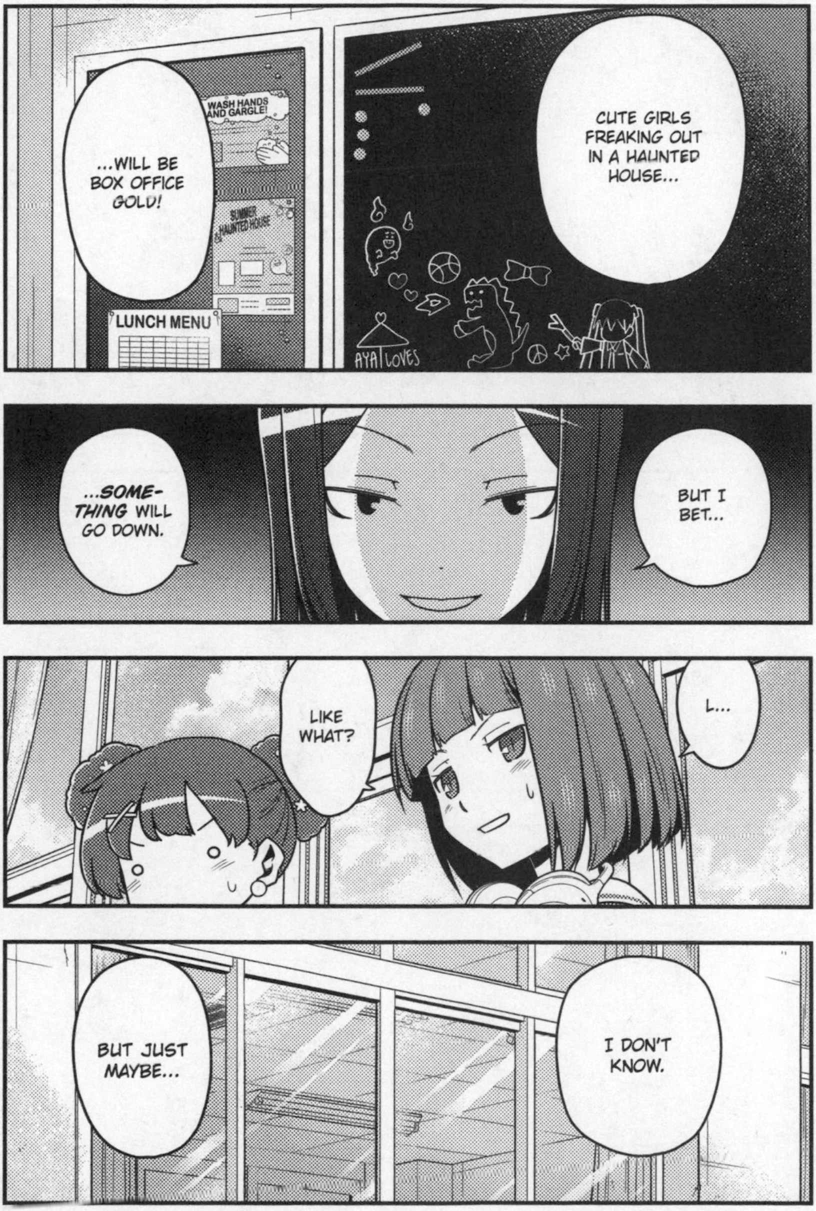
CUTE GIRLS FREAKING OUT IN A HAUNTED HOUSE...
WASH HANDS AND GARGLE!
...WILL BE BOX OFFICE GOLD!
SUMMER HAUNTED HOUSE
LUNCH MENU
AYA LOVES
BUT I BET...
...*SOME-THING* WILL GO DOWN.
I...
LIKE WHAT?
I DON'T KNOW.
BUT JUST MAYBE...

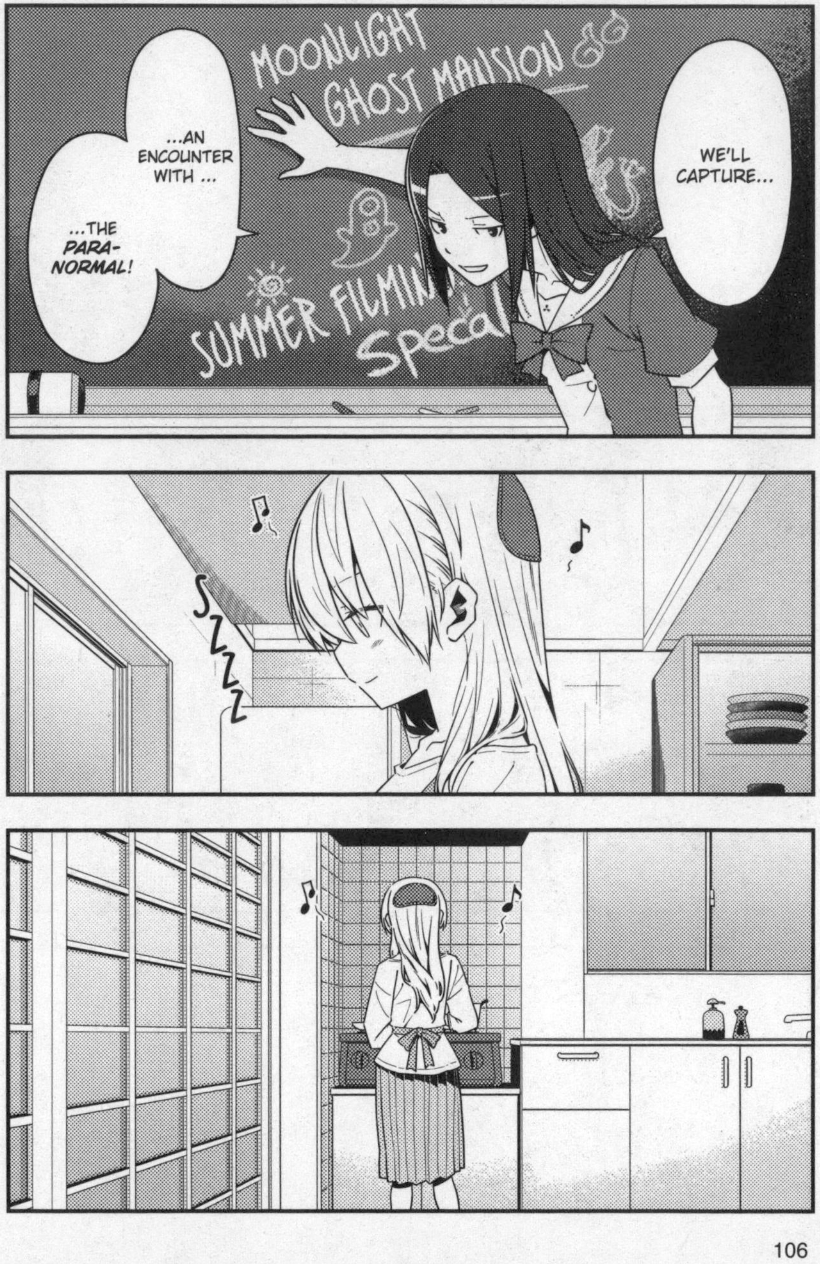
WE'LL CAPTURE...
MOONLIGHT GHOST MANSION
SUMMER FILMIN
Specal
...AN ENCOUNTER WITH ...
...THE PARA-NORMAL!
SZZZZ

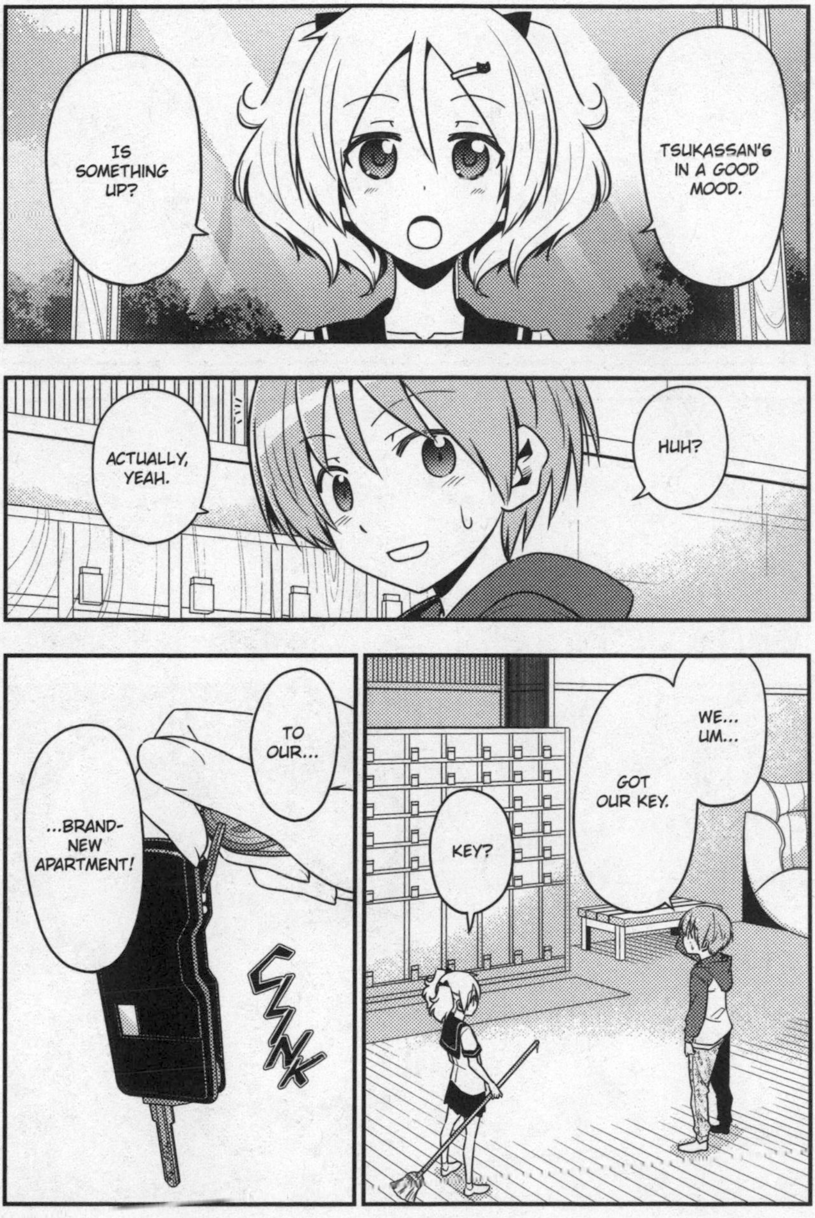
TSUKASSAN'S IN A GOOD MOOD.
IS SOMETHING UP?
HUH?
ACTUALLY, YEAH.
WE... UM...
GOT OUR KEY.
KEY?
TO OUR...
...BRAND-NEW APARTMENT!
CLINK

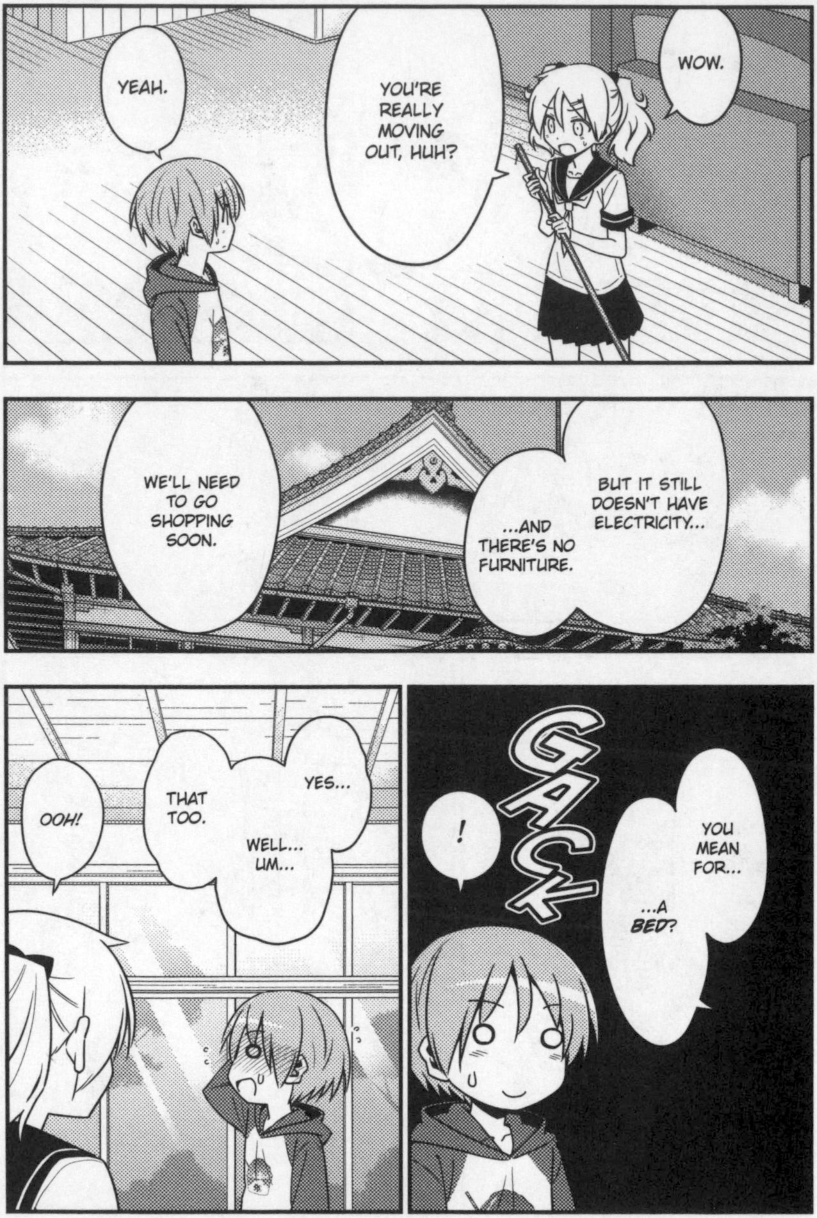
WOW.
YOU'RE REALLY MOVING OUT, HUH?
YEAH.
BUT IT STILL DOESN'T HAVE ELECTRICITY...
...AND THERE'S NO FURNITURE.
WE'LL NEED TO GO SHOPPING SOON.
YOU MEAN FOR... ...A BED?
GACK
!
YES... THAT TOO.
WELL... UM...
OOH!

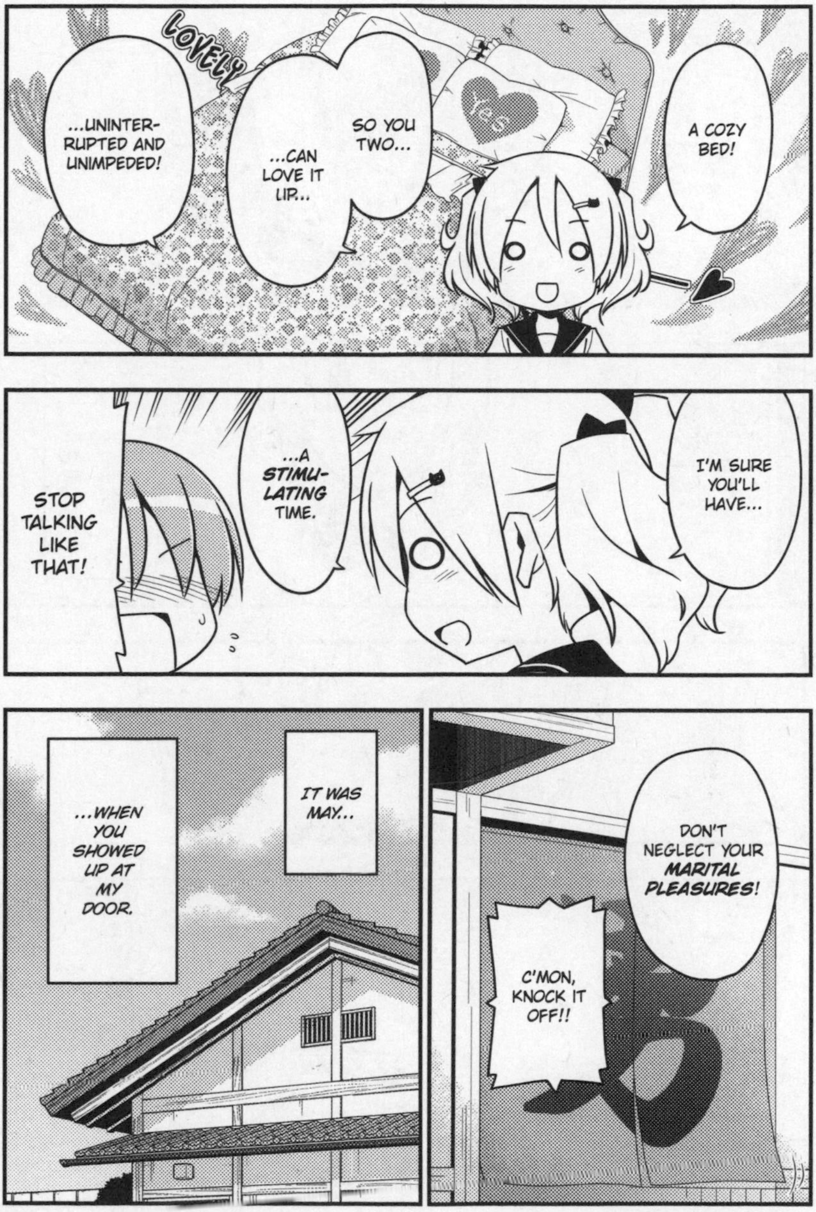
A COZY BED!
SO YOU TWO...
...CAN LOVE IT UP...
...UNINTERRUPTED AND UNIMPEDED!
LOVELY
I'M SURE YOU'LL HAVE...
...A STIMULATING TIME.
STOP TALKING LIKE THAT!
DON'T NEGLECT YOUR MARITAL PLEASURES!
C'MON, KNOCK IT OFF!!
IT WAS MAY...
...WHEN YOU SHOWED UP AT MY DOOR.

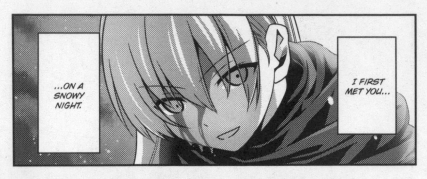

I FIRST MET YOU...
...ON A SNOWY NIGHT.
FOR THE PAST TWO SUMMER MONTHS...
...I'VE GOTTEN TO KNOW YOU.
WHAT IS IT?
UH...
NOTHING.

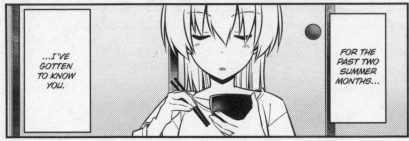

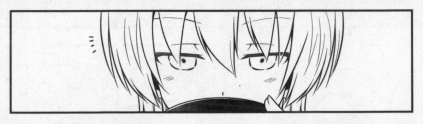

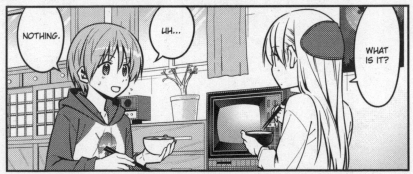

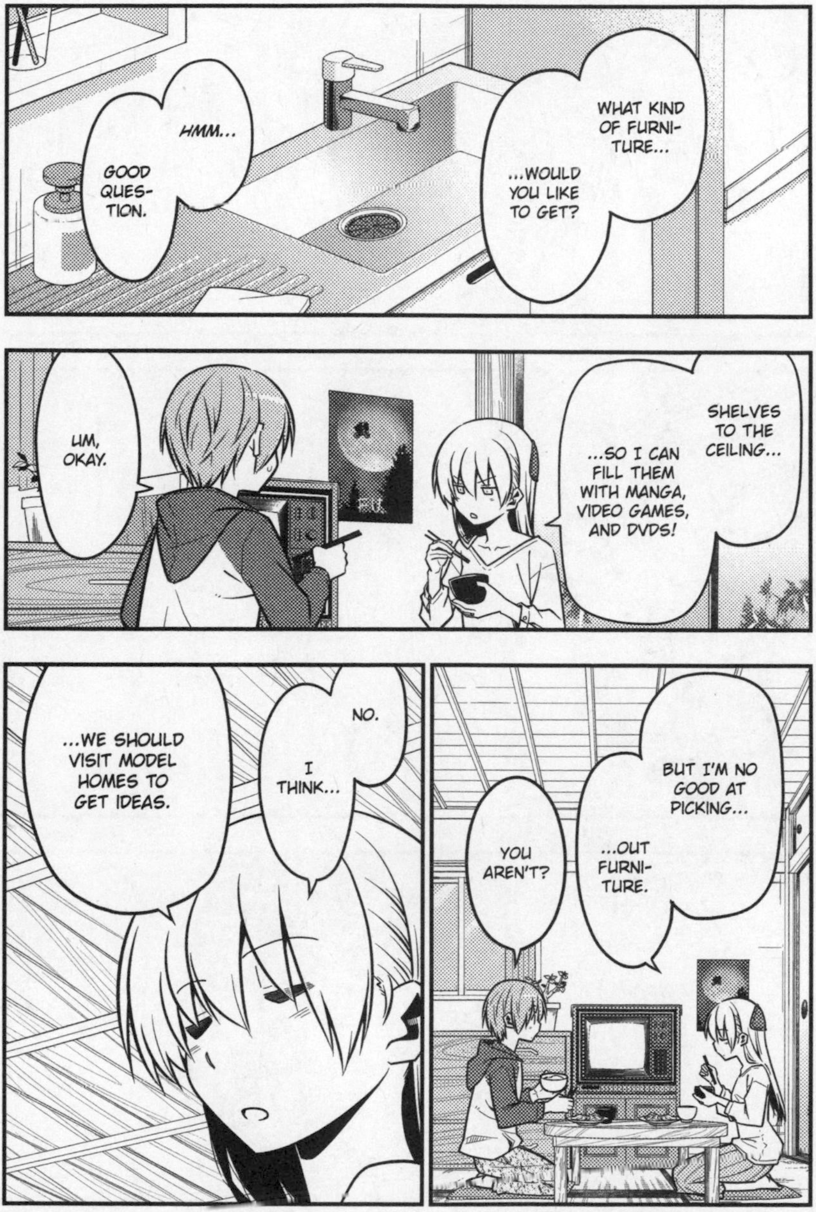
WHAT KIND OF FURNI-TURE...
...WOULD YOU LIKE TO GET?
HMM...
GOOD QUES-TION.
SHELVES TO THE CEILING...
...SO I CAN FILL THEM WITH MANGA, VIDEO GAMES, AND DVDS!
UM, OKAY.
BUT I'M NO GOOD AT PICKING...
...OUT FURNI-TURE.
YOU AREN'T?
NO.
I THINK...
...WE SHOULD VISIT MODEL HOMES TO GET IDEAS.

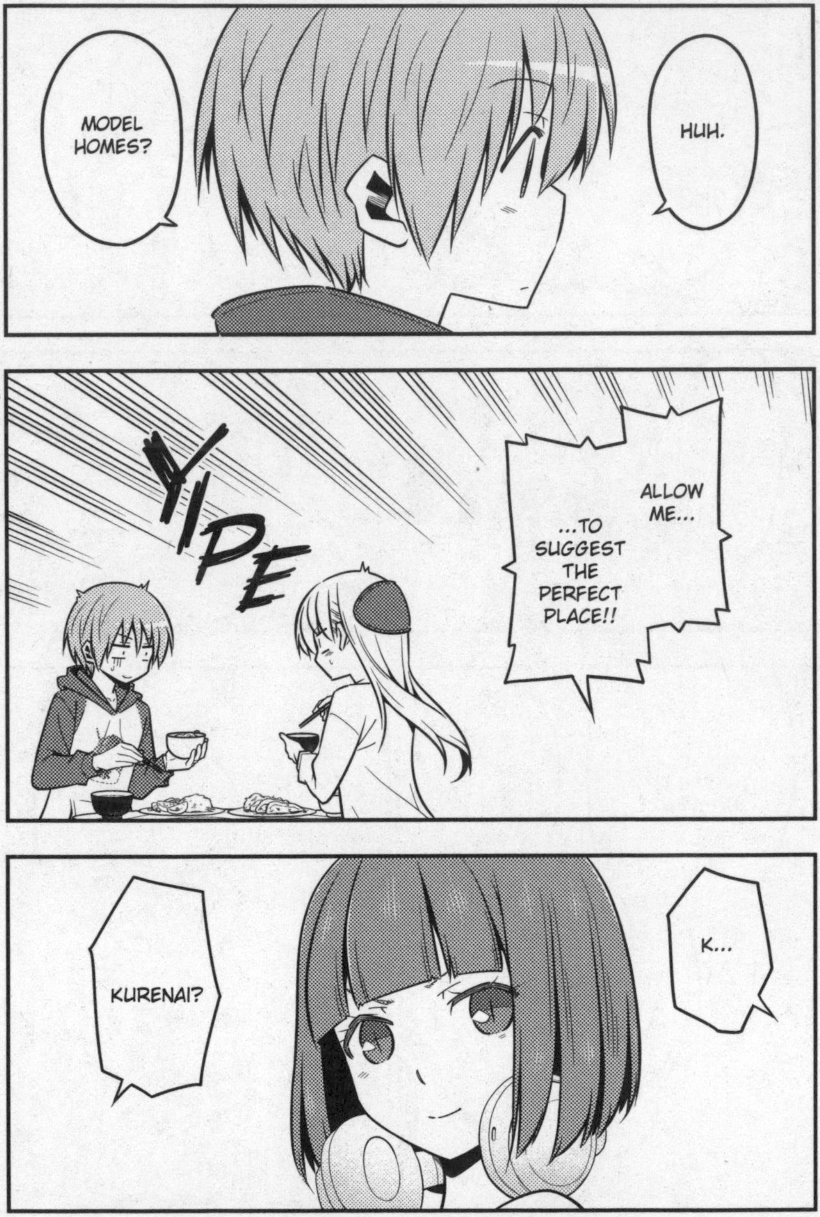
HUH.
MODEL HOMES?
ALLOW ME... ...TO SUGGEST THE PERFECT PLACE!!
YIPE
K...
KURENAI?

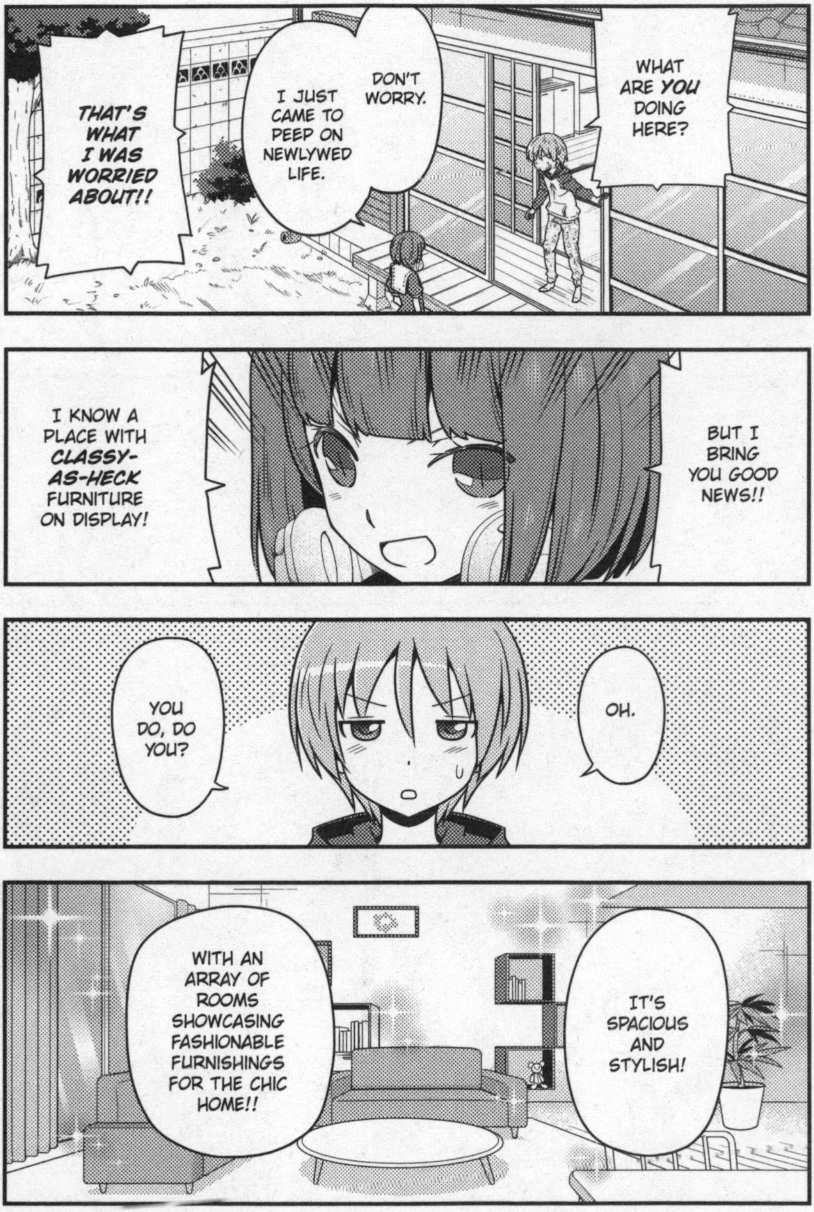
WHAT ARE YOU DOING HERE?
DON'T WORRY. I JUST CAME TO PEEP ON NEWLYWED LIFE.
THAT'S WHAT I WAS WORRIED ABOUT!!
BUT I BRING YOU GOOD NEWS!!
I KNOW A PLACE WITH CLASSY-AS-HECK FURNITURE ON DISPLAY!
OH.
YOU DO, DO YOU?
IT'S SPACIOUS AND STYLISH!
WITH AN ARRAY OF ROOMS SHOWCASING FASHIONABLE FURNISHINGS FOR THE CHIC HOME!!

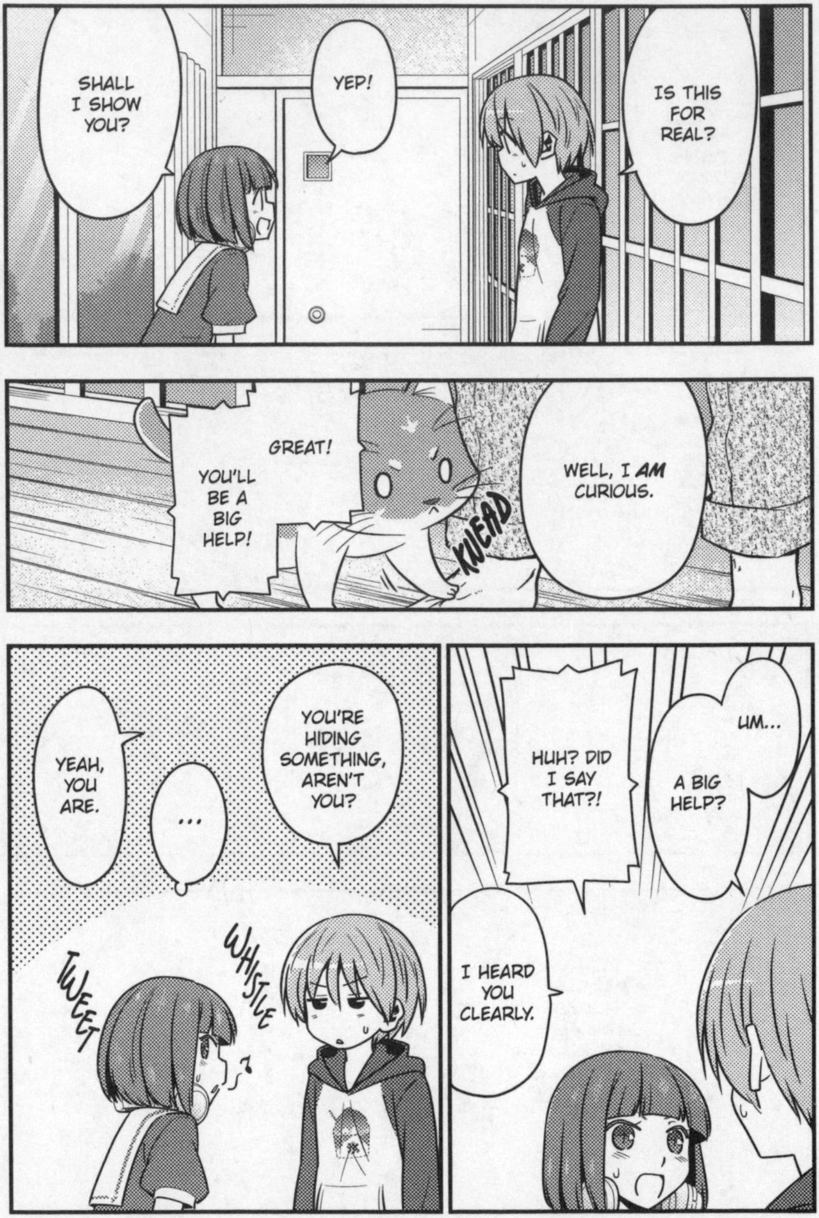
IS THIS FOR REAL?
YEP!
SHALL I SHOW YOU?
WELL, I AM CURIOUS.
KNEAD
GREAT!
YOU'LL BE A BIG HELP!
UM...
A BIG HELP?
HUH? DID I SAY THAT?!
I HEARD YOU CLEARLY.
YOU'RE HIDING SOMETHING, AREN'T YOU?
...
YEAH, YOU ARE.
WHISTLE
TWEET

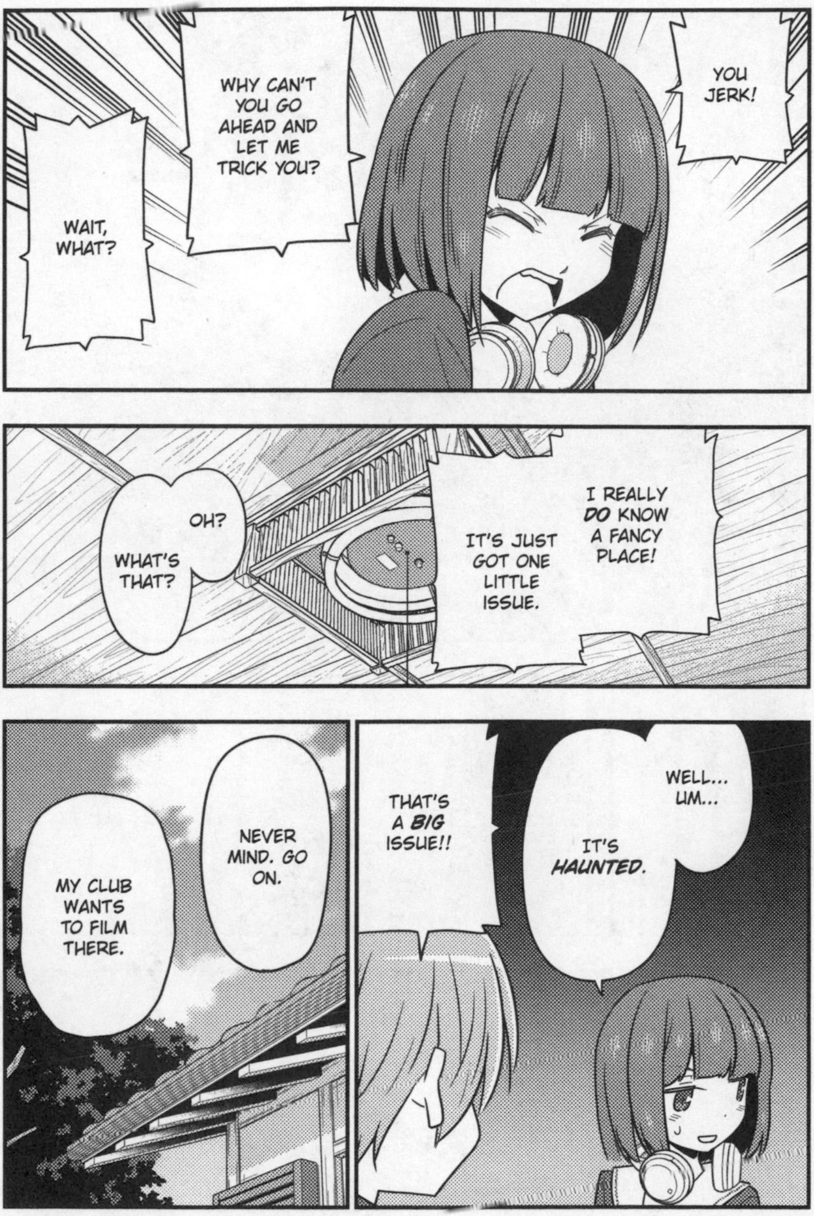
YOU JERK!
WHY CAN'T YOU GO AHEAD AND LET ME TRICK YOU?
WAIT, WHAT?
I REALLY DO KNOW A FANCY PLACE!
IT'S JUST GOT ONE LITTLE ISSUE.
OH? WHAT'S THAT?
WELL... UM...
IT'S HAUNTED.
THAT'S A BIG ISSUE!!
NEVER MIND. GO ON.
MY CLUB WANTS TO FILM THERE.

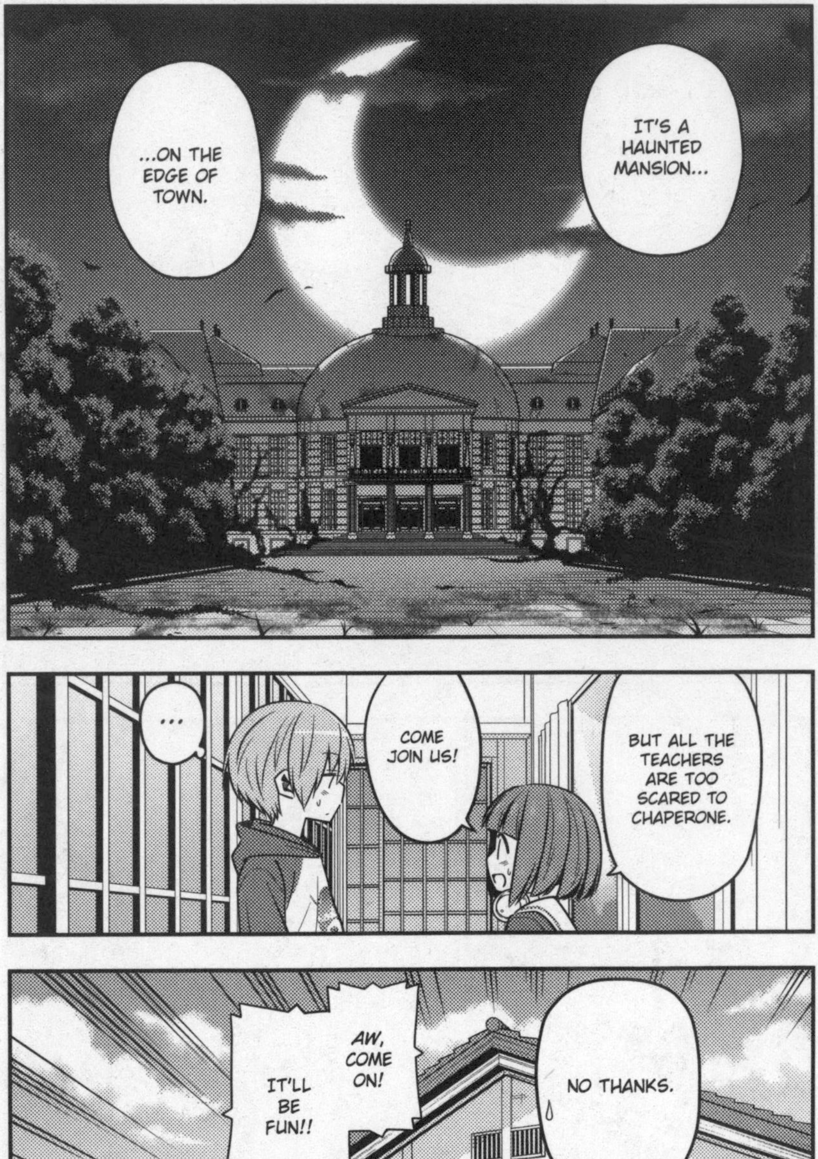
IT'S A HAUNTED MANSION...
...ON THE EDGE OF TOWN.
BUT ALL THE TEACHERS ARE TOO SCARED TO CHAPERONE.
COME JOIN US!
...
NO THANKS.
AW, COME ON!
IT'LL BE FUN!!

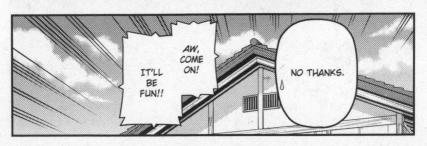

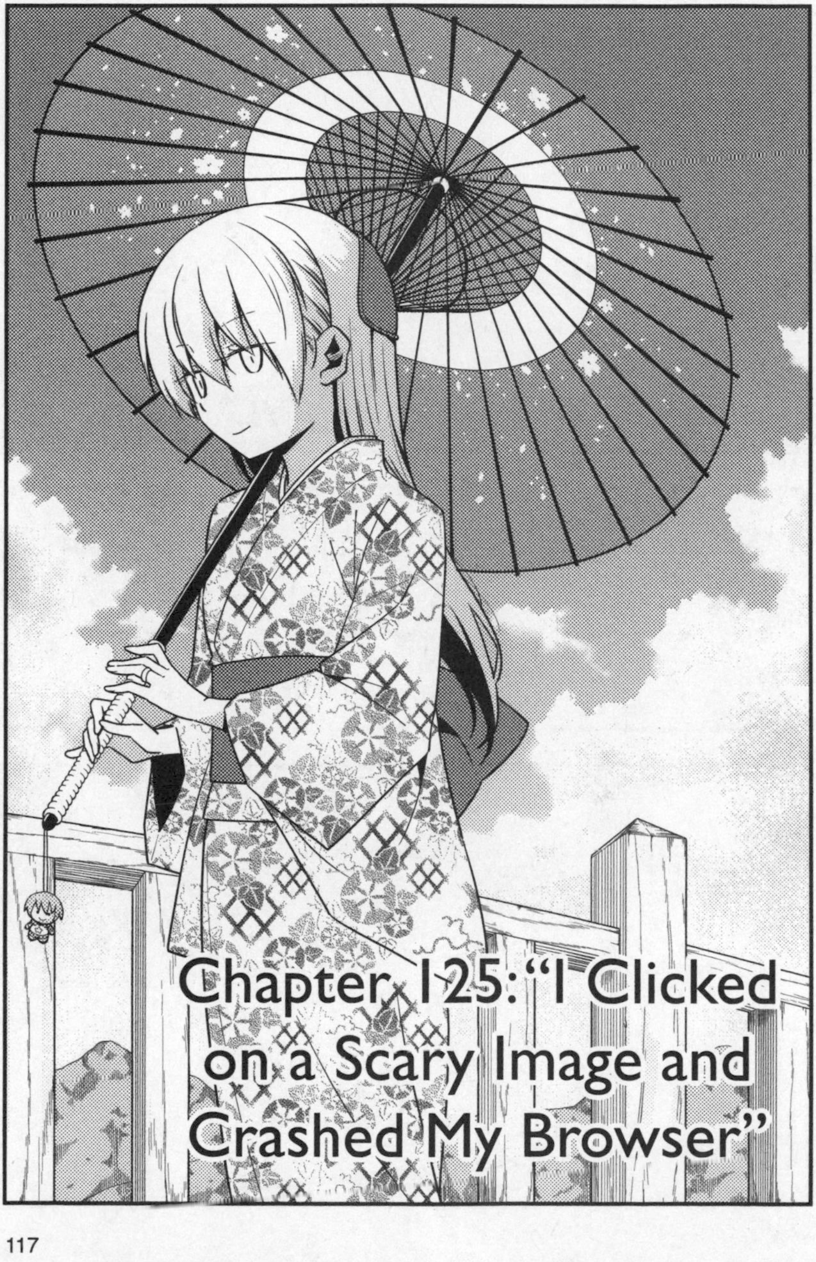
Chapter 125: "I Clicked on a Scary Image and Crashed My Browser"

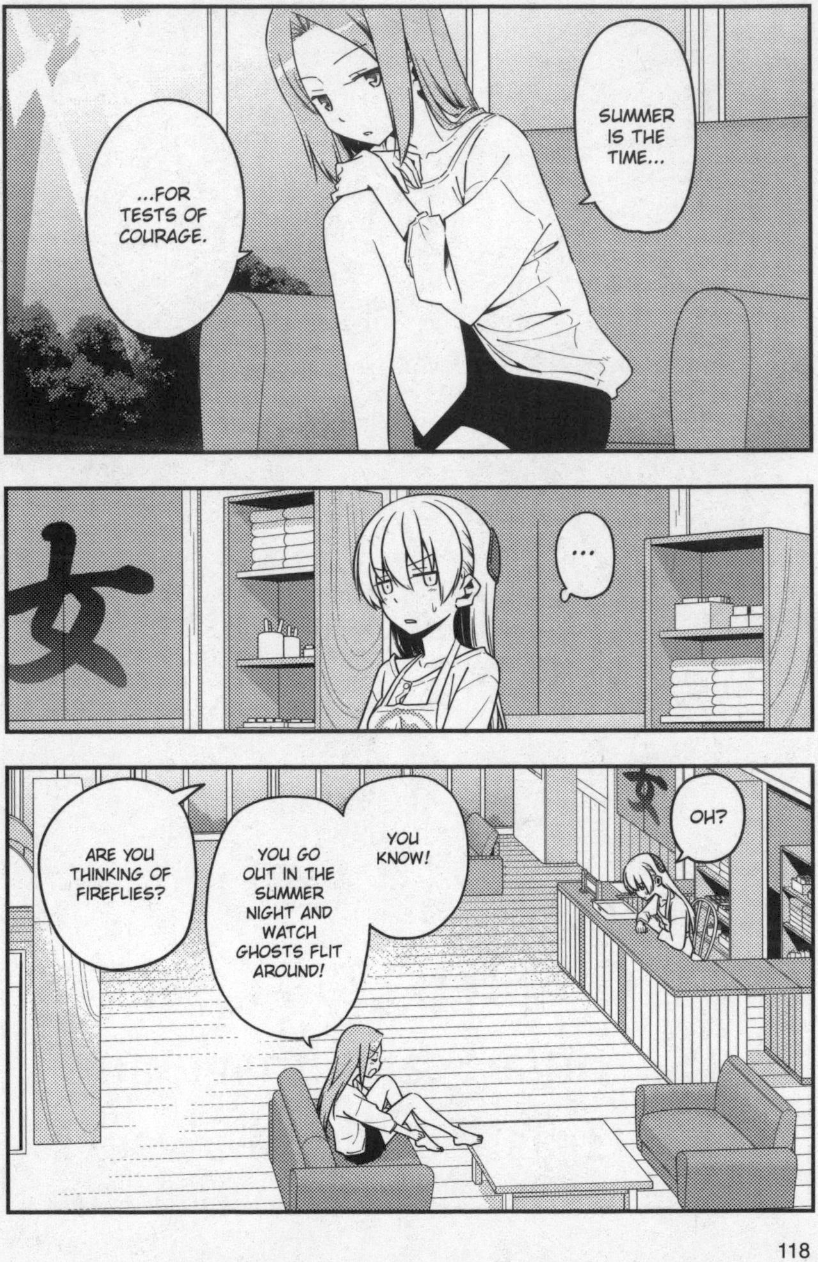
SUMMER IS THE TIME...
...FOR TESTS OF COURAGE.
...
OH?
YOU KNOW!
YOU GO OUT IN THE SUMMER NIGHT AND WATCH GHOSTS FLIT AROUND!
ARE YOU THINKING OF FIREFLIES?

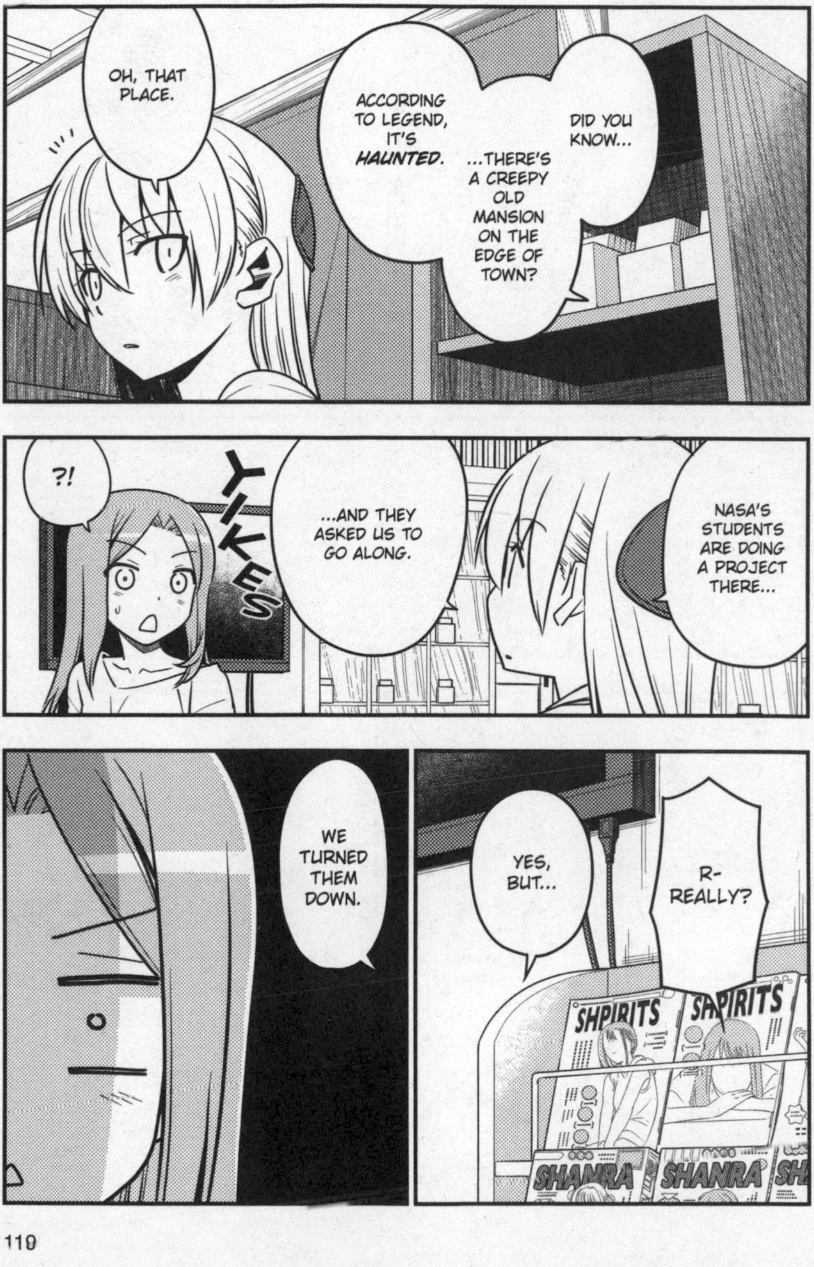
DID YOU KNOW...
...THERE'S A CREEPY OLD MANSION ON THE EDGE OF TOWN?
ACCORDING TO LEGEND, IT'S ***HAUNTED***.
OH, THAT PLACE.
NASA'S STUDENTS ARE DOING A PROJECT THERE...
...AND THEY ASKED US TO GO ALONG.
YIKES
?!
R-REALLY?
YES, BUT...
SHPIRITS
SHPIRITS
SHANRA
SHANRA
WE TURNED THEM DOWN.

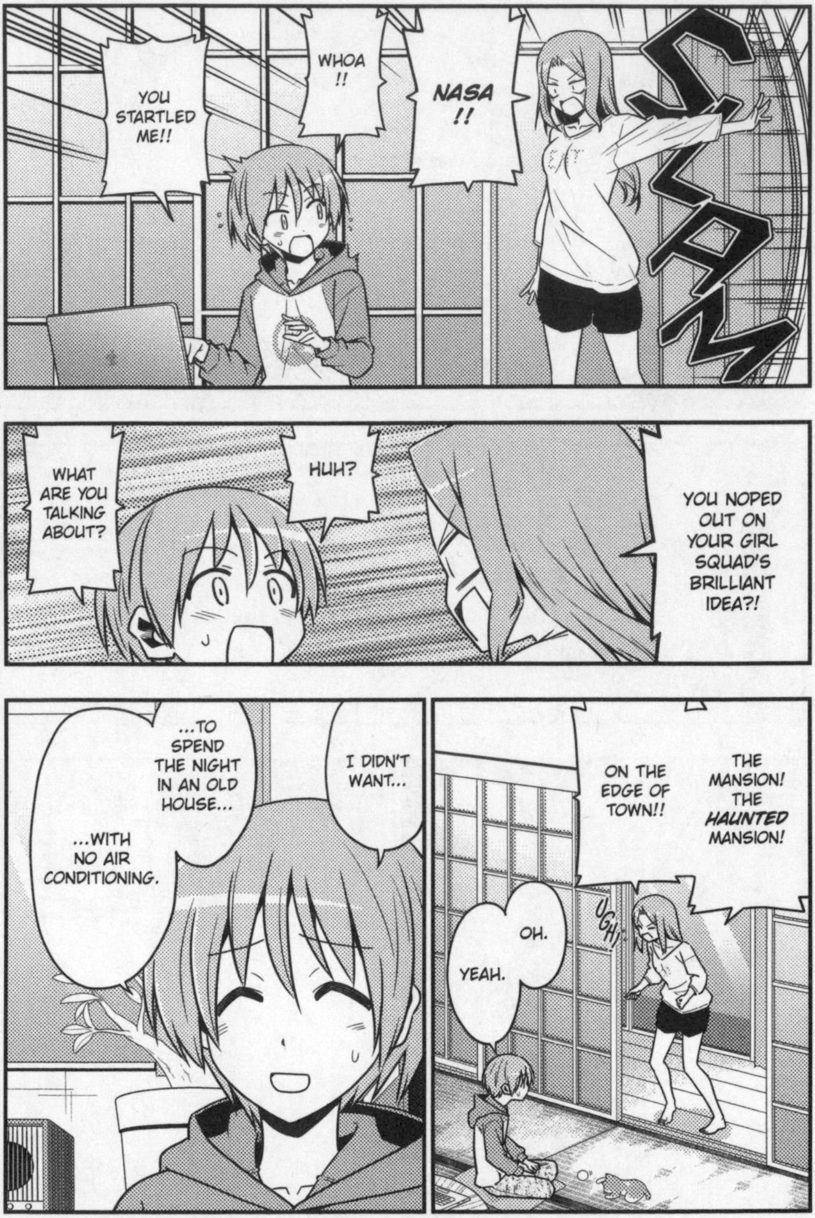
SLAM
NASA!!
WHOA!!
YOU STARTLED ME!!
YOU NOPED OUT ON YOUR GIRL SQUAD'S BRILLIANT IDEA?!
HUH?
WHAT ARE YOU TALKING ABOUT?
THE MANSION! THE HAUNTED MANSION!
ON THE EDGE OF TOWN!!
UGH!
OH.
YEAH.
I DIDN'T WANT...
...TO SPEND THE NIGHT IN AN OLD HOUSE...
...WITH NO AIR CONDITIONING.

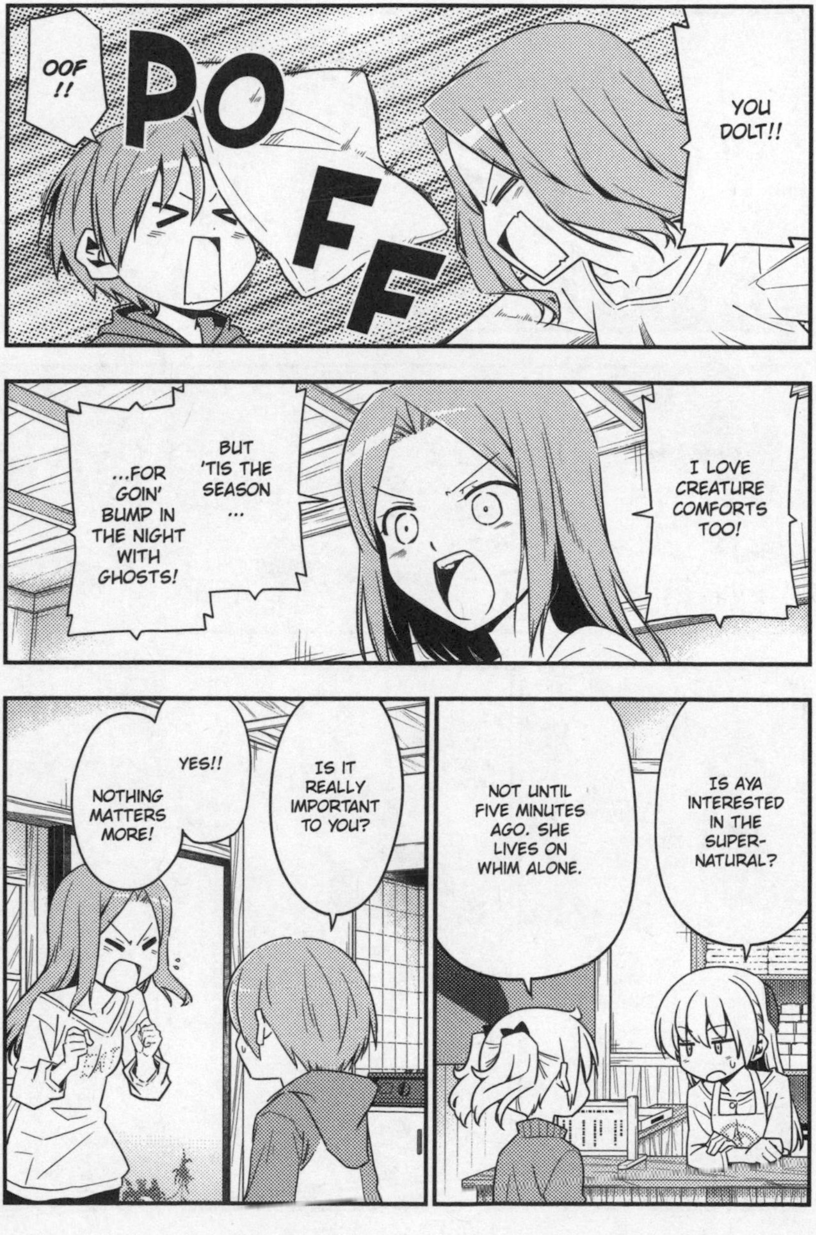
YOU DOLT!!
POFF
OOF !!
I LOVE CREATURE COMFORTS TOO!
BUT 'TIS THE SEASON ...
...FOR GOIN' BUMP IN THE NIGHT WITH GHOSTS!
IS AYA INTERESTED IN THE SUPER-NATURAL?
NOT UNTIL FIVE MINUTES AGO. SHE LIVES ON WHIM ALONE.
IS IT REALLY IMPORTANT TO YOU?
YES!!
NOTHING MATTERS MORE!

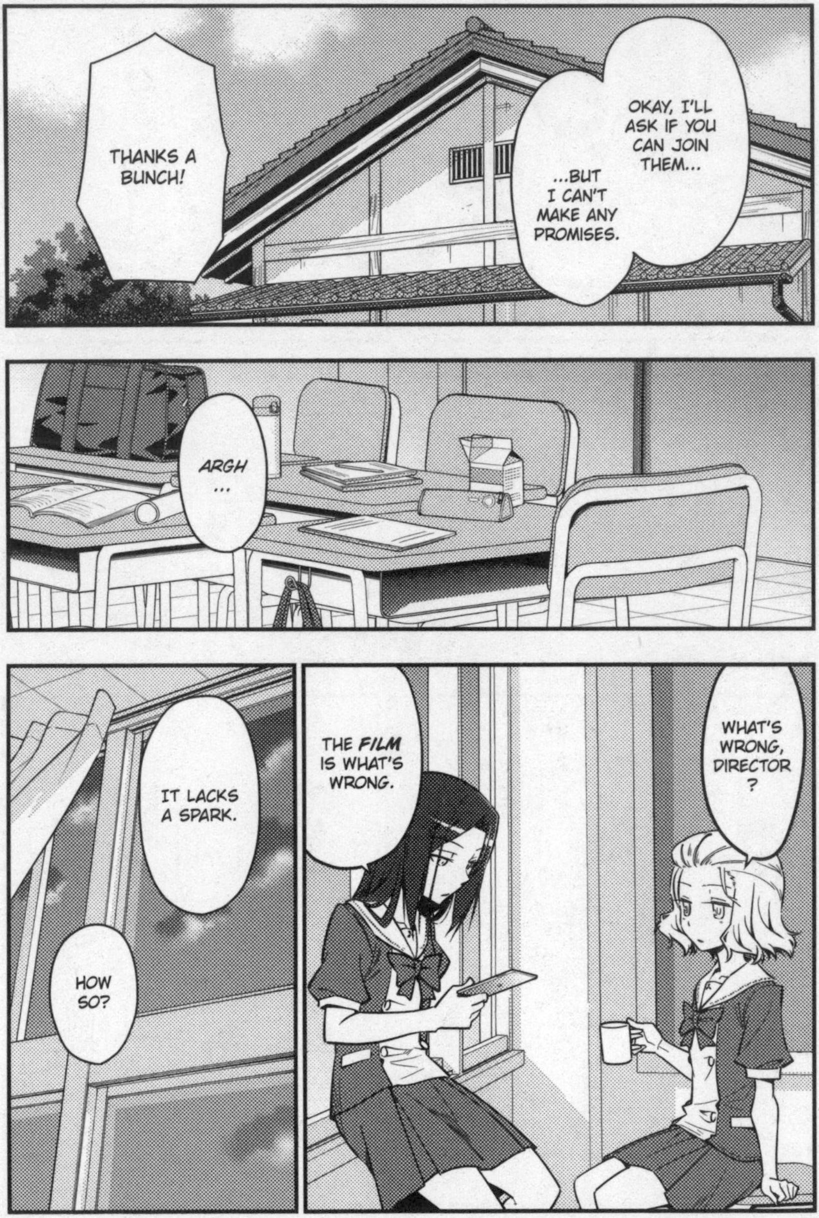
OKAY, I'LL ASK IF YOU CAN JOIN THEM...
...BUT I CAN'T MAKE ANY PROMISES.
THANKS A BUNCH!
ARGH ...
WHAT'S WRONG, DIRECTOR ?
THE *FILM* IS WHAT'S WRONG.
IT LACKS A SPARK.
HOW SO?

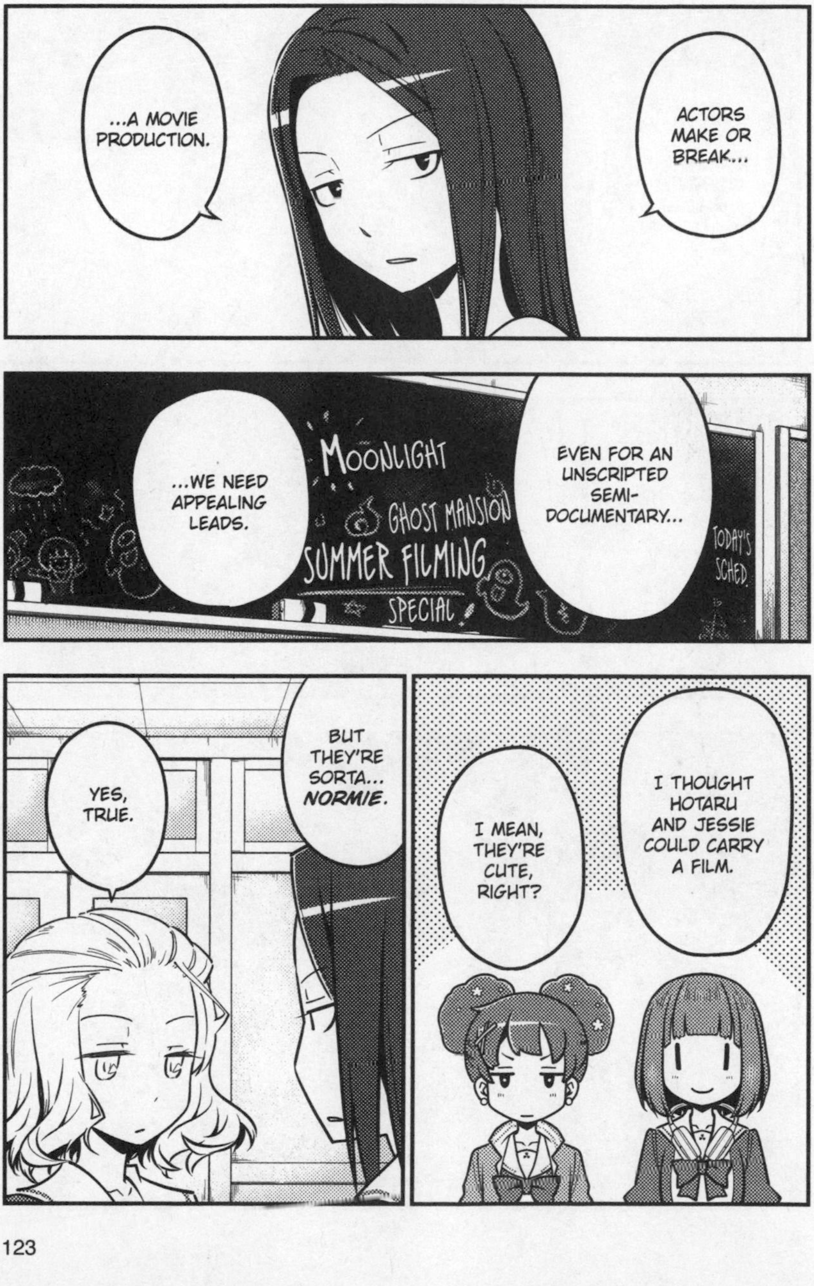
ACTORS MAKE OR BREAK...
...A MOVIE PRODUCTION.
EVEN FOR AN UNSCRIPTED SEMI-DOCUMENTARY...
TODAY'S SCHED.
MOONLIGHT
GHOST MANSION
SUMMER FILMING
SPECIAL
...WE NEED APPEALING LEADS.
I THOUGHT HOTARU AND JESSIE COULD CARRY A FILM.
I MEAN, THEY'RE CUTE, RIGHT?
BUT THEY'RE SORTA... *NORMIE*.
YES, TRUE.

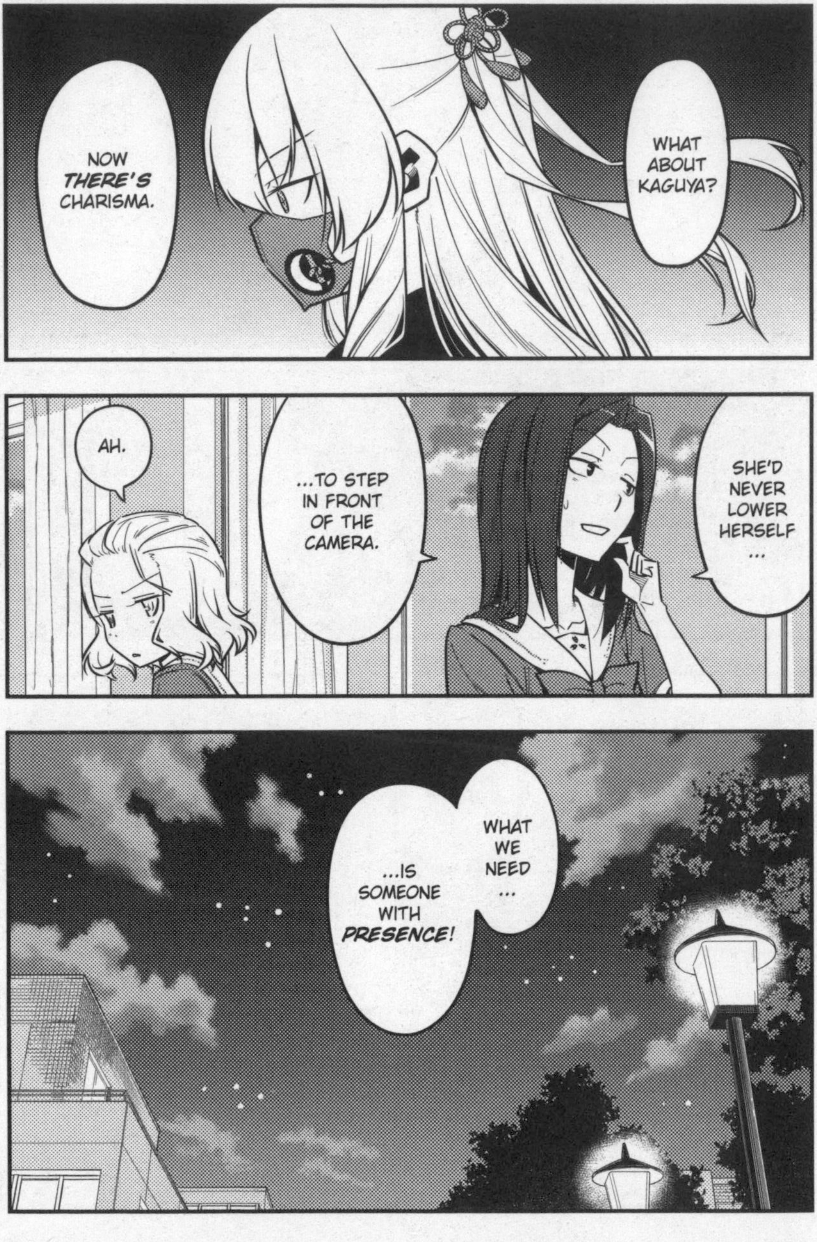
WHAT ABOUT KAGUYA?
NOW *THERE'S* CHARISMA.
SHE'D NEVER LOWER HERSELF...
...TO STEP IN FRONT OF THE CAMERA.
AH.
WHAT WE NEED...
...IS SOMEONE WITH *PRESENCE*!

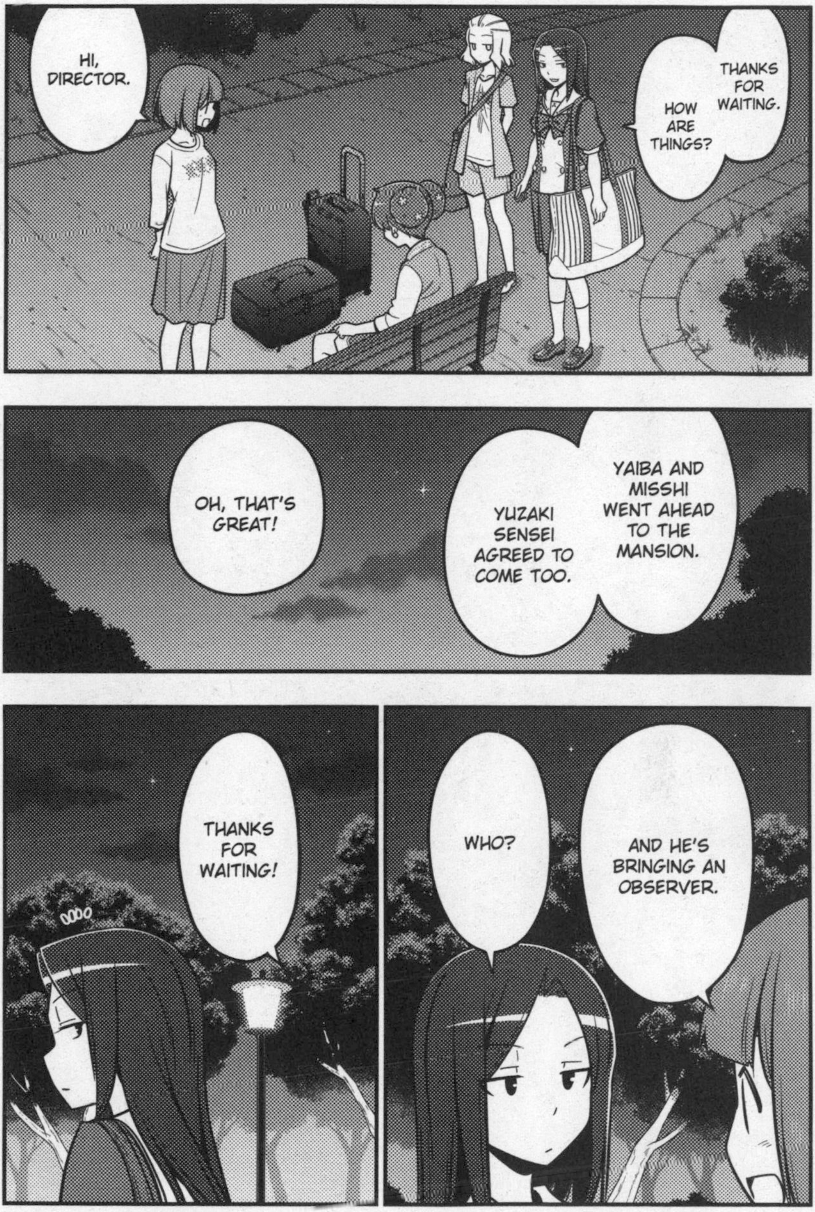
THANKS FOR WAITING.
HOW ARE THINGS?
HI, DIRECTOR.
YAIBA AND MISSHI WENT AHEAD TO THE MANSION.
YUZAKI SENSEI AGREED TO COME TOO.
OH, THAT'S GREAT!
AND HE'S BRINGING AN OBSERVER.
WHO?
THANKS FOR WAITING!

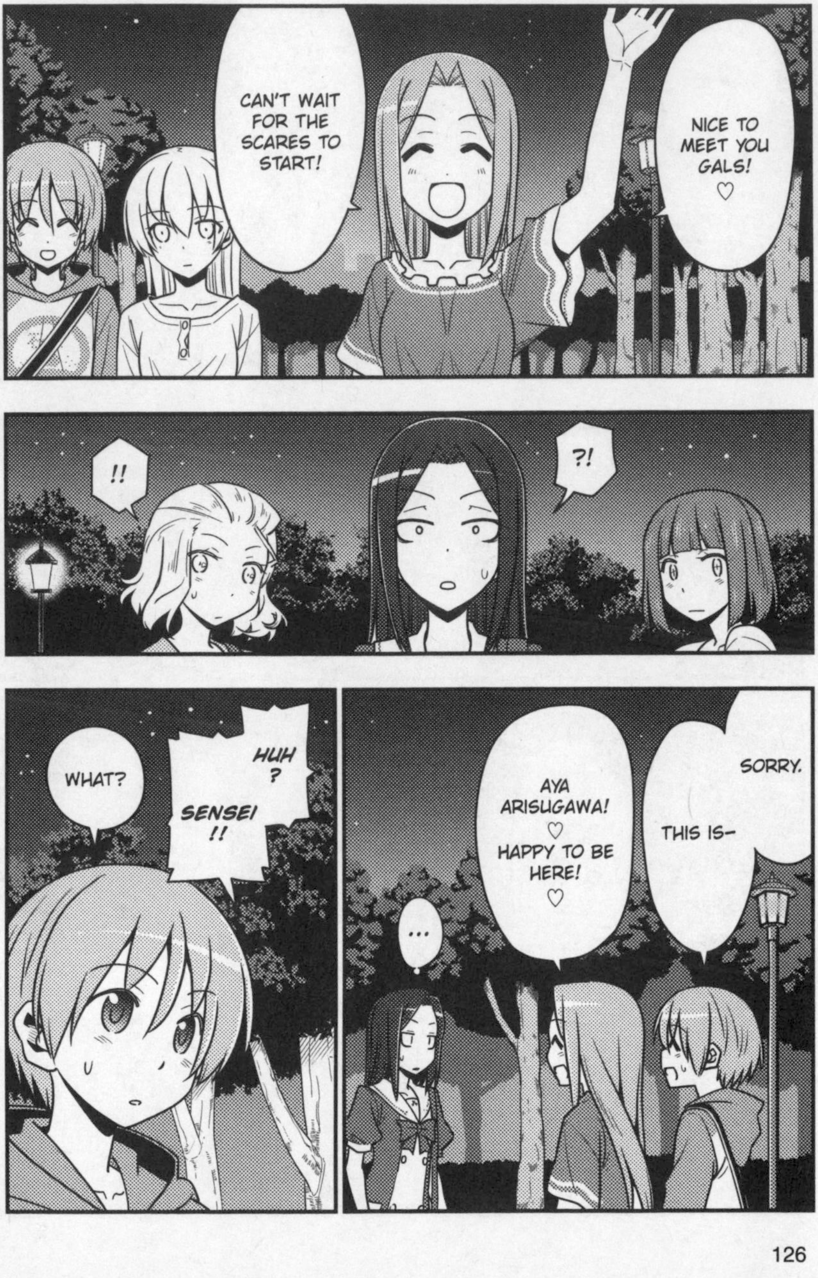
NICE TO MEET YOU GALS! ♡
CAN'T WAIT FOR THE SCARES TO START!
?!
!!
SORRY. THIS IS-
AYA ARISUGAWA! ♡ HAPPY TO BE HERE! ♡
...
HUH? SENSEI!!
WHAT?

THAT'S *AYAPI*!!
?
THE YOUTUBE STAR!
SENSEI, YOU KNOW AYAPI?!
WHO?
COOL.
SOME OF MY FANS!
HIYA, EVERYBODY!!
WEE HEE! COO! ♡
IT'S ME, AYAPI! ♡
WOW!! IT'S REALLY HER!!
KYAAAH ♡
HOW DOES SHE MAKE THOSE HEARTS APPEAR?

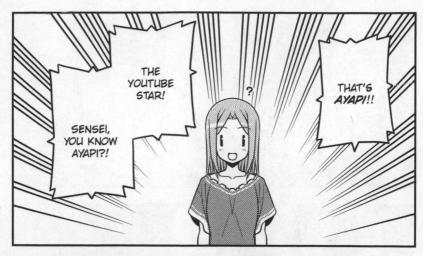

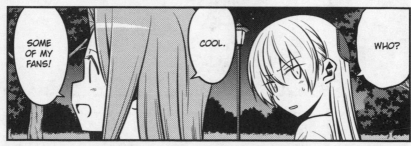

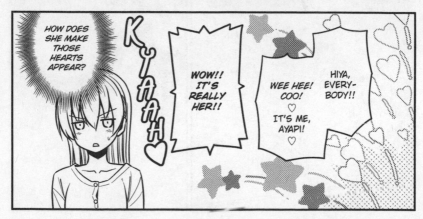

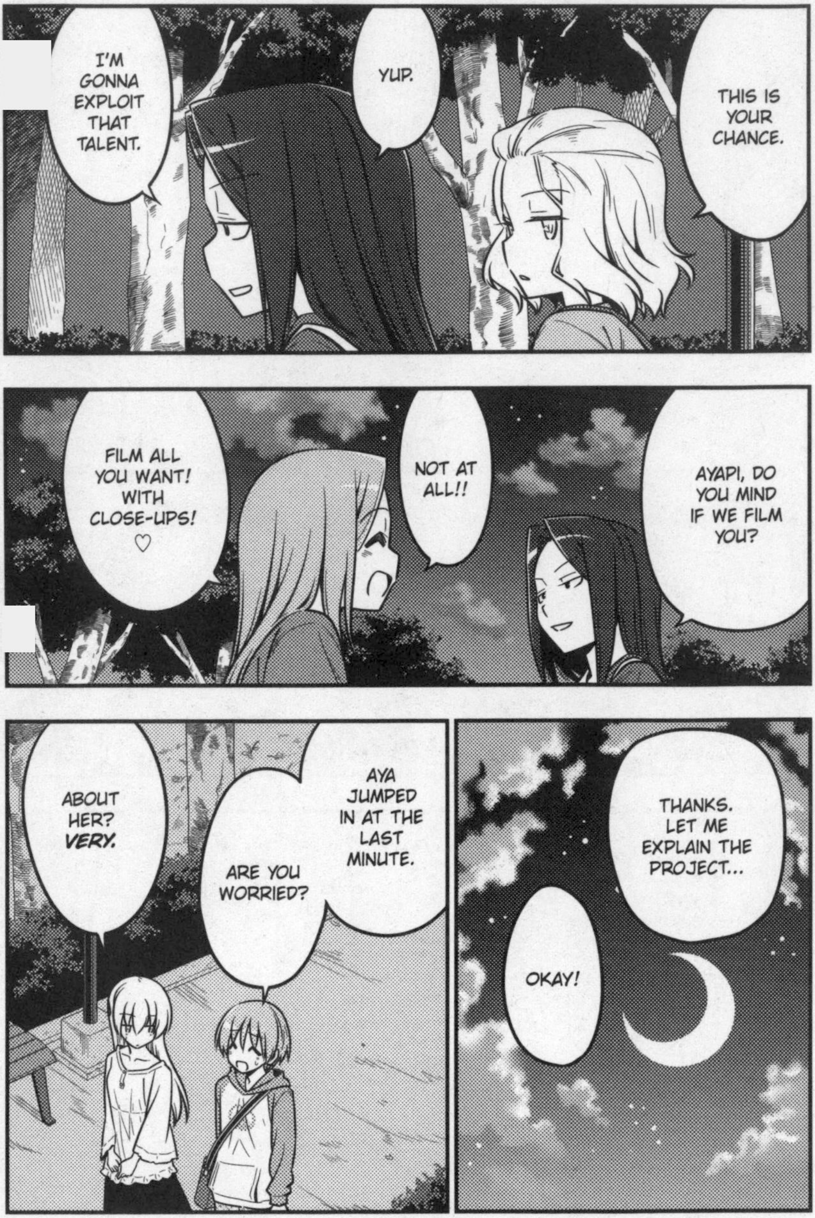
THIS IS YOUR CHANCE.
YUP.
I'M GONNA EXPLOIT THAT TALENT.
AYAPI, DO YOU MIND IF WE FILM YOU?
NOT AT ALL!!
FILM ALL YOU WANT! WITH CLOSE-UPS! ♡
THANKS. LET ME EXPLAIN THE PROJECT...
OKAY!
AYA JUMPED IN AT THE LAST MINUTE.
ARE YOU WORRIED?
ABOUT HER? *VERY.*

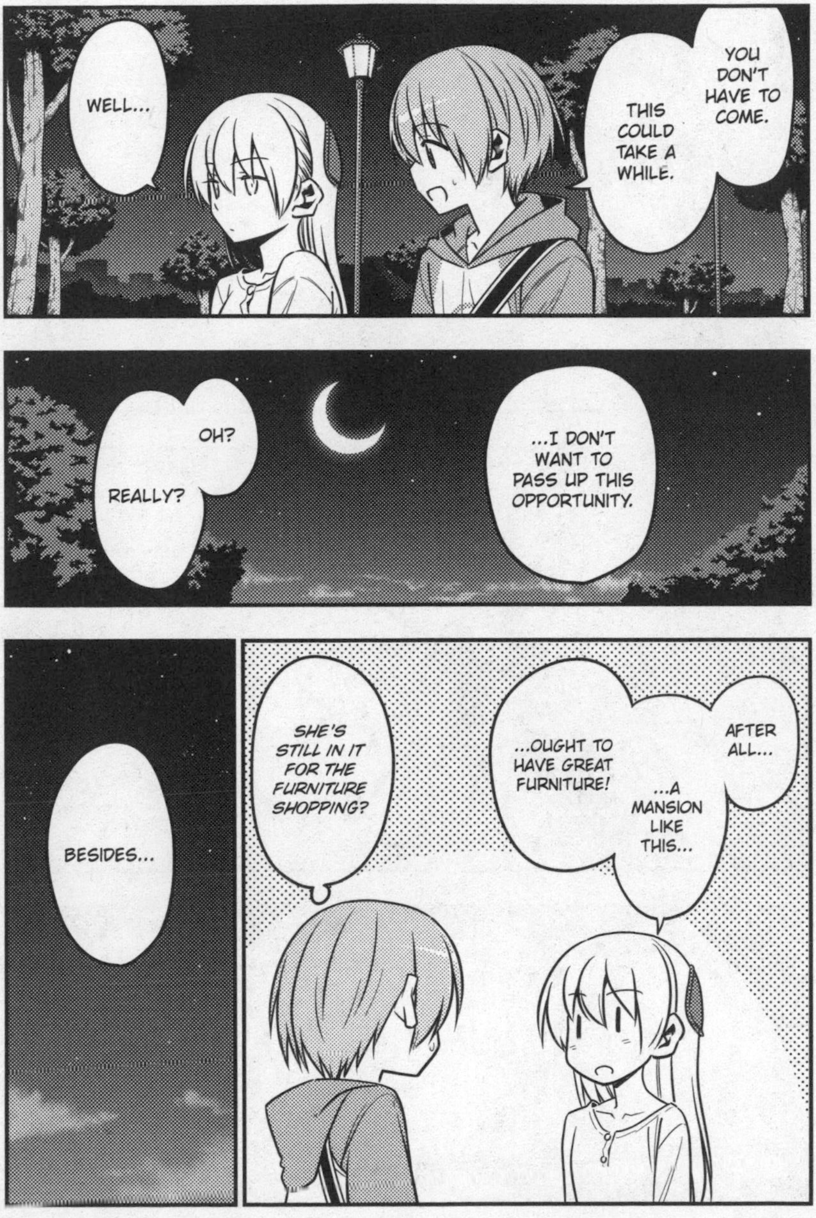
YOU DON'T HAVE TO COME.
THIS COULD TAKE A WHILE.
WELL...
...I DON'T WANT TO PASS UP THIS OPPORTUNITY.
OH?
REALLY?
AFTER ALL...
...A MANSION LIKE THIS...
...OUGHT TO HAVE GREAT FURNITURE!
SHE'S STILL IN IT FOR THE FURNITURE SHOPPING?
BESIDES...

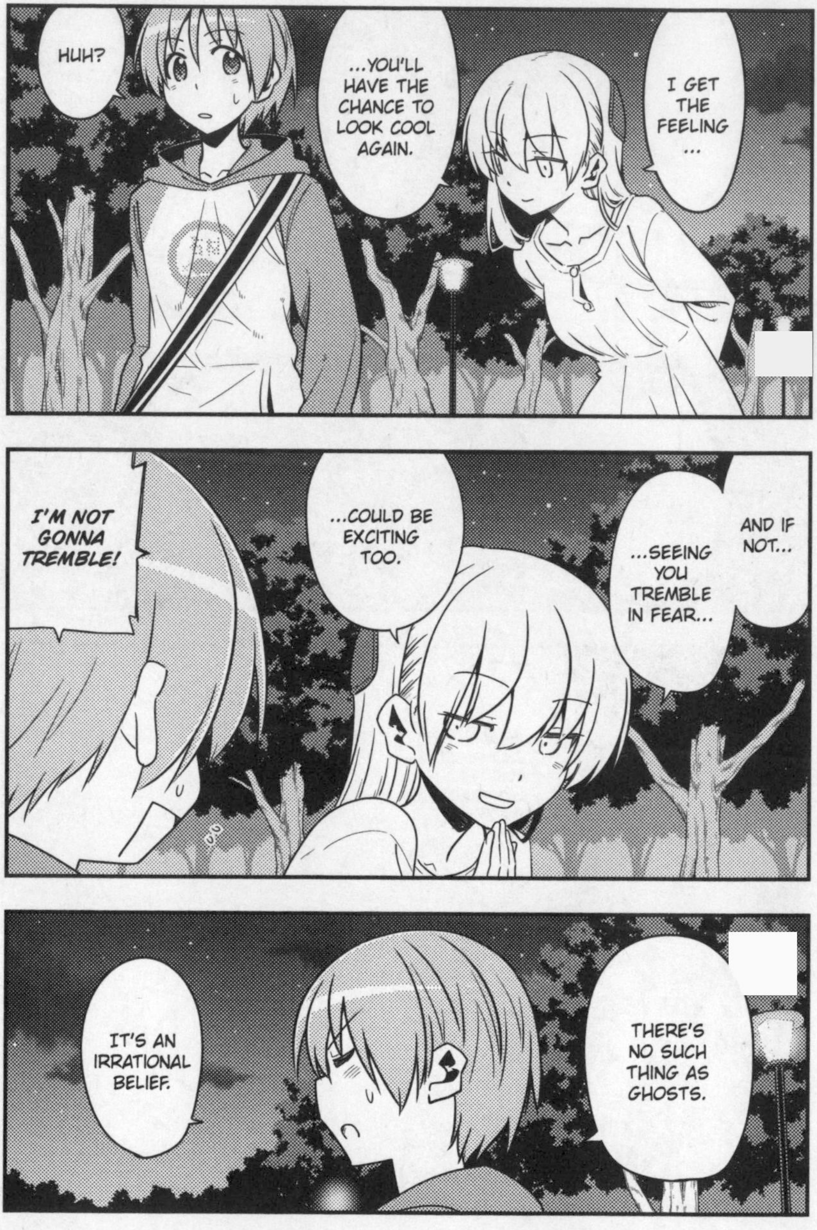
I GET THE FEELING ...
...YOU'LL HAVE THE CHANCE TO LOOK COOL AGAIN.
HUH?
AND IF NOT...
...SEEING YOU TREMBLE IN FEAR...
...COULD BE EXCITING TOO.
I'M NOT GONNA TREMBLE!
THERE'S NO SUCH THING AS GHOSTS.
IT'S AN IRRATIONAL BELIEF.

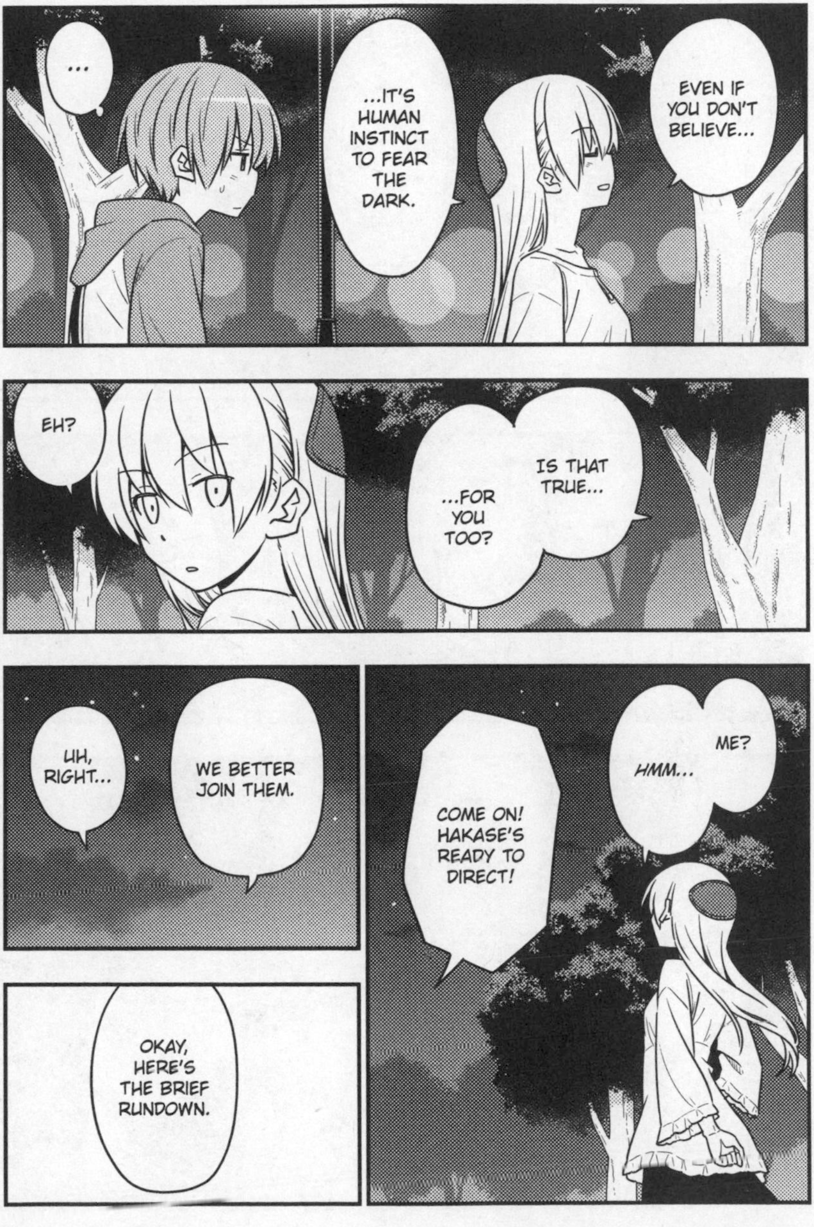
EVEN IF YOU DON'T BELIEVE...
...IT'S HUMAN INSTINCT TO FEAR THE DARK.
...
IS THAT TRUE... ...FOR YOU TOO?
EH?
HMM... ME?
COME ON! HAKASE'S READY TO DIRECT!
WE BETTER JOIN THEM.
UH, RIGHT...
OKAY, HERE'S THE BRIEF RUNDOWN.

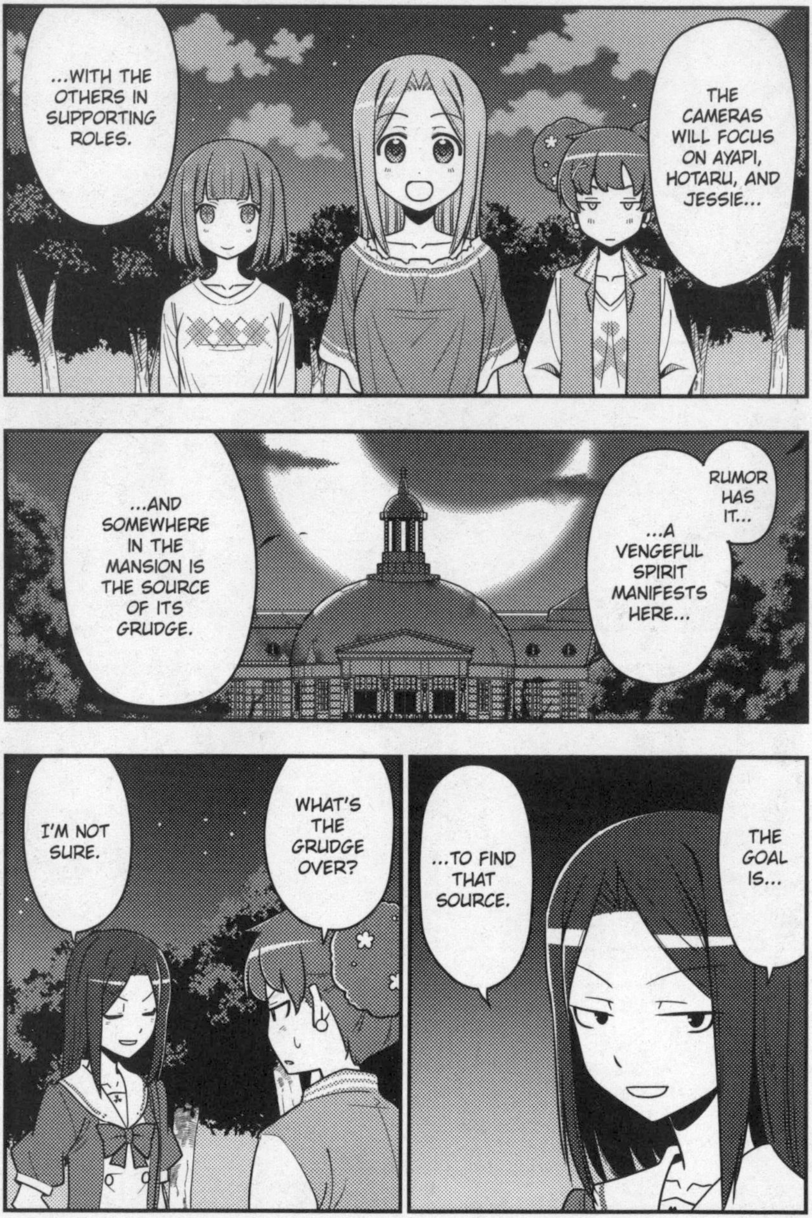
THE CAMERAS WILL FOCUS ON AYAPI, HOTARU, AND JESSIE...
...WITH THE OTHERS IN SUPPORTING ROLES.
RUMOR HAS IT...
...A VENGEFUL SPIRIT MANIFESTS HERE...
...AND SOMEWHERE IN THE MANSION IS THE SOURCE OF ITS GRUDGE.
THE GOAL IS...
...TO FIND THAT SOURCE.
WHAT'S THE GRUDGE OVER?
I'M NOT SURE.

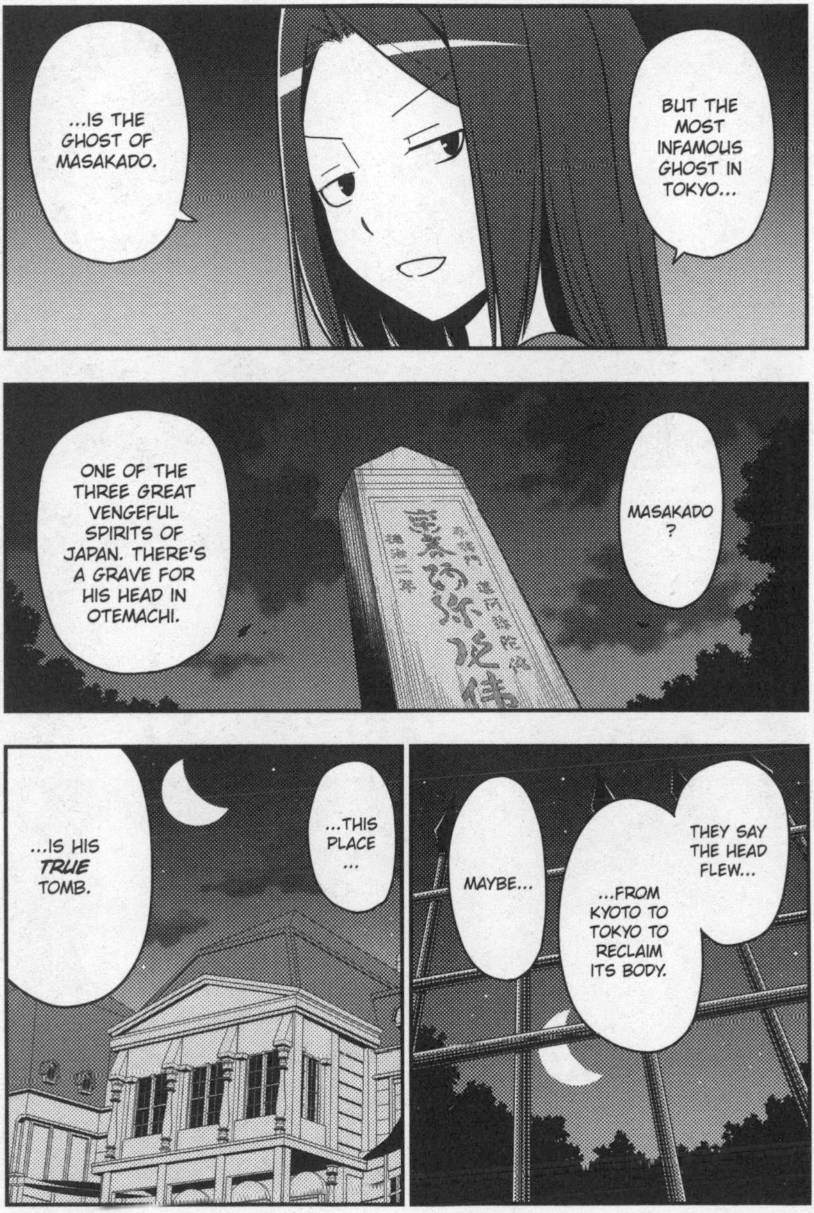
BUT THE MOST INFAMOUS GHOST IN TOKYO...
...IS THE GHOST OF MASAKADO.
MASAKADO?
ONE OF THE THREE GREAT VENGEFUL SPIRITS OF JAPAN. THERE'S A GRAVE FOR HIS HEAD IN OTEMACHI.
THEY SAY THE HEAD FLEW...
...FROM KYOTO TO TOKYO TO RECLAIM ITS BODY.
MAYBE...
...THIS PLACE...
...IS HIS *TRUE* TOMB.

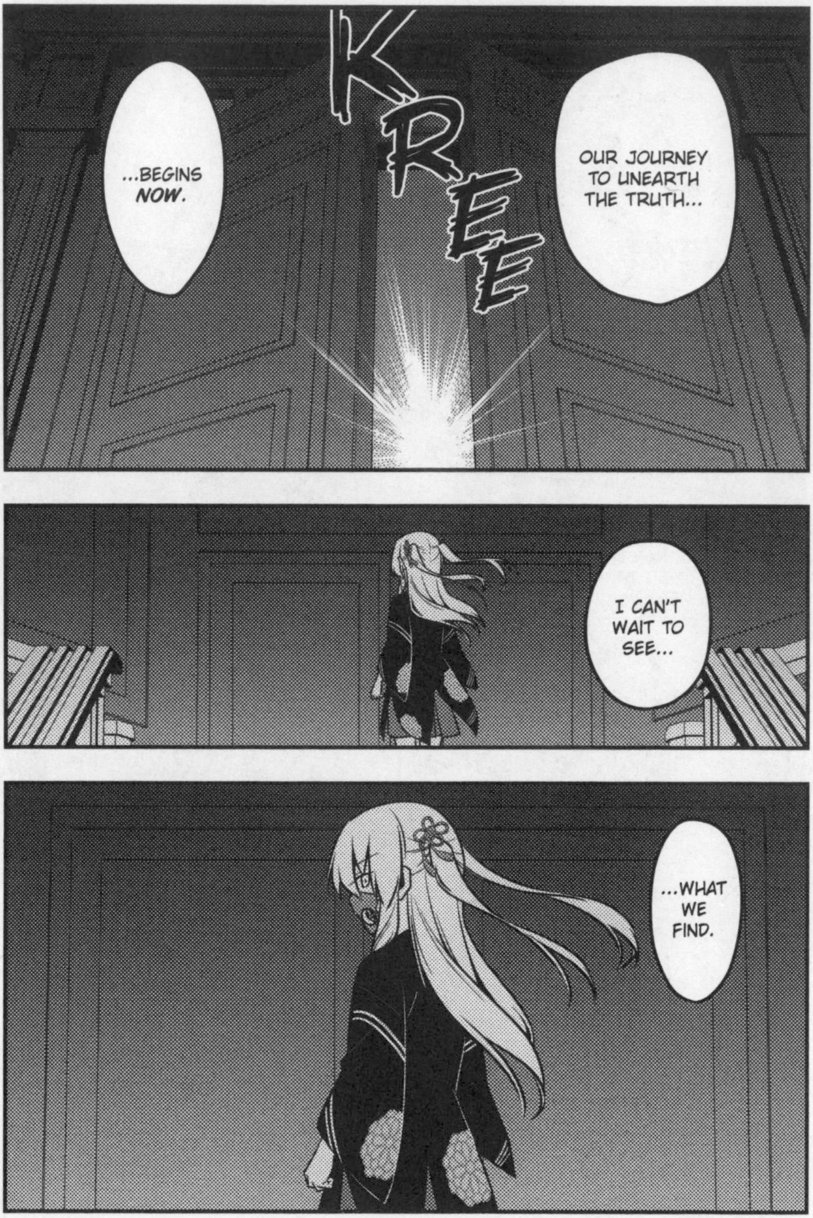
OUR JOURNEY TO UNEARTH THE TRUTH...
KREE
...BEGINS NOW.
I CAN'T WAIT TO SEE...
...WHAT WE FIND.

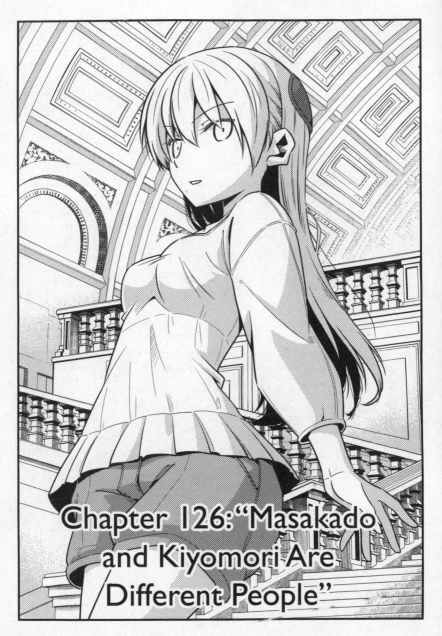

Chapter 126: "Masakado and Kiyomori Are Different People"

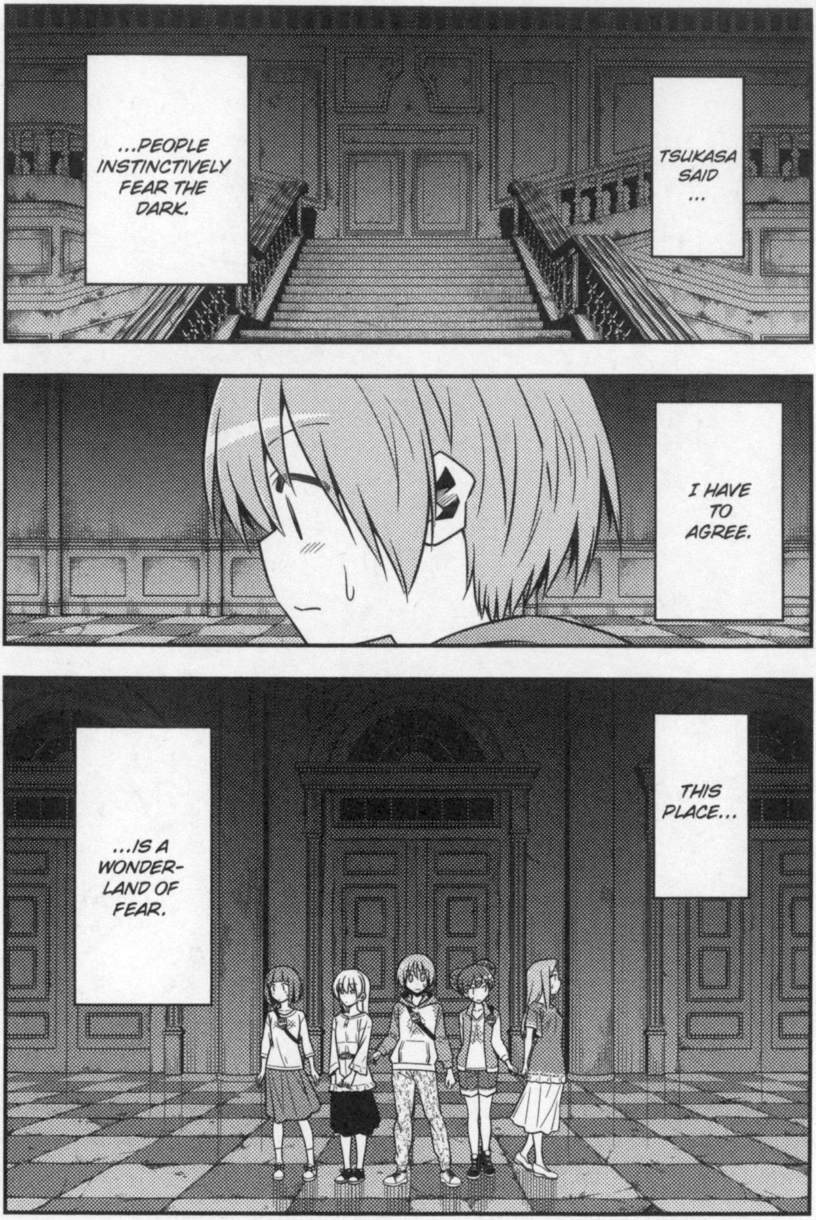
TSUKASA SAID ...
...PEOPLE INSTINCTIVELY FEAR THE DARK.
I HAVE TO AGREE.
THIS PLACE...
...IS A WONDER-LAND OF FEAR.

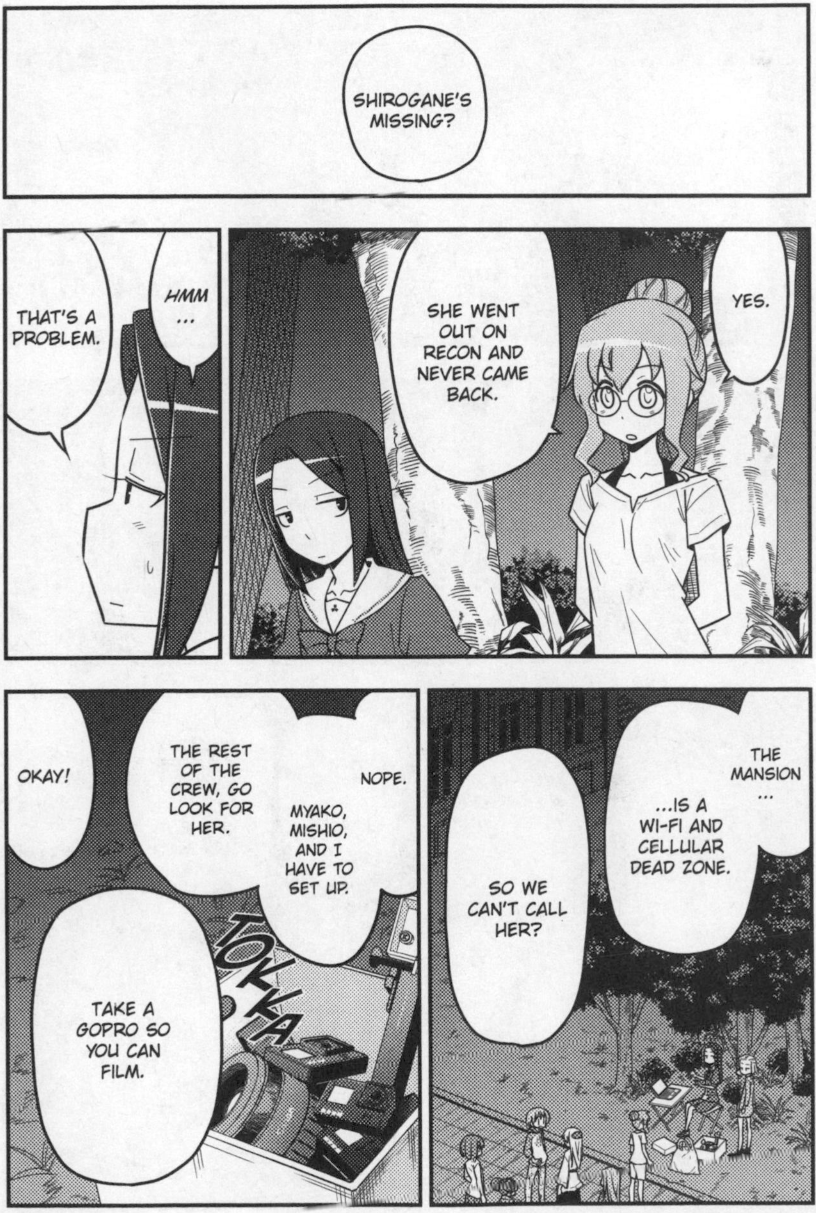
SHIROGANE'S MISSING?
YES.
SHE WENT OUT ON RECON AND NEVER CAME BACK.
HMM ...
THAT'S A PROBLEM.
THE MANSION ...
...IS A WI-FI AND CELLULAR DEAD ZONE.
SO WE CAN'T CALL HER?
NOPE.
MYAKO, MISHIO, AND I HAVE TO SET UP.
THE REST OF THE CREW, GO LOOK FOR HER.
OKAY!
TOKKA
TAKE A GOPRO SO YOU CAN FILM.

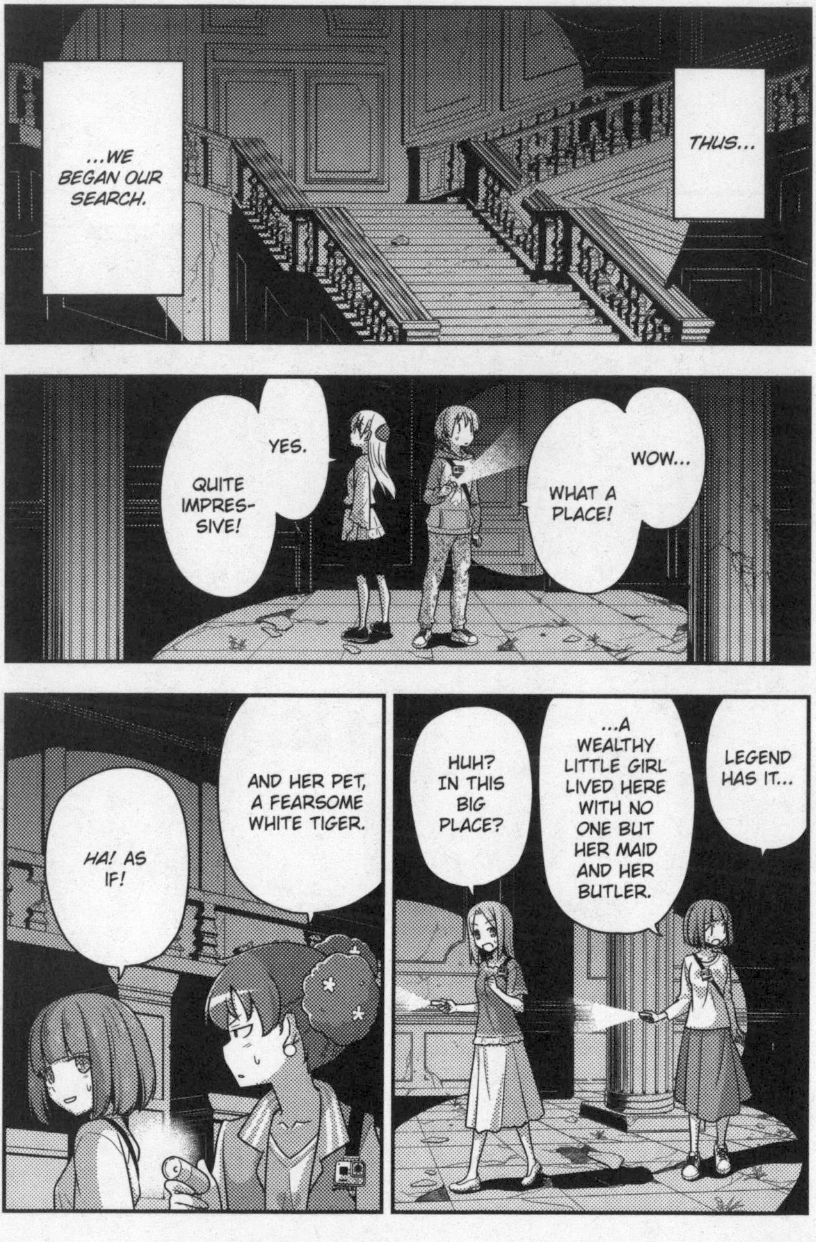
THUS...
...WE BEGAN OUR SEARCH.
WOW... WHAT A PLACE!
YES. QUITE IMPRES-SIVE!
LEGEND HAS IT...
...A WEALTHY LITTLE GIRL LIVED HERE WITH NO ONE BUT HER MAID AND HER BUTLER.
HUH? IN THIS BIG PLACE?
AND HER PET, A FEARSOME WHITE TIGER.
HA! AS IF!

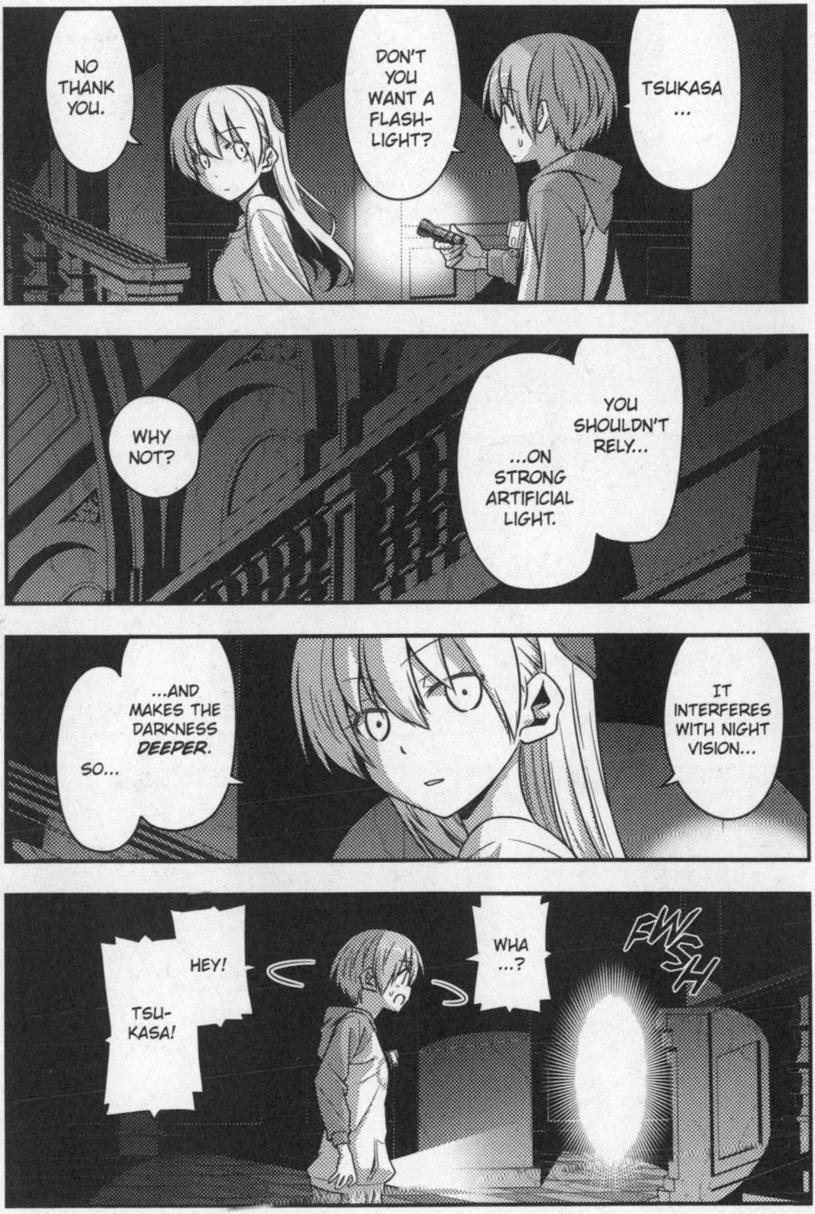
TSUKASA ...
DON'T YOU WANT A FLASH-LIGHT?
NO THANK YOU.
YOU SHOULDN'T RELY...
...ON STRONG ARTIFICIAL LIGHT.
WHY NOT?
IT INTERFERES WITH NIGHT VISION...
...AND MAKES THE DARKNESS DEEPER.
SO...
FWSH
WHA ...?
HEY!
TSU-KASA!

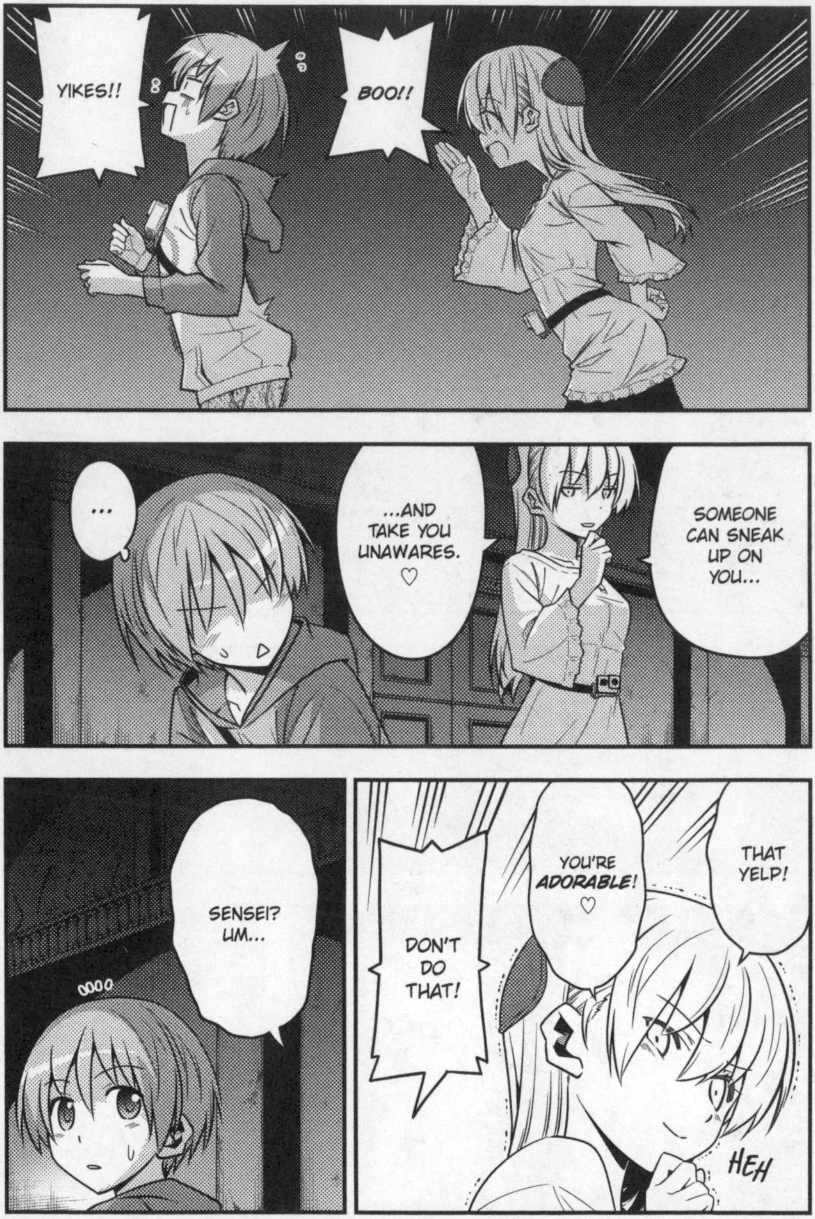
BOO!!
YIKES!!
SOMEONE CAN SNEAK UP ON YOU...
...AND TAKE YOU UNAWARES. ♡
...
THAT YELP!
YOU'RE ADORABLE! ♡
DON'T DO THAT!
HEH
SENSEI? UM...

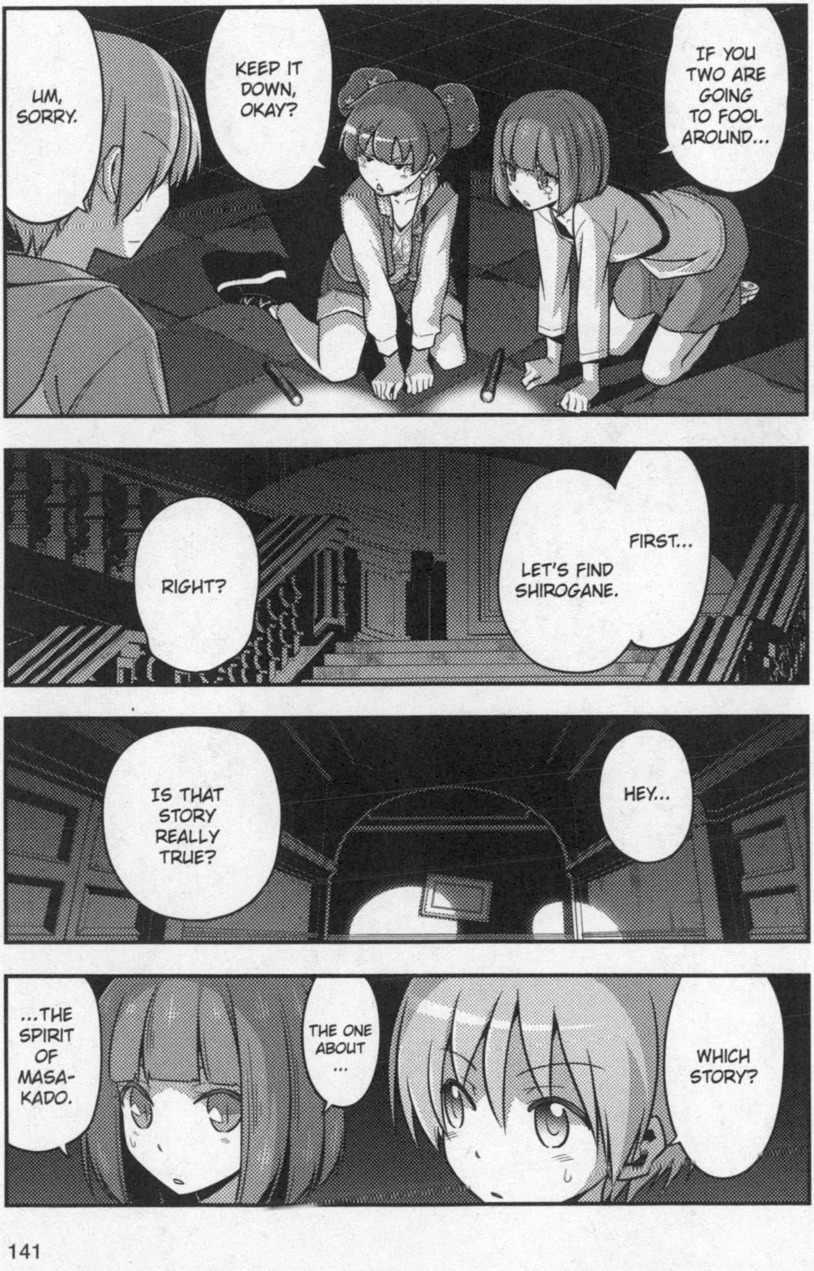
IF YOU TWO ARE GOING TO FOOL AROUND...
KEEP IT DOWN, OKAY?
UM, SORRY.
FIRST...
LET'S FIND SHIROGANE.
RIGHT?
HEY...
IS THAT STORY REALLY TRUE?
WHICH STORY?
THE ONE ABOUT ...
...THE SPIRIT OF MASA-KADO.

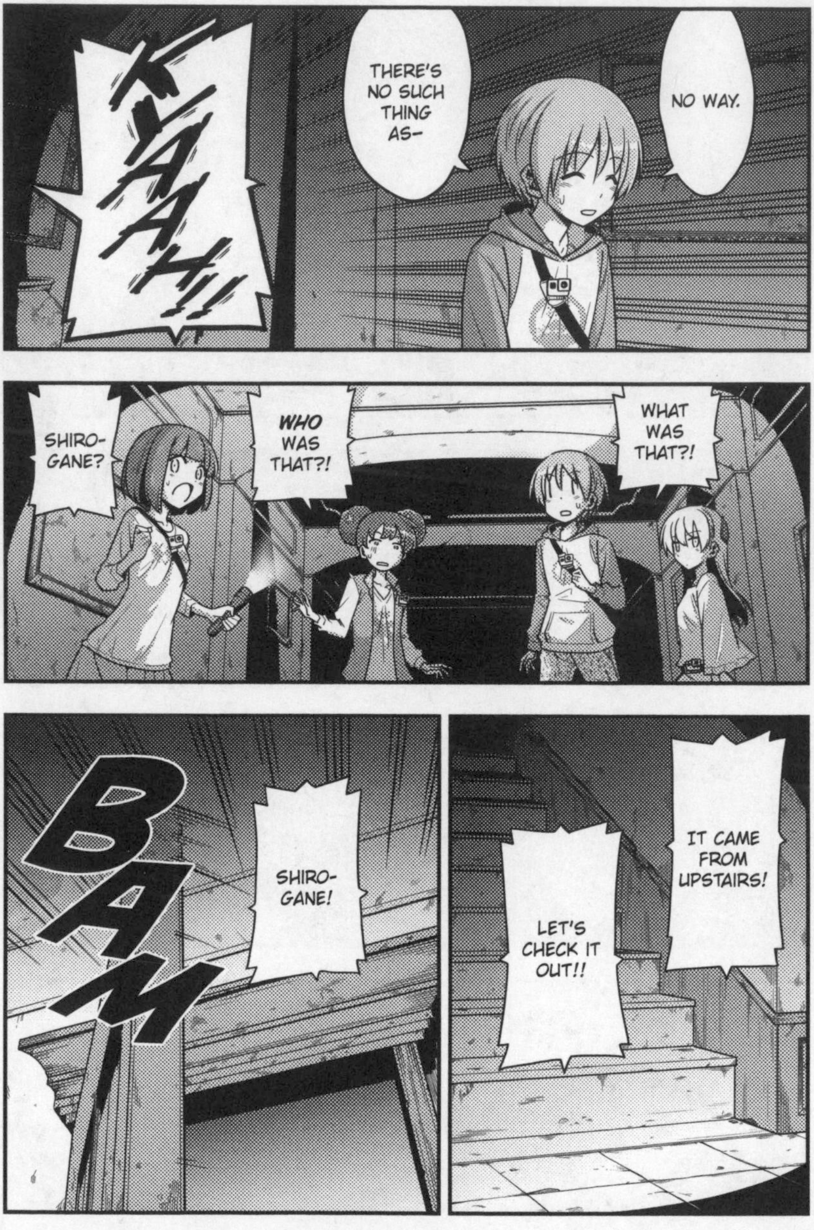
NO WAY.
THERE'S NO SUCH THING AS–
KYAAAH!!
WHAT WAS THAT?!
WHO WAS THAT?!
SHIRO-GANE?
IT CAME FROM UPSTAIRS!
LET'S CHECK IT OUT!!
SHIRO-GANE!
BAM

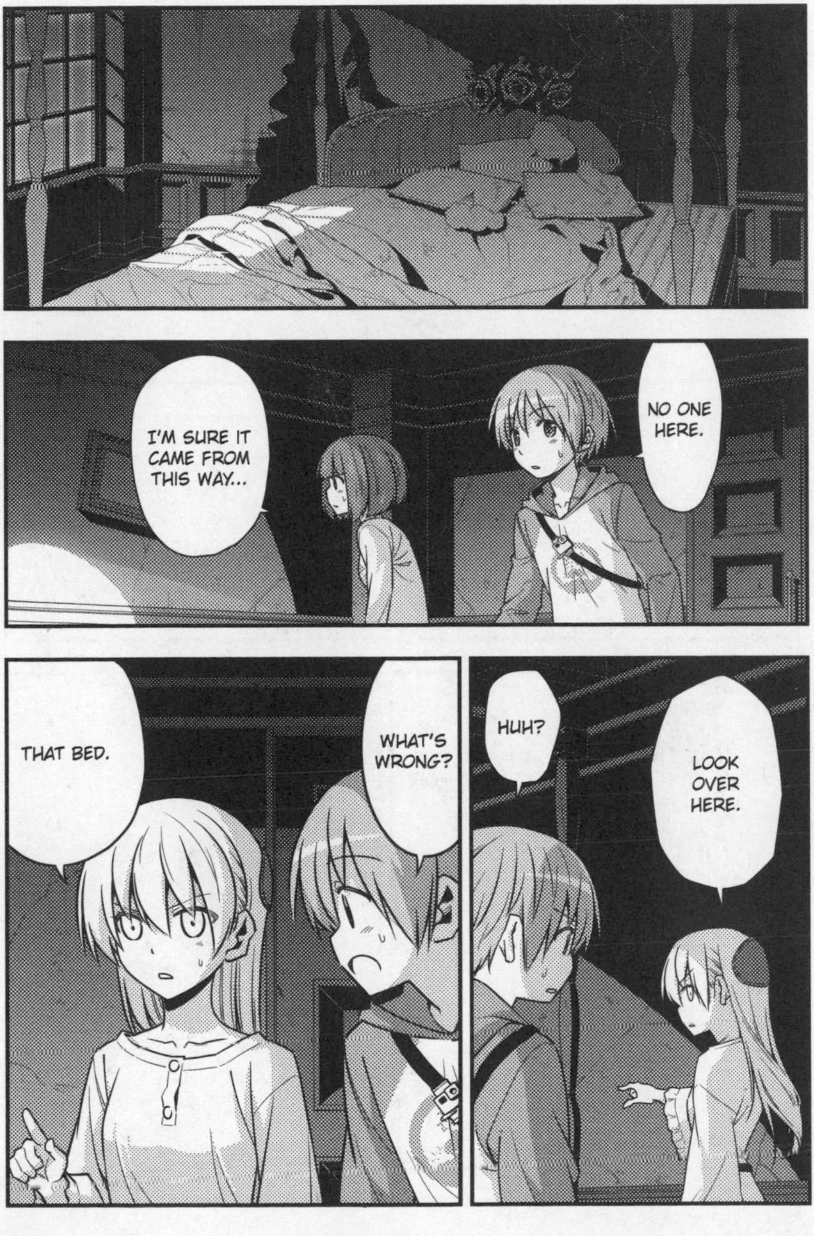
NO ONE HERE.
I'M SURE IT CAME FROM THIS WAY...
LOOK OVER HERE.
HUH?
WHAT'S WRONG?
THAT BED.

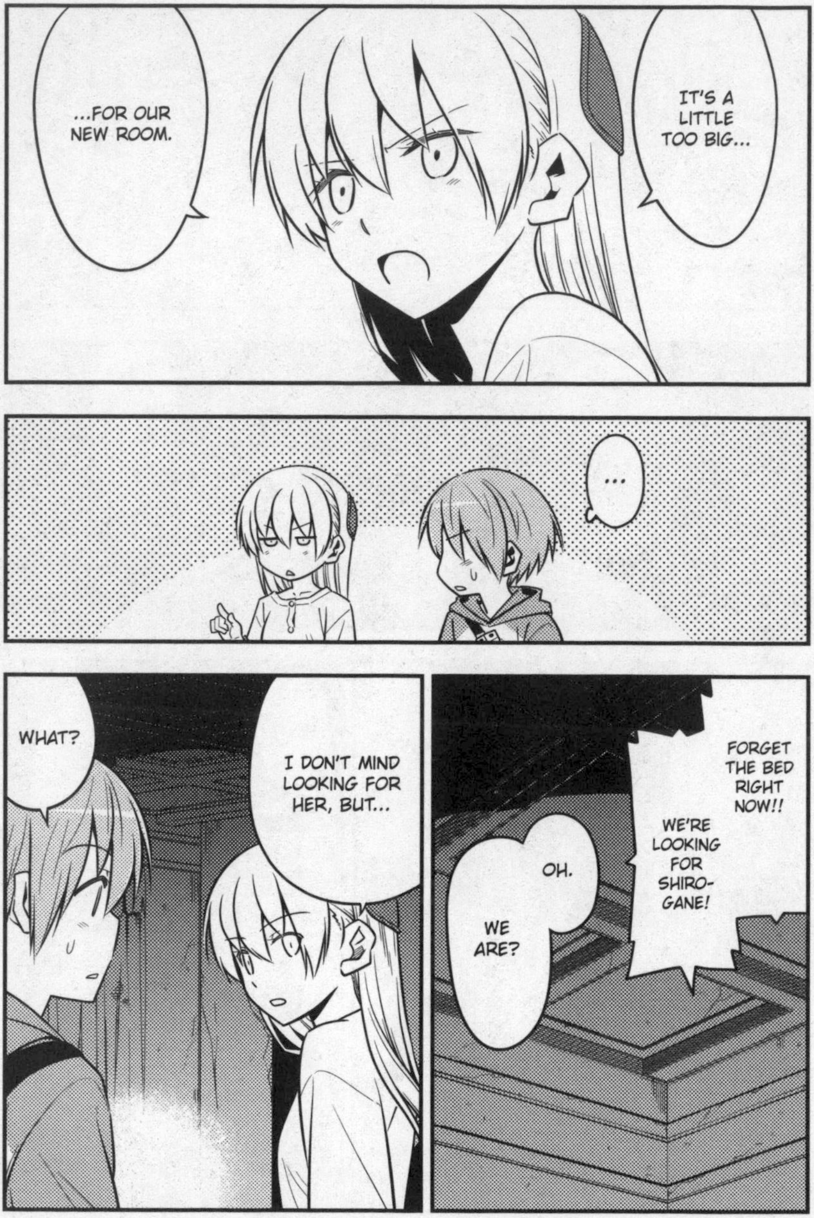
IT'S A LITTLE TOO BIG...
...FOR OUR NEW ROOM.
...
FORGET THE BED RIGHT NOW!!
WE'RE LOOKING FOR SHIRO-GANE!
OH.
WE ARE?
I DON'T MIND LOOKING FOR HER, BUT...
WHAT?

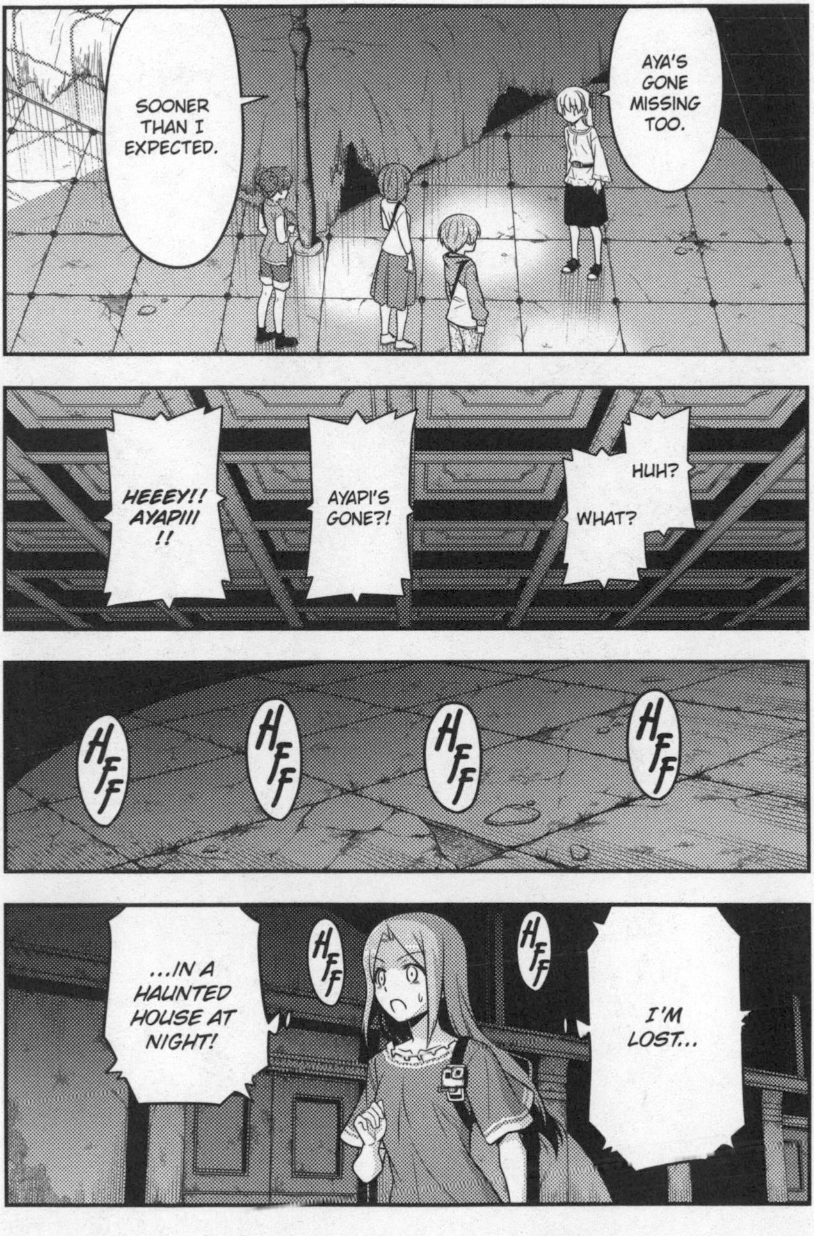
AYA'S GONE MISSING TOO.
SOONER THAN I EXPECTED.
HUH?
WHAT?
AYAPI'S GONE?!
HEEEY!! AYAPIII !!
HFF
HFF
HFF
HFF
I'M LOST...
HFF
HFF
...IN A HAUNTED HOUSE AT NIGHT!

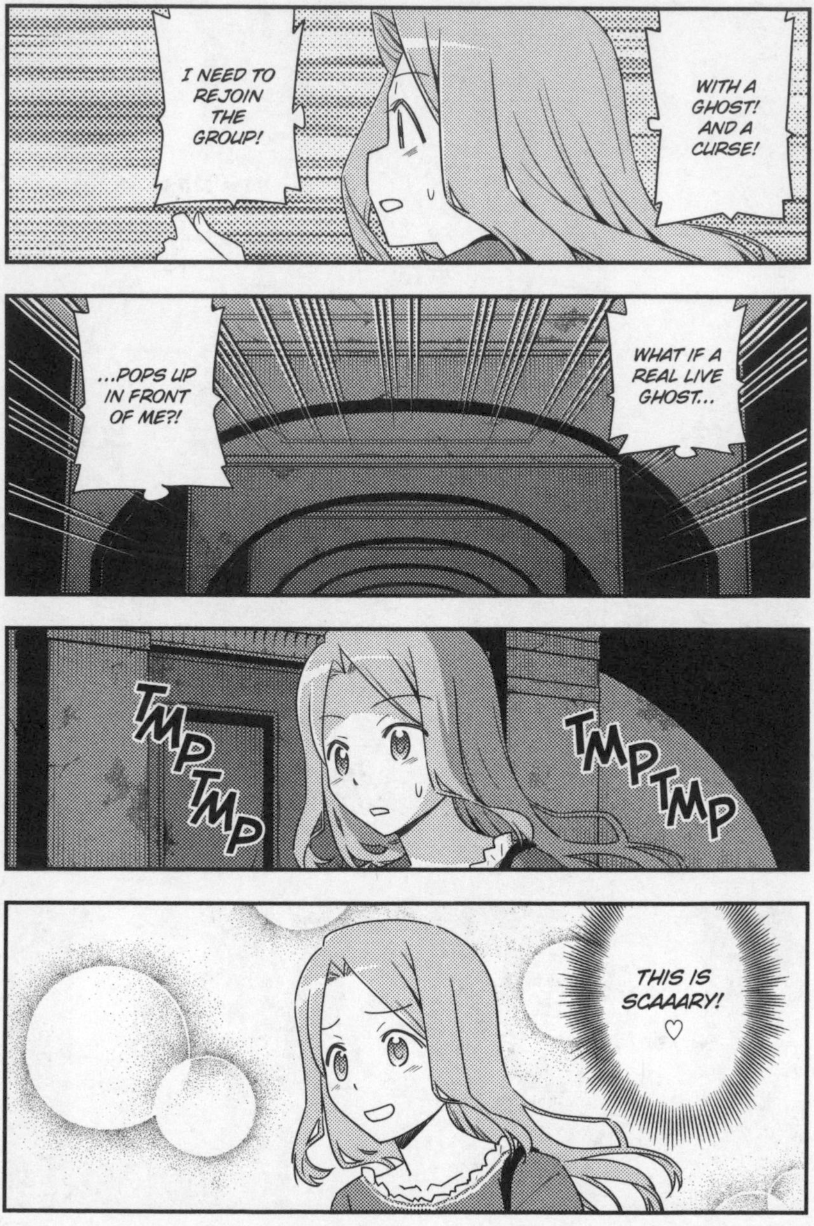
WITH A GHOST! AND A CURSE!
I NEED TO REJOIN THE GROUP!
WHAT IF A REAL LIVE GHOST...
...POPS UP IN FRONT OF ME?!
TMPTMP
TMPTMP
THIS IS SCAAARY! ♡

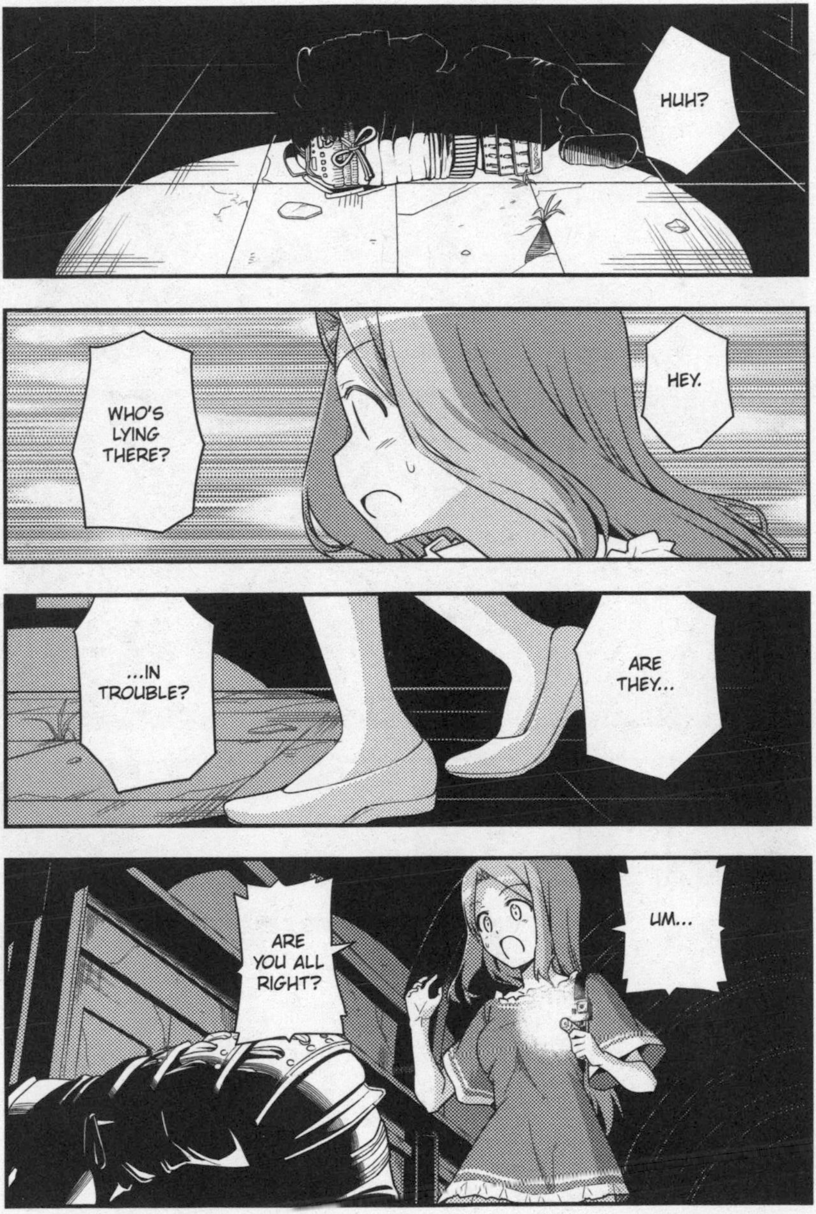
HUH?
HEY.
WHO'S LYING THERE?
ARE THEY...
...IN TROUBLE?
UM...
ARE YOU ALL RIGHT?

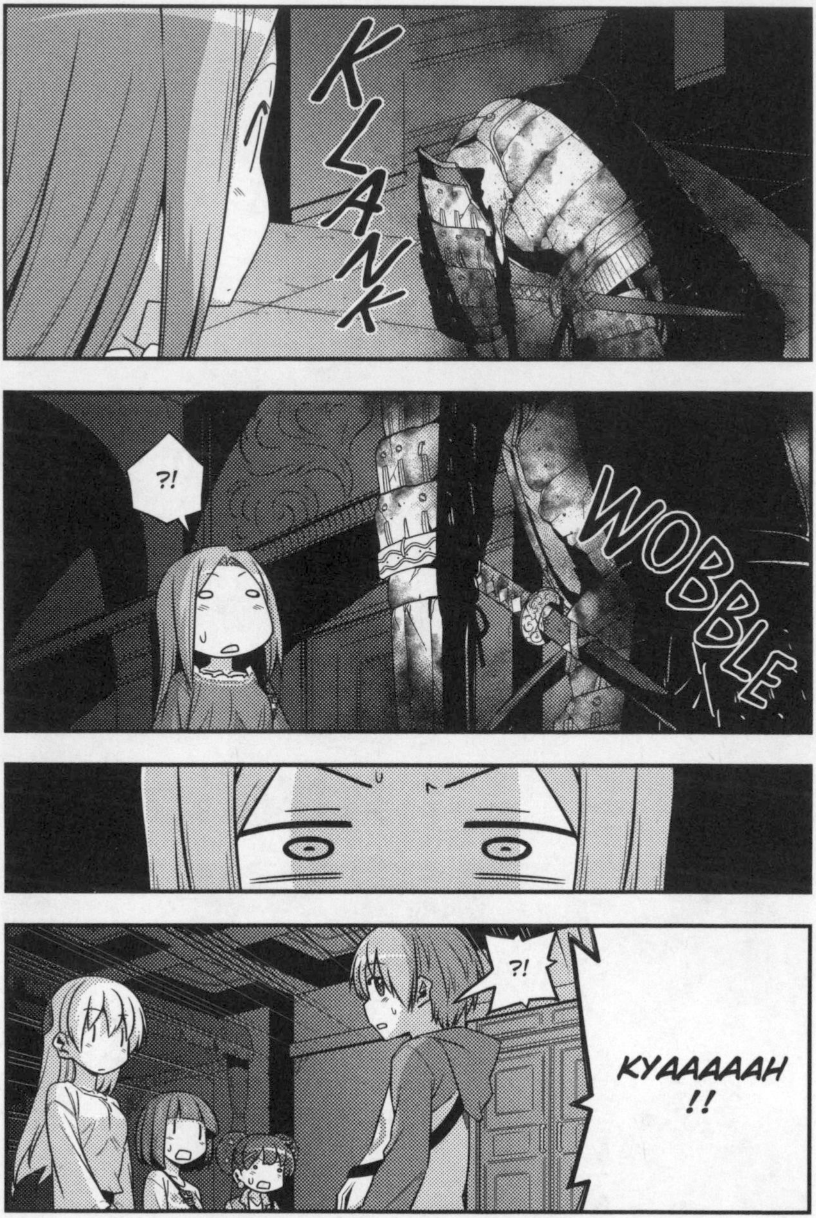
KLANK
WOBBLE
?!
?!
KYAAAAAH !!

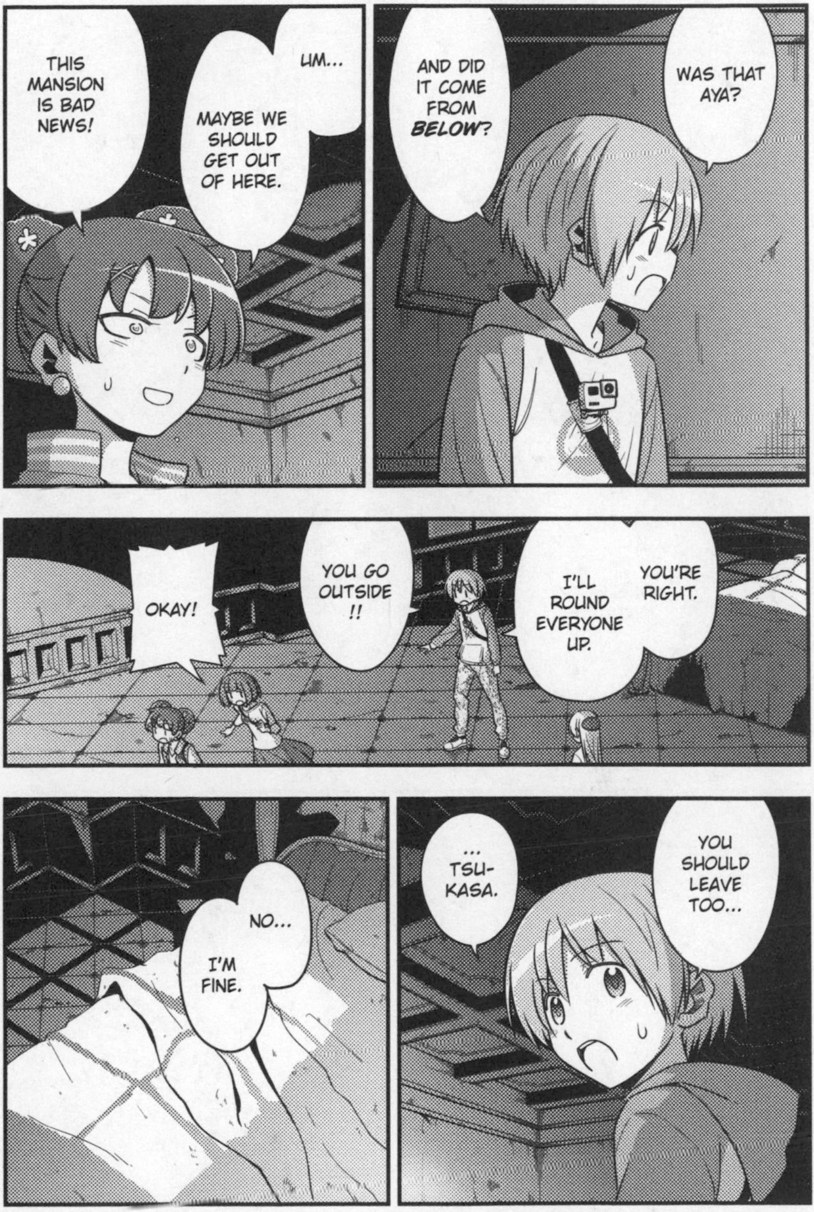
WAS THAT AYA?
AND DID IT COME FROM *BELOW*?
UM...
MAYBE WE SHOULD GET OUT OF HERE.
THIS MANSION IS BAD NEWS!
YOU'RE RIGHT.
I'LL ROUND EVERYONE UP.
YOU GO OUTSIDE !!
OKAY!
YOU SHOULD LEAVE TOO...
... TSU-KASA.
NO...
I'M FINE.

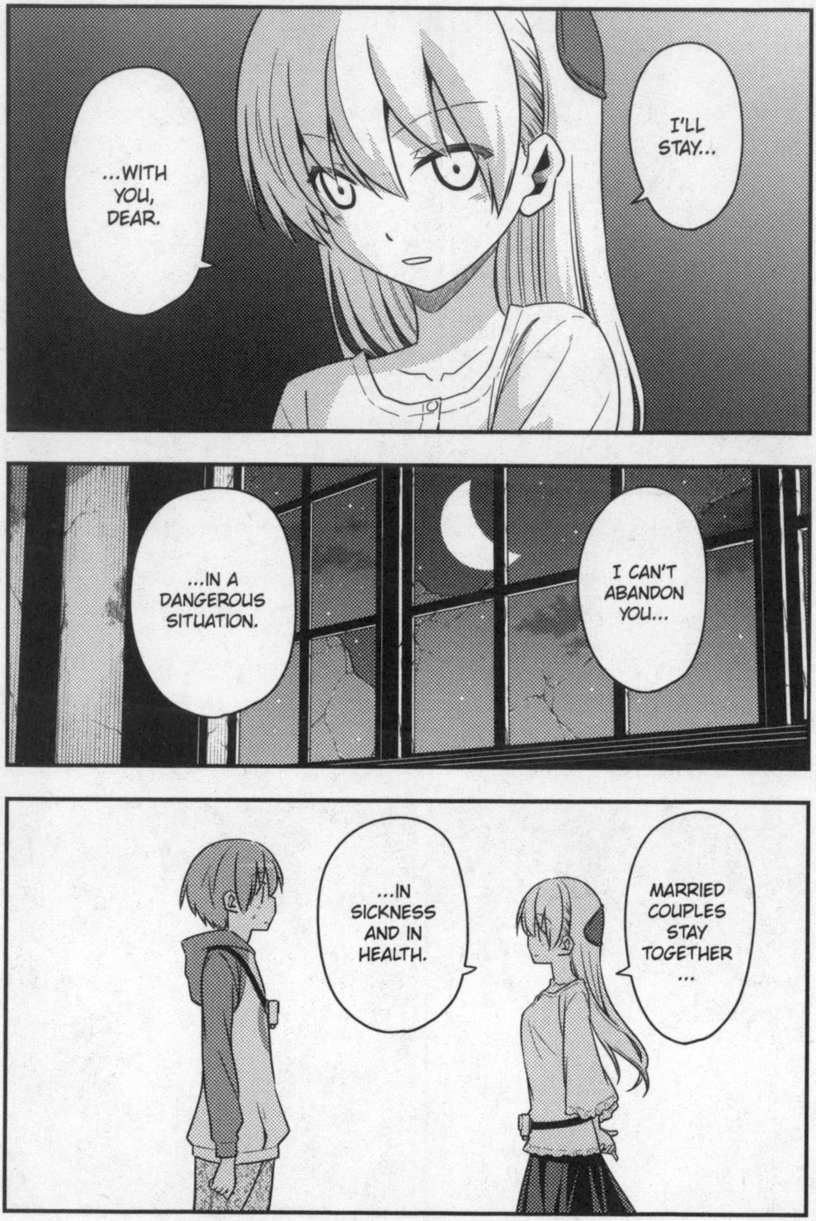
I'LL STAY...
...WITH YOU, DEAR.
I CAN'T ABANDON YOU...
...IN A DANGEROUS SITUATION.
MARRIED COUPLES STAY TOGETHER ...
...IN SICKNESS AND IN HEALTH.

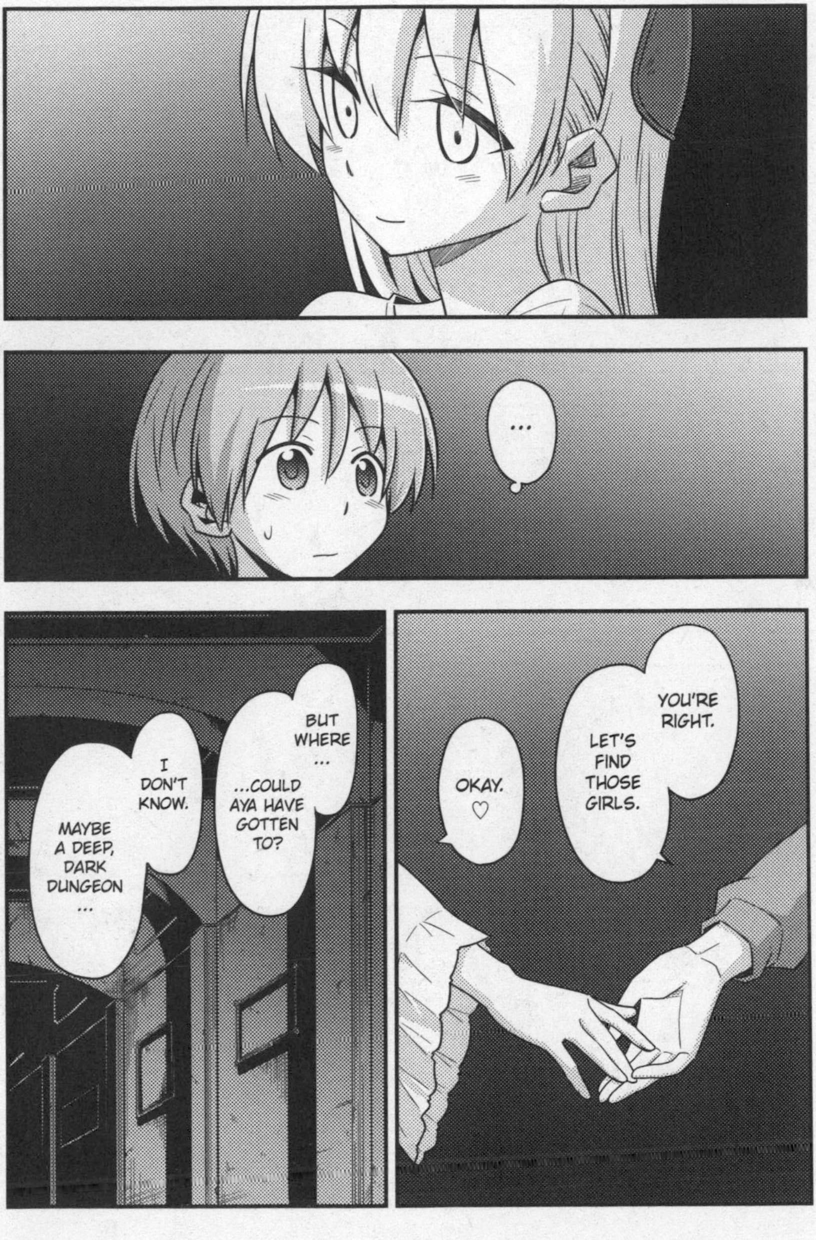
...
YOU'RE RIGHT.
LET'S FIND THOSE GIRLS.
OKAY. ♡
BUT WHERE ...
...COULD AYA HAVE GOTTEN TO?
I DON'T KNOW.
MAYBE A DEEP, DARK DUNGEON ...

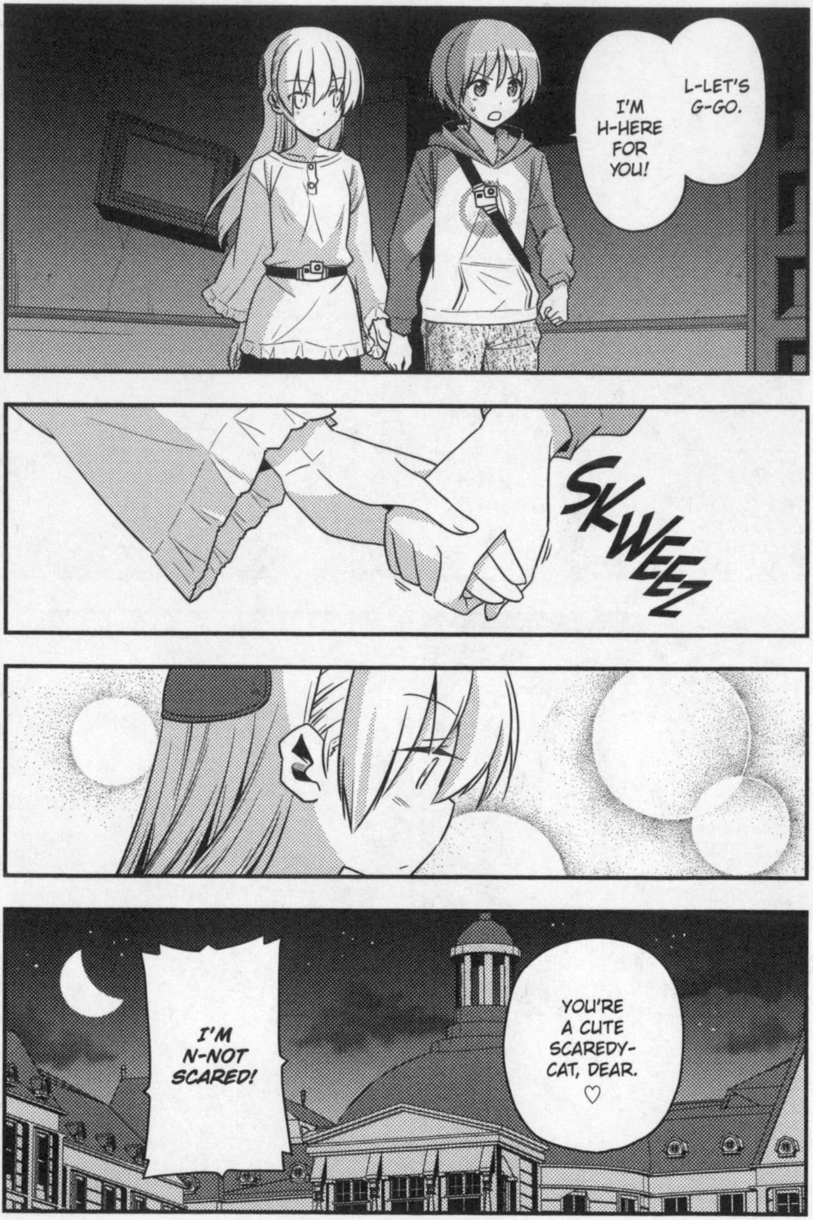
L-LET'S G-GO.
I'M H-HERE FOR YOU!
SKWEEZ
YOU'RE A CUTE SCAREDY-CAT, DEAR. ♡
I'M N-NOT SCARED!

FLY ME TO THE MOON

Chapter 127: "The Manga's Good, but Watch the Anime Too, Okay?"

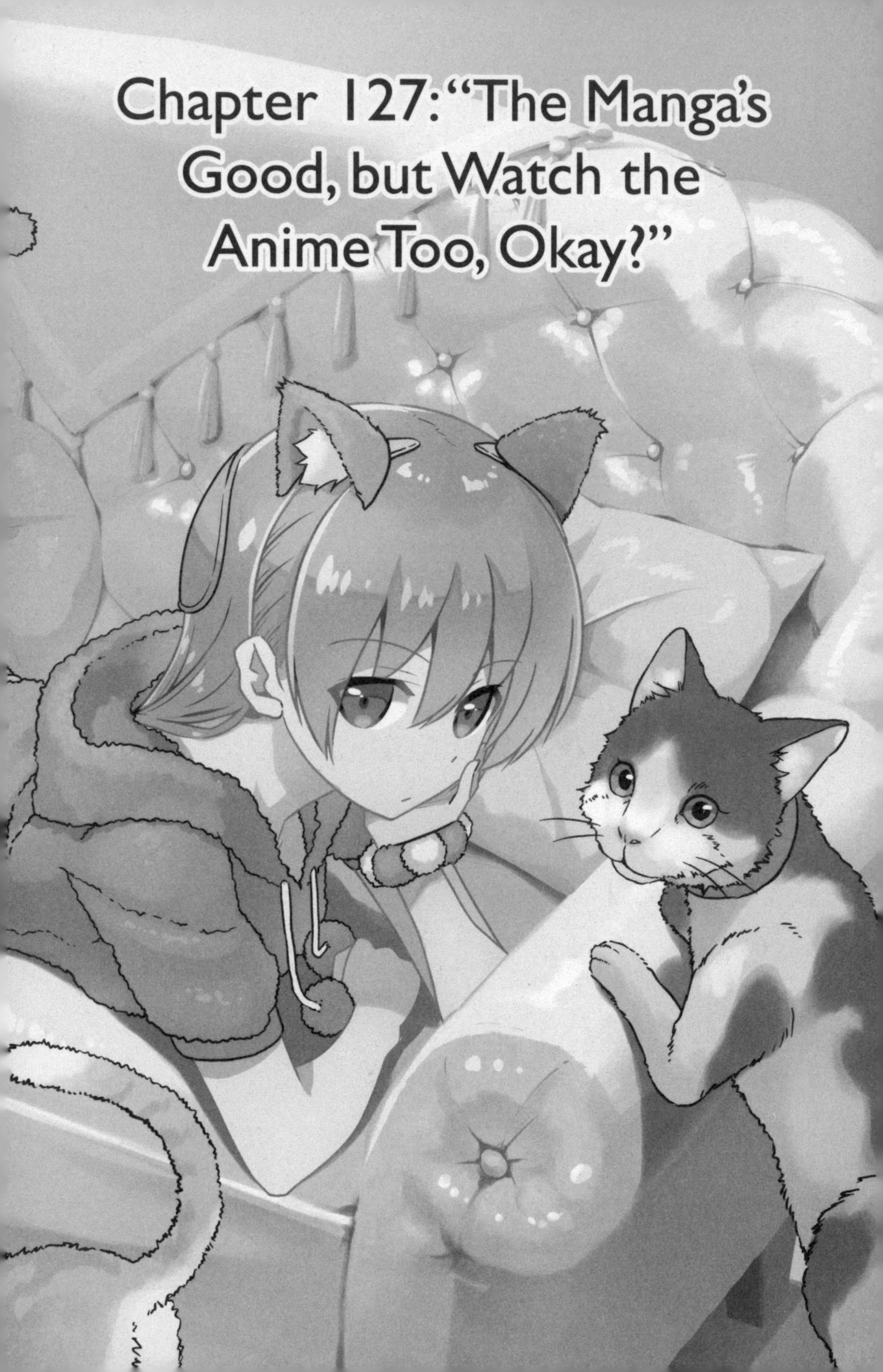

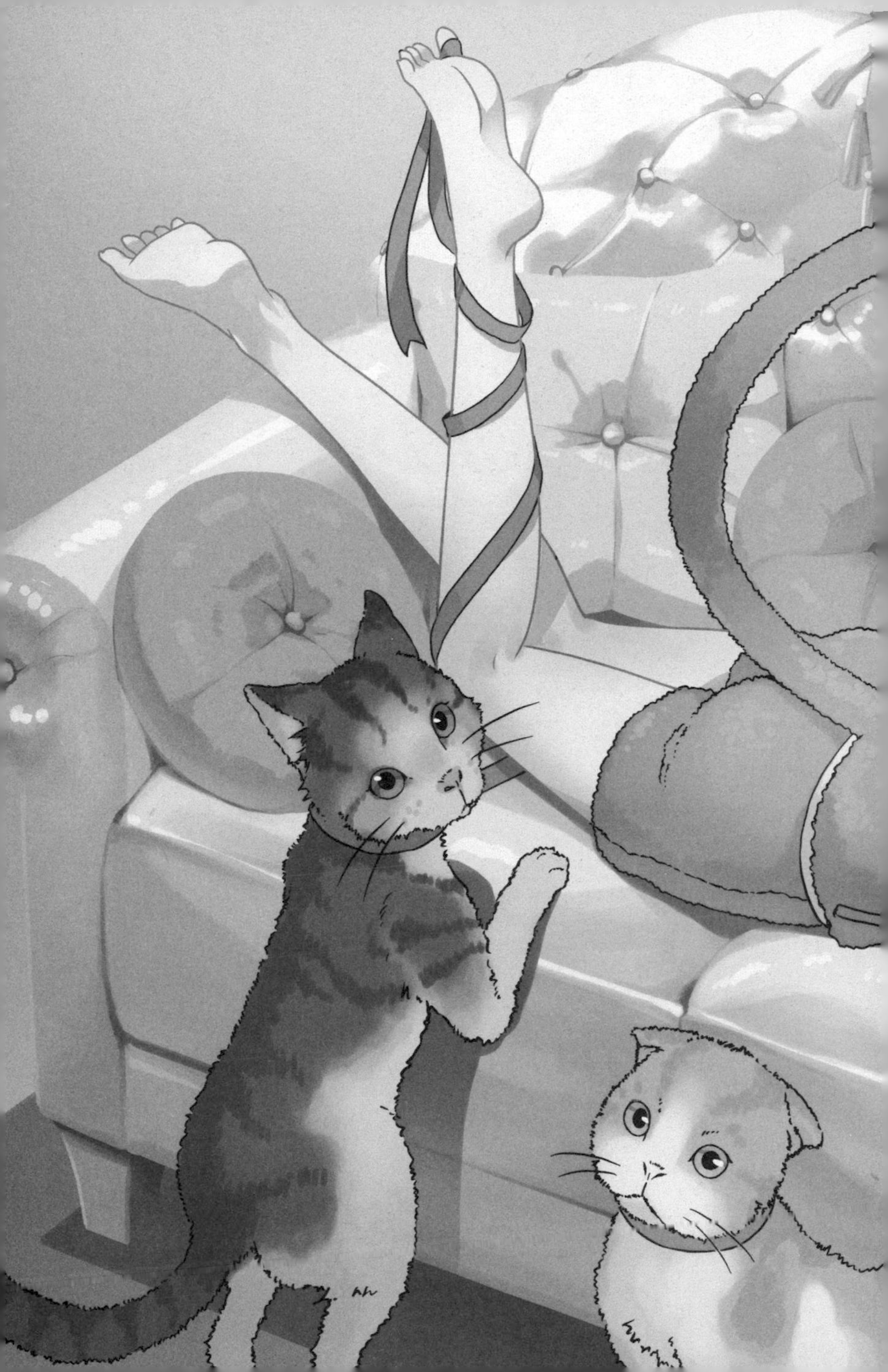

FLY ME $_{TO}^{THE}$ MOON

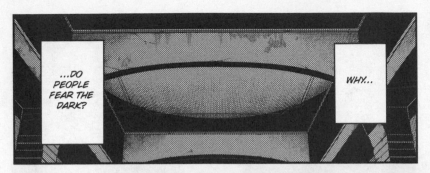

...DO PEOPLE FEAR THE DARK?

WHY...

...I DON'T BELIEVE IN GHOSTS.

I SWEAR...

BUT...

...I GET SCARED WHEN THE LIGHTS GO OUT.

EVEN SO...

157

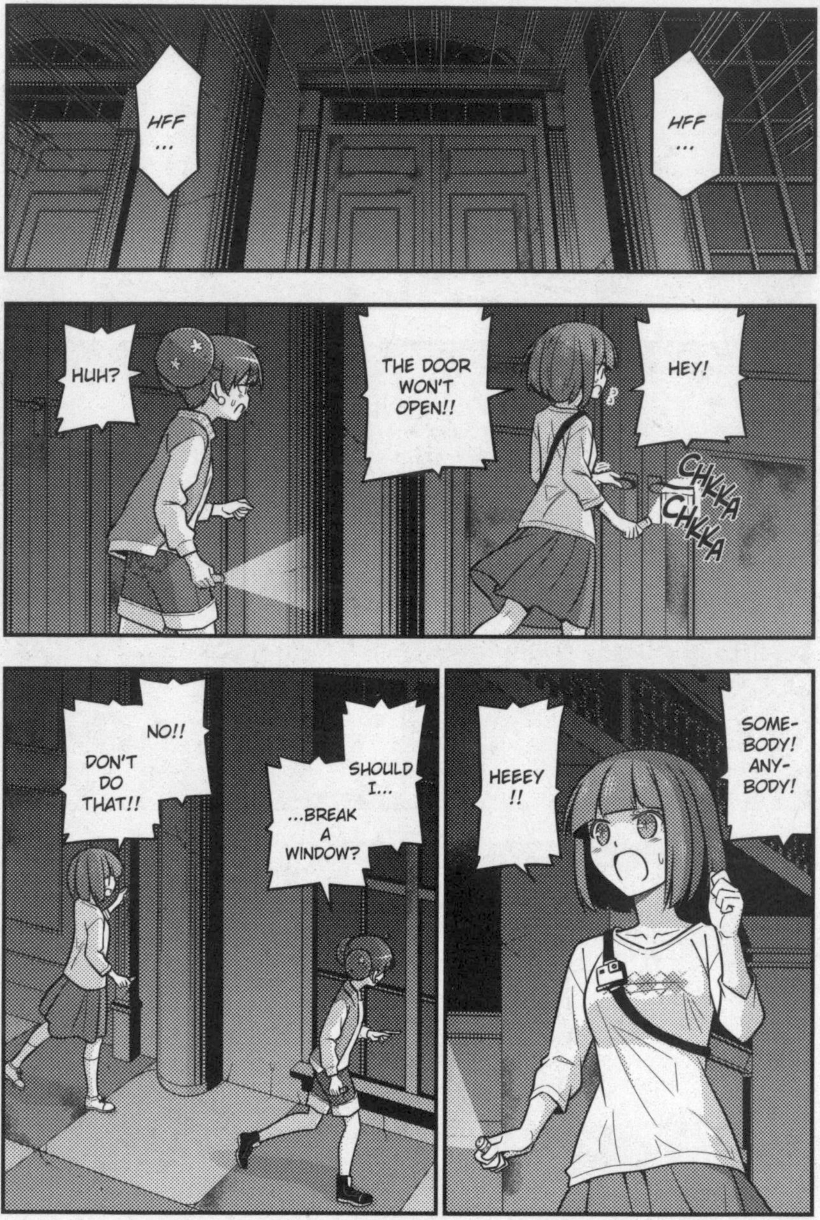
HFF ...
HFF ...
HEY!
THE DOOR WON'T OPEN!!
CHKKA CHKKA
HUH?
SOME-BODY! ANY-BODY!
HEEEY !!
SHOULD I...
...BREAK A WINDOW?
NO!!
DON'T DO THAT!!

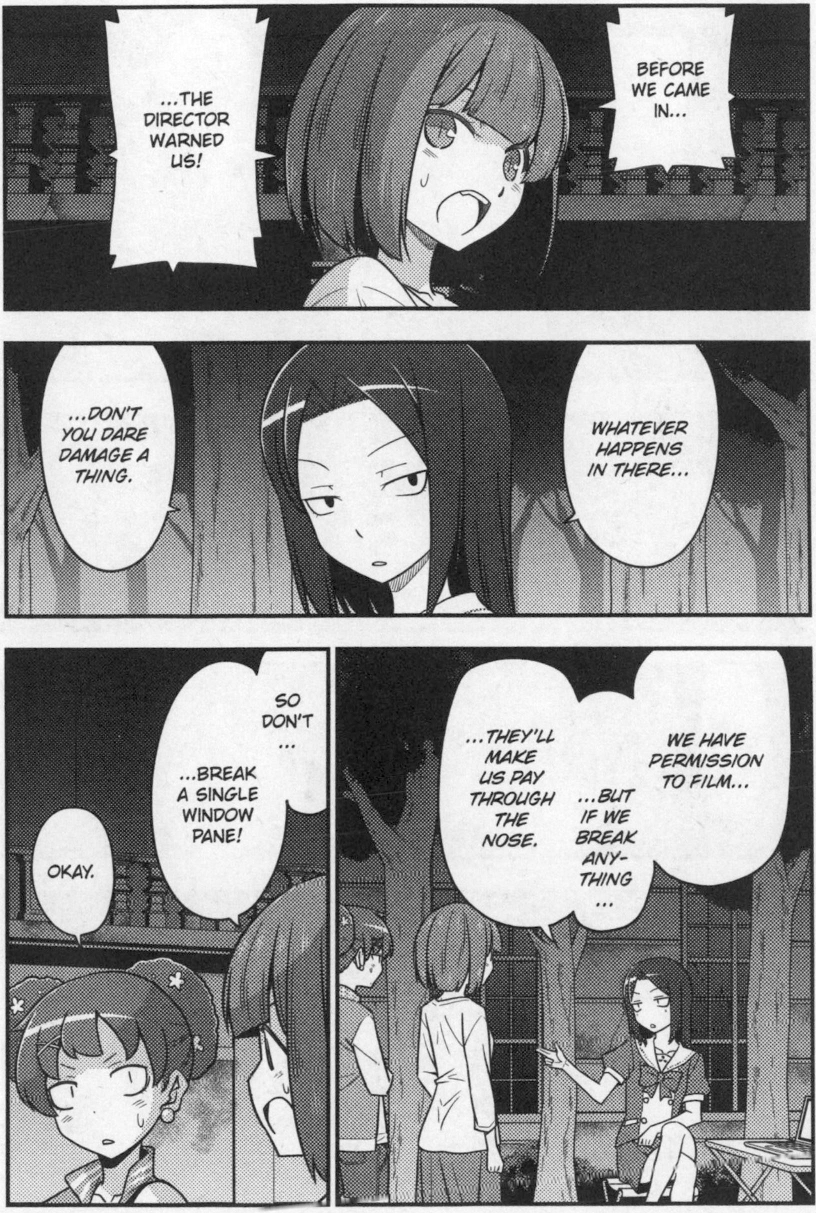
BEFORE WE CAME IN...
...THE DIRECTOR WARNED US!
WHATEVER HAPPENS IN THERE...
...DON'T YOU DARE DAMAGE A THING.
WE HAVE PERMISSION TO FILM...
...BUT IF WE BREAK ANYTHING...
...THEY'LL MAKE US PAY THROUGH THE NOSE.
SO DON'T ...
...BREAK A SINGLE WINDOW PANE!
OKAY.

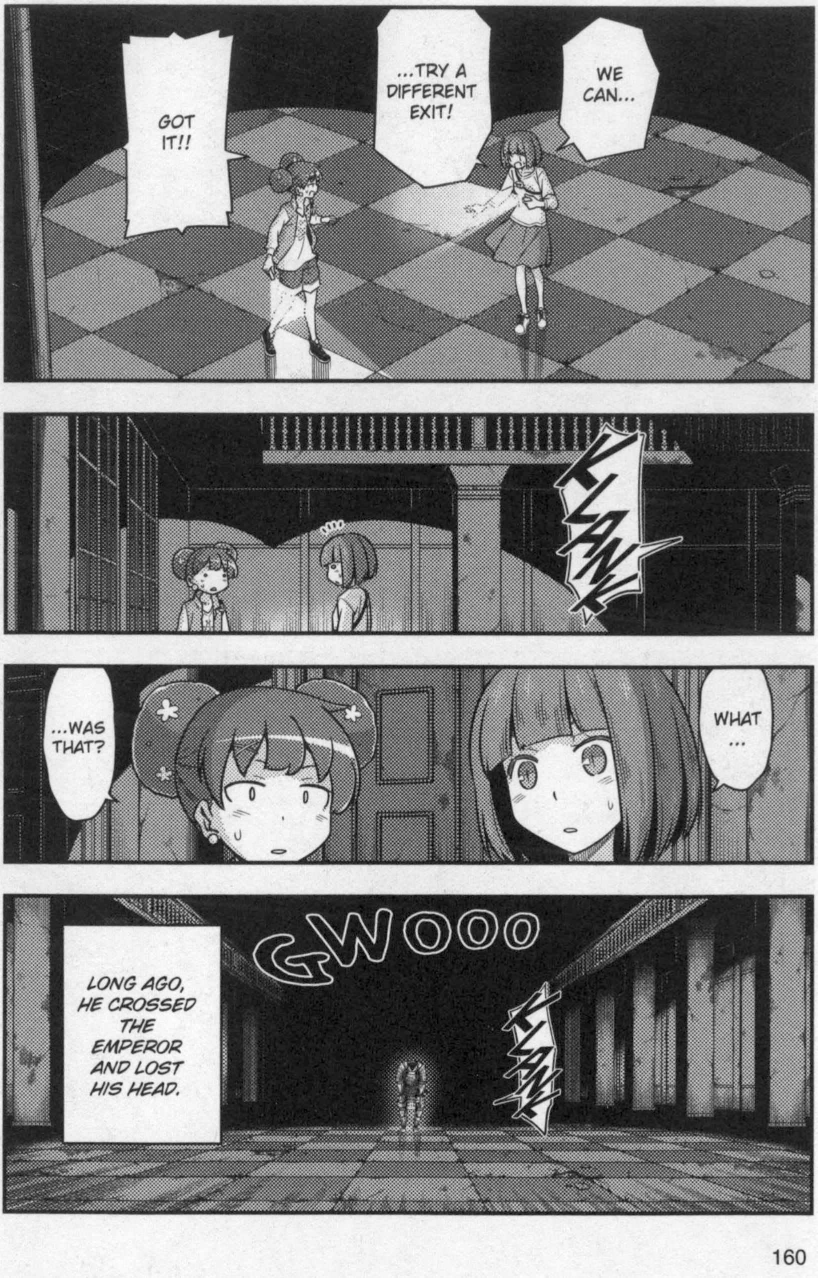
WE CAN...
...TRY A DIFFERENT EXIT!
GOT IT!!
KLANK
WHAT...
...WAS THAT?
GWOOO
KLANK
LONG AGO, HE CROSSED THE EMPEROR AND LOST HIS HEAD.

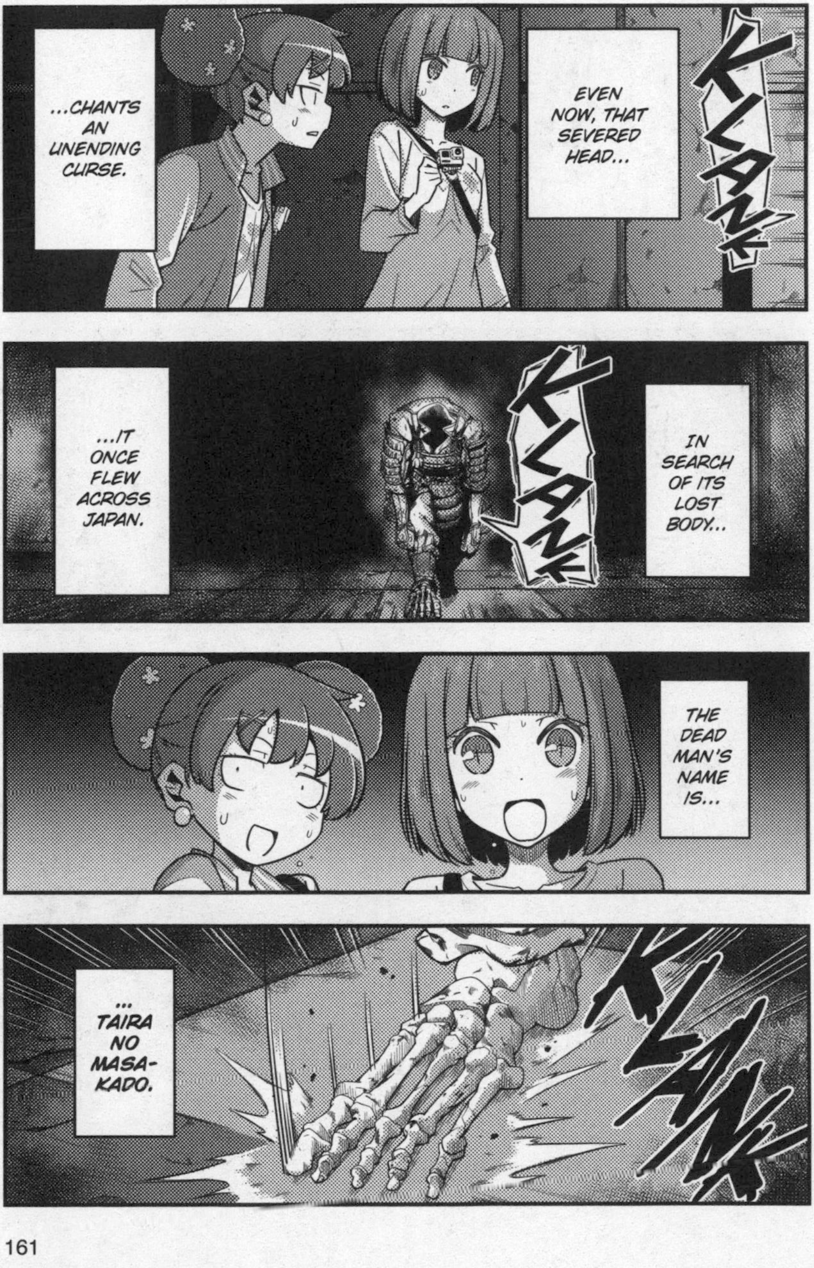
KLANK
EVEN NOW, THAT SEVERED HEAD...
...CHANTS AN UNENDING CURSE.
IN SEARCH OF ITS LOST BODY...
KLANK
...IT ONCE FLEW ACROSS JAPAN.
THE DEAD MAN'S NAME IS...
KLANK
...TAIRA NO MASA-KADO.

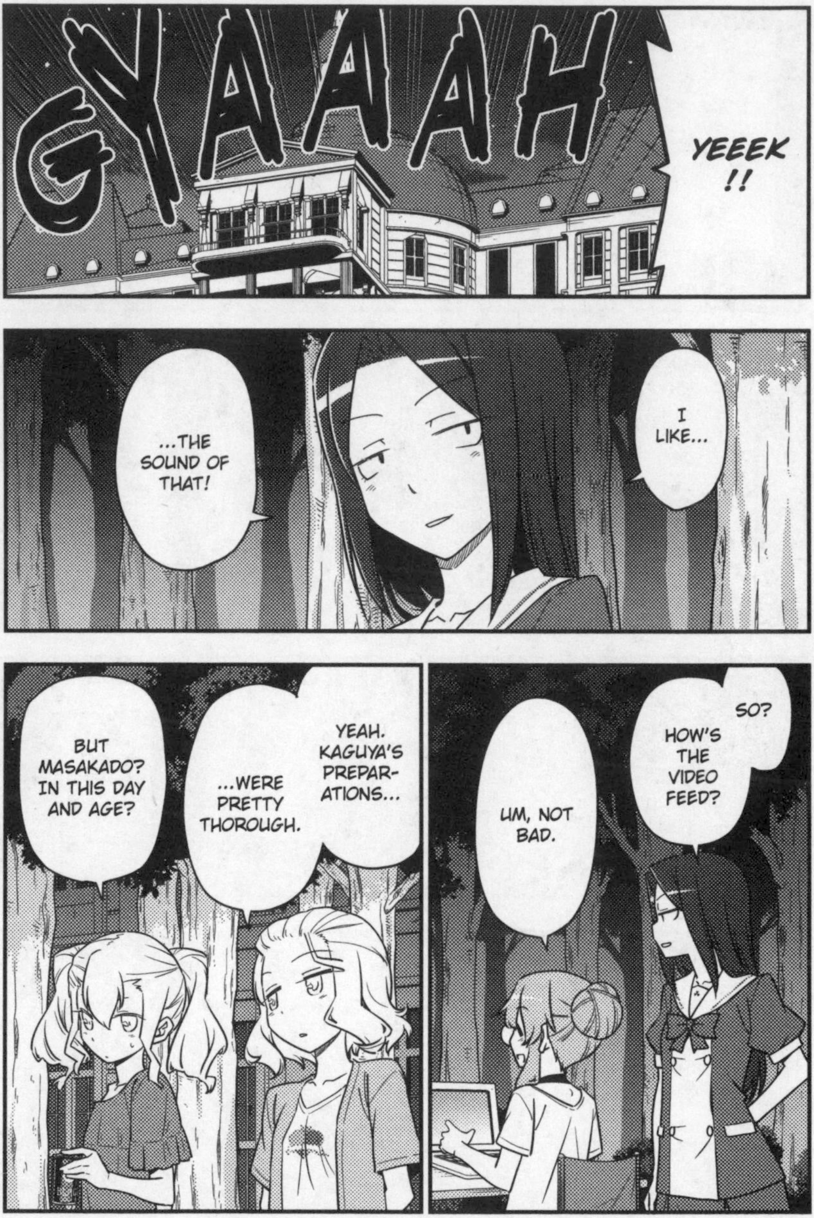
YEEEK !!
GYAAAH
I LIKE...
...THE SOUND OF THAT!
SO? HOW'S THE VIDEO FEED?
UM, NOT BAD.
YEAH. KAGUYA'S PREPARATIONS...
...WERE PRETTY THOROUGH.
BUT MASAKADO? IN THIS DAY AND AGE?

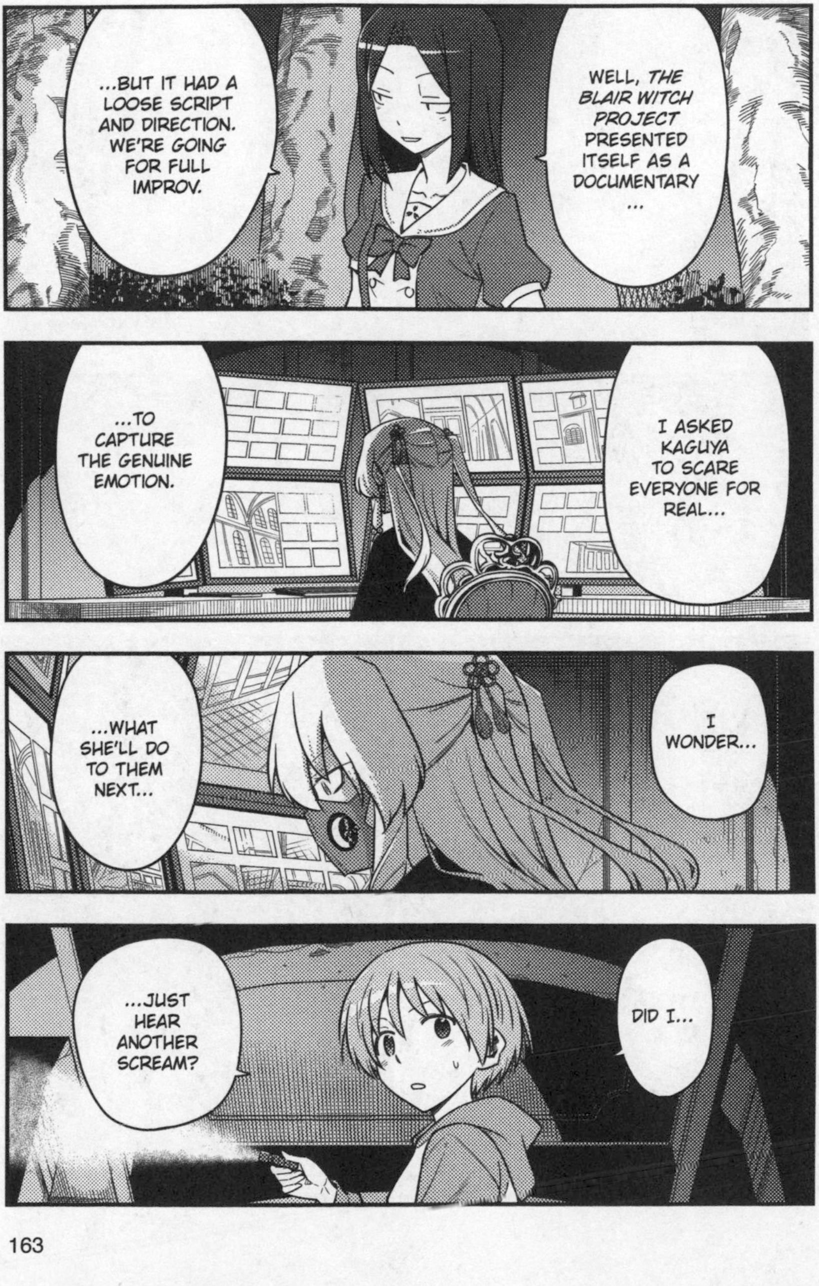
WELL, *THE BLAIR WITCH PROJECT* PRESENTED ITSELF AS A DOCUMENTARY ...
...BUT IT HAD A LOOSE SCRIPT AND DIRECTION. WE'RE GOING FOR FULL IMPROV.
I ASKED KAGUYA TO SCARE EVERYONE FOR REAL...
...TO CAPTURE THE GENUINE EMOTION.
I WONDER...
...WHAT SHE'LL DO TO THEM NEXT...
DID I...
...JUST HEAR ANOTHER SCREAM?

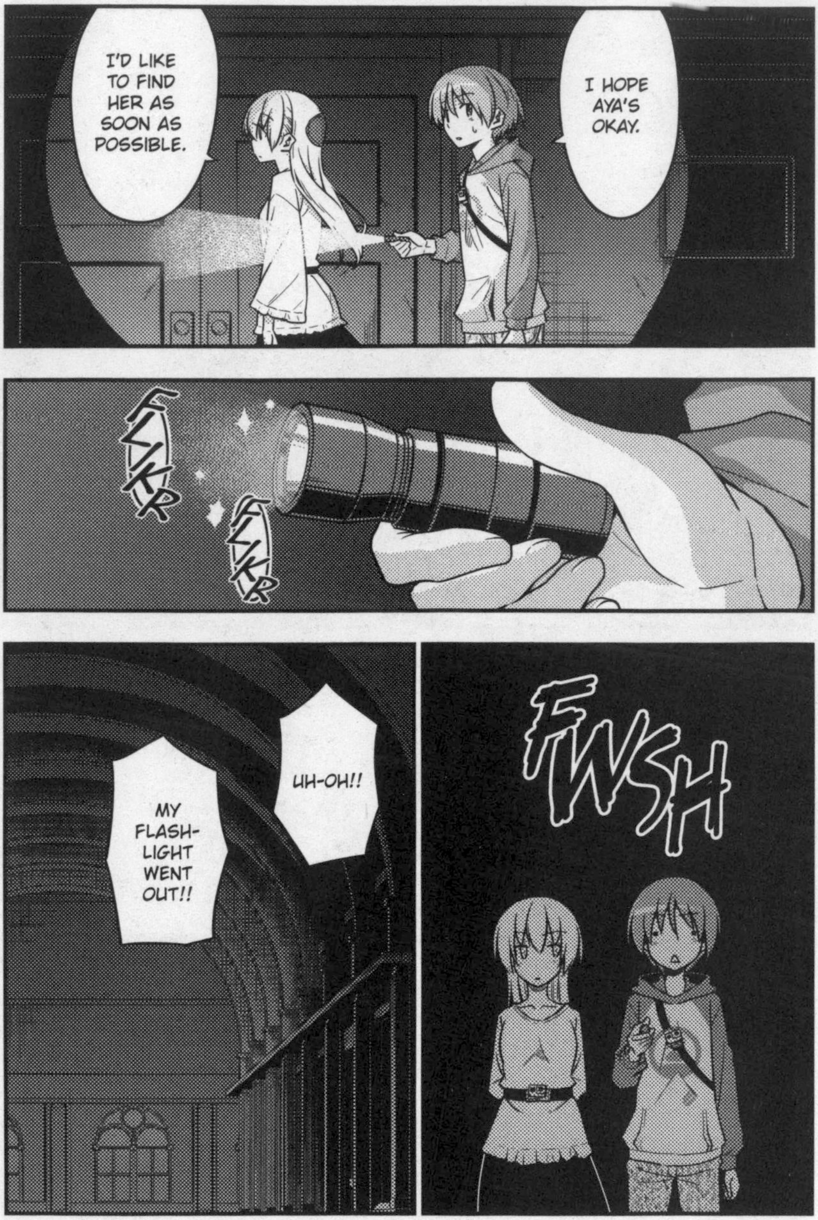
I HOPE AYA'S OKAY.
I'D LIKE TO FIND HER AS SOON AS POSSIBLE.
FLIKR
FLIKR
FWSH
UH-OH!!
MY FLASH-LIGHT WENT OUT!!

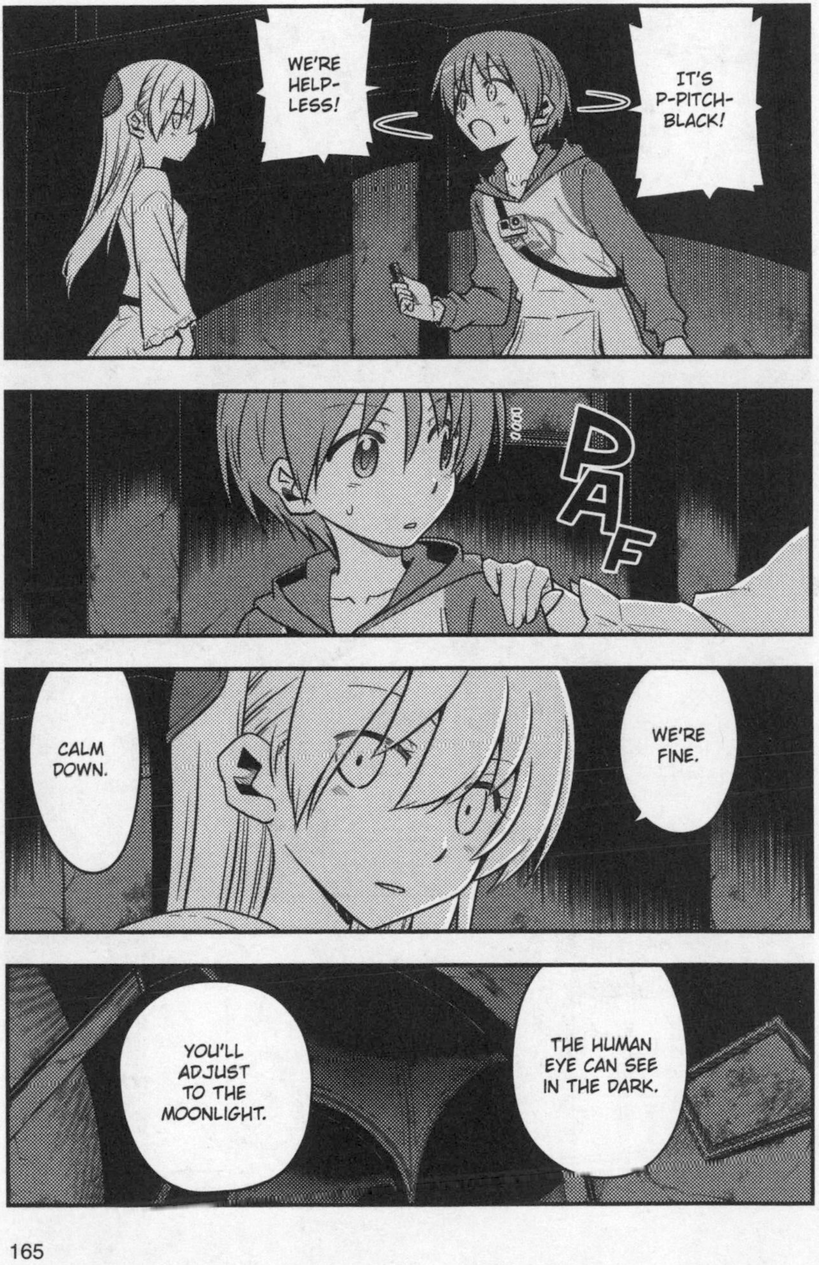
IT'S P-PITCH-BLACK!
WE'RE HELPLESS!
DAF
WE'RE FINE.
CALM DOWN.
THE HUMAN EYE CAN SEE IN THE DARK.
YOU'LL ADJUST TO THE MOONLIGHT.

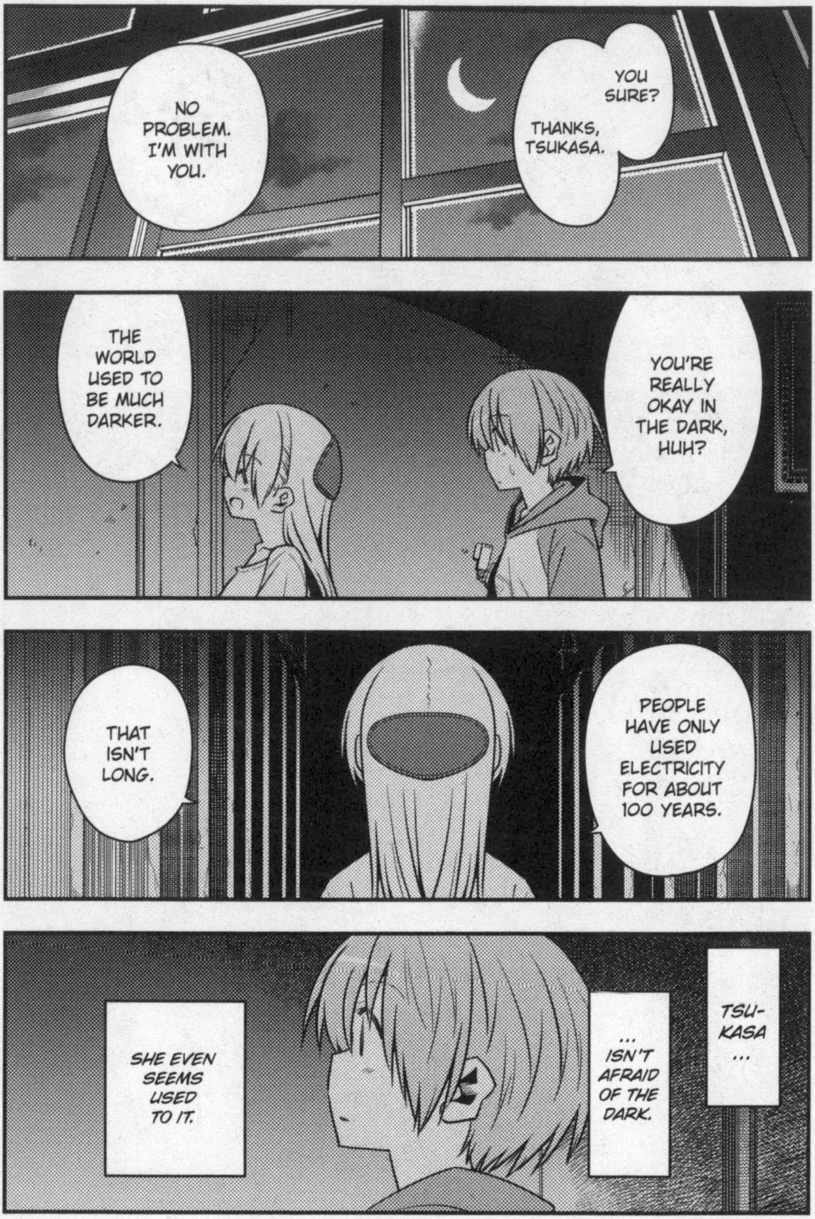
YOU SURE?
THANKS, TSUKASA.
NO PROBLEM. I'M WITH YOU.
YOU'RE REALLY OKAY IN THE DARK, HUH?
THE WORLD USED TO BE MUCH DARKER.
PEOPLE HAVE ONLY USED ELECTRICITY FOR ABOUT 100 YEARS.
THAT ISN'T LONG.
TSU-KASA...
...ISN'T AFRAID OF THE DARK.
SHE EVEN SEEMS USED TO IT.

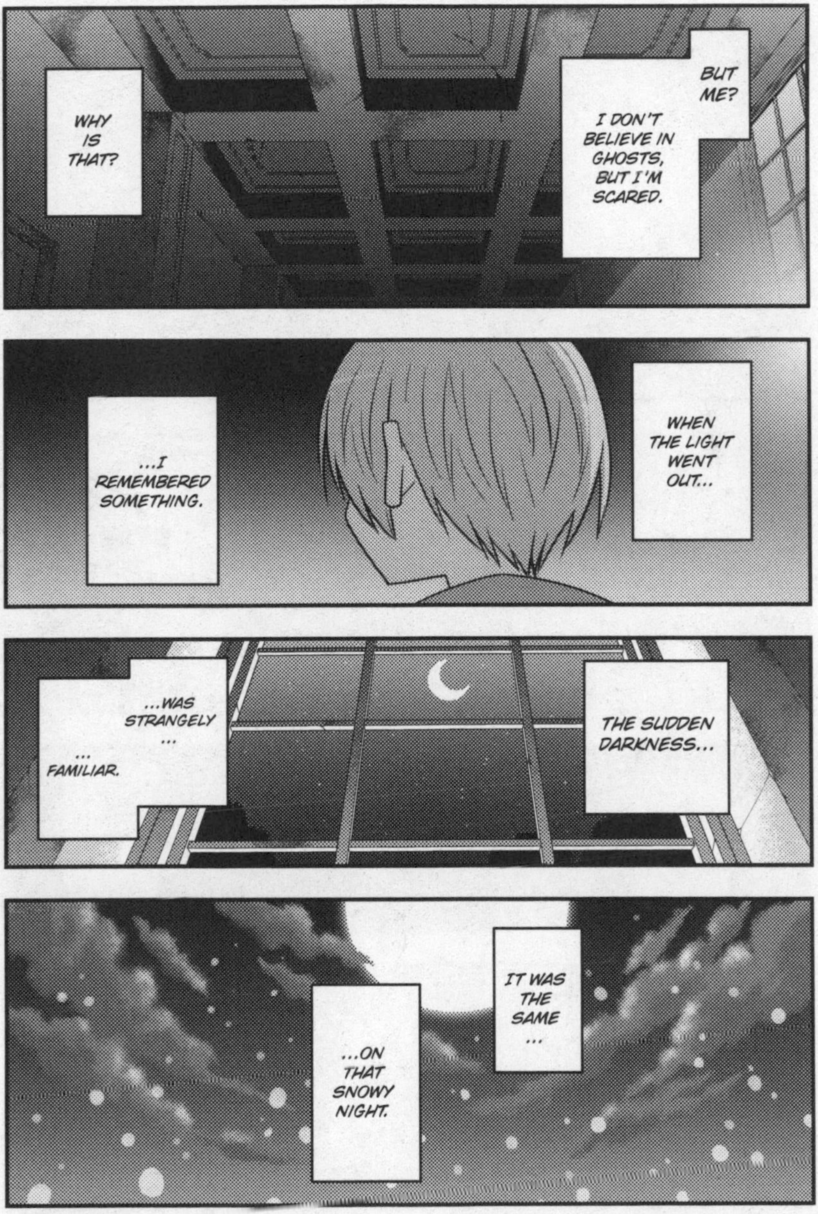
BUT ME?
I DON'T BELIEVE IN GHOSTS, BUT I'M SCARED.
WHY IS THAT?
WHEN THE LIGHT WENT OUT...
...I REMEMBERED SOMETHING.
THE SUDDEN DARKNESS...
...WAS STRANGELY ... ... FAMILIAR.
IT WAS THE SAME ...
...ON THAT SNOWY NIGHT.

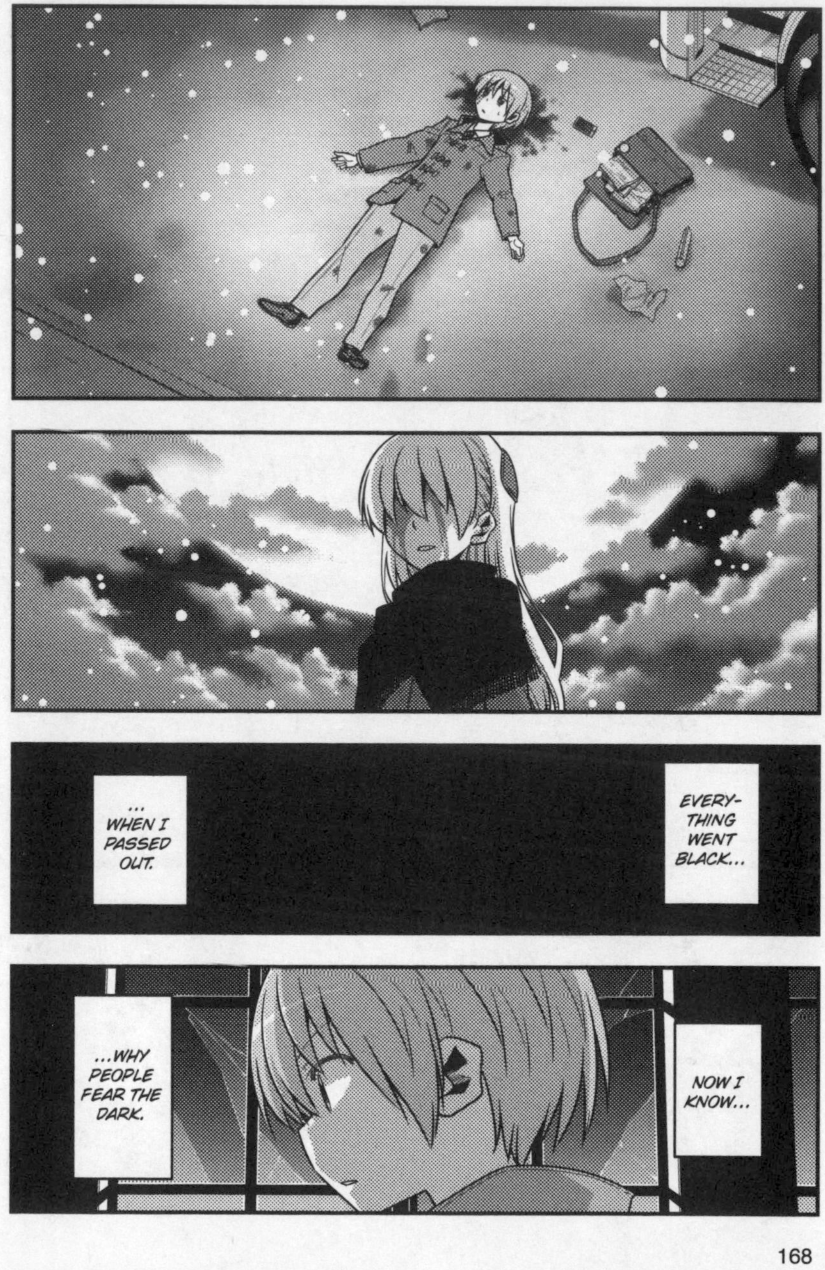
EVERY-THING WENT BLACK...
... WHEN I PASSED OUT.
NOW I KNOW...
...WHY PEOPLE FEAR THE DARK.

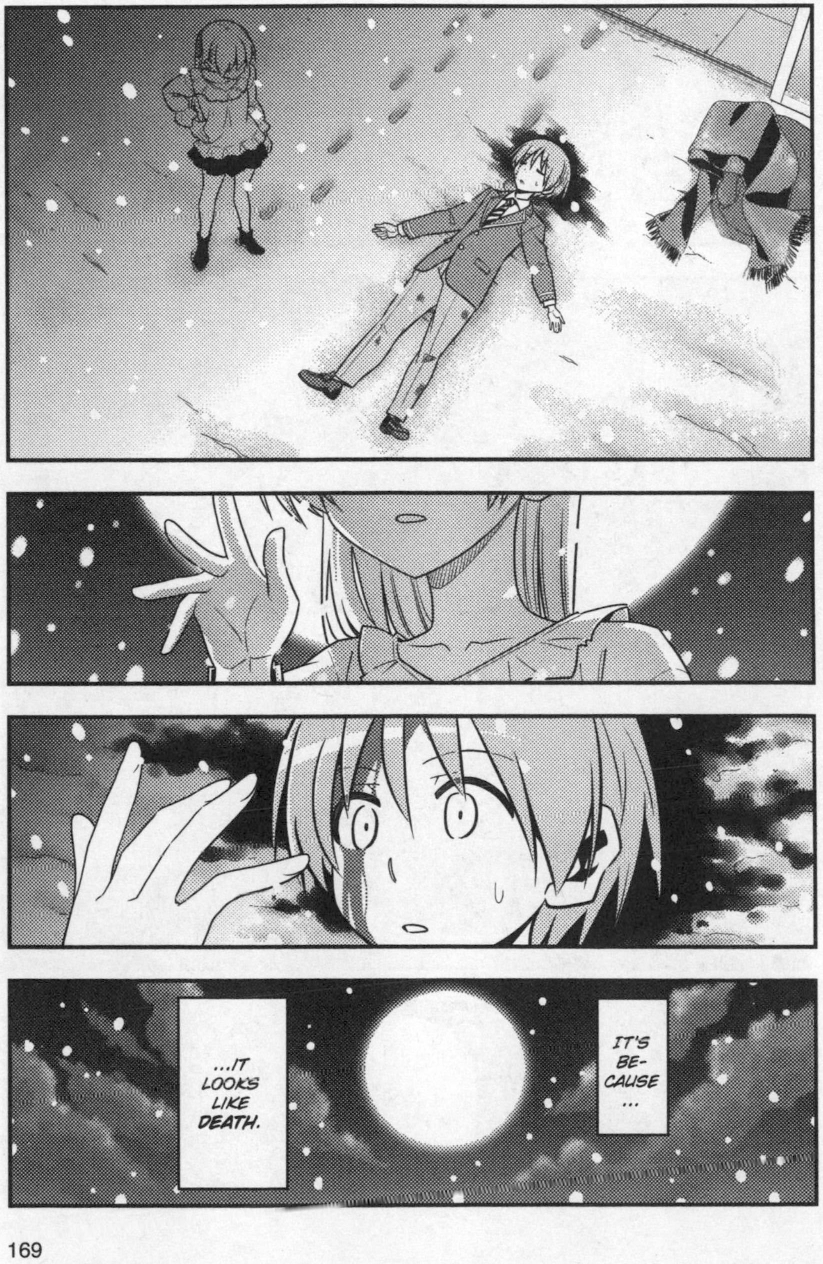
IT'S BE-CAUSE ...
...IT LOOKS LIKE DEATH.

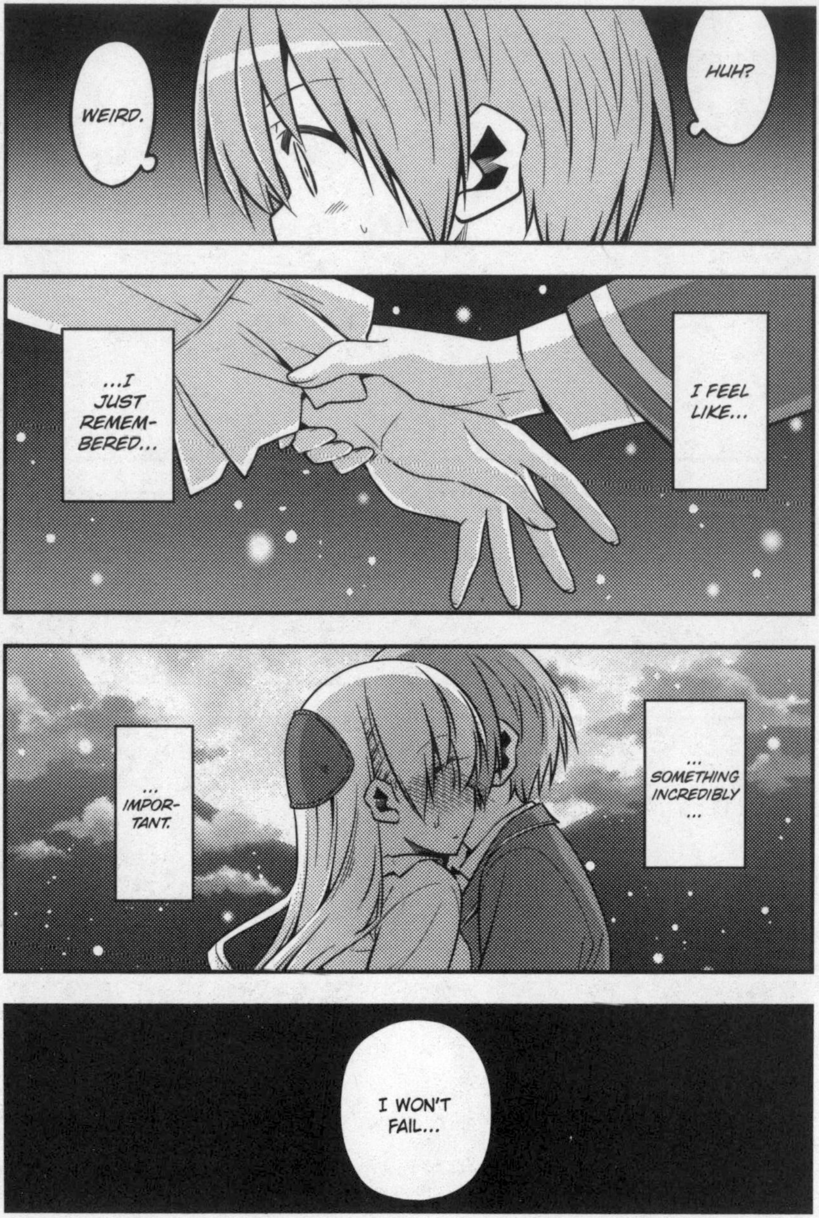
HUH?
WEIRD.
I FEEL LIKE...
...I JUST REMEMBERED...
... SOMETHING INCREDIBLY ...
... IMPORTANT.
I WON'T FAIL...

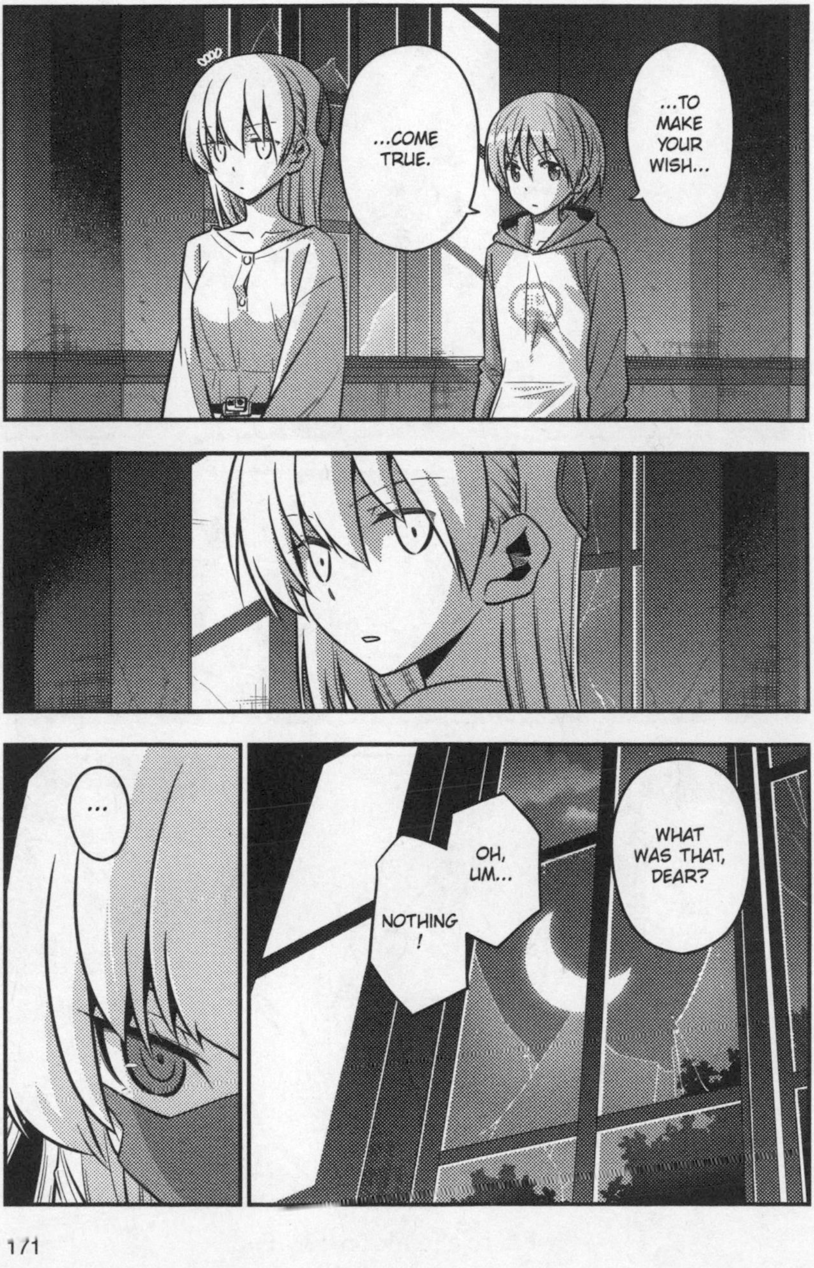
...TO MAKE YOUR WISH...
...COME TRUE.
WHAT WAS THAT, DEAR?
OH, UM...
NOTHING!
...

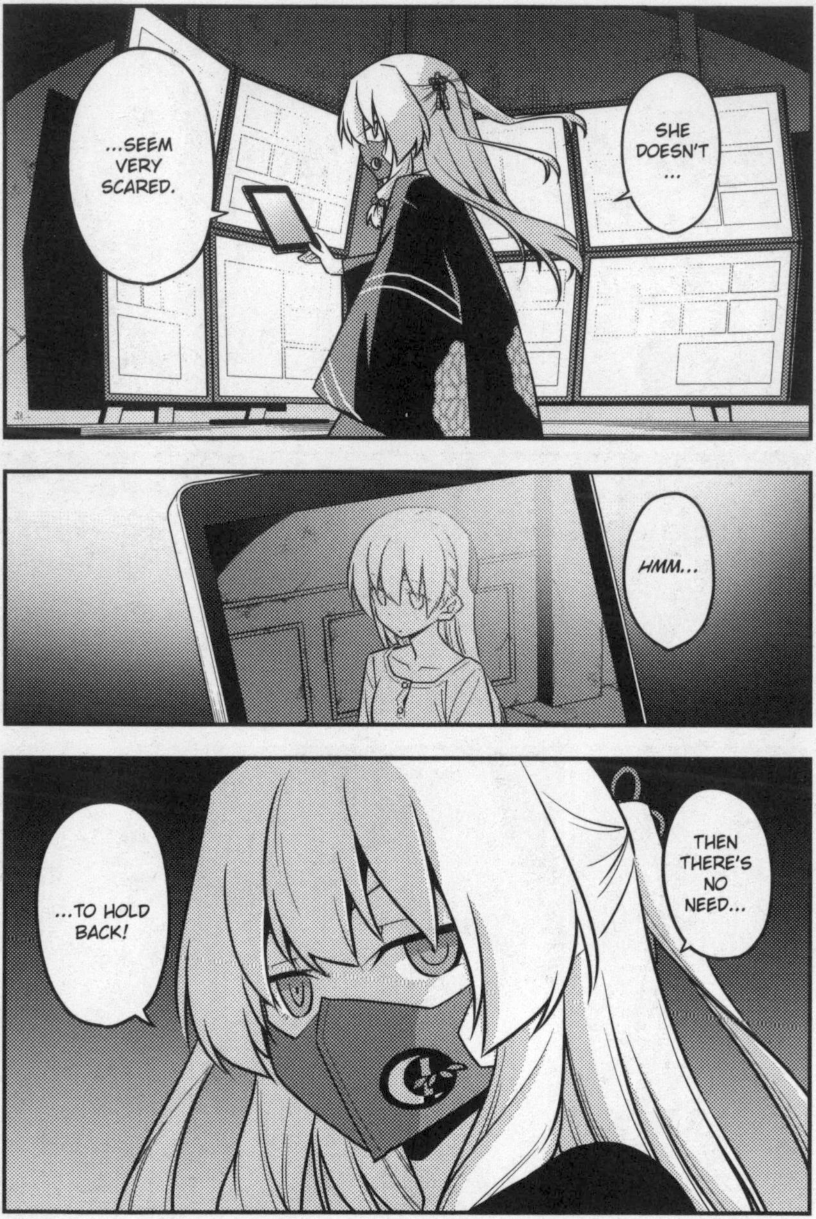
SHE DOESN'T ...
...SEEM VERY SCARED.
HMM...
THEN THERE'S NO NEED...
...TO HOLD BACK!

—Fly Me to the Moon 13 / End—

Chapter 123 ½: "Growing Girls Need Sleep"

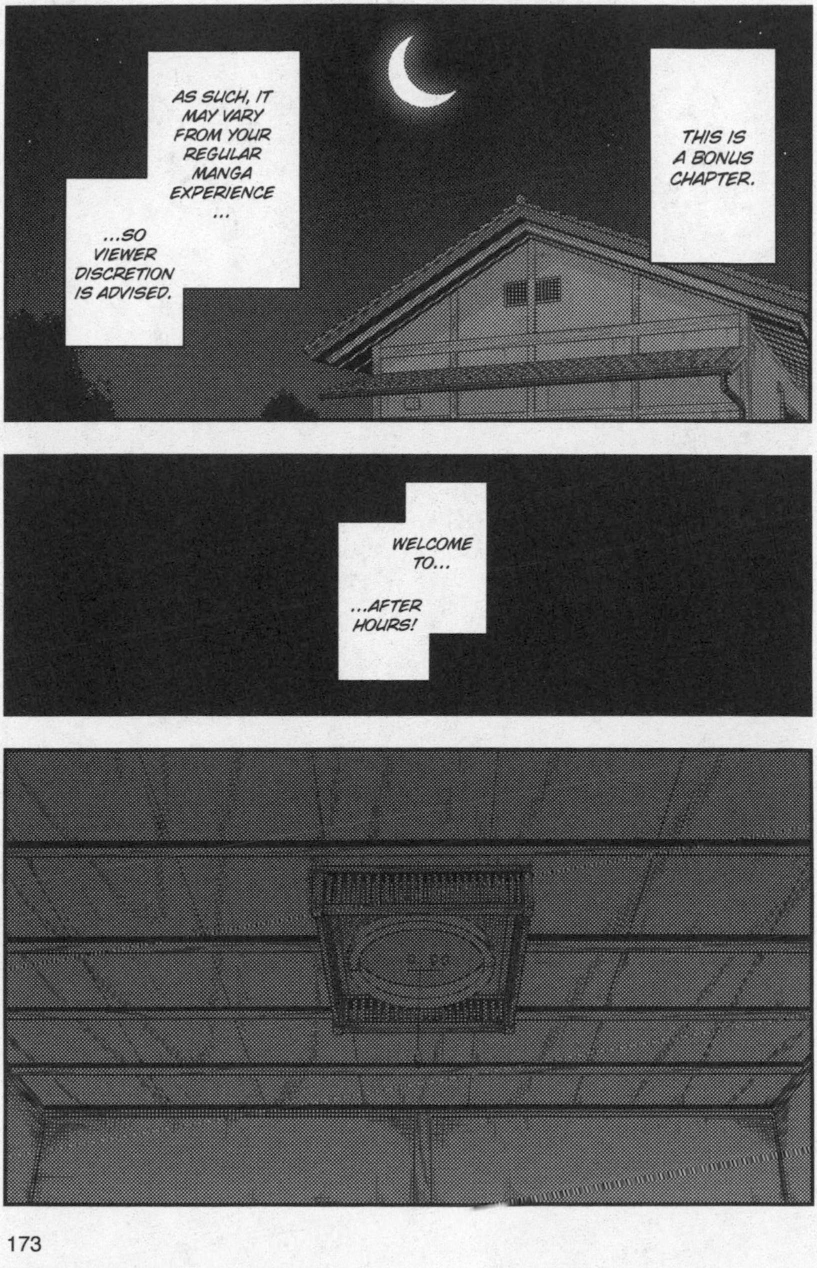

THIS IS A BONUS CHAPTER.
AS SUCH, IT MAY VARY FROM YOUR REGULAR MANGA EXPERIENCE...
...SO VIEWER DISCRETION IS ADVISED.
WELCOME TO...
...AFTER HOURS!

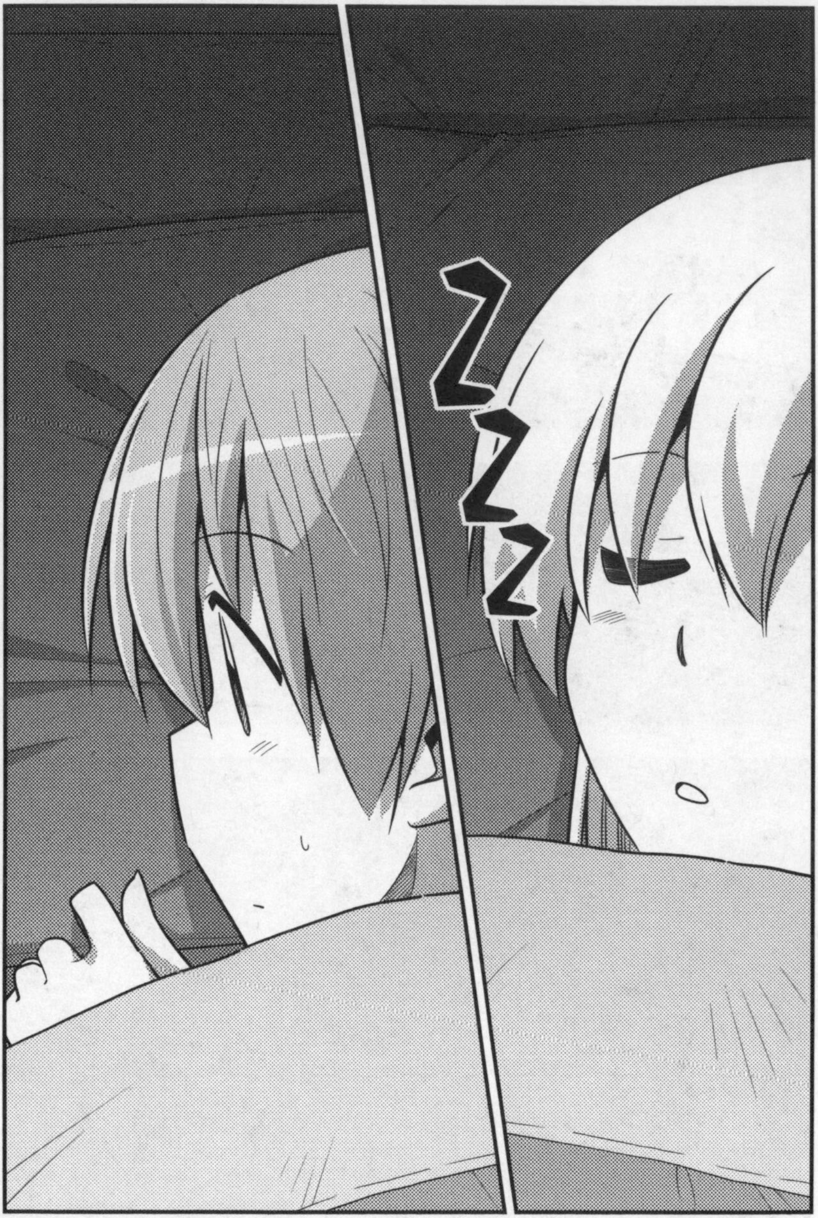
ZZZ

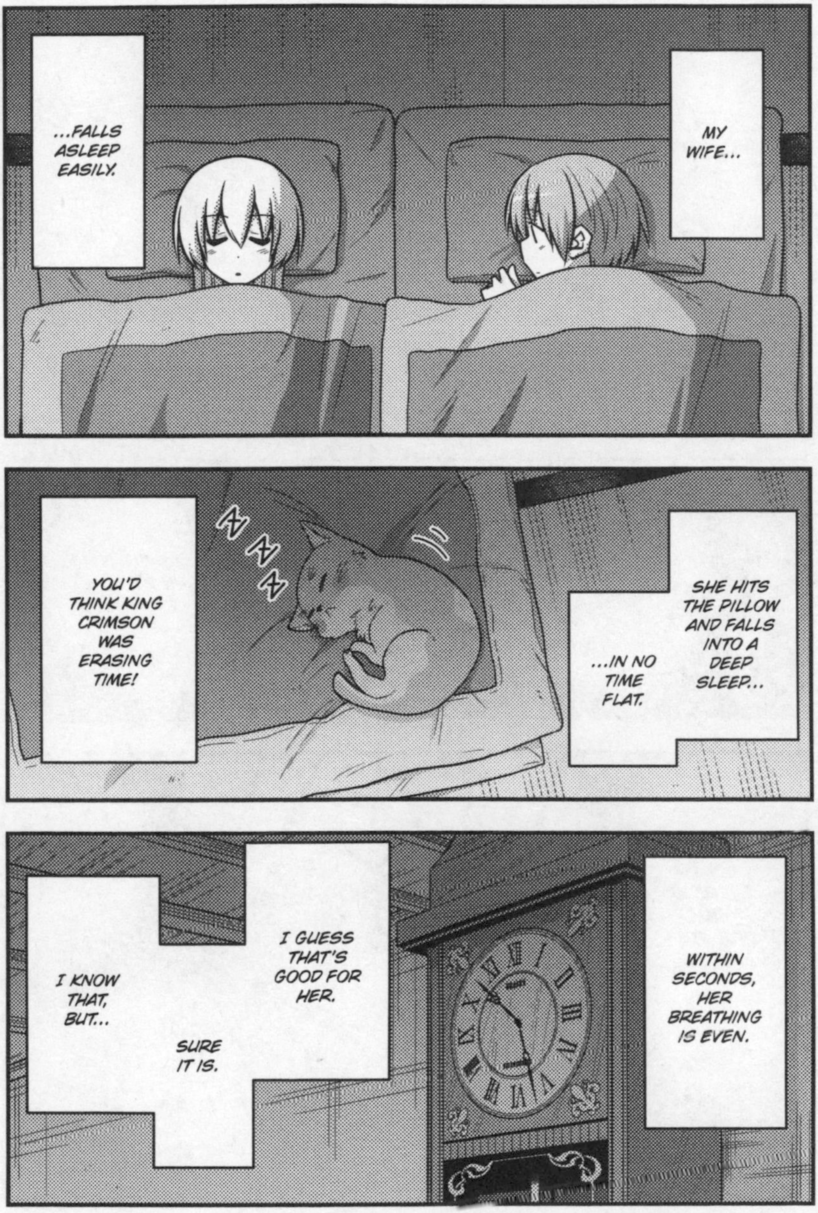
MY WIFE...
...FALLS ASLEEP EASILY.
SHE HITS THE PILLOW AND FALLS INTO A DEEP SLEEP...
...IN NO TIME FLAT.
YOU'D THINK KING CRIMSON WAS ERASING TIME!
WITHIN SECONDS, HER BREATHING IS EVEN.
I GUESS THAT'S GOOD FOR HER.
SURE IT IS.
I KNOW THAT, BUT...

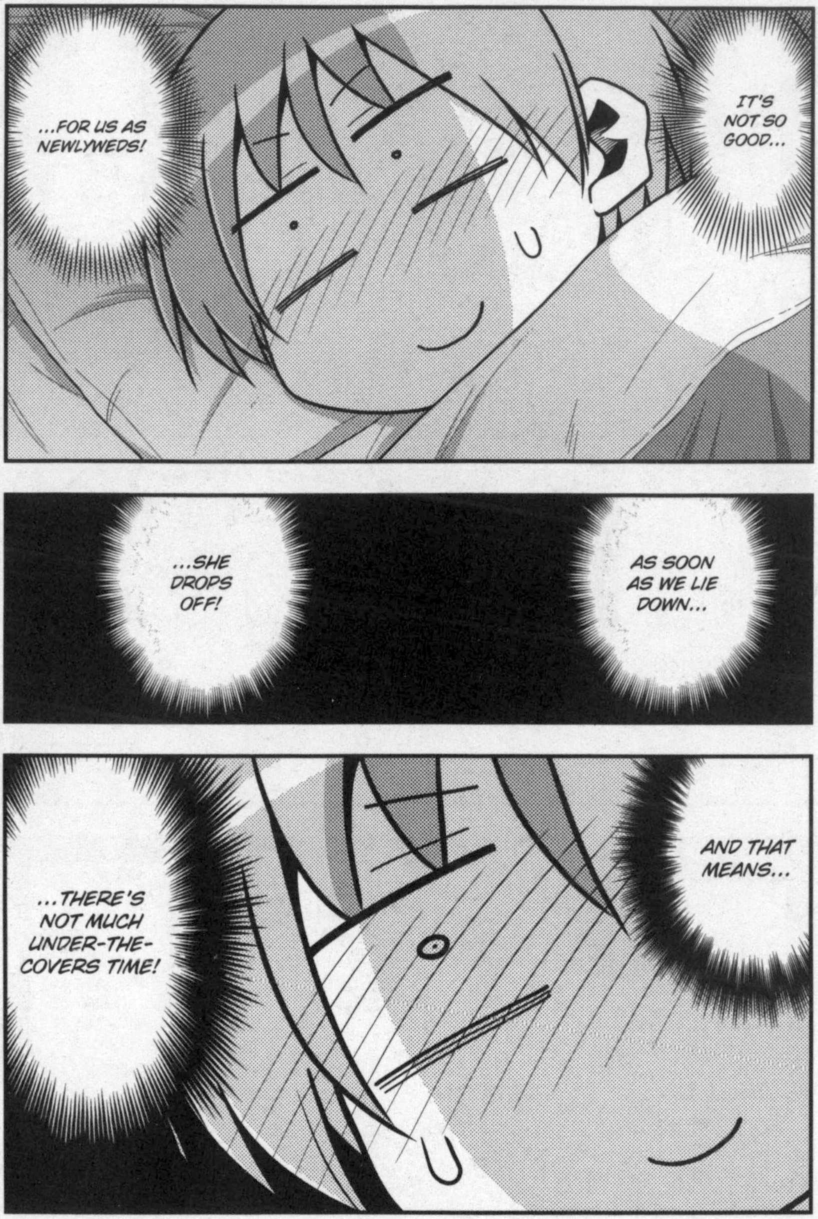
IT'S NOT SO GOOD...
...FOR US AS NEWLYWEDS!
AS SOON AS WE LIE DOWN...
...SHE DROPS OFF!
AND THAT MEANS...
...THERE'S NOT MUCH UNDER-THE-COVERS TIME!

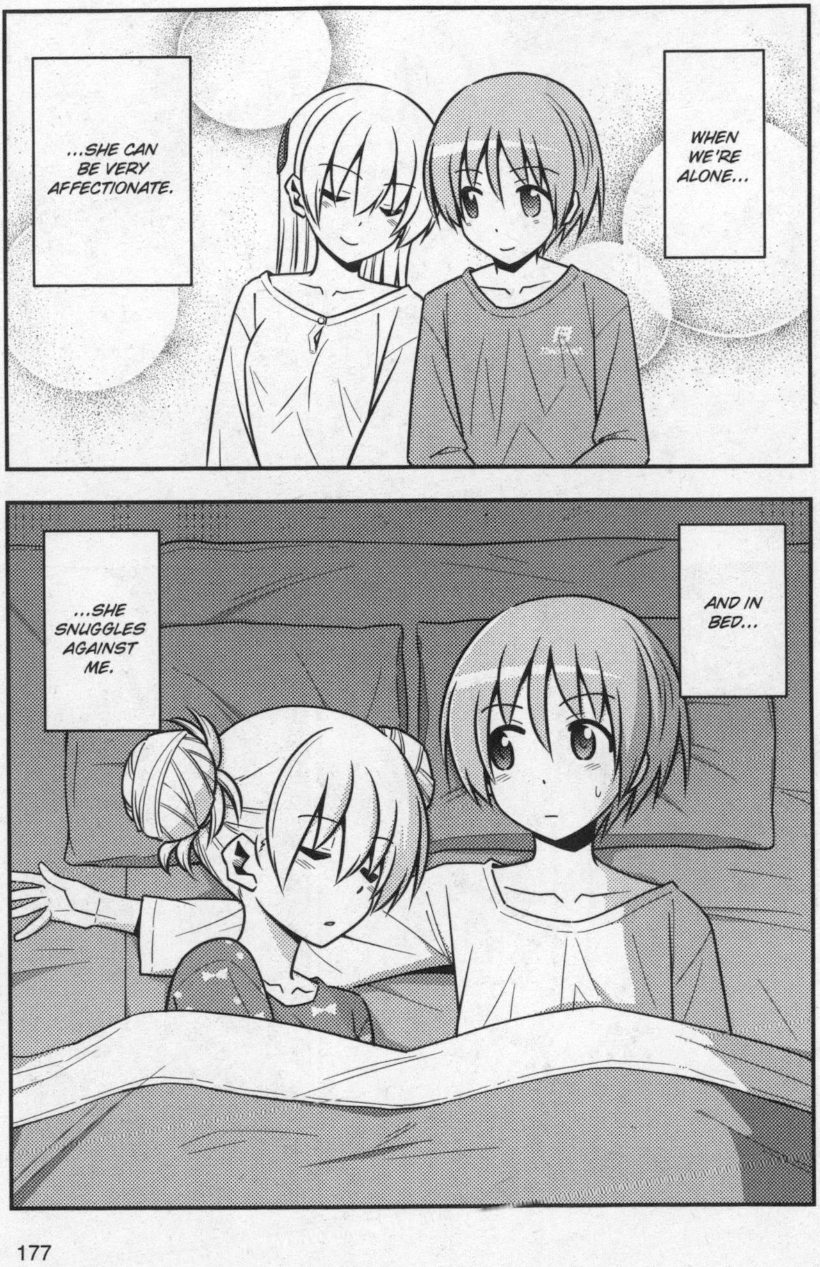
WHEN WE'RE ALONE...
...SHE CAN BE VERY AFFECTIONATE.
AND IN BED...
...SHE SNUGGLES AGAINST ME.

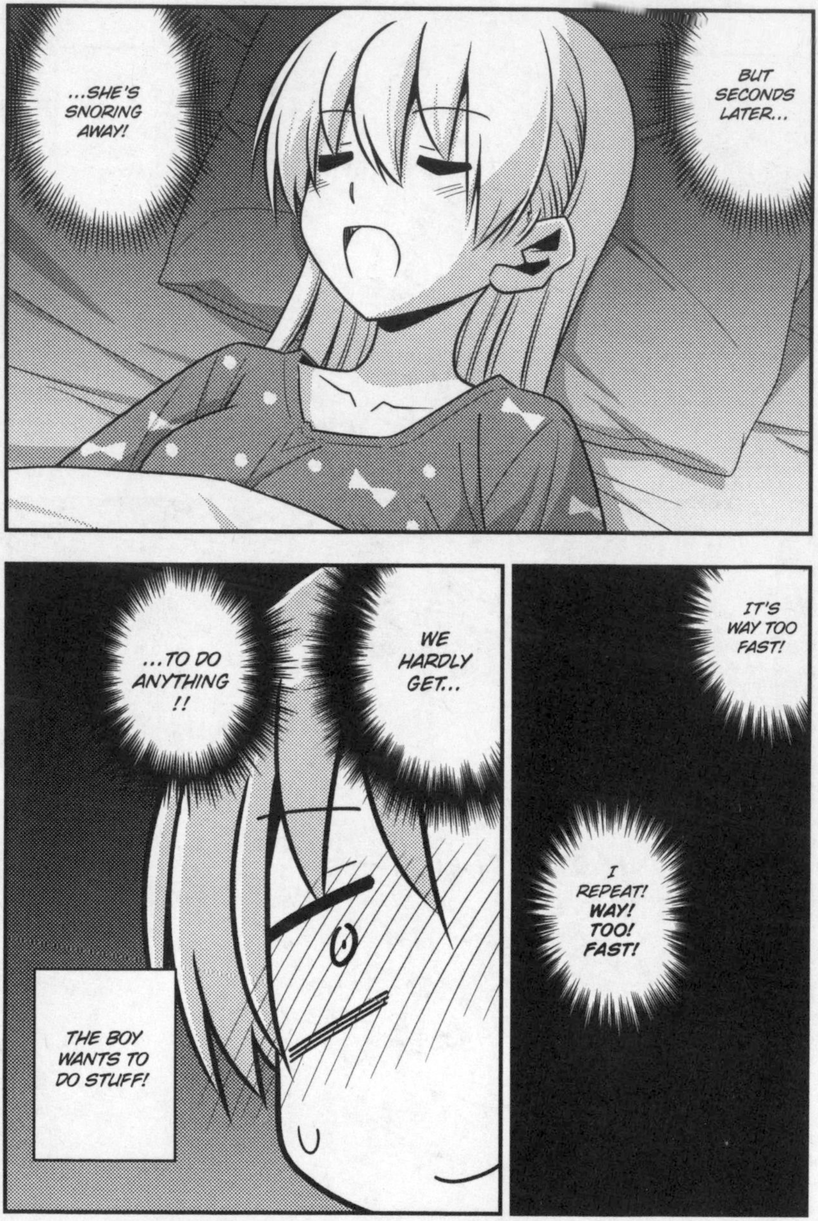
BUT SECONDS LATER...
...SHE'S SNORING AWAY!
IT'S WAY TOO FAST!
I REPEAT! WAY! TOO! FAST!
WE HARDLY GET...
...TO DO ANYTHING!!
THE BOY WANTS TO DO STUFF!

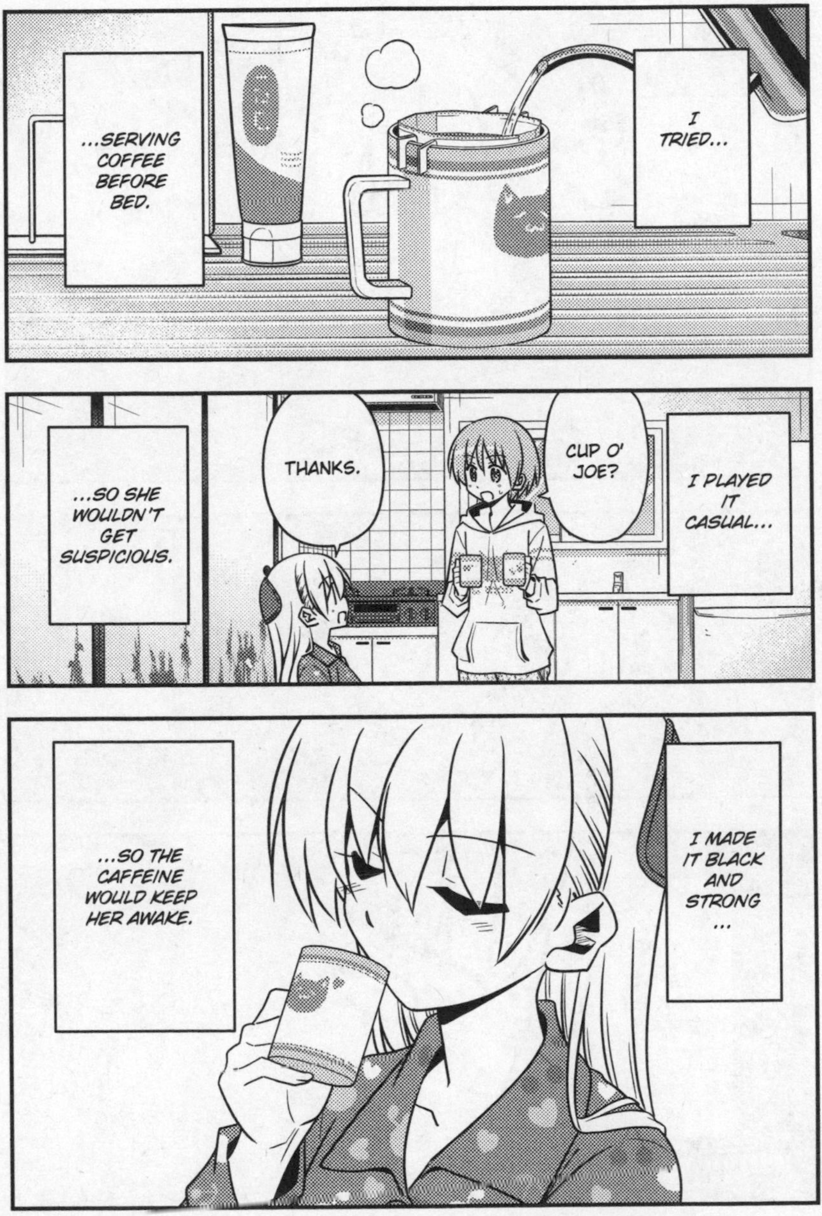
I TRIED...
...SERVING COFFEE BEFORE BED.
I PLAYED IT CASUAL...
CUP O' JOE?
THANKS.
...SO SHE WOULDN'T GET SUSPICIOUS.
I MADE IT BLACK AND STRONG...
...SO THE CAFFEINE WOULD KEEP HER AWAKE.

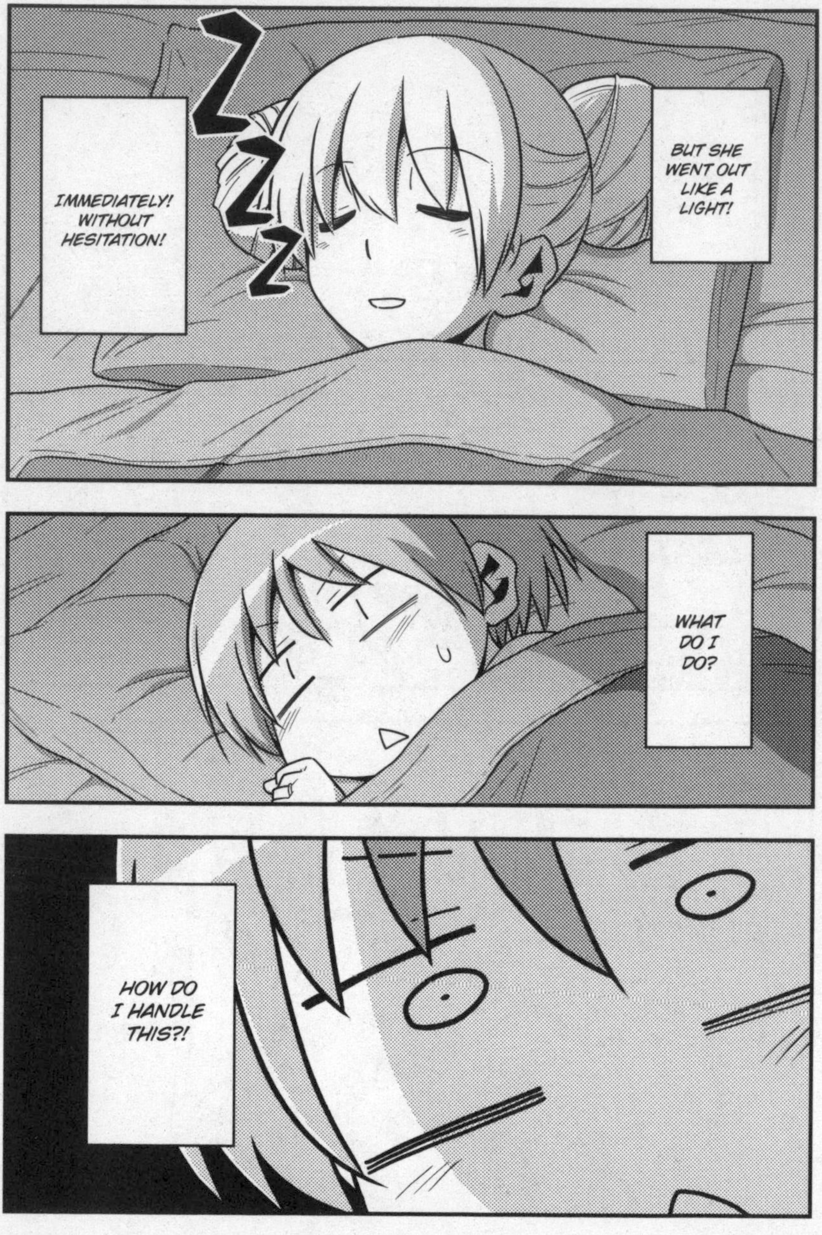
BUT SHE WENT OUT LIKE A LIGHT!
IMMEDIATELY! WITHOUT HESITATION!
WHAT DO I DO?
HOW DO I HANDLE THIS?!

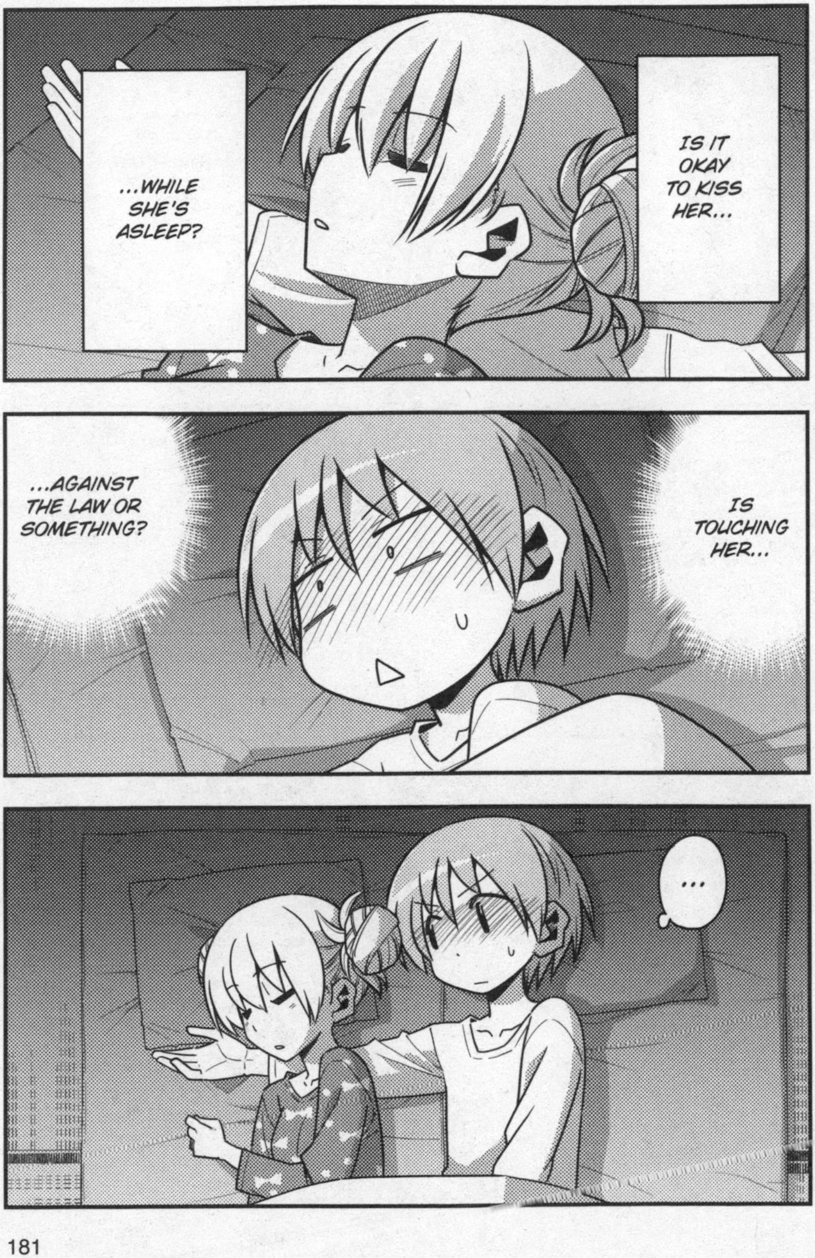
IS IT OKAY TO KISS HER...
...WHILE SHE'S ASLEEP?
IS TOUCHING HER...
...AGAINST THE LAW OR SOMETHING?
...

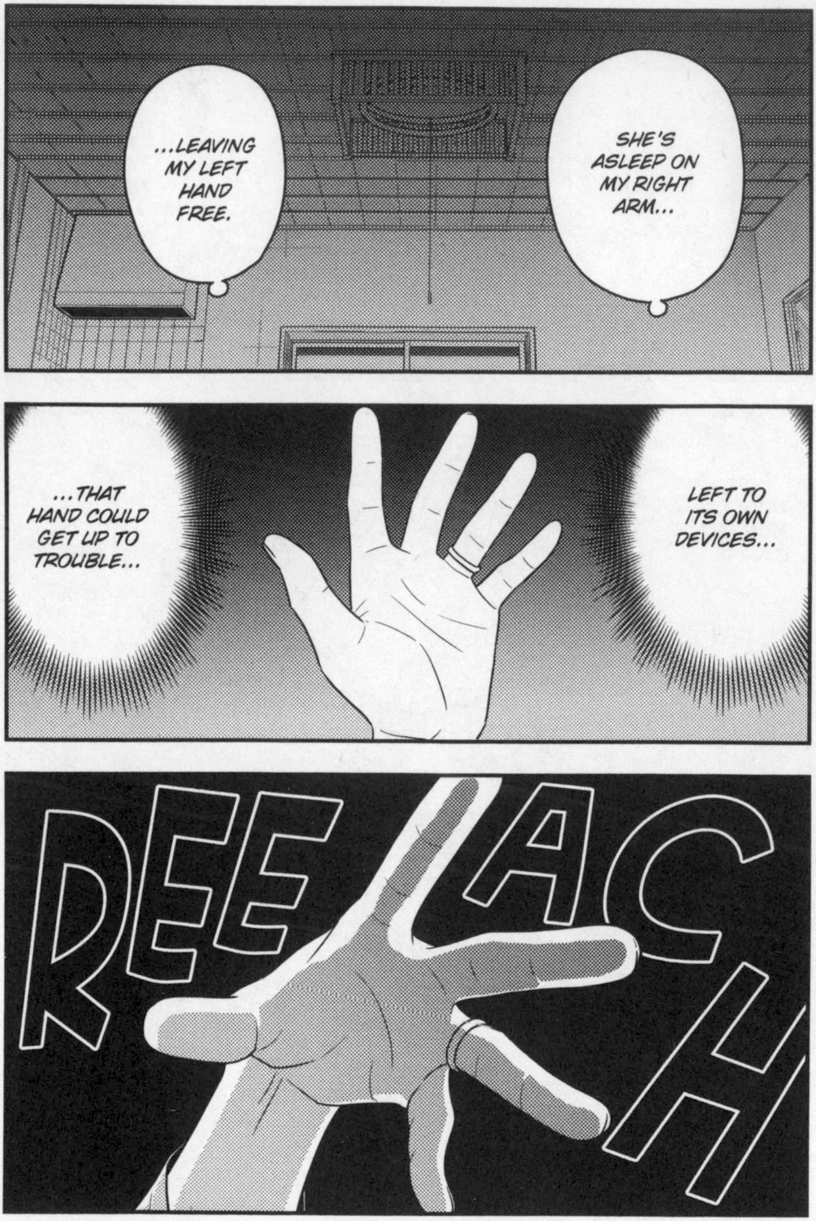
SHE'S ASLEEP ON MY RIGHT ARM...
...LEAVING MY LEFT HAND FREE.
LEFT TO ITS OWN DEVICES...
...THAT HAND COULD GET UP TO TROUBLE...
REEACH

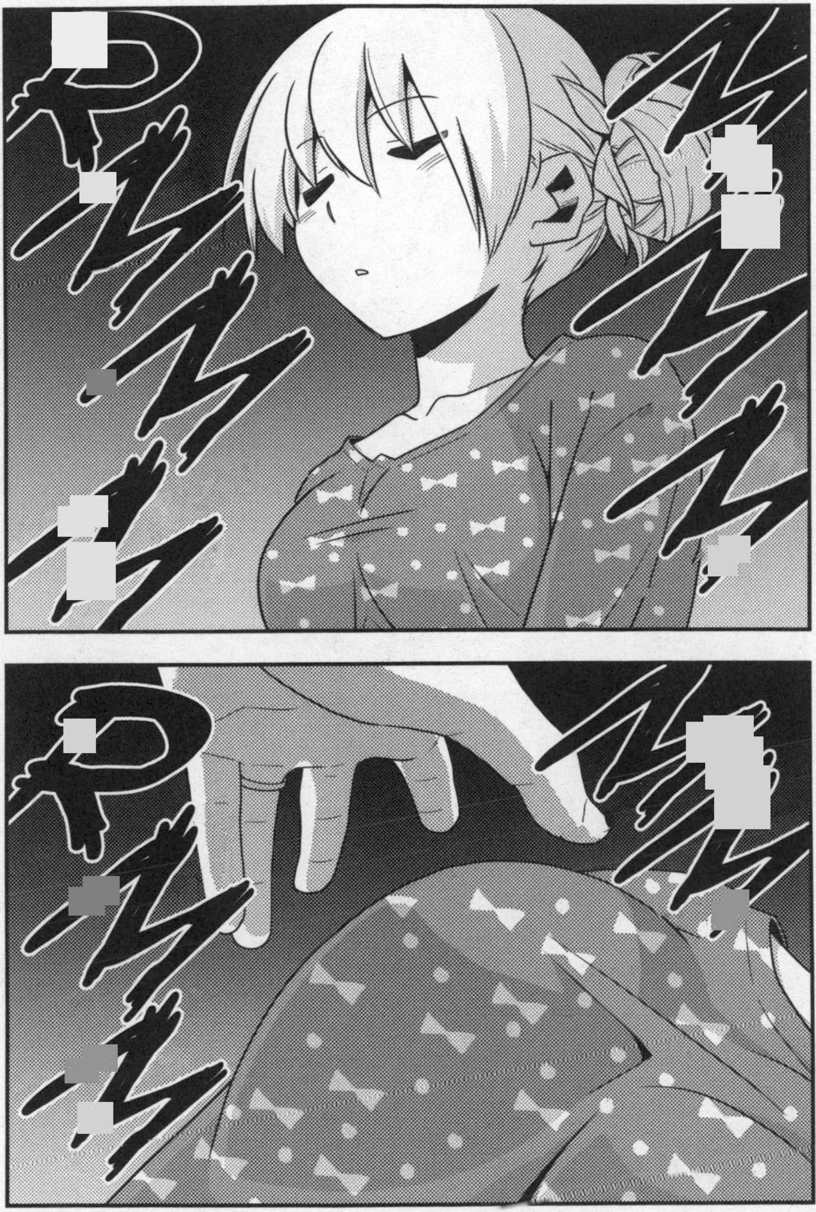

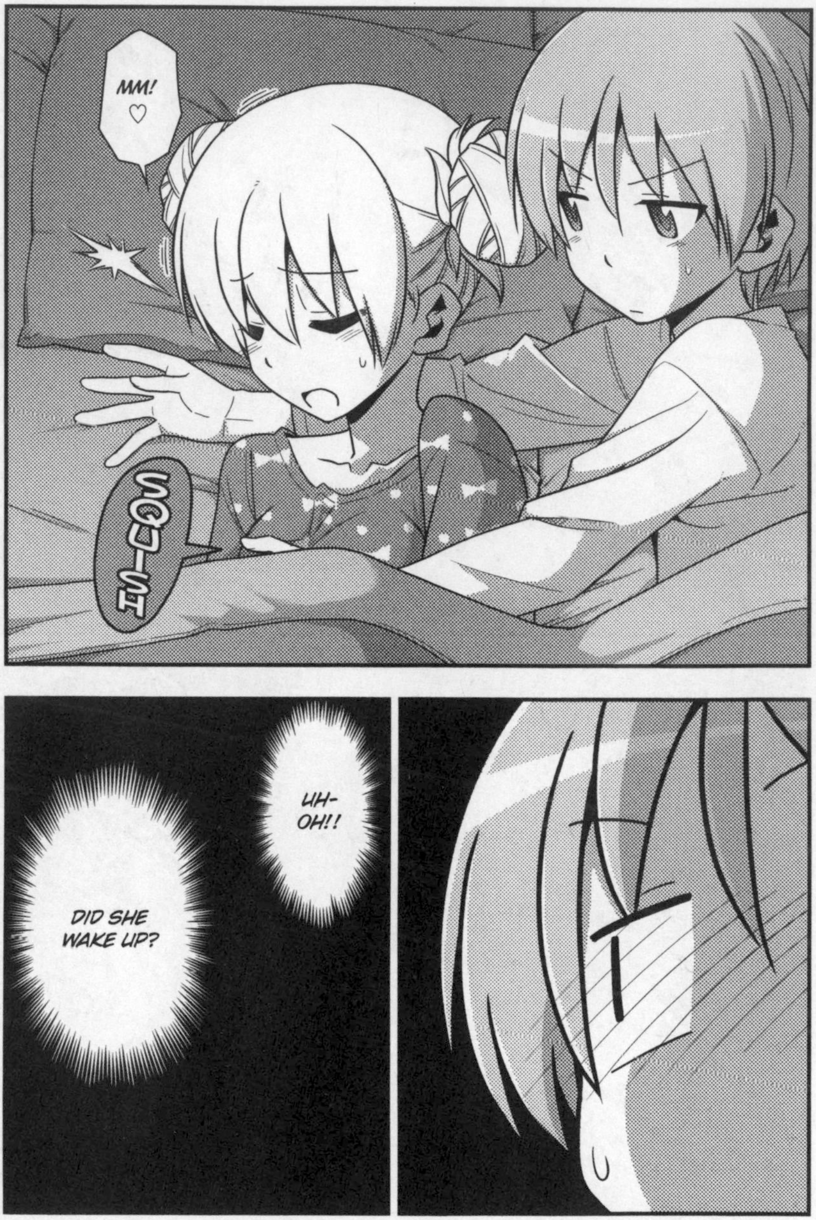
MM! ♡
SQUISH
UH-OH!!
DID SHE WAKE UP?

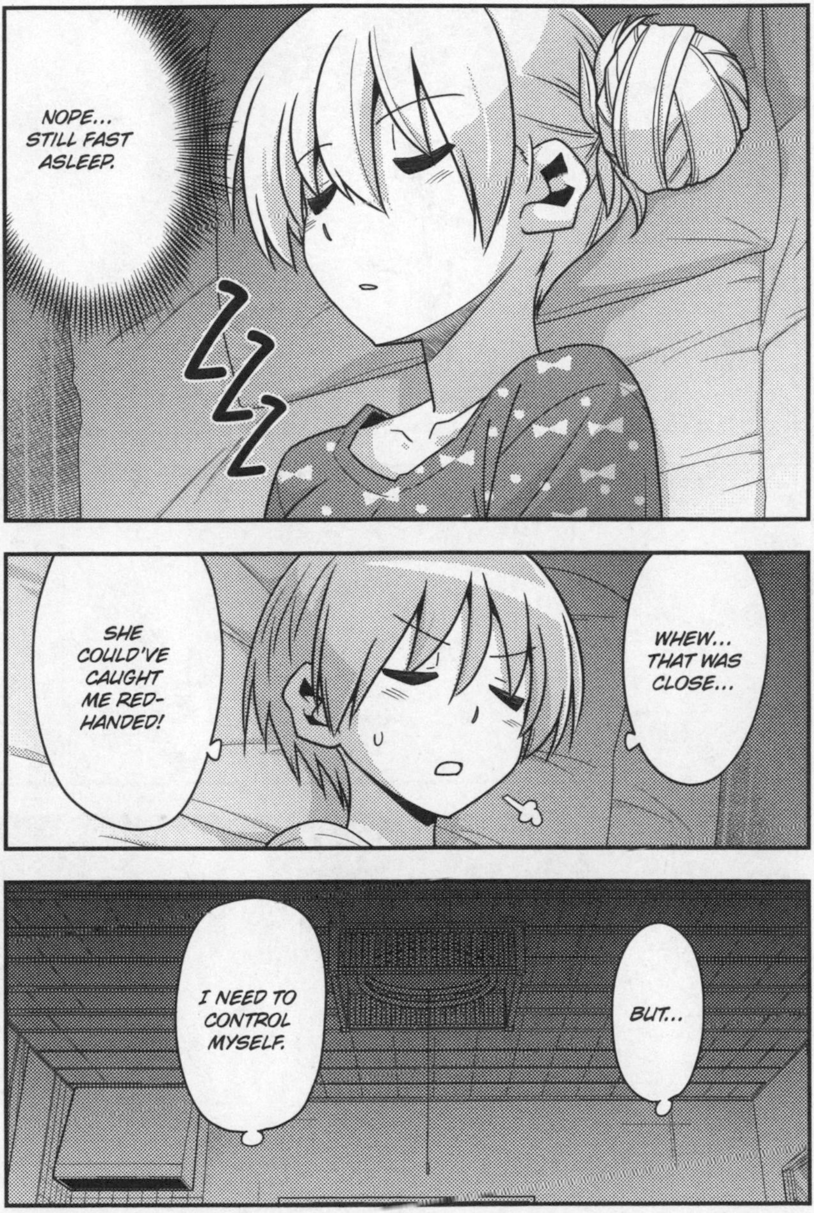
NOPE... STILL FAST ASLEEP.
WHEW... THAT WAS CLOSE...
SHE COULD'VE CAUGHT ME RED-HANDED!
BUT...
I NEED TO CONTROL MYSELF.

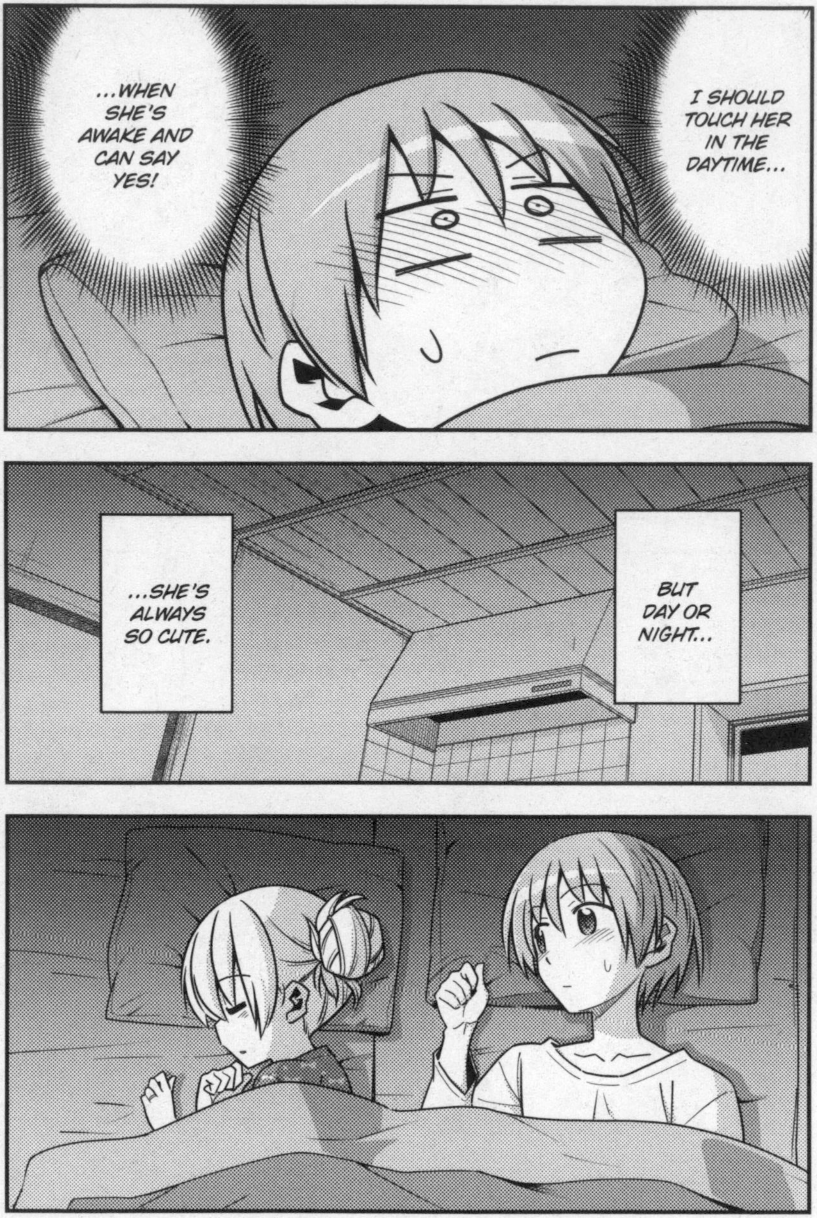
I SHOULD TOUCH HER IN THE DAYTIME...
...WHEN SHE'S AWAKE AND CAN SAY YES!
BUT DAY OR NIGHT...
...SHE'S ALWAYS SO CUTE.

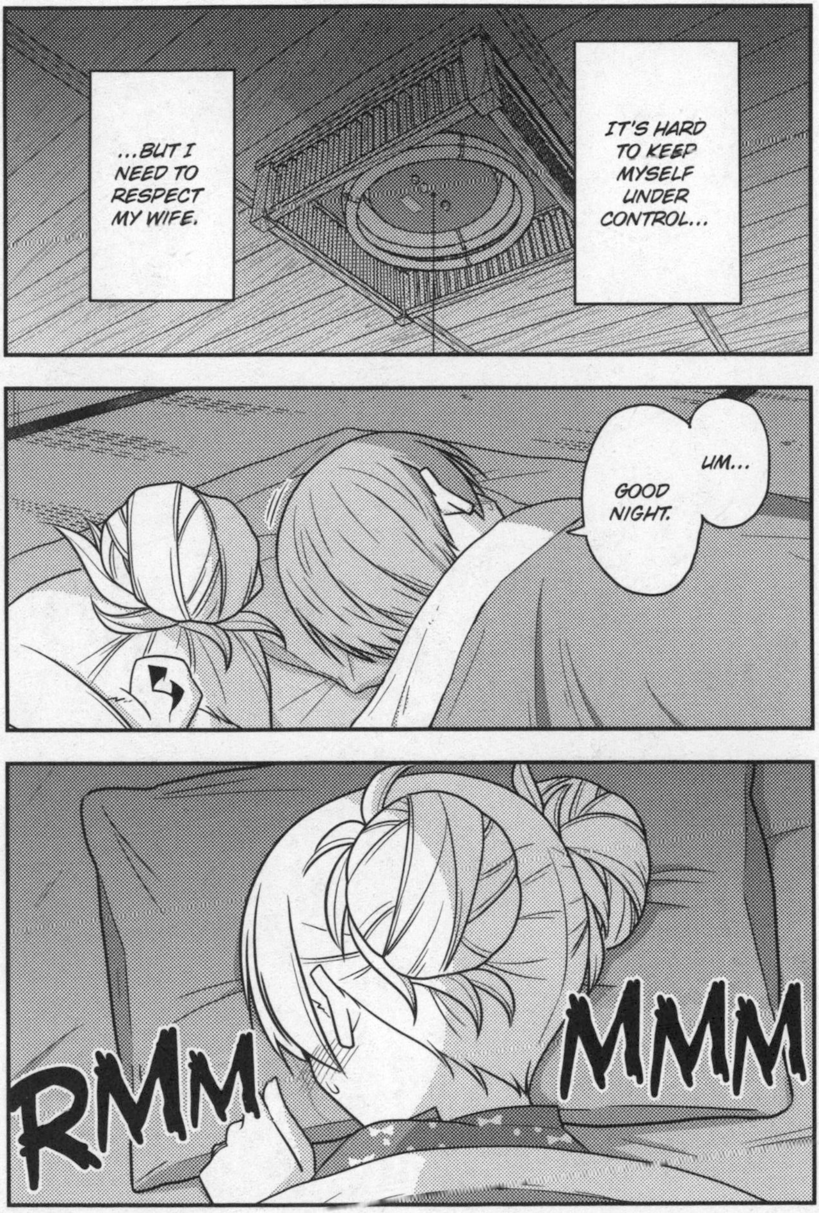
IT'S HARD TO KEEP MYSELF UNDER CONTROL...
...BUT I NEED TO RESPECT MY WIFE.
UM... GOOD NIGHT.
RMM MMM

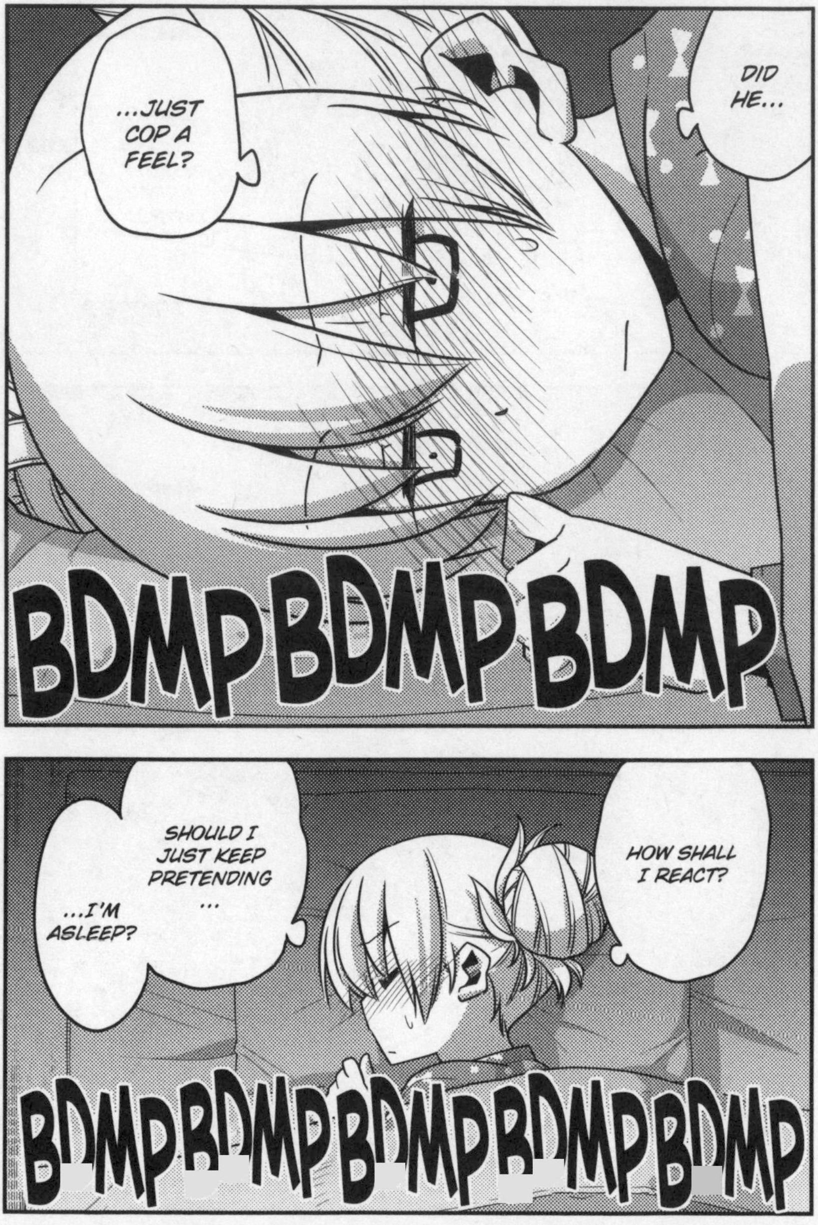
DID HE...
...JUST COP A FEEL?
BDMP BDMP BDMP
HOW SHALL I REACT?
SHOULD I JUST KEEP PRETENDING...
...I'M ASLEEP?
BDMP BDMP BDMP BDMP BDMP

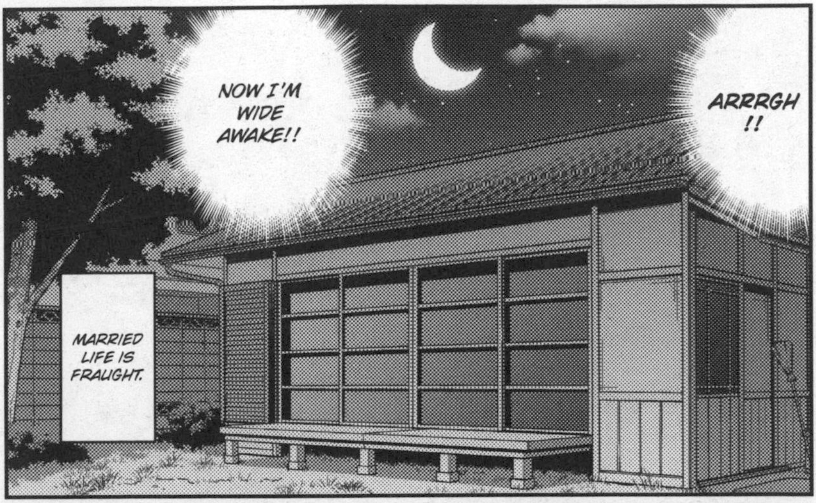
ARRRGH !!
NOW I'M WIDE AWAKE!!
MARRIED LIFE IS FRAUGHT.

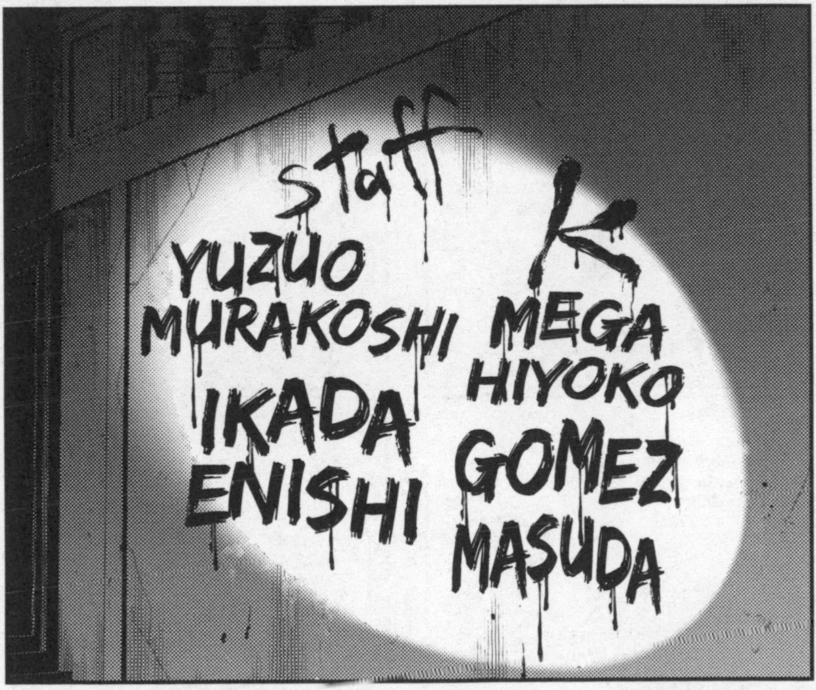
staff K
YUZUO MURAKOSHI
IKADA
ENISHI
MEGA
HIYOKO
GOMEZ
MASUDA

Chapter 123 ½ / End

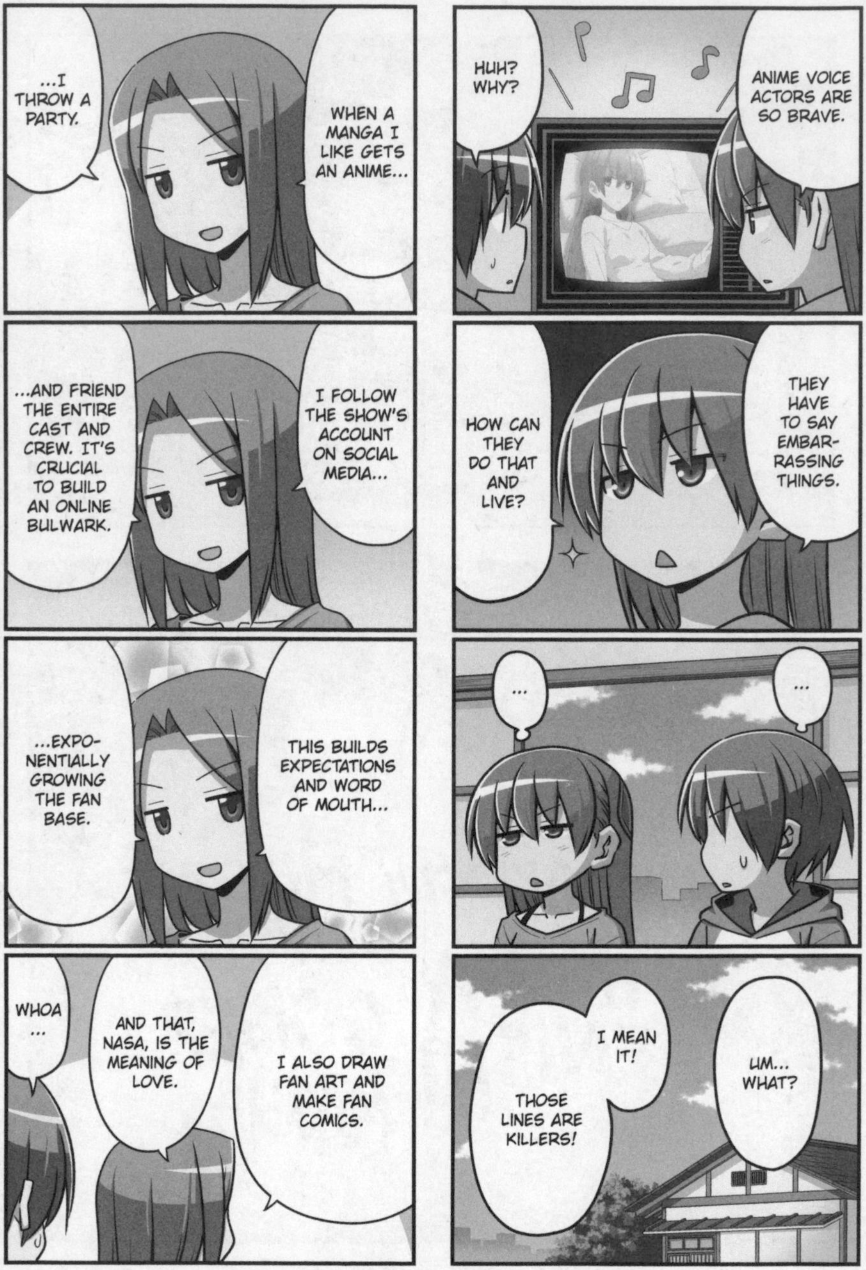
ANIME VOICE ACTORS ARE SO BRAVE.
HUH? WHY?
THEY HAVE TO SAY EMBARRASSING THINGS.
HOW CAN THEY DO THAT AND LIVE?
...
...
UM... WHAT?
I MEAN IT!
THOSE LINES ARE KILLERS!
WHEN A MANGA I LIKE GETS AN ANIME...
...I THROW A PARTY.
I FOLLOW THE SHOW'S ACCOUNT ON SOCIAL MEDIA...
...AND FRIEND THE ENTIRE CAST AND CREW. IT'S CRUCIAL TO BUILD AN ONLINE BULWARK.
THIS BUILDS EXPECTATIONS AND WORD OF MOUTH...
...EXPONENTIALLY GROWING THE FAN BASE.
I ALSO DRAW FAN ART AND MAKE FAN COMICS.
AND THAT, NASA, IS THE MEANING OF LOVE.
WHOA...

Fly Me to the Moon

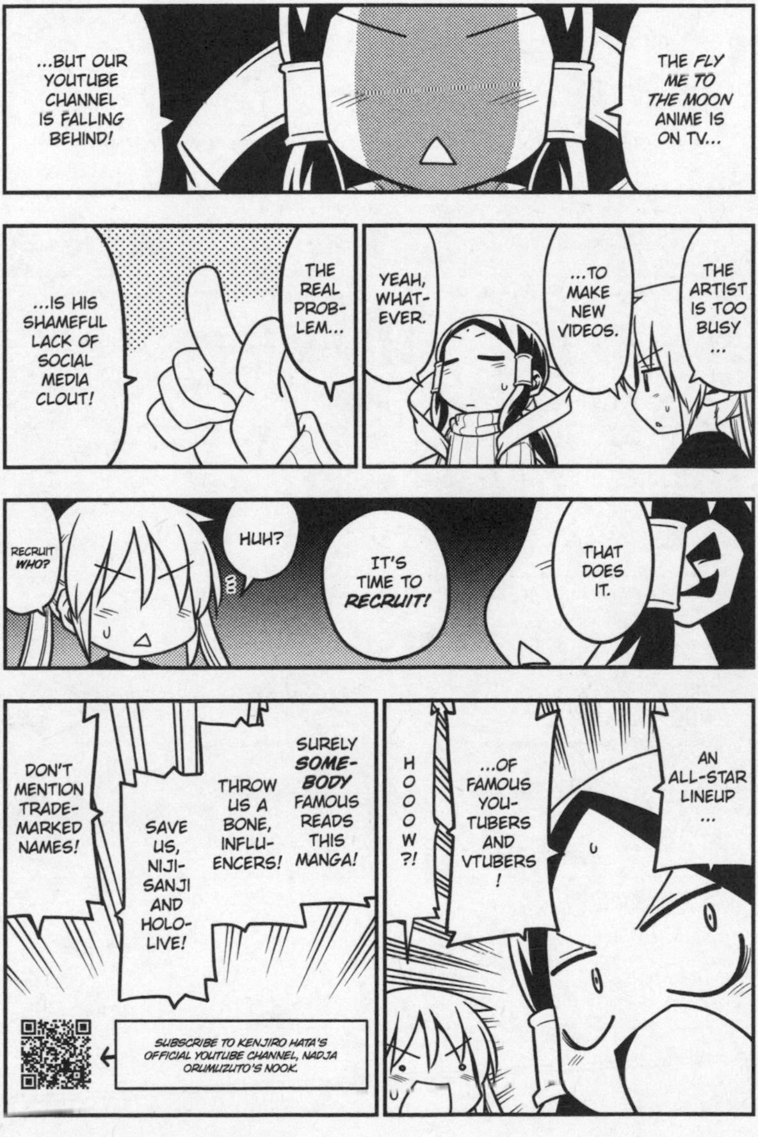
THE FLY ME TO THE MOON ANIME IS ON TV...
...BUT OUR YOUTUBE CHANNEL IS FALLING BEHIND!
THE ARTIST IS TOO BUSY ...
...TO MAKE NEW VIDEOS.
YEAH, WHATEVER.
THE REAL PROBLEM...
...IS HIS SHAMEFUL LACK OF SOCIAL MEDIA CLOUT!
THAT DOES IT.
IT'S TIME TO RECRUIT!
HUH?
RECRUIT WHO?
AN ALL-STAR LINEUP ...
...OF FAMOUS YOUTUBERS AND VTUBERS!
HOOOOW?!
SURELY SOMEBODY FAMOUS READS THIS MANGA!
THROW US A BONE, INFLUENCERS!
SAVE US, NIJISANJI AND HOLOLIVE!
DON'T MENTION TRADEMARKED NAMES!
SUBSCRIBE TO KENJIRO HATA'S OFFICIAL YOUTUBE CHANNEL, NADJA ORUMUZUTO'S NOOK.

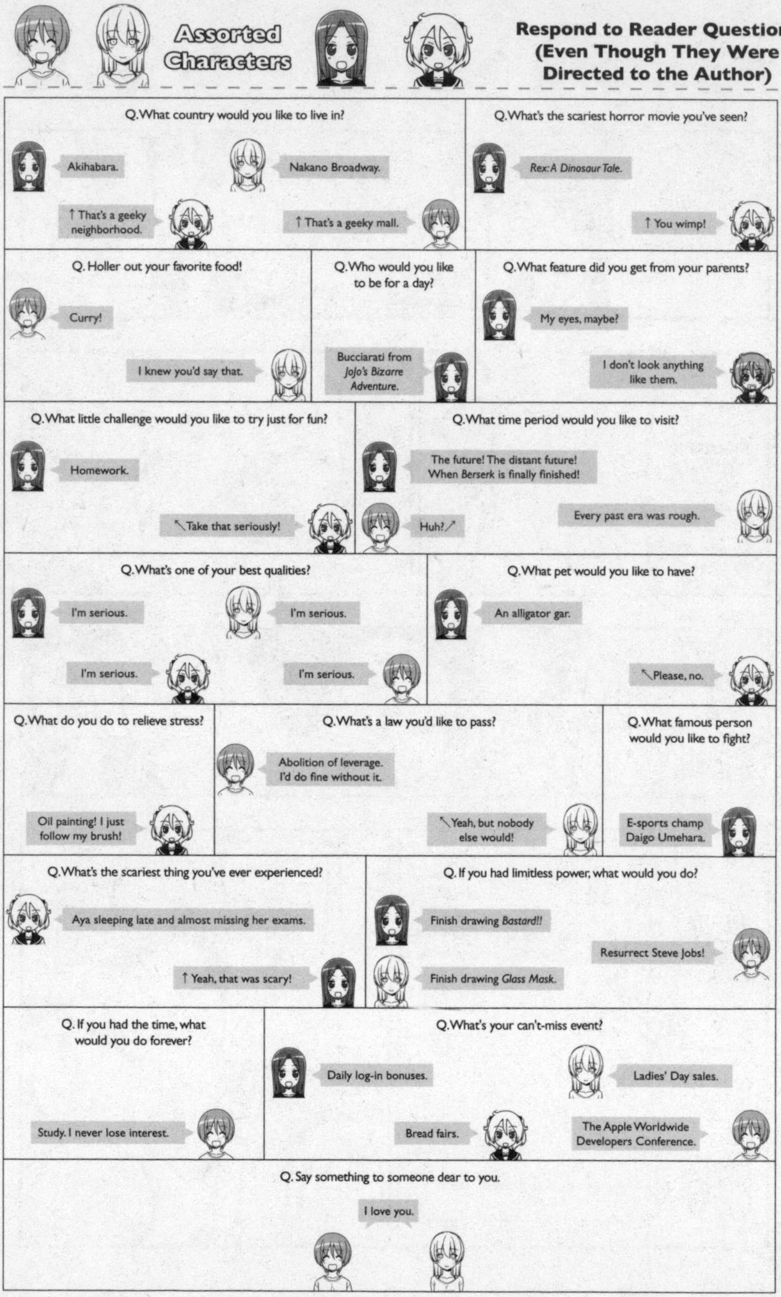
Assorted Characters
Respond to Reader Questions (Even Though They Were Directed to the Author)
Q.What's the scariest horror movie you've seen?
Rex: A Dinosaur Tale.
↑ You wimp!
Q.What country would you like to live in?
Nakano Broadway.
Akihabara.
↑ That's a geeky mall.
↑ That's a geeky neighborhood.
Q.What feature did you get from your parents?
My eyes, maybe?
I don't look anything like them.
Q.Who would you like to be for a day?
Bucciarati from JoJo's Bizarre Adventure.
Q. Holler out your favorite food!
Curry!
I knew you'd say that.
Q.What time period would you like to visit?
The future! The distant future! When Berserk is finally finished!
Every past era was rough.
Huh?↗
Q.What little challenge would you like to try just for fun?
Homework.
↖Take that seriously!
Q.What pet would you like to have?
An alligator gar.
↖Please, no.
Q.What's one of your best qualities?
I'm serious.
I'm serious.
I'm serious.
I'm serious.
Q.What famous person would you like to fight?
E-sports champ Daigo Umehara.
Q.What's a law you'd like to pass?
Abolition of leverage. I'd do fine without it.
↖Yeah, but nobody else would!
Q.What do you do to relieve stress?
Oil painting! I just follow my brush!
Q. If you had limitless power, what would you do?
Finish drawing Bastard!!
Resurrect Steve Jobs!
Finish drawing Glass Mask.
Q.What's the scariest thing you've ever experienced?
Aya sleeping late and almost missing her exams.
↑ Yeah, that was scary!
Q.What's your can't-miss event?
Ladies' Day sales.
Daily log-in bonuses.
The Apple Worldwide Developers Conference.
Bread fairs.
Q. If you had the time, what would you do forever?
Study. I never lose interest.
Q. Say something to someone dear to you.
I love you.

ABOUT THE AUTHOR

Without ever receiving any kind of manga award,
Kenjiro Hata's first series, *Umi no Yuusha Lifesavers*,
was published in *Shonen Sunday Super*. He followed
that up with his smash hit *Hayate the Combat Butler*.
Fly Me to the Moon began serialization in 2018
in *Weekly Shonen Sunday*.

FLY ME TO THE MOON

VOL. 13

Story and Art by **KENJIRO HATA**

SHONEN SUNDAY EDITION

TONIKAKUKAWAII Vol. 13
by Kenjiro HATA

Original Japanese edition published by SHOGAKUKAN.
English translation rights in the United States of America, Canada, the United Kingdom, Ireland, Australia and New Zealand arranged with SHOGAKUKAN.

Original Cover Design: Emi Nakano (BANANA GROVE STUDIO)

Translation
John Werry

Touch-Up Art & Lettering
Evan Waldinger

Design
Jimmy Presler

Editor
Shaenon K. Garrity

Printed in the U.S.A.

Published by VIZ Media, LLC
P.O. Box 77010
San Francisco, CA 94107

10 9 8 7 6 5 4 3 2 1
First printing, September 2022

PARENTAL ADVISORY
FLY ME TO THE MOON is rated T+ for Older Teen and is recommended for ages 16 and up. This volume contains sexual situations.

RATED T+ OLDER TEEN ratings.viz.com

VIZ MEDIA
viz.com

MANGA STARTS ON SUNDAY SHONEN SUNDAY
shonensunday.com

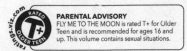

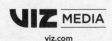

A hilarious tale of butlers, love and battles!

Hayate the Combat Butler

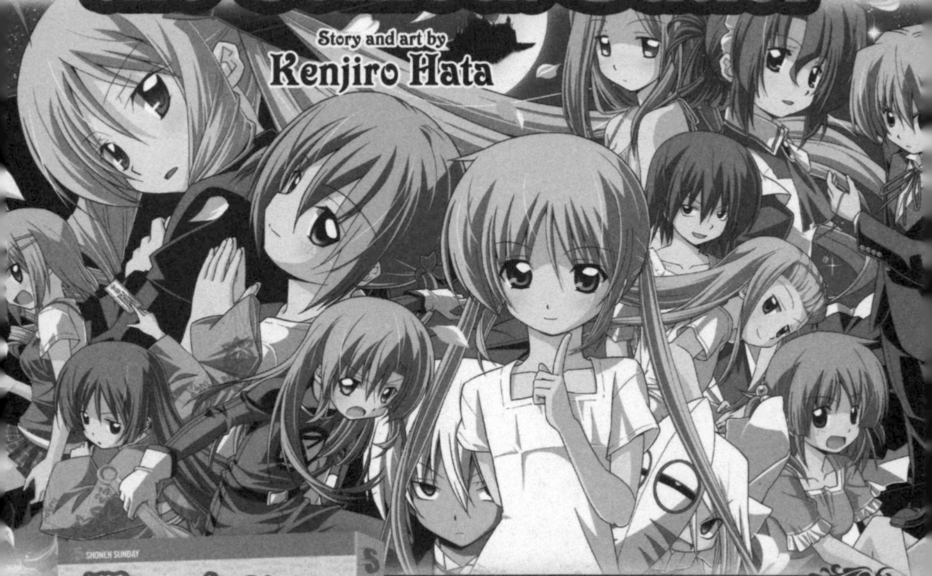

Story and art by
Kenjiro Hata

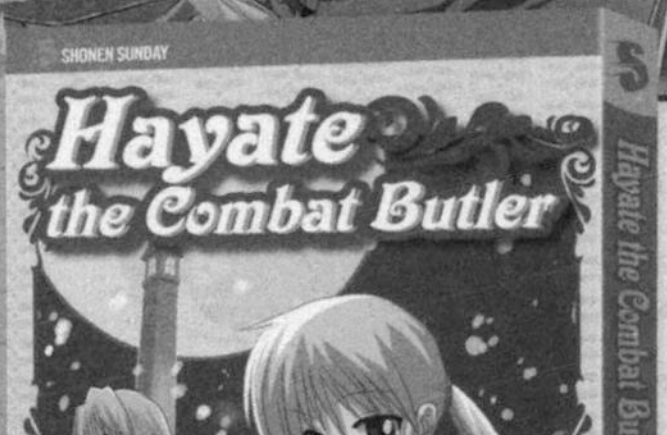
SHONEN SUNDAY
Hayate the Combat Butler
Hayate the Combat Butler
1
Kenjiro Hata
Story and art by
Kenjiro Hata
1
VIZ

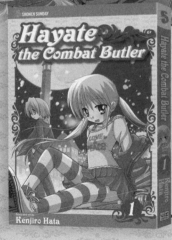

Since the tender age of nine, Hayate Ayasaki has busted his behind at various part-time jobs to support his degenerate gambler parents. And how do they repay their son's selfless generosity? By selling his organs to the yakuza to cover their debts! But fate throws Hayate a bone… sort of. Now the butler of a wealthy young lady, Hayate can finally pay back his debts, and it'll only take him 40 years to do it.

RATED T+ OLDER TEEN

VIZ

MAO

Exorcise your destiny in an era-spanning supernatural adventure from manga legend Rumiko Takahashi!

Story and Art by
RUMIKO TAKAHASHI

When Nanoka travels back in time to a supernatural early 20th century, she gets recruited by aloof exorcist Mao. What is the thread of fate that connects them? Together, they seek answers...and kick some demon butt along the way!

RATED
T+
OLDER TEEN

VIZ

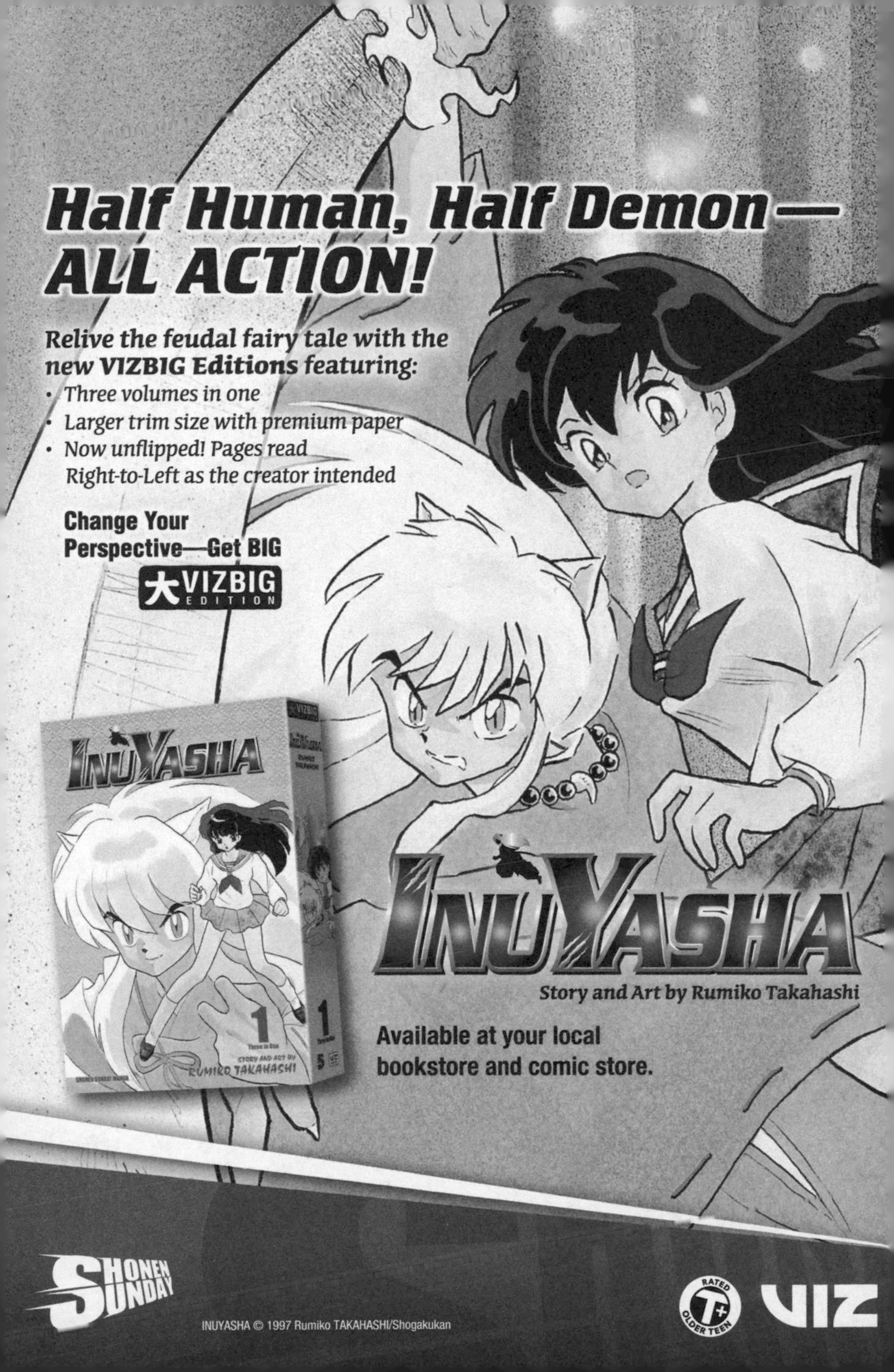

Half Human, Half Demon—
ALL ACTION!
Relive the feudal fairy tale with the new VIZBIG Editions featuring:
• Three volumes in one
• Larger trim size with premium paper
• Now unflipped! Pages read Right-to-Left as the creator intended
Change Your Perspective—Get BIG
大 VIZBIG EDITION
INUYASHA
1
Three in One
STORY AND ART BY RUMIKO TAKAHASHI
SHONEN SUNDAY MANGA
INUYASHA
Story and Art by Rumiko Takahashi
Available at your local bookstore and comic store.
SHONEN SUNDAY
INUYASHA © 1997 Rumiko TAKAHASHI/Shogakukan
RATED T+ OLDER TEEN
VIZ

Kidnapped by the Demon King and imprisoned in his castle, Princess Syalis is...bored.

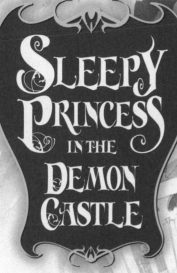

SLEEPY PRINCESS IN THE DEMON CASTLE

Story & Art by
KAGIJI KUMANOMATA

Captured princess Syalis decides to while away her hours in the Demon Castle by sleeping, but getting a good night's rest turns out to be a lot of work! She begins by fashioning a DIY pillow out of the fur of her Teddy Demon guards and an "air mattress" from the magical Shield of the Wind. Things go from bad to worse—for her captors—when some of Princess Syalis's schemes end in her untimely—if temporary—demise and she chooses the Forbidden Grimoire for her bedtime reading...

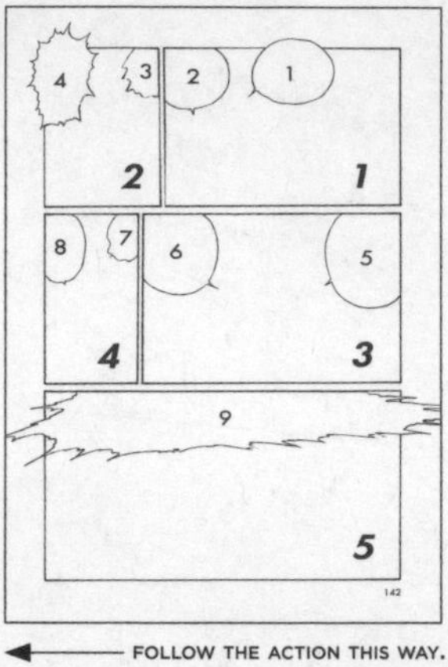
FOLLOW THE ACTION THIS WAY.

Fly Me to the Moon has been printed in the original Japanese format in order to preserve the orientation of the original artwork. Please turn it around and begin reading from right to left.

Unlike English, Japanese is read right to left, so Japanese comics are read in reverse order from the way English comics are typically read. Have fun with it!

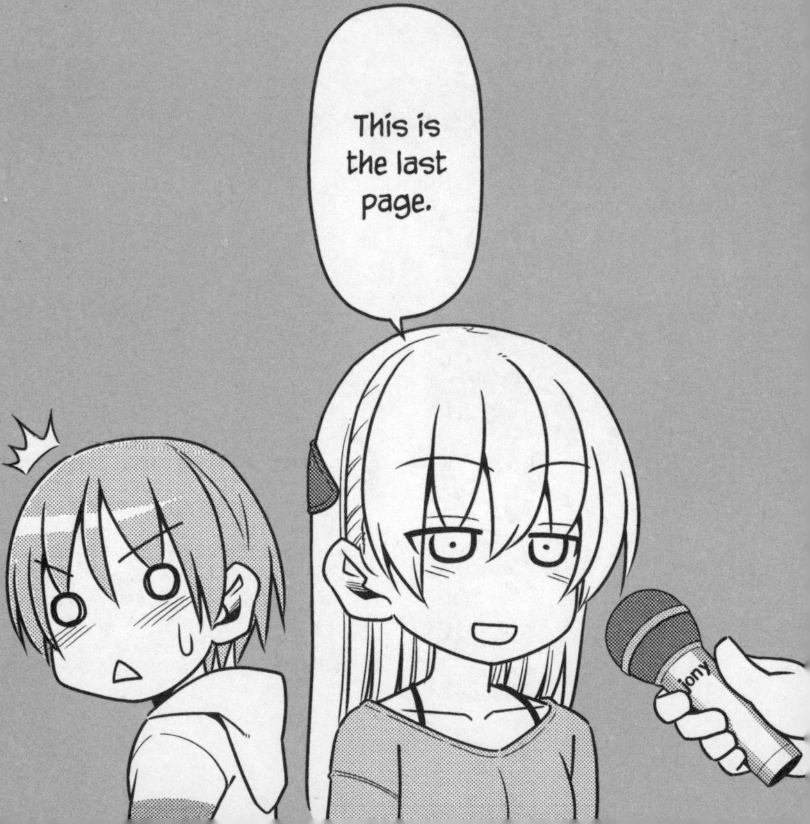
This is the last page.